STRINDBERG
AND GENRE

STRINDBERG
AND GENRE
EDITED BY MICHAEL ROBINSON

Norvik Press
1991

Other books in Series A include:

(Paperback)

Michael Robinson: *Strindberg and Autobiography*
Irene Scobbie (ed.): *Aspects of Modern Swedish Literature*
James McFarlane: *Ibsen and Meaning*
Robin Young: *Time's Disinherited Children*
Egil Törnqvist and Barry Jacobs: *Strindberg's Miss Julie*
Georg Brandes: *Selected Letters*
Knut Hamsun: *Selected Letters I (1879-98)*
Ludvig Holberg: *Moral Reflections and Epistles*

Our logo is based on a drawing by Egil Bakka (University of Bergen) of a Viking ornament in gold foil, paper thin, with impressed figures (size 16 x 21 mm). It was found in 1897 at Hauge, Klepp, Rogaland, and is now in the collection of the Historisk museum, University of Bergen (inv.no.5392). It depicts a love scene, possibly (according to Magnus Olsen) between the fertility god Freyr and the maiden Gerðr; the large penannular brooch of the man's cloak dates the work as being most likely 10th century.

Cover design by V & A Vargo

British Library Cataloguing in Publication Data
International Strindberg Conference
(10th 1990 Norwich)
   Strindberg and Genre
   I. Title   II. Robinson, Michael
   839.7

ISBN 1-870041-18-6

First published in 1991 by Norvik Press, University of East Anglia, Norwich, NR4 7TJ, England
Managing Editors: James McFarlane and Janet Garton

Norvik Press has been established with financial support from the University of East Anglia, the Danish Ministry for Cultural Affairs, the Norwegian Cultural Department, and the Swedish Institute. Publication of this book has been aided by a grant from the Anglo-Swedish Literary Foundation.

Printed in Great Britain by Billing & Sons Ltd., Worcester.

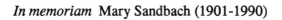

In memoriam Mary Sandbach (1901-1990)

Contents

Preface

The essays collected here were originally presented as papers at the Xth International Strindberg Conference, held jointly by the Universities of Loughborough and East Anglia in Norwich, in April 1990. They have been largely revised for publication together with the appropriate annotation. What the volume unfortunately does not document, however, is the sequence of performances which complemented the giving of these formal papers, from an example of the Stockholm Royal Dramatic Theatre's classic Strindberg tradition with Marie Göranzon and Jan Malmsjö in scenes from *Fröken Julie* and *Dödsdansen* to the interrogation of such established performance genres in an evening of improvisations on Strindbergian themes by Helge Skoog, Pia Johansson and Peder Falk, and the transposition of the Swedish text and its performance expectations into English by way of a production of *Pelikanen* by students from Leeds University and a rehearsed reading of Eivor Martinus' new translation of *Stora landsvägen*.

These performances, like the theme of the Conference in general, were designed to open up as many aspects as possible of a writer whose reception in this country has been both tardy and partial. Indeed, even where the plays are concerned, only a small proportion have entered the general repertoire here, and a number of the most significant still await an adequate professional British production, while Strindberg's contribution to other genres, as novelist, autobiographer, essayist, letter writer and historian, remains for the most part largely unknown. If his contemporaries Ibsen and Chekhov have been long (though not always happily) domesticated, Strindberg has not.

There are many reasons why this should be so. One of the most obvious is the sheer variety of Strindberg's production and the seeming lack of consistency that he displays, even within a single kind of literature. Quite simply, the multiplicity of his discourses is disconcerting, as is his apparent failure ever to remain faithful to a single point of view or any one way of expressing it. Moreover, if genre is, as Alastair Fowler suggests, primarily to do with communication, and hence an instrument not of classification or prescription, but of meaning, then Strindberg's refusal to settle (like Ibsen) into a single, recognizable, if developing, genre through which to conduct his transactions with the reader or spectator, is certainly of relevance where his British reception has been concerned.

Not that Strindberg ignored categories, literary or otherwise. In fact, he was a passionate taxonomist and shared with many of his protagonists (notably Axel Borg in *I havsbandet*) an intense concern for conceptual classification, continually seeking and sometimes finding in the consonance of form and the rightness of expression the appropriate generic mould for his own, frequently very immediate and personal concerns, but only in time to question the categories he had evolved, as he had always been accustomed to question received categories in general. Thus, having sought, like Borg, to achieve an inventory of the world along Naturalist lines during the 1880s, he then embarked, between 1894 and 1897, upon the religious and occult reclassification of the Inferno Crisis, transforming himself in the process from the nineteenth-century writer of *Tjänstekvinnans son* and *Fröken Julie* into the Modernist of *Till Damaskus*, *Taklagsöl* and *Ett drömspel*, in which, however, what frequently appears to be a radical generic break with the immediate past awakens in fact (as Strindberg himself acknowledges) an echo of some older literary model.

Nevertheless, as many of the essays here reveal, his approach to literary genres was often provokingly personal and at times disturbingly idiosyncratic. Although he declared in 1907 that the secret of all his novels and stories was that they were really dramas in disguise, written in narrative form for future use during those frequent periods when he could not gain an audience in the theatre, he may also be heard, during the early 1880s, arguing in favour of the primacy of other genres, and insisting (for example, in a letter to Pehr Staaff from 1883) that drama was not to be regarded as the alpha and omega of a radical writer's project. Meanwhile, expediency and an anxious publisher would sometimes compel him to redefine or retouch an autobiographical work as fiction (witness his many and various comments on both *Tjänstekvinnans son* and *En dåres försvarstal*, and the transposition of *Klostret* into 'Karantänmästarns andra berättelse'), and *Svarta handsken* was redesignated a Chamber Play simply because he had already spent the advance he had been given some years previously against a future successor to *Spöksonaten* and *Pelikanen*. His eye for a new genre, however, was sharp. In 1886, for example, he seized eagerly upon the pioneering photo-reportage about the chemist Eugène Chevreul, which Nadar and his son, Paul, had published in *Le Journal Illustré* on 5 September; by 15 November he had collected and despatched a series of photographs of himself and family, with captions, to Albert Bonnier, the publisher of his recently completed literary autobiography, *Tjänstekvinnans son*, with a view to a complementary volume. In the belatedly published Preface to his autobiographical narrative, meanwhile, he invented an interviewer interrogating its author (who is thus himself engaged in fictional discourse) about the nature of the book in hand: 'Vad är detta nu för en bok herrn kommer med? Är det roman, biografi, memoar eller vad?' (What kind of book have you written, sir? Is it a novel, a biography, a memoir or what?). And though the 'Author' stubbornly insists that the book is merely what it declares itself to be on its title page ('A History of a Soul's Development 1849-67', that is, at once the unique account of a singular life and a representative narrative of a specific historical period), he in fact artfully eludes all the categories within which the envisaged interviewer would imprison him.

As Kerstin Dahlbäck points out, in her contribution to this volume, with Strindberg we are confronted by a canon which continually mingles fact with fiction, and one of the questions he raises with immediate urgency is the relationship of private experience to the literary institution, of which the available genres are one manifestation. Much of the fascination of his work resides in the tension between the form that experience seems to take (for Strindberg, the indefatigable spectator of his own life, lived experience could sometimes be observed — or so he claimed — following the contours of a particular genre) and the literary forms, with all their cultural freight, that were available to him when he came to recuperate this experience in language.

What consequently emerges from these pronouncements by Strindberg on genre (and this is something which is confirmed by almost all the contributions to this volume) is that he was a professional writer, confronted by the exigencies and opportunities of the literary and theatrical institutions of his day. The Norwich Conference was thus fortunate in having Jan Myrdal, who is in certain respects the most Strindbergian of contemporary Swedish authors, to open the proceedings. Not only does Myrdal emulate Strindberg in his professionalism as a '*brödskrivare*', he has also contributed to a similarly wide range of genres including, in *Report from a Chinese Village*, the tradition of reportage that Strindberg enriched with *Bland franska bönder* and, most recently, in the autobiographical trilogy *Barndom*, *En annan värld*, and *Tolv på det trettonde*, the form of personal writing which Strindberg established with *Tjänstekvinnans son* as (in Myrdal's words) 'the exemplary Swedish genre'.

Commencing with Myrdal's opening address, the papers have been grouped under four broad headings. Although many of the later essays also raise more issues and investigate more works than their respective titles may indicate, the first section is devoted to contributions of a comparative or more theoretical nature, ranging over several aspects or periods of Strindberg's work, including the short story, the autobiographical fictions, and the way in which Strindberg habitually mixes different genres at different periods of his career. Not surprisingly, however, the majority of the contributions focus on the drama, and this section is therefore followed by a series of essays on the way in which Strindberg extended the notion of what might be expressed or presented verbally and scenically in the late nineteenth-century and early modern theatre. They range over a number of comparatively lesser-known works, including his comedies and fairy-tale plays, or *sagospel*, as well as key texts like *Till Damaskus* and the Chamber Plays, which emerge as perhaps Strindberg's single most original compositions and yet part of a general movement in the theatre of the time bringing drama closer to music.

The third section, which focuses on the non-dramatic works, considers a sequence of the early poetry, analyses the extraordinary prose work *Inferno*, which changes genre in mid-flow, from 'un roman occulte d'après nature' to exemplary autobiography, and the tetralogy of *En blå bok*, the most flexible and capacious of Strindberg's genres, which Göran Printz-Påhlson aptly describes as a 'glorious ragbag' characterized by serendipity. In the final section, Strindberg's associative, visual imagination is explored in relation both to his writing and to the painting which forms an essential aspect of his project, and the latter is here placed within the context of Scandinavian art of the period.

Two aspects of editorial practice require comment. Firstly, since in many significant instances the transposition of Strindberg into English has not yet been accomplished (even where his plays are concerned, there remains a surprising lack of consistency in the translation of titles), the titles of all Strindberg's separately published works are given throughout in Swedish only. However, there is a comprehensive list of these works, with their dates and an English equivalent, following this introduction. In accordance with the theme of this volume, they have been arranged in broad generic categories. (Hopefully, this listing may serve as a source of reference beyond the uses of this volume.) Secondly, throughout the collection, quotations from Strindberg's works are identified in parenthesis following a translation of the Swedish original. Where a work has already appeared in the new edition of *Samlade Verk* currently being issued (hereafter SV), this edition is used in preference to John Landquist's edition of *Samlade Skrifter* (Stockholm 1912-20, hereafter SS). The volume number is in each case given in arabic numerals, thus: SV 16, p.137 or SS 16, p.137. For Strindberg's letters, references are to *August*

Strindbergs brev (Stockholm, 1948-), originally edited by Torsten Eklund and now happily in progress again under the caring editorship of Björn Meidal. In quotations from the letters, the volume number is denoted by Roman numerals and references are likewise incorporated within the text.

A number of debts have been incurred, both in arranging the Conference and publishing the papers. At the University of East Anglia, Jon Cook, Julian Hilton and Anthea Iveson gave much appreciated assistance. The Swedish Institute, and Björn Westeson in particular, made it possible for a number of Swedish performers and speakers to attend the Conference, as did the British Academy. The Anglo-Swedish Literary Foundation, with Torsten Kälvemark as a generous intermediary, supported both ventures from the outset, and Margareta Brundin at Kungliga Biblioteket and Gunilla Norming at the Strindberg Museum were - as always - endlessly helpful in providing me with material for the exhibition of Strindberg's life and works which was mounted to accompany the Conference. My most immediate debt, however, is to Heather Rees who gave so generously of her time, care and energies over the last two years, initially in arranging the Conference and latterly in the publication of these papers.

Finally, this volume is dedicated, although alas *in memoriam*, to Mary Sandbach, who was happily able to receive the recently instituted but prestigious Strindberg Prize in person at the Conference. As an intermediary between Swedish and British culture, her contribution was unique, not least through her alert and faithful renderings of a whole sequence of Strindberg's major prose works, including *Giftas*, *I havsbandet*, *Inferno* and *Klostret*, into English. She is sorely missed.

January 1991   M.G.R.

STRINDBERG'S WORKS

Strindberg's principal works, with their dates and an English equivalent, arranged chronologically according to Genre, although as several of the following articles indicate, the status of many of these works (e.g. *En blå bok* or *Vivisektioner*) frequently raises difficulties concerning their definition in conventional generic terms. The date given is generally that in which a work was written, although where there was a significant delay in publication, it has sometimes been appropriate to indicate when it may have been published.

PLAYS

Fritänkaren (1869)	The Free Thinker
Den sjunkande Hellas (1869)	Greece in Decline
(orig version of *Hermione*)	
Hermione (1870)	Hermione
I rom (1870)	In Rome
Den fredlöse (1871)	The Outlaw
Mäster Olof (prose version, 1872,	Master Olof
revised version, 1874, verse	
version, 1876, Epilogue, c.1877)	
Anno fyrtioåtta (1876-77)	Anno '48
Gillets hemlighet (1880)	The Secret of the Guild
Lycko-Pers resa (1882)	Lucky Peter's Journey
Herr Bengts hustru (1882)	Sir Bengt's Wife
Marodörer (1886)	Marauders
Kamraterna (1886-87)	Comrades
Fadren (1887)	The Father
Fröken Julie (1888)	Miss Julie
Fordringsägare (1888)	Creditors
Den starkare (1888-89)	The Stronger
Paria (1889)	Pariah
Hemsöborna (1889)	The People of Hemsö
Samum (1889)	Simoom
Himmelrikets nycklar (1892)	The Keys of Heaven
Debet och kredit (1892)	Debit and Credit
Första varningen (1892)	The First Warning
Inför döden (1892)	Facing Death
Moderskärlek (1892)	Motherly Love
Leka med elden (1892)	Playing with Fire
Bandet (1892)	The Bond
Till Damaskus (Part I, 1898,	To Damascus
Part II, 1898)	
Advent (1898)	Advent
Brott och brott (1899)	Crimes and Crimes
Folkungasagan (1899)	The Saga of the Folkungs
Gustav Vasa (1899)	Gustav Vasa
Erik XIV (1899)	Erik the Fourteenth

Gustav Adolf (1900)	Gustav Adolf
Midsommar (1900)	Midsummer
Kaspers fet-tisdag (1900)	Casper's Shrove Tuesday
Påsk (1900)	Easter
Dödsdansen (Part I, 1900 Part II, 1900)	The Dance of Death
Kronbruden (1901)	The Crown Bride
Svanevit (1901)	Swanwhite
Carl XII (1901)	Charles the Twelfth
Till Damaskus Part III (1901)	To Damascus III
Engelbrekt (1901)	Engelbrekt
Kristina (1901)	Queen Christina
Ett drömspel (1901)	A Dream Play
Gustav III (1902)	Gustav the Third
Holländarn (1902)	The Flying Dutchman
Näktergalen i Wittenberg (1903)	The Nightingale of Wittenberg
Världshistoriska dramer (*Moses, Sokrates, Kristus,* wr 1903, publ 1918)	World Historical Dramas (Moses, Socrates, Christ)
Oväder (1907)	Thunder in the Air
Brända tomten (1907)	The Burned Site
Spöksonaten (1907)	The Ghost Sonata
Toten-Insel (1907)	The Isle of the Dead
Pelikanen (1907)	The Pelican
Siste riddaren (1908)	The Last Knight
Abu Casems tofflor (1908)	Abu Casem's Slippers
Riksföreståndaren (1908)	The Protector
Bjälbo-Jarlen (1909)	The Earl of Bjälbo
Svarta handsken (1909)	The Black Glove
Stora landsvägen (1909)	The Great Highway

POETRY

Dikter på vers och prosa (1883)	Poems in Verse and Prose
Sömngångarnätter på vakna dagar (1884-90)	Somnambulistic Nights in Broad Daylight
Ordalek och småkonst (1902)	Word Play and Minor Art

NOVELS

Röda rummet (1879)	The Red Room
Hemsöborna (1887)	The People of Hemsö
I havsbandet (1890)	By the Open Sea
Götiska rummen (1904)	Gothic Rooms
Svarta fanor (wr 1904, publ 1907)	Black Banners
Taklagsöl (1907)	The Roofing Feast
Syndabocken (1907)	The Scapegoat

16

SHORTER FICTIONAL PROSE

'Början av Ån Bogsveigs saga' (1872)	The Beginning of Ån Bogsveig's Saga
Från Fjärdingen och Svartbäcken (1877)	Town and Gown
Det nya riket (1882)	The New Kingdom
Svenska öden och äventyr (1882-91)	Swedish Destinies and Adventures
including *Tschandala* (1889)	Tschandala
Giftas I (1884), II (1885)	Getting Married
Utopier i verkligheten (1885)	Utopias in Reality
Fabler (orig wr in French as 'Contes et Fabliaux' 1885, publ in Swedish 1891)	Fables
Genvägar (1887)	Short Cuts
Skärkarlsliv (1888)	Life in the Skerries
Fagervik och Skamsund (1902)	Fairhaven and Foulstrand
Sagor (1903)	Fairy Tales
Historiska miniatyrer (1905)	Historical Miniatures
Hövdingaminnen (1906)	Memories of the Chieftains
- originally *Nya svenska öden*	- originally New Swedish Destinies
Armageddon (unfinished, 1908)	Armageddon

AUTOBIOGRAPHICAL WORKS

Tjänstekvinnans son - comprising	The Son of a Servant
I *Tjänstekvinnans son* (1886)	
II *Jäsningstiden* (1886)	Time of Ferment
III *I Röda rummet* (wr 1886, publ 1887)	In the Red Room
IV *Författaren* (wr 1886, publ 1909)	The Author
Han och hon (S's correspondence with Siri von Essen 1875-76, edited 1886, publ 1921)	He and She
En dåres försvarstal (orig wr 1887-88 in French, publ in Swedish transl by John Landquist (1914), Tage Aurell (1962), and Hans Evander (1976), in German (as *Die Beichte eines Thoren*) in 1893, and French (as *Le Plaidoyer d'un fou*) in 1895.	A Madman's Defence
Inferno (wr in French, publ 1898 in Swedish)	Inferno
Legender (partly wr in French and incl *Jakob brottas*, 1898)	Legends Jacob Wrestles

Klostret (wr 1898, publ 1966; original version of 'Karantän-mästarns andra berättelse')	The Cloister
'Karantänmästarns andra berättelse' (1902, in *Fargervik och Skamsund*)	The Quarantine Master's Second Story
Ensam (1903)	Alone
Ockulta dagboken (21 Feb 1896-11 Nov 1908, publ 1977)	The Occult Diary

DISCURSIVE PROSE

Gamla Stockholm (1880-82)	Old Stockholm
Kulturhistoriska studier (1881)	Studies in Cultural History
Bland franska bönder (1886)	Among French Peasants
Vivisektioner (1887)	Vivisections
Blomstermålningar och djurstycken (1888)	Flower Paintings and Animal Pieces
Antibarbarus (1893)	Antibarbarus
Vivisektioner II (wr 1894, in French, publ 1958)	Vivisections II
Sylva Sylvarum (1896, in French)	Sylva Sylvarum
Jardin des plantes (1896)	Jardin des plantes
Världshistoriens mystik (1903)	The Mysticism of World History
En blå bok (1907)	A Blue Book
En ny blå bok (1907)	A New Blue Book
En blå bok, avdelning III (1908)	A Blue Book, Part III
Öppna brev till Intima teatern (1909)	Open Letters to the Intimate Theatre
En blå bok, avdelning IV (1912)	A Blue Book, Part IV

Strindberg's principal essays from the 1880s on Politics, Society, Literature, and the Woman Question, including 'Om det allmänna missnöjet' (On the General Discontent, 1884), *Kvarstadsresan* (The Sequestration Journey, 1884), 'Om modernt drama och modern teater (On Modern Drama and Modern Theatre, 1889), and the *Lilla katekes för underklassen* (Little Catechism for the Underclass, 1884) are collected in *Likt och olikt* (Alike and Unlike, Volumes 16 and 17 of Samlade Skrifter). Likewise Volume 27, *Prosabiter från 1890-talet* (Prose Pieces from the 1890s), contains a wide selection of the stories and works of history, speculative science and natural history which Strindberg wrote, in both French and Swedish, during the 1890s, including *Antibarbarus* and *Jardin des plantes*. His polemical writings of 1910-12, *Tal till svenska nationen* (Speeches to the Swedish Nation, 1910), *Folkstaten* (The People's State, 1910), *Intima teatern* (The Intimate Theatre, 1910-11), *Religiös renässans*, (Religious Renaissance, 1910), and *Tsarens kurir* (The Tsar's Courier, 1912) are collected in Volume 53 (Volume 68 of Samlade Verk). Finally, Strindberg's miscellaneous writings on linguistics, including *Bibliska egennamn* (Biblical Proper Names, 1910), *Modersmålets anor* (The Origins of our Mother Tongue, 1910), and *Världsspråkens rötter* (The Roots of World Languages, 1911) are contained in Volume 52, *Språkvetenskapliga studier* (Studies in Linguistics).

I

Without Bounds?

General Issues

August Strindberg and his Tradition in Swedish Literature

Beyond Fiction, Autobiography and the Literature of the Established Truth

Jan Myrdal

I shall begin by saying something that many of you will not agree with. Nevertheless it is, I believe, necessary to point out that it is not possible to understand Strindberg — or Gorky, Sartre, Dreiser, Brecht, take any name — without accepting the determining reality of national roots. We might have to change countries like shoes; exchange one passport for another; swear allegiance to this, that or another flag; start talking in a new language and even find that we have begun to dream in that other language. But our nationality remains like the colour of our eyes or the way we react in anger, love and sorrow. I can settle in the United States or China, in England, France or Russia, but I remain a Swede.

That Swedish literature is specific is not surprising. Though languages are related, there is no such thing as a language in general, a language beyond and above the people who speak it. Nor is there a literature in general, a literature above and beyond its language, though writers from different literatures deeply influence one another. Reading Swedish twentieth-century literature, you will find that it is not only specific in this sense; you will find that it differs from the literature of other European nations in two ways.

During a large part of the century, the main stream of Swedish literature was formed by what we call the proletarian writers. They were not proletarian writers in the political meaning that the German Left gave to the expression, not all would even call themselves socialist. Nor did they come mainly from the industrial proletariat as such. But their class background was different from that of the intellectuals floating socially near the dominant class; their road to literature differed from that of the academic writers. They told other stories and they told them better. They were all very different from each other but they not only reached a mass audience in the Nordic countries, they dominated our literature for many decades, and anyone interested in Swedish writing during this century knows their names. Writers like Jan Fridegård (1897-1968), Ivar Lo-Johansson (1901-1990), Moa Martinson (1890-1964); but also Eyvind Johnson (1900-1976), Harry Martinson (1904-1976) and even a writer of peasant background like Vilhelm Moberg (1896-1973).

As a trend, they were not quite unique even if they were so in Europe. If you look at the literary scene in the United States during the early Roosevelt years you will see something similar. But in Sweden they really dominated the whole literary scene and continued to do so long after the literature of the New Deal had passed into history. In Sweden they could determine writing in this way for many reasons. An important factor lay in the fact that the academic and aesthetic upper-class hegemony over literature had been broken at the turn of the century by August Strindberg.

In France as in England, language was a barrier to keep the uppity from the underclass outside literature. Strindberg liberated our language as well. He wrote at a time when the academic strata in Sweden tried to make Swedish a more rigid language. By turning against and partly smashing official literature he had opened a way out of the academic prison, and even if writers such as Ivar Lo-Johansson found Strindberg a petty-bourgeois writer, they all followed him through that breech out to the public. In most other European countries the barriers were formidable and the gates were kept shut. There, proletarian literature was written by socialist academic writers depicting the proletariat.

The second specific trait is that of the dominant literary genre. But genre is a dangerous word. It not only helps you state the fact that there are differences in style, it also makes you think that there are different kinds of literature, separated one from another by strict borders: essay, reportage, novel, autobiography.

But you all know that we who write in Swedish tend to write stories based on our own lives, our own experiences, using the self as a basis for our work and those near us as raw material. Some of us call these texts autobiographies, some call them novels, some write in the first person singular, others find another name for that self which is the central figure. This is the exemplary Swedish genre. There are few real novels in our literature. Those that do exist are also in the main not very interesting. But there are many fascinating works based on the experiences of the self. It is typical that even those works which most strongly proclaim collectivity (Ivar Lo-Johansson's, for example) are of this character.

Of course, autobiographical novels are not unique to Sweden. Though in Sweden they differ from the *Erziehungsromane, Bildungs-romane, Entwicklungsromane* — to express it in German — of the continental tradition. They are more refractory. You might say that our stories can all trace their ancestry to the Jacques Vingtras trilogy of Jules Vallès through August Strindberg. But in France, Vallès remains outside official literature. Strindberg, who took inspiration from him when he began writing *Tjänstekvinnans son*, was not only as truly refractory as Vallès, he also succeeded in winning out against that literary establishment which still keeps Vallès outside its walls. He thus opened a way to writing for us. To write more directly and with less consideration for the academic rules.

This means that to understand us and the way we are both as a people and as writers, to feel the tradition behind the manner in which we write, you have to go to August Strindberg.

This spring it will be seventy-eight years since Strindberg died. He was born long ago, when the revolution of 1848 that was to give him his political parameters had already turned into the reaction of 1849. And those European writers who were to become his real contemporaries once he began writing were then already passing away.

At Strindberg's birth, Honoré de Balzac was for the last time refused entry to the French Academy; during Strindberg's first seven years Heinrich Heine lay dying on his mattress grave in Paris; when the young Strindberg in 1870 had finished *I Rom*, the first of his plays to be staged at the Royal Dramatic Theatre, Charles Dickens died.

But August Strindberg still determines our literature, and the pattern he set for us remains valid. Officially Sweden has both had a Democratic Breakthrough and built a People's Home (*folkhem*) since his death, and might now, nearing the twenty- first century, be dragged into some kind of neo-liberal, continental, European era, yet Strindberg remains the paradigm for Swedish writing.

This may seem strange since many critics, especially the well tempered ones, those who have been formed according to European standards, have pointed out that his verse is no verse, that his novels are no novels, that his autobiography is no autobiography, that his essays are no essays, that none of his dramatic works really is a *pièce bien faite*. They are right.

As right, by the way, as the historians who have criticized his great national historical dramas — which have given three generations of Swedes their view of national history — for not being written according to the then most recent historical evidence. He knew his sources and was good at finding references, but he wrote in an early nineteenth-century democratic tradition. (Though the official critics were wrong when they believed what the academic historians of his time said: that what Strindberg wrote on popular traditions in *Svenska folket* and other works was unhistorical. In these works he was anti-academic and partisan, but he also broke new ground and was as far ahead of his time there as in the impressive reportage from the mid-1880s, *Bland franska bönder*.)

It is true that nothing Strindberg wrote was well tempered or well done according to the rules. Thus it can be held as proven that Strindberg wrote no real literature. He wrote a text here and a text there that may be of interest to the educated public. But that is all.

I agree. He is not a real European writer, moulded in one piece like, say, an Ibsen or a Thomas Mann or some other among all those collecting medals, honours and prestige, who look into the mirror over the washstand each morning after dabbing the sleep out of their eyes, and say, with satisfaction: 'There, standing before me, I can recognize a truly classic modern European author!'

Nevertheless, his works in Swedish take more than six feet of my bookshelf in the old edition, and will take still more in the new one. His books appear in one popular edition after another. They are being read and reread. His Swedish contemporaries like Gustaf af Geijerstam (1858-1909), Verner von Heidenstam (1859-1940), Oscar Levertin (1862-1906) and the others live a ghostly life in academic seminars, but Strindberg lives among his people.

A paradigm I said. How come he could set the pattern for us? The language is one reason. He wrote us our living Swedish language. He played our language by ear. Swedish is not a language you can truly learn at universities. Swedish is not like French, a language correctly written by ten men each generation. There is no such thing as 'correct' Swedish. Our language is continuously being formed by the people and their writers in symbiosis. August Strindberg wrote us our Swedish language. He formed the popular and literary language as had the brothers Olof and Lars Pettersson in the sixteenth century: Olaus Petri (1493-1552) the reformer and chancellor who wrote our first prose history and our first drama, and Laurentius Petri (1499-1573), the archbishop who supervised the Bible translation of 1541. He gave us our language fresh and alive as did Georg Stjernhjelm (1598-1672), the father of Swedish poetry, in the seventeenth century. This is a key to his immense power over Swedish thought and feeling. Had he written Swedish only ploddingly like an af Geijerstam, pretentiously like a von Heidenstam, or 'correctly' like our Frenchified critics and Germanized academics of the time, Strindberg would now have been literally dead and forgotten like them.

This was not just a natural gift. He had trained himself as an actor when he was a young man. Learnt the secret of rhythm and resonance in the language. That which can let words echo down far beyond the conscious memory of the audience. And as Brecht turned to Luther and his Bible in order to write German, Strindberg drew on the Swedish Bible of 1541. The clear and loud words our people had listened to — and used — over four hundred years.

There is more to this than just a question of language. The relationship between the writer and the people in Swedish is closer to the Russian context than the English. There is a deep communion which makes a writer like Strindberg more than a writer; he becomes a spokesman. Thus he could not only survive against the establishment; he could set a pattern against them. As he wrote, in a poem that generations of young Swedish writers have quoted to themselves as they began writing:

> I han makten, jag har ordet,
> Jag har ordet i min makt . . .
>
> (You have the power, I have the word,
> I have the word in my power . . .)

This also explains how he could both develop and succeed as a refractory writer. The educated Swedish upper classes had been but a thin layer, their academic tradition was weak. Strindberg was strong as he could commune with the people. Thus he could set a lasting pattern. Take, for instance, how he viewed the Swedish Academy. Strindberg did not enter the Academy. He considered the Academy to have a malign influence on literature. It had slush funds that it used to further upper-class, academic, bloodless and a-sexualized literature. The Nobel Prize was awarded by the wrong jury because a man, even a writer, ought to have the right to be judged by his peers, not by such men as the members of the Swedish Academy alone.

Many thought so. It was the kind of talk one can still hear about institutions at literary gatherings the world over. Strindberg though didn't only say it. He wrote it. He published his words. And he stood by them. A man stands by his word, a wretch by his bag, as people said about him and von Heidenstam.

He thus set us a standard of behaviour towards the academics and the officials. We who move inside the popular tradition have found his judgement correct. The Academy has a bad influence on the development of the Swedish language and its literature, and those of us who have respect for our work don't enter that body. 'The Academy,' said Ivar Lo-Johansson, the greatest novelist of these decades, 'the Academy is not my table!'

Over the years there have been academicians of literary worth. Some of them were openly on the other side like the explorer Sven Hedin (1865-1952), a great explorer and a great pro-fascist whom

Strindberg unmasked in a series of articles just before his death. Some were less reactionary. Pär Lagerkvist (1891-1974), for instance. Eyvind Johnson and Harry Martinson were already passing away as writers of value when they entered the Academy. Today, Lars Forssell (b.1928) is a member. I can understand why. He is a Forssell, but his father was considered by the other, proud Forssells to have married beneath them. This hurt, and the son had thus to vindicate them by entering the Swedish Academy. Artur Lundqvist (b.1906) also accepted membership; he thought he could use the Academy for international literary politics. That, too, I can understand, even if I don't agree with it. For the rest, the Academy consists now as formerly of the second-raters. But second-rate writers who dispose over large funds to distribute among themselves and to the more well behaved of the Swedish poets, translators and other writers. And of course they control the Nobel Prize in the annual world championship in the literature of the ideal.

The refractory pattern which Strindberg set did make it possible for writers outside the academic tradition to form the mainstream of Swedish literature. But Sweden is not an absolute exception. Many refractory writers are silenced as effectively in Sweden as in other countries. You can take David Sprengel (1860-1941) and Per Meurling (1906-1984) as typical examples. Both were brilliant. I don't agree with them on every question. Why should I? But both transgressed and then took one step too many, and went too far against the establishment. Thus David Sprengel, who was not only one of our most brilliant critics and translators, but also the best of essayists, who introduced Voltaire, Rousseau and Diderot to the Swedish public, was silenced. His edition of Rousseau is superb — but the last volume of notes is still unpublished. Even today, nearly fifty years after his death, when a young generation of intellectuals is now reprinting his words (see David Sprengel, *Från sidan*, edited by Crister Enander, Solna: Cogito, 1990), David Sprengel is pushed aside by those who were and remain less intelligent and less knowledgeable. Per Meurling, the philosopher and essayist who shaped the Swedish intellectual left of the thirties, but who broke with Moscow, has shared the same fate. Just before he died, I tried to get some of his essays republished (Per Meurling, *Den goda tonens pingviner. Artiklar 1931-46*, Stockholm: Kulturfront, 1984), he just laughed at me and said: 'They never forgive me for being brilliant. Even if you manage it, they will try to kill the words by just keeping silent. The only sound you will hear will be the gnashing of teeth.'

He was right, of course. They did as he said they would. Kept quiet and hated. Because as I was the editor, they knew I could hit back at them if they said it out loud. So they preferred silence. But taking our time, our tradition wins out. We shall reinstate them in the tradition. After all, the establishment did not manage to keep them unpublished. We who work in a Strindbergian tradition will surely see to it that they are given their rightful place. After all, we have the word in our power!

This aspect of Strindberg has had very little influence outside the country. Not that he otherwise was unknown abroad. He had people like his German translator Emil Schering (1873-1951) working for him, and in Germany and Russia he was one of the important foreign writers up to around 1920. An Expressionist before the fact. A representative of the new theatre. O'Neill was his pupil.

The French have now and then taken a slice here, the Italians a slice there, but despite Bernard Shaw and O'Neill the official Anglo-Saxon critics have usually looked with monumental incomprehension on what they have seen of what has been picked out of him. See the notes on Strindberg in *The Reader's Encyclopedia* from 1948, edited by William Rose Benét, or the fifth edition of *The Oxford Companion to English Literature* from 1985, edited by Margaret Drabble. 'A Swedish novelist and dramatist, known for his pessimistic and realistic works influenced by the school of NATURALISM and the theories of NIETZSCHE', according to *The Reader's Encyclopedia*. Or in the smug words of *The Oxford Companion*: '. . . his works . . . are marked by a deeply neurotic response to religion, social class, and sexuality'.

Not a sensible word! Just literary officialese! Truth for students!

Now though, when it will soon be eighty years since his death, Strindberg is at last emerging internationally on his own conditions, as a great world writer. Neither pessimistic nor specifically neurotic. This conference is itself a sign of this. He is now also being extensively translated into other languages besides Russian and German. He is close to becoming the French writer he once hoped to be. Even his *Bland franska bönder*, one of the most important reports on France during the nineteenth century, a counterpart to Arthur Young's *Travels in France* of a century earlier, can no longer be suppressed in France by those Swedish academic critics who for aesthetic — read political! — reasons found Strindberg's text unliterary, uninteresting, and unworthy of the Strindberg they wanted to present.

A reason for his emergence is that he is not a solid writer like Ibsen or Mann, a man cast in one metal which can thus crack and become neurotic. He is — somewhat like Sartre if you want to make comparisons — a pliable, changeable, shimmering writer who cannot be easily labelled. I will take a typical example. Typical because it shows a situation when his words emerge in their own right.

André Mathieu, who has studied the reception of Strindberg in France, has pointed out that *Dödsdansen* opened at the Théâtre de l'Œuvre on 29 July 1944 in Paris, as the great battles after the Invasion were continuing to the west. The critics in the fascist press of occupied Paris were enthusiastic. Not only enthusiastic. The critic of the *Cri du*

Peuple — Doriot's organ — wrote that *Dödsdansen* now appeared even younger and more relevant than it had when first presented. In *Le Franciste* of Marcel Bucard, Simone Mohy pointed out that Strindberg's personages were more human than those of Ibsen. Only the critics of *Combats*, the organ of the murderous *milice* of Darnand, who intelligently discussed the relationship between Strindberg and Sartre, and praised the theatrical force of Strindberg's writing, also wrote that Strindberg, despite all this, had to be rejected as utterly foreign to 'our race', and that *Dödsdansen* was a piece from 'another world'.

Less than a month after the opening of the play, Paris was liberated. The political world was turned upside down. Doriot was later killed in Germany, Darnand and Bucard were executed as traitors. Rightly so, by the way; I don't pretend to agree with Amnesty that Quisling ought not to have been shot. The critics now were different but their reactions to the play were the same as those of the fascist critics. In Aragon's *Ce Soir*, Jean Tardieu wrote that *Dödsdansen* was a masterpiece and stated that Strindberg was one of the first who, in his work, admitted the inexplicable in human nature.

I say this because it shows how Strindberg's words force themselves through at a decisive historical moment when they prove tuned to the need of the public. Then the ideological prejudices or beliefs of the critics matter very little.

We know how his words were charged with that force. As usual Strindberg used his life and drew on his personal experiences when he wrote *Dödsdansen*. He also borrowed from earlier works. Then he did as he was accustomed to. As he did when he stood looking closely at Siri, his first wife, the mother of his children, in order to be able to sit down at his desk and write *En dåres försvarstal*. This time he took his sister, his beloved sister Anna, by the way, and his brother-in-law Hugo von Philp as material. He loaded them with his experience and projected their possibilities on stage.

It is this technique of not hedging, not holding back, not behaving as one 'should' behave in writing, but instead using himself and everyone around him as raw material for the literary work that gives his words such an extraordinary force. The second thoughts on how relatives or friends might react privately can come afterwards, when they do not harm the work any longer, when the black letters have already been permanently printed on the silent white paper.

Strindberg thus does not construe; he writes. In *Dödsdansen* he writes beyond fiction; he works on the basis of the self. A psychoanalyst would — of course — think that this is not a grown-up way to behave and write. He might even believe as the *Oxford Companion* has it, that it is neurotic. But then the psychoanalysts, like the poor novelists who become their patients, have seldom shown an ability to write like Strindberg.

It was late in Strindberg's life that he wrote *Dödsdansen*, but he worked there as he had done in *Tjänstekvinnans son*. To write effectively, he consciously drew on his experience and used all those close to him as his material without really caring to write an autobiography. This charges his words with power. His figures are inseminated by him, and come alive. There is more to this though than the conscious intent.

Even if he tried to keep clear of political and literary loyalties that could bind him, Strindberg was both an observer and a participant in the intellectual life of his time, and if one wants to know something about the literary and academic scene of Sweden today, *Götiska rummen* and *Svarta fanor* of eighty years ago are still as reliable guides as *Röda rummet* and *Det nya riket* which were written two decades earlier.

This is not to say that *Götiska rummen* and *Svarta fanor* are only guides to the literary life of Stockholm, like the guide to Oslo that the Norwegian writer Sigurd Hoel (1890-1960) wrote in *Sesam, sesam*, just before the Second World War. Hoel's well-written novel is a good historical guide to a dead literary life. But even I, who knew many of the people in question when I lived in Oslo in 1945, find it difficult to sustain an interest all the way through. As for Gustaf af Geijerstam, whom the official press of the time pitied as the innocent victim of the cruel Strindberg, and who whined to the publisher Bonnier that his old friend Strindberg had behaved badly to him in *Svarta fanor*, he is dead and so entirely forgotten that it is as if he had never existed, and the other 'real names' behind the personages in the novel have all long since sunk down to footnotes. Nevertheless, the book is continually reaching new readers, who have never heard of af Geijerstam. But this is not because the novel is a well-made piece: as a novel *Svarta fanor* follows few of the academic rules for good fiction, and in that respect Hoel's is better made.

No, the novel is read because of Zachris, whose name evokes the changeling Little Zaches in the E.T.A. Hoffmann tale 'Klein Zaches genannt Zinnober' from 1819. But through *Svarta fanor* Zachris has become one of the great literary figures in the Swedish language. Thus af Geijerstam himself is gone to oblivion with all his works, but the figure of Zachris that he once saw as his image lives. That is not so strange. Strindberg took only a couple of traits from af Geijerstam when he created Zachris. The eyes. The face. Out of the af Geijerstam family reality he also lifted a couple of scenes. For instance, the one in the eighteenth chapter, when the dying wife comes down and dances for the guests. Or at least he took that from the Geijerstam family reality as noted by Strindberg. But the greatness of Zachris is far beyond the possible for the insignificant af Geijerstam. And the truly great scenes are taken from Strindberg's own life; Zachris is a projection of Strindberg, of his fears and his disgust at seeing the self of former years. Zachris in *Svarta fanor* is as much autobiography as Johan in *Tjänstekvinnans son*. The self in *Svarta fanor*, though, is not a beloved self like Johan. By using the self through the disgusting medium of af Geijerstam, the changeling self as Zachris is reflected larger than life, distorting the figure. As Strindberg goes on writing, this distorted mirror image is throwing the self out of its normal proportions, and so discloses new dimensions. Zachris observes and writes about his dying wife as Strindberg once observed and wrote about Siri. The charge is there, but now the perspective has changed. Zachris becomes a monumental figure; a mythical hero.

Much of Swedish literature would be difficult for an English writer to write in England. Much of our literary criticism would be unpublishable in London, where writers can sue critics for criminal libel. Much also of what we in Sweden write on the doings of the state bureaucracy would be illegal if it were published about the British state in England. That is due to what are to us your strange laws on libel and official secrets. That is not the only difference between us. After all, it is easy enough to learn how to write so they cannot jail you. I know from experience. The real difference is that most of us use our parents, relatives, wives, friends and enemies as raw material in a much freer fashion. Whether we accept it or not, Strindberg is the paradigm. Ivar Lo-Johansson, writing about how Artur Lundqvist sits behind drawn curtains writing primitivist poetry and then eating and drinking, is a beautiful story. The story would not have been written that simply in French or English. An English Lundqvist also would — and could! — have reacted violently against this invasion of his privacy. My childhood trilogy probably would have caused sharper and still more irrational and emotional reactions in England than it did in Sweden, where the volumes, after some initial conflict, have been treated as the writing, the literature, they are. (Something about honouring your father and mother and Exodus 20, verse 12, I imagine.) There is in the Strindbergian tradition a greater acceptance of the necessity of regardlessly — ruthlessly, your critics would say — using your private life and the private lives of anyone around you so as not to construe, not to write artificially.

To most of us in Sweden, Strindberg is a very personal experience. We have read him from early childhood onwards. All of him. *Röda rummet* and the volumes of *Tjänstekvinnans son, Det nya riket* as well as *Ett drömspel* and *Till Damaskus*. As for *Inferno* and *Legender*, they are books no one in their early teens does not understand. You feel them. You also experiment with those explanations in growing up inside our culture. Thus you become enmeshed in his words. That is as it should be. Literature is not something for seminars. We live what we read. He himself lived secondary lives through the words of Heinrich

Heine and Honoré de Balzac, and others. (Being 'impregnated', as he would say, by others as widely different as Chernyshevsky and Joséphin Péladan, E.T.A. Hoffmann and Mark Twain.) To me, the Paris of those Inferno years of Strindberg blend into my Paris of the post-war years. During my second marriage it even so happened that my then wife, May, and I came to live at the Pension Hôtel Orfila. It was still just as Strindberg had described it. *Confort moderne. Prix modéré.* Catholic students from the provinces eating steamed fish on Friday. My daughter was born there. I did not choose to go there. It just so happened. Why it so happened that May and I had to move to rooms at the Hôtel Orfila is a long story that has not directly to do with Strindberg. I will write it another time. But: coming from the Bar Monaco one winter night nearly forty years ago, caught in the middle of an emotional mess of my own making, I looked up and found myself walking past the Luxembourg gardens towards my home where my wife and child were waiting for me in his rooms. Then I knew how that marriage would end. That is not something unique to me. Strindberg is for many, maybe for a majority, in Sweden a factor in our private lives.

My maternal grandfather was a strict and organized teetotaller, a socialist and strong atheist who never allowed a word of religion or other superstition under his roof, whatever my grandmother tried to say. At the same time, of course, he read *Inferno* and *Legender* and *En blå bok.* They were by Strindberg. Strindberg was different. If he dabbled in occultism that was no superstition; if he wrestled with God that was no religion. Strindberg was one of us whatever he did. My grandfather had even seen him in Furusund once. He had gone there just to look at him. Gone with his brother who was a gilder at a bookbinder binding books for Strindberg. They had met him and given him a packet of books but they had not spoken to him. 'There was no need. We had read his words. I simply wanted to see him just once.'

There is a very deep national love for Strindberg. This has to be explained when the very word national has been made doubtful. I remember what a Jewish-Russian writer once told me when we were travelling together in Turkmenistan thirty years ago. Just after the war he was a political officer in a small town in the Soviet Occupation Zone of Germany. The new German cultural league was on his initiative playing *Boris Godunov* by Pushkin as part of the effort to reeducate the Germans after Hitler. Suddenly a Soviet soldier from the Russian countryside rose from his seat. He drew his gun and shot at the ceiling: 'You Germans,' he shouted, 'you cannot be allowed to steal our Pushkin.'

'Of course he was drunk,' my friend said, 'drunk as a Russian peasant. But I understand him. I felt a little like that myself. After all, I had marched and marched from Moscow to Berlin the war through.

From the day I matriculated 22 June 1941 I had marched during four years until I could at last enter Berlin. Even if I knew that it was politically necessary, I felt how it hurt deep inside me having to look at and hear those Germans handling our Pushkin.'

Our feeling for Strindberg is of the same kind. He is Swedish very deeply inside us. Not that every Swede feels like that. Victor Svanberg (1896-1985) was literary critic who became a professor at the provincial university of Uppsala. Some people — he himself at least — considered him daring and radical because he stated openly that the great liberal Swedish nineteenth-century writer Viktor Rydberg (1825-1895) was homosexual and loved boys. The far more brilliant critic and real radical, Erik Blomberg (1894-1965), who was one of the great Swedish poets this century, replied that he didn't care if it was cats Viktor Rydberg had loved. The only important thing was the words he left behind him. Strindberg used to state the same truth about life and words, and tried to say it just as death cut his last sentence short: 'I am no more. Only what I have written exists.'

Victor Svanberg, who had difficulties in understanding words, also struggled against the Strindbergian influence in Swedish life. We lived, he said, Strindbergian lives, had Strindbergian marriages and Strindbergian divorces. He was right, of course, in general but utterly wrong in fact. Most of us have lived in a Strindbergian marriage at one time. Not because we have read too much Strindberg and thus destroyed our marriage. But because Strindberg was a normal Swedish man of his time, describing marital problems, or rightly, marital horrors, that continue to be our normality.

He was married three times. Each time with an independent, intellectual working woman. Someone who was not only a female body walking around or standing in the kitchen and bearing children, like the ones that most of his contemporaries on the literary scene used to seek. He was a sane man who did not only want some kind of quickened sexual mattress. The women he fell in love with were women he could talk to. This makes life and marriage difficult now — as many of us know — and it was still more difficult then.

Who among us quite normal men today, having lived through both the happiness of marriage and the hell of divorce, is unable to understand Strindberg's behaviour when every door is closed to him, when his first marriage is in total crisis, when his wife drinks too much, has other interests, and has tried to get rid of him by having a doctor declare him insane (Siri, a von Essen and thus born into the nobility, was originally married to Baron Wrangel, and has been awarded a halo in literary history that she did not deserve), and when, finally, he lives in a state of married celibacy and asks himself what the hell he should do when he feels the rut coming except masturbate - who cannot understand Strindberg? He seeks no new relationship and does not wish to pay for sex (he is, in any case, sufficiently aristocratic to prefer girls who use toothpaste and soap, and needs to be able to talk intelligently with a woman), and nor is he a pederast, who can turn to boys. I remember the situation very clearly myself from a divorce which took place many years ago. I don't consider this a neurotic response to sexuality.

Strindberg thus both set us a pattern in our lives and remains a paradigm for Swedish writing. For us there is also the national dimension and the social. Not only the national language or the refractory tradition of: 'Another is as good as Another.'

I will try to explain this because many foreigners do not know how to place Strindberg. Also those Swedish critics of Strindberg who become too European and thus lose the possibility of seeing, of visualizing, of living in our words, try their best to get Strindberg to fit into what they consider to be a normal European left-right scheme. First, he is religious as a young man (on the Right), then he is radical and rational (on the Left), then he is occult (on the Right), then he is again a radical, though still religious (some kind of Left). It all becomes very confusing, and they have to do as the stepmother did with her daughters in Andersen's tale. Chop off a toe here and a heel there. In the end, they transform him into their likeness; with bowels filled with fear and the hope that one God or another will show mercy on him who has lived among honourable men, leaving him to die with a good pension.

They say that they understand how we 'on the Left' can read *Röda rummet* and *Det nya riket* and the other writings from Strindberg's early period, but what they absolutely cannot understand is how we, people like me, can read and like and identify with the Strindberg of *Inferno*, *Legender*, *En blå bok* and *Ockulta dagboken*. They even sometimes believe that we on the Left — now or in the youth movement of eighty years ago — accept *Götiska rummen* and *Svarta fanor* only for tactical reasons; because Strindberg there unmasks the liberals.

The political importance of Strindberg is that he transgresses this simple dichotomy of left-right. He belonged in part to the movement that in Sweden was called *åttiotal*, the Eighties. But only partly. And he changed direction when it became the establishment. Hjalmar Branting and the other survivors of that radicalism never understood what he then wrote. But it was *Inferno* and *Legender* that made it possible for him both to become a truly national writer and to join up with the young workers' movement in the new century. They were Marxists, not liberal republicans like Branting, or anarchists like the petty-bourgeois students. Thus they did not mind that Strindberg believed in God. Their own fathers were more often than not both socially rebellious and Free Church believers. This real Left of the 1910s saw what Strindberg stood for: the unmasking of the established upper class and their faked truths. *Inferno* was not a step backward from *Röda rummet*; it was part of a necessary dialectical leap out of an old radicalism that was changing hue, becoming established and reactionary, to a new consciousness. In this necessary change, Strindberg refused to consider the liberal consensus, his literary career, or to let himself be bound by any loyalty, any friendship or love.

Twenty years ago, when I thought it necessary to try and make those of the student movement — and the anti-imperialists — of that time conscious, I wrote at length about this dialectical leap of Strindberg's out of the eighties towards a new century. I wanted to show them a precedent. To clarify what Strindberg did when the radicalism of the eighties was turning into a new establishment and it was thus — in Mao Zedong's words — necessary to act according to the understanding that: To keep Yenan is to lose Yenan; to give up Yenan is to win Yenan.

'Tragical-Comical-Historical-Pastoral'

Strindberg and the Absurdity of Categories

Inga-Stina Ewbank

University of Leeds

My brief for this paper was to provide a table of contents for the conference on 'Strindberg and Genre'. For this purpose Polonius' catalogue seems, for once, not long enough — even if it is allowed to run on to 'scene individable, or poem unlimited'. If those last two Polonian terms are correctly described as bringing 'the already ridiculous categories to a climax in an all-inclusive (*unlimited*) and unclassifiable (*individable*) drama',[1] then they might just do to categorize the *plays* Strindberg wrote after his Inferno crisis. But a major purpose of this conference, I take it, is to dispel the notion, particularly prevalent in English-speaking countries, that Strindberg was primarily a dramatist and would have been wise to remain exclusively so: that he 'wasted' his time on novels, poems and discursive prose — let alone paintings — when he should have been writing *Fadren*, *Fröken Julie*, and perhaps *Ett drömspel*, over and over again. This is a conference to celebrate the range and variousness of the Strindberg corpus; and to attempt to find categories for everything within that huge body of works — verbal and visual, fictive and non-fictive — would seem to be to out-polonius Polonius in absurdity.

And yet, if such an exercise is absurd, it is not so in the sense defined by Ionesco in his essay on Kafka: 'Absurd is that which is devoid of purpose.'[2] Polonius' list is absurd only in so far as it is a ridiculous self-parody. It is not devoid of purpose: it reminds us of the importance of genre theory in the Renaissance, when Italian critics like

Scaliger did not think it absurd to identify and describe more than a hundred genres, both traditional and new generic forms.[3] It reminds us, too, that Shakespeare — while not a theorist — wrote within genre assumptions, an improver rather than an inventor of genres. And, finally, that creative artists have always worked by adjusting, stretching and recombining the genres available to them. Milton in *Samson Agonistes* told the story of himself and of his country through a Hebrew folk tale structured as a Greek tragedy. Strindberg in *Fadren* told the story of his own marriage, as he saw it at a particular moment, through the form of a 'naturalistic tragedy' which he thought would please Zola, and in which his protagonist at one point expresses himself through a serious travesty of a speech from a Shakespearean comedy. Strindberg may always have been telling his own story, but the form he chose to do it in — tragical, comical, historical, or even pastoral — conditioned the story told and controlled its subjectivity. Throughout his career — in letters, diary entries and published writings — he scattered discussions of his own art and that of others; and these are more often than not preoccupied with interaction, with influences and models, giving and taking. If *Rosmersholm* and *Othello* both provided the dynamism of 'själamord' (soul murder — SS 22, p.195) for *Fadren*, Strindberg saw *Hedda Gabler* as the product of 'min säd' (my seed) fertilising Ibsen's 'hjärna' (brain — VIII, p.205);[4] and his own history plays were written 'efter läraren Shakespere' (following the model of my teacher Shakespeare — SS 50, p.240). Strindberg's art was shaped by, and helped to shape, European literary traditions; and for him, as much as for anyone, literary kinds 'may be regarded as institutional imperatives which both coerce and are in turn coerced by the writer.'[5]

Like Polonius, I will deal here with *literary* genres, but the word 'categories' in the title is intended to signal that to do so is in itself a major restriction. Not only does it mean leaving out Strindberg's non-verbal art, but within the verbal category it means sorting literature from non-literature: a daunting task since so much of his writing is the meeting-place for creative urges and theoretical concepts — philosophical, historical, scientific (or pseudo-scientific), critical, and so on — which intermingle in apparent defiance of traditional kinds. How, for example, do we assign *En blå bok* to a genre? At this point the question threatens to become one for Swedish speakers only, as the absence of translations of most of these writings — with the exception of the more spectacularly 'Strindbergian' ones, such as *En dåres försvarstal* — becomes an insurmountable obstacle. This is all the more regrettable, since recent critical developments, rejecting the concept of literature as a canonical body of works, should be a genuine stimulus to Strindberg studies. We must be grateful to Michael Robinson for showing, in his book on *Strindberg and Autobiography*,[6] the complex interweaving of stimuli, subjective and objective, personal and literary, throughout

Strindberg's writings, and we can look forward to his forthcoming translation of Strindberg's letters for continued illumination. What we can learn from works like these, and from any sustained contact with the Strindberg corpus, is that his challenge to 'normal' categories goes hand in hand with a profound and often self-conscious interest in genres. It becomes important, then, not to reject, but to hold on to, the notion of genre as a way into understanding Strindberg. He was, of course, not unwilling to categorize his own work. When he does, the underlying principles tend to be both formal and experiential, as can be seen in the tabulated literary biography which forms the Preface to the fourth part of *Tjänstekvinnans son*, entitled *Författaren* (The Author). The Preface was composed in 1909 when this part of his autobiography, though written in 1886, was first published. Given the distance in time and the potentially misleading title (for *Författaren* deals only with the years 1877-86), he feels the need to 'ställa Författaren rätt i ledet' (to put the Author in his right place in the ranks — SS 19, p.147). There is an interesting ambiguity about the image he uses: 'ställa . . . rätt i ledet', with its implication of inserting himself as an author in a pre-existing, orderly row of people (such as school-children, or soldiers), would seem to refer as much to defining his place in a developing literary tradition as to describing the course of his own life. Even so, some of the labels he gives are entirely experiential, defining works in terms of his own spiritual and ideological position at the time of writing: thus, for example:

Himmelrikets Nycklar (1892). Mörker, sorg, förtvivlan; absolut skepsis.

(*The Keys of Heaven* (1892). Darkness, sorrow, despair; absolute scepticism. — SS 19, p.148)

Some, on the other hand, are entirely formal, as when *Fadren*, *Fröken Julie* and *Fordringsägare* are brought together as 'Försök till Dramats ombildning i tidsenlig form' (Attempts at finding a contemporary form for drama — p.148); and some define works entirely in terms of the development of literary tradition, as when *Svenska öden och äventyr* is labelled 'I Romantikens stil-art, men med nutida innehåll och syn på tingen' (In a Romantic form and style, but with contemporary content and view of things — p.148). And even the most experiential definition tends to slide over into literary history, even if only to disclaim the idea of formal models:

Inferno 1898	Stora krisen vid 50 år; revolutioner i själslivet, ökenvandringar, ödeläggelsen. Svedenborgs Helveten
Legender 1899	och Himlar. Icke influerad av Huysmans' En Route, ännu mindre
Advent	av Peladan som då var Förf. okänd, liksom "En Route", utan byggd på
Damaskus 1, 2	personliga upplevelser.

(The great crisis at the age of 50; spiritual upheavals, wanderings in the desert, devastation, Swedenborg's Hells and Heavens. Not influenced by Huysman's *En Route*, still less by Péladan, who was unknown to the Author at that time, as was *En Route*, but built on personal experiences. — p.149)

It is not difficult to deconstruct the disclaimer, especially as we know that Strindberg was familiar with both Huysmans and Péladan well before 'that time'.[7] The anxiety of influence[8] helps to shape Strindberg's thinking about his own works, even as, in the writing of them, genre expectations help to shape the material: if *Himmelrikets nycklar* is an outpouring of 'sorrow, despair', etc., these emotions have been transmuted and structured into a satirical 'sagospel i fem akter' (A Fairy-Tale Play in Five Acts — title page, SS 25, p.113), looking back to *Lycko-Pers resa* and forward to *Till Damaskus*. Much pain seems to have accompanied that process of structuring,[9] but the struggle to contain his material must in the end also have given him a sense of commanding genre; of using, rather than being used by, genre expectations. And this must be even more true for the plays he wrote in the following summer — the summer of his divorce from Siri von Essen — plays such as *Bandet*, 'Sorgespel i en akt' (A Tragedy in One Act — title page, SS 25, p.291), and *Leka med elden*, 'Komedi i en akt' (A Comedy in One Act — title page, SS 25, p.401). That in the same summer he also began to paint 'more seriously than before'[10] is evidence of the multiple strengths of his creativity. In the list of works in *Författaren*, all the one-act plays of this period are lumped together under the label 'Ur det cyniska livet' (From the Cynical Life — SS 19, p.148); but anyone who has read, or better still, seen *Bandet* and *Leka med elden* knows that these plays move the boundary stakes of the genres of, respectively, tragedy and comedy, thus confirming that

In truth the prison unto which we doom
Ourselves no prison is.[11]

If, then, Strindberg saw genre as a challenge, rather than a confinement to 'a narrow room', this is, of course, not unique to him. Alastair

Fowler has stated the general point with a clarity that justifies a lengthy quotation:

> Every work of literature belongs to at least one genre. Indeed, it is sure to have a significant generic element. For genre has quite a different relation to creativity from the one usually supposed, whereby it is little more than a restraint upon spontaneous expression. Rightly understood, it is so far from being a mere curb on expression that it makes the expressiveness of literary works possible. Their relations to the genres they embody is not one of passive membership but of active modulation. Such modulation communicates. And it probably has a communicative value far greater than we can ever be directly aware of.[12]

Not that Strindberg had always been convinced of the 'communicative value' of genre. It is worth remembering that there was a period in the mid-1880s when he came close to rejecting literature and longed, almost untranslatably 'att få skriva, utan att författa' (to be allowed to write without writing literature — SS 16, p.143). He satisfied this longing in quantities of polemical writing, like the essay on 'Nationalitet och svenskhet' (Nationality and Swedishness) from which the just quoted phrase is taken, and this opens with a triumphant assertion of the rights conferred on him by journalism, 'att få nedsätta tankar i tidens frågor utan att behöva inlägga dem i skönlitteraturens konfektaskar' (to set down my thoughts on the questions of the age without having to package them in the chocolate boxes of fiction — p.143). At much the same time (spring and early summer 1884) he wrote to his publisher, Karl Otto Bonnier: 'Jag tycker det är omoraliskt skrifva noveller' (I think writing short stories is immoral — IV, p.210). Fortunately he continued to be, in this sense, extremely immoral. Theoretically, he held the extreme position that truth and reality lie only in each individual's experience and can only be falsified by literature; hence literature should in future be replaced by 'varje medborgares självbiografi vid viss ålder, anonymt . . . inlämnad till kommunalarkivet' (each citizen's autobiography, written at a certain age and anonymously . . . submitted to the municipal archive — SS 18, p.457). Looking back at that position in 1886 he sees himself as having held it 'på tre fjärdedels allvar' (three-quarters convinced — SS 18, p.457), although a couple of months later he could still write to Gustaf Steffen: 'Skönlitteraturen är död för mig' (For me, fiction is a dead art form — VI, p.9). In 'Över mölnen' (Above the Clouds), one of the four short stories which make up the volume *Utopier i verkligheten* from 1885, the position of fiction and poetry is debated; and it is interesting to note that the story, so far from being programmatic, deconstructs itself.

Two poet-playwrights, Henri and Aristide, both desperately ill with tuberculosis, meet at a Swiss mountain hotel-cum-sanatorium. Previously mortal enemies, they now talk, helpless in their wheelchairs, about the state of literature, about the kind of works they have been writing, and about the kind of literature the age needs. Henri is the spokesman for doing away with literature as fiction, form and style — as something which makes the real, however beautiful, vague and hazy. Poetry, he says, must be abolished, for:

> Det kittlar inbillningen men ger icke någon klar föreställning, det vaggar begreppen i en domning, där verklighet och drömmar blandas; det är sålunda med vår poesi som med den lasten som kallas rus.

> (It tickles the imagination but gives us no clear ideas; it lulls our conceptual powers into a state of semi-consciousness where reality and dreams merge; it is with our poetry as with the vice called intoxication — pp.169-70)

The idea of poetry rejected here is curiously like that which will be exalted in *Ett drömspel*.[13] Henri makes his rejection the thematic centre of the story as he proceeds to contrast his and Aristide's poetic activity with that which is useful: 'det arbetar i jorden, men det höjer oss över molnen; vi arbetade över molnen och komma lika fullt i jorden' (it works in the earth, but raises us above the clouds; we were working above the clouds but will still end up in the earth — SS 15, p.171). There is irony here, in Henri's use of the poetic devices of metaphor and antithesis to condemn poetry, which prevents us from taking it as the author's own statement. This becomes even more obvious in the blatantly symbolical ending, a strikingly visual scene where Henri, left at the hotel, watches and tries to wave to the departing Aristide and his family, their carriage travelling ever higher:

> Ett ofantligt moln svävade som en pappersdrake däruppe framför hästens huvud och i nästa ögonblick skulle åkdonet med de resande försvinna. Henri såg det; öppnade munnen till ett rop, men fick ej fram ett ljud. Då syntes något vitt röra sig inne i vagnen, och snart viftade fyra näsdukar, viftade som farande vänner, när skeppet går till havs, och så försvann åkdonet in i molnet.

(A gigantic cloud hovered, like a paper kite, up there, in front of the horse's head, and in the next moment the carriage with the travellers would have vanished. Henri saw this; he opened his mouth to call after them, but no sound would come. Then something white could be seen moving inside the carriage, and soon four handkerchiefs were waving, waving as do departing friends when their ship sets sail, and then the carriage vanished — p.175)

If this story was meant to advocate a rejection of literature and its formal, structural and verbal devices, then it very effectively deconstructs itself. Strindberg will not have known that he was creating a new genre of narrative literature — one which we might call tragicomical-dialectical-sanatorial and see continued in Thomas Mann's short story 'Tristan', let alone in *The Magic Mountain* — but I doubt very much that the basic irony was unconscious. To support that doubt there is the tongue-in-cheek 'Interview' which serves as a Preface to the first volume of *Giftas*, in 1884:

Interv. : Nå herrn har gått och skrivit en romanbok igen nu?
Förf. : Ja, kära herre, så illa är det! Jag vet att det är stort straff på det, men jag kunde inte hålla mig!
Interv. : Men jag tycker det är inkonsekvent att hugga på författeri och sedan själv gå och författa. Medger herrn det?
Förf. : Medgives!

(*Interviewer* : So, sir, you have gone and written yet another novel?
Author : Yes, my dear sir, I'm afraid I have. I know it's a punishable offence, but I couldn't help myself.
Interviewer : But I think it's inconsistent to be trying to do away with literature and then to go and write a book yourself. Do you admit it, sir?
Author : I admit it! — SV 16, p.9)

Having admitted his inconsistency, the Author explains his novel as an 'återfall' (relapse) and promises to stop writing novels, plays and poems 'om ett par år . . . om det är möjligt' (in a couple of years . . . if possible). And when asked what he will then do with himself, he replies: 'Jag tänker bli intervjuare' (I'm thinking of becoming an interviewer — p.9).

Strindberg would have been a very bad interviewer, preoccupied with himself rather than with his interviewee, and he knows it, just as he must have known that it was not 'possible' for him to stop being an author. Novels, plays and poems — as well as many other forms of writing — were to continue to pour from his pen. In just over two years from this fictive interview he had finished *Tjänstekvinnans son* (December 1886), and two months later he had completed *Fadren*. The fourth part of the autobiographical fiction spans the years in which he had discovered that he was, ineluctably, a writer; by the end of it the hero, Johan, is launched into the present. At this point there is nothing to indicate that Strindberg saw himself primarily as a dramatist. He has indeed little to say on genres as such: they are, it would seem, part of the process which the last chapter of the book describes as a 'search'. In this context the nature and function of a writer are defined in words which, from our vantage point, seem uncannily to describe his own entire authorship, pre- and post-Inferno:

> Där finns motsägelser! Ja, där skall finnas motsägelser, ty sakerna skola betraktas från motsatta sidor, emedan sakerna icke äro lika på två sidor, och författaren är en experimentator. . .

> (There are contradictions! Indeed, there have to be contradictions, as things have to be seen from two sides, since the two sides of a thing are different; and a writer is an experimenter — SS 19, p.278)

The author is an experimenter, grappling with old forms to express new thoughts and feelings, not afraid to present unresolved contradictions: this seems to me the key to Strindberg's relationship with genres. It may be easier to demonstrate this in the works of the post-Inferno period. When, for example, Strindberg first conceived the work he was to call *Inferno*, he saw it as 'ett poem på prosa' and 'i stor hög ton' (a poem in prose . . . in a grand high tone — XI, p.307), and as a response to the call to become 'Ockultismens Zola' (the Zola of the occult — p.307). In the same letter, of 23 August 1896, he is quite clear about the thematic structure and didactic bearings of the proposed work. But only a few weeks later, on 12 September, he feels he 'synes drifvas fram till skrifningen af Inferno' (is being driven forward to the writing of Inferno — XI, p.323); and when he finally sits down to compose *Inferno* in the summer of 1897, it is indeed a prose poem, but one finding, under the pressure of experience, its own organic form — combining, contradictorily, the wonderful and the grotesque, the nightmarish and the comic — rather than the tendentious one originally envisaged. The genre thus created, and its transmutation into dramatic form in *Till Damaskus*, may be new; but the principle of freedom to create is not. Strindberg had practised it all along and preached it in the 1880s, most explicitly in the essay 'Om modernt drama och modern teater' (On Modern Drama and the Modern Theatre, 1889), where he hails the achievement of the Théâtre Libre as 'en konstens frigörelse, en renässans, en förlossning från en gruvlig estetik' (a liberation of art, a renaissance, a delivery from a terrible aesthetic — SS 17, p.302) and prays that his own country may also acquire such a theatre,

> ... där man kan rysa åt det rysligaste, le åt det löjliga, leka med leksaker; där man kan få se allt ... även om gamla konvenanslagar skola brytas, må vi få en fri teater, där man har frihet till allt, utom att sakna talang och vara hycklare eller dumbom!

(where one is allowed to shudder at horrors, smile at the ludicrous, play with toys; where one is allowed to see anything ... even if it means breaking the established laws of decorum, may we acquire a free theatre, one where you have the freedom to do anything, except lack talent, or be a hypocrite or an idiot! — p.303)

Nearly twenty years later, he was to define the genre of the Chamber Play in very similar terms: 'Ingen bestämd form skall binda författaren, ty motivet betingar formen. Alltså frihet i behandlingen, endast bunden av konceptionens enhet och stilkänslan' (No predetermined form is to limit the writer; the content will determine the form. Thus, freedom in the treatment of the material, limited only by the unity of the writer's conception and his feeling for style — SS 50, p.12).

There are many aspects to Strindberg's exercise of this freedom; but, in pursuit of the idea of genre, I will dwell on only two. The first is his modernity: the impact of his iconoclasm and innovatory power on European thought and literary tradition. Thomas Mann best sums this up when he refers to the works of Strindberg as 'ein unerlässliches Bildungszubehör zur Zeit meiner Jugend' (an indispensable element of the *Bildung* [culture and education] of the time of my youth).[14] The impact has, of course, lasted beyond the generation of Thomas Mann. We tend to think, and write, of him mostly as an influence on twentieth-century drama, from the German Expressionists to Beckett and beyond; his impact as an 'experimenter' in prose fiction and in verse needs much more exploration.[15] It is, for example, worth remembering how strangely 'modern', in the age of Vietnam, or the Gulf War, can seem even an early story like 'Samvetskval' (Pangs of Conscience) — another of the stories in *Utopier i verkligheten*, in which a Prussian officer has to execute three French *franc-tireurs* and finds, because of Strindberg's use of a technique of merging inner and outer reality which looks forward to his post-Inferno period, that their blood is everywhere — on the vines outside, in his food, in his mind.

The second aspect of Strindbergian 'freedom' that we might note is his ability to treat the same subject in different genres. Sometimes this is a very specific phenomenon, as when the stories of an early play, *Herr Bengts hustru* (1882) and a late one, *Gustav III* (1902), also exist as prose fiction in *Svenska öden och äventyr*. More often it is a more general question of central Strindberg themes being explored in one genre after another: the amorphous nature of the self both enacted and discussed in *Tjänstekvinnnans son*, determining the structure of *Inferno* and *Ett drömspel* respectively, and translated into lyric poetry in 'Molnbilder' (Cloud Pictures).[16] Or, as no one needs reminding, the nature of marriage is obsessively explored in work upon work, through a variety of genres — in the plays, from the pseudo-historical *Herr Bengts hustru* to the Chamber Plays, via the naturalistic plays and *Dödsdansen*; in prose ranging from the most raw and autobiographical to the most historical-fictional; and in verse, where the marriage of true minds can change into hatred at the adjusting of a shoulder strap. In this last example I am referring to the poem called 'Jag drömde' (I dreamed) which is part of that wonderful poetic medley, 'Trefaldighetsnatten' (The Night Before Trinity Sunday, 1902). Moving a piece of ribbon on his beloved's shoulder, which has been irritating him as a blot on her perfection, the lover suddenly finds that

> med ett, förvandlades min brud,
> ett ansikte så grymt som väl Gorgonens.

> (at a stroke, my bride was transformed,
> a face as cruel as the Gorgon's — SS 37, p.288)

'Jag drömde' reminds one of (and may indeed have its roots in) Shakespeare's Cleopatra, who sees Anthony under two simultaneous aspects: 'Though he be painted one way like a Gorgon, / The other way's a Mars' (*Anthony and Cleopatra*, II.v.117-18). It reminds one, too, of Strindberg's vision of the writer as an 'experimenter' driven by his sense of the doubleness of things. Here, I repeat, seems to lie a key to his use of genres: his urge to bend and stretch and recombine existing forms until they fit what he wishes to pour into them. The deep structure underlying whatever genre he uses would seem to be one of transformation: a perception of life, characters, even things, as fragmentary and forever liable to change into their opposites. And as they do, love may change into hatred, or fear into exaltation; tragedy may change into comedy, or vice versa.

Perhaps the most spectacular such transformation is in *Till Damaskus II*, where the triumph of the protagonist, the Unknown, turns to shame as the banqueting hall in which he is seated turns into a bar, then a brothel, and eventually a prison cell. The theatre is, of course, the vehicle of transformation *par préférence*; and the clash between the two halves (pre- and post-seduction) of *Fröken Julie*, or the incongruity of the ball in hell in *Advent*, is each in its way also a clash between genres — but of the kind that creates a new and richer genre in the process. Yet Strindbergian transformations are just as prevalent outside his plays: at the level of linguistic detail, for example, as when the author of the semi-fictional story 'Hjärnornas kamp' (The Battle of the Brains) in the first collection of *Vivisektioner*, sums up the contradictory possibilities of human relationships by saying, of the young man Schilf: 'Jag ville gagna honom och begagna honom' (I wanted to be of use to him *and* use him — SV 29, p.37). And it is also operative at the level of narrative detail. Striking examples of this abound in Strindberg's later, more obviously experimental, fiction, such as *Taklagsöl*; but they are richly evident in the early stories of *Svenska öden och äventyr*, like the remarkable 'Högre ändamål' (Higher Purposes), in the agonies of the priest forced by papal decree to put away his wife and children. The marital bed, thrust out into the snow, becomes both 'en ofantlig likkista' (a gigantic coffin — SS 11, p.106) and 'en vällustig bädd. Här skulle Cleopatra hava firat bröllop med Goliath' (a lustful bed. In it, Cleopatra should have celebrated her marriage with Goliath — p.106). A scrap of red material, torn off his wife's skirt as it caught on a bush at a *fête champêtre* in happier days, looks to the priest first like a bright butterfly; then, turned by the wind, it becomes 'ett blodigt hjärta; ett hjärta ryckt ur bröstet på ett offer och upphängt i lundens träd' (a bleeding heart; a heart torn from the breast of a victim and hung in one of the trees of a sacrificial grove — SS 11, pp.110-11).

This piece of red material functions much as do the transformations of objects in *Ett drömspel*: one of many possible reminders of the cross-currents within the Strindberg corpus and of the continuity of his associative imagination, whether it expresses itself in narrative, dramatic or lyrical art. It is a reminder, too, of how often that art is both tragic and comic (for the priest is in the end reunited with his wife), both historical and pastoral.

In a letter to Verner von Heidenstam from 4 August 1886, Strindberg tells a story which, if it does not sum up this table of contents, will at least serve to point any discussion of 'Strindberg and Genre' in the direction of a 'both'- 'and':

Igår vid table d'hôten satt en gubbrackare midt emot mig och glodde. Slutligen sade han på tyska:
 ''Entweder ein Dichter oder ein Demagogue!''
 ''Alles Beides!'' svarade jag.

(Yesterday at the table d'hôte an old chap sat opposite me and
stared. Finally he said in German:
"Either a poet or a demagogue!"
"Both!" I replied. — VI, p.6)

Notes

1. *Hamlet*, ed. Harold Jenkins, The Arden Shakespeare (London, 1982), notes
   to II.ii.391-96: 'The best actors in the world, either for tragedy,
   comedy, history, pastoral, pastoral-comical, historical-pastoral,
   tragical-historical, tragical-comical-historical-pastoral, scene
   individable, or poem unlimited.'
2. Quoted in Martin Esslin, *The Theatre of the Absurd* (London, 1962), p.17.
3. On genre theory in the Renaissance generally, see Madeleine Doran,
   Endeavours of Art: A Study of Form in Elizabethan Drama (Madison,
   Wisc., 1954), in Shakespeare in particular, see Rosalie L. Colie,
   Shakespeare's Living Art (Princeton N.J., 1974).
4. All translations from the Swedish are my own.
5. René Wellek and Austin Warren, *The Theory of Literature* (Peregrine
   Books edition, Harmondsworth, 1978), p.226, quoting N.H. Pearson,
   'Literary Forms and Types . . .', *English Institute Annual*, 1940
   (1941), p.70.
6. *Strindberg and Autobiography: Writing and Reading a Life* (Norwich,
   1986).
7. According to the last chapter of *Inferno*, discovering Péladan was part of
   the resolution of Strindberg's religious crisis: 'Den 1 maj [1897] läste
   jag för första gången Sar Peladans [sic] book "Comment on devient
   mage". Sar Peladan, dittills okänd för mig, kommer som en
   stormvind. . . .' (On 1 May [1897] I read for the first time Sâr
   Péladan's book *Comment on devient mage*. Sâr Péladan, till that time
   unknown to me, comes like a storm wind — SS 28, p.201). See my
   discussion of Strindberg and Péladan in 'German Poets in Strindberg's
   Theatre: The Repertoire That Never Was', in Dorothy James and Silvia
   Ranawake, eds., *Patterns of Change: German Drama and the
   European Tradition* (New York, 1990), pp.150-163, esp. pp.156-57.
   — Georg Brandes talked with Strindberg of Huysmans and occultism
   in November 1896 (the year after *En Route*, Huysmans' novel of
   monastic life, was published); see Stellan Ahlström, ed., *Ögonvittnen:
   August Strindberg*, II (Stockholm, 1961), pp.115-18.
8. Cf. Harold Bloom, *The Anxiety of Influence* (New York, 1973). Strindberg
   so assumes the notion of influence, or literary parallels, that he can
   acknowledge it, in this list, in almost shorthand fashion. Thus, '*Gustav
   Adolf* = Nathan den Vise' (*Gustav Adolf* = [Lessing's] *Nathan der
   Weise*).

The Absurdity of Categories

See Strindberg's letter to Fredrik Vult von Steijern: 'Drog mig sjelf i håret upp ur förtviflan och skref med raseri och tre fastkörningar andra akten — som jag nu måste kassera!' (I dragged myself up from my despair by the hair and wrote, furiously and getting stuck three times, the second act — which I must now destroy! — VIII, p.388).
10. Olof Lagercrantz, *August Strindberg* (Stockholm, 1979), p.273.
11. William Wordsworth's sonnet, 'Nuns fret not at their narrow room'.
12. Alastair Fowler, *Kinds of Literature: An Introduction to the Theory of Genres and Modes* (Oxford, 1982), p.20.
13. Cf. the dialogue between Indra's Daughter and the Poet in the Fingal's Cave scene. The Daughter defines poetry as 'Ej verklighet men mer än verklighet . . . ej dröm men vakna drömmar. . .' (Not reality, but more than reality . . . not dream, but dreams dreamed when awake — SV 46, p.91).
14. Thomas Mann, 'August Strindberg', in *Gesammelte Werke*, X (Frankfurt, 1960), p.371. Cf. also Leopold von Weise, *Strindberg und die Junge Generation* (Cologne, 1921).
15. Two notable recent Swedish contributions in this area are Barbro Ståhle Sjönell, *Strindbergs Taklagsöl — Ett prosaexperiment* (Stockholm, 1986) and John Eric Bellquist, *Strindberg as a Modern Poet: A Critical and Comparative Study* (Berkeley and Los Angeles, 1986).
16. 'Molnbilder', in *Ordalek och småkonst* (1902), has an uncanny resemblance to the passage in Shakespeare's *Anthony and Cleopatra*, IV.xiv.2ff., where Anthony feels his identity dissolving: 'Sometime we see a cloud that's dragonish.'

Strindberg's Mixing of Genres

Barbro Ståhle Sjönell

Stockholm University

Strindberg's relationship to literary genres was at times somewhat ambivalent, as this dialogue from the introduction to volume one of *Giftas* reveals:

> Interv. : Nå herrn har gått och skrivit en romanbok igen nu?
> Förf. : Ja, kära herre, så illa är det! Jag vet att det är stort straff på det, men jag kunde inte hålla mig!
> Interv. : Men jag tycker det är inkonsekvent att hugga på författeri och sedan själv gå och författa. Medger herrn det? [. . .]
> Förf. : Javisst! Jag är liksom allt skapat underkastad utvecklingens lag, och utvecklingen går fram genom återfall! Den här romanboken är ett litet återfall (en rechute), men herrn skall inte vara ond på mig för det. Om ett par år skall jag sluta med romanböcker, pjäsböcker och versböcker, om det är möjligt!
> Interv. : Vad tänker herrn ta sig till sedan då?
> Förf. : Jag tänker bli intervjuare.

(*Interviewer*: Now, Sir, you've gone and written another novel. *Author*: Yes, my friend, that's the sad truth. I know I shall be severely punished for it, but I couldn't stop myself. *Interviewer*: But isn't it inconsistent of you to attack the writing of novels, and then go and write a novel yourself. Don't you agree? [. . .] *Author*: Of course I do! Like everything else in creation, I'm subject to the laws of evolution, and it's through our relapses that we advance. This book of stories is a slight relapse (a *rechute*), but you mustn't be angry with me because of it. In a couple of years I shall stop producing novels, and plays, and poetry, that is if I can! *Interviewer*: And what will you turn to then, Sir? *Author*: I'm thinking of becoming an interviewer. — SV 16, p.9)

Since *Giftas* is a collection of short stories, the word 'novel' is here evidently synonymous with 'prose'. In future, therefore, I shall avoid Strindberg's terminology and keep instead to the definitions used by Morten Nøjgaard in *Litteraturens Univers*, in which those genres not associated with a definite era — lyric, prose and drama — are referred to as the lyrical, narrative and dramatic registers. Nøjgaard adds a fourth register, the didactic, to cover non-literary texts, i.e. letters, diaries, historical writings, travel books, works of popular science, newspaper and magazine articles. He also includes 'real' autobiography in this register and points out that such narrative texts as autobiographical novels often claim to belong to the didactic register. This register is especially convenient for our purposes since Strindberg produced work in all these fields. Nøjgaard reserves the term 'genre' for a group of texts associated with specific periods, for instance 'the well-made play' or 'the picaresque novel',[1] though I prefer to use the term to define the sub-groups in a particular register: novel, short story, saga, fable, etc.

However, I entirely subscribe to Nøjgaard's view that there are no texts which represent pure registers or genres. Furthermore, authors are continually creating new genres. If one therefore wishes to ascertain how and to what extent registers are mixed, one is obliged to employ some practical tool such as a constructed term. The main object of my investigation is to discover how Strindberg's works fit into these four registers, taking *Inferno* (1897) as the dividing line between his early and late works. This is partly because the so-called Inferno crisis led to a certain shift in his writing, even though there are motifs, themes, symbols and genres that are common to both periods, and partly because this division is practical if one wishes to trace a development in his writing.[2] A further reason is that, after writing *Inferno*, Strindberg returned to Sweden to find a new literary climate dominated by the writers of the nineties.

Strindberg's early writing covers all four registers. He may well have essayed the didactic register first as his earliest known text, a letter written when he was nine, suggests.[3] Twelve years later he preached several sermons in Ösmo church, but unfortunately they have not been preserved, and between 1868 and 1872 he tried writing in all three literary registers, and also made his debut as a journalist.[4] Indeed, Strindberg moved from one register to another during the greater part of his career, although the lyrical, concentrated to two periods — an early one between 1869 and 1883 and a late one between 1902 and 1905 — is the least well represented.[5] When Strindberg was working as a journalist during the 1870s he was also writing plays, and when he made his breakthrough at the beginning of the 1880s with the novel *Röda rummet* (1879) he alternated imaginative literature with cultural history. In the mid-1890s he did in fact stop writing 'romanböcker, pjäsböcker och versböcker', as the introduction to *Giftas* had prophesied, and devoted himself to scientific research. About the turn of the century he concentrated entirely on writing drama, but within a few years he resumed writing novels and stories as well. The last six years of his life were dominated by works in the didactic register, the essays of *En blå bok*, the open letters to the Intimate Theatre, his studies in philology, and his polemical contributions to the press in what became known as 'the Strindberg Feud'. If one compares the works written before *Inferno* with those from the following period, however, one can say that about two thirds of what he wrote in the narrative register dates from before 1897 while works in the didactic and lyrical registers are fairly evenly distributed between both periods, but that two thirds of his work in the dramatic register was written after *Inferno*. This prompts the following question: did the fact that Strindberg had complete mastery of the different registers mean that he set up sharp dividing lines between them? I shall endeavour to answer this by examining works belonging to various registers in order to see whether there is a mixing of registers, or whether some works are particularly difficult to assign to a specific category. Since space is limited, I must rely on a limited number of illuminating examples.

The Didactic and Narrative Registers

It is often difficult to set a dividing line between the didactic and the narrative registers. This is especially true where Strindberg is concerned. For example, in a work of cultural history such as *Gamla Stockholm*, he writes several chapters, like the introductory 'En Stockholmspromenad på 1730-talet' (A Walk in Stockholm in the 1730s), in the form of short stories. His letters, too, often have pronounced literary qualities, and in some cases can be regarded as the preliminaries to a literary work. The so-called Hedlund letters, written to Torsten Hedlund during 1896 on numbered manuscript paper, are a particularly good example. They may be regarded as the first draft of *Inferno*.[6] The autobiographical works *Tjänstekvinnans son, En dåres försvarstal, Inferno, Legender, Klostret*[7], and *Ensam* can be assigned to the narrative register without much difficulty. To a greater or lesser extent, and in various ways, they are all arranged in a literary manner. But how should we classify the epistolary novel *Han och hon* which was intended to form part of *Tjänstekvinnans son*? It is based on the correspondence between Strindberg and Siri von Essen in 1875 and 1876, and differs from the original letters only in the substitution of fictitious names and the addition of chapter headings. Does it belong to the narrative or the didactic register? In any case, it offers an example of mixed registers since several of the letters include fragments of poetry.

Among the scientific works, meanwhile, there are also several with distinct literary features. When The Svedberg, the Nobel Prize winning chemist, summed up his impressions of Strindberg's works on chemistry, he declared that their value was 'helt och hållet av litterär och psykologisk natur' (entirely of a literary and psychological nature),[8] and called the essays in *En blå bok* 'små stilistiska mästerstycken av bestickande idioti' (small stylistic masterpieces of seductive idiocy).[9] It was unquestionably the literary qualities to which he attached importance.[10] By making the principal character a scientist, Strindberg was able to introduce scientific argument into several of his works, for example the story 'Samvetskval' in *Utopier* and the novel *I havsbandet*. However, it was not until after *Inferno* that he began to include extended sequences belonging to the didactic register in his literary prose. This was done in various ways. In *Svarta fanor*, for example, the whole composition of the novel is characterized by the fact that Strindberg has mixed two registers. It is set in two distinct milieux. The first nine chapters depict a false clique of writers and journalists in a world dominated by materialism. In the tenth chapter the action switches to a cloister where an order of intellectual brothers carry on learned discussions reminiscent of Platonic dialogues. Subsequent chapters alternate between the clique of writers and the group in the cloister,[11] whose discussions of (among other things) ornithology, astronomy, Frauenhofer's lines and chemistry (complete with technical terms and figures) evidently belong to the didactic register. For example:

> Nu återvänder jag till tennet. Tenn smälter vid 236°, men tennets molekularvikt är 236. Vad innebär detta? Det rår icke min tanke ännu att uträkna, men likvisst synes med varje ökad värmegrad molekularattraktionen minskas med talet 1 . . . bom! Men, vidare, framåt i mörkret, jag vet att det skall ljusna.

> (I now return to tin. Tin melts at 236°, but the molecular weight of tin is 236. What does that imply? My thoughts are not yet able to work it out, but nevertheless the molecular attraction seems to decrease by 1 unit for every degree of increased heat . . . a miss! But onwards through the darkness,

I know it will grow lighter. — SS 41, p.250)

In *Taklagsöl*, meanwhile, there is also a section in the didactic register, but its inclusion in the text is justified in a quite different way from *Svarta fanor*. In *Taklagsöl* the main character, a curator, is dying as the result of an accident. To ease his pain, he takes morphine and the hallucinations it induces lead him to talk almost unceasingly. Towards the end of the story the monologue becomes more and more incoherent. It is here that Strindberg inserts purely scientific material containing complicated chemical calculations:

> ... nu skall du se siffror: gallan håller bland annat Biliprasin vars formel är $C_{16}H_{22}O_5 + N_2O$, och malörten håller Absintin vars formel är $C_{16}H_{22}O_5$. Tala de siffrorna, och vet du var malörten växer? Ja, om du hittar ett malörtstånd i skogen, så vet du vad som hänt på den platsen, där någon deponerat Exkretin, vars karaktär bestämmes av gallan. Gallan blir malört! Naturens kretslopp, symbiosen mellan djuret och växten, uttryckt i siffror $C_{16}H_{22}O_5$ ...

> (... now I'm going to show you the figures: Bile contains, among other things, biliprasine, whose formula is $C_{16}H_{22}O_5 + N_2O$, and wormwood contains absinthine, whose formula is $C_{16}H_{22}O_5$. Let those figures speak for themselves. Do you know where wormwood grows? Well, if you find a clump of wormwood in the forest, then you know what happened on that spot there, somebody has deposited excretine, whose characteristics are determined by bile. The bile becomes wormwood! The cycle of Nature, the symbiosis between animals and plants, expressed in the figures $C_{16}H_{22}O_5$ ... — SV 55, pp.52-3)[12]

In a letter that Strindberg wrote to his German translator Emil Schering in 1907, he indicates that he had 'deponerat upptäckter' (deposited discoveries) in *Taklagsöl*, one of which is the section on wormwood. He also requested Schering to pass the discoveries on to two scientists.[13] In the so-called Green Sack in the Royal Library in Stockholm which contains Strindberg's papers, among the many manuscripts, drafts and notes there are also several sheets of formulae for biliprasine and absinthine, showing that he had been working on his discoveries. Indeed, *Taklagsöl* is not the only work in which he discussed the relationship between wormwood and bile. The argument recurs in *En blå bok*, under the heading 'Serumväxter' (serum Plants). It was here that Strindberg finally found a form and a genre suited to preserving discoveries of this nature. *En blå bok* consists of short sections, often no longer than one or two pages, discussing mainly religious and scientific problems. The index lists eighteen different fields, among them philosophy, art, botany, astronomy, physics and medicine. Almost a third of the sections deal with scientific subjects. Furthermore, within the framework provided, Strindberg could mix texts belonging to the didactic register with others that are purely narrative in character. The book contains short stories like 'I vindskontoret' (In the Attic), in which an abandoned husband goes up into the attic and, on seeing furniture and other objects that once stood in the family home, recalls the years spent with his wife and children. A similarity with the short story 'Ett halvt ark papper' (A Half-sheet of Paper) in *Sagor* is striking, for both are constructed on a mental review of a chain of events. Other texts bear a greater resemblance to the stories in *Giftas*. The fate of a married couple is described, often with the same type of concentrated opening as in the short stories of the 1880s. For example, 'Korsdragaren' (The Cross Bearer) begins: 'När han gifte sig med henne, var hon 23 år, alltså en gammal flicka, men även med ett riksbekant förflutet' (When he married her, she was 23, that is to say an old maid, but with a past notorious throughout the country — SS 48, p.885). There are also instances where a sketch in *En blå bok* was later expanded into a complete work. This is the case with 'Staden Tofet' (The City of Tophet) which later became the drama *Stora landsvägen*.[14] But the mixture of registers in *En blå bok* is naturally not the same as in *Svarta fanor* or *Taklagsöl*, in which the didactic register is introduced into a narrative text. The sections in *En blå bok* can generally be ascribed to one register or the other.[15]

The Dramatic and the Lyrical Registers

If one wishes to determine whether there is a mixture of the dramatic and the lyrical registers in Strindberg one immediately runs into difficulty since verse drama has been an established form since Antiquity. Three of Strindberg's oldest historical plays are verse dramas: *Hermione, I Rom* and the third version of *Mäster Olof*. The fairy-tale plays *Himmelrikets nycklar*, *Abu Casems tofflor*, *Svarta handsken*, and the fragment entitled *Starkodder skald* also belong to this category. In these plays roughly the same proportion of verse to prose can be observed as in Shakespeare. *Stora landsvägen* is a cross between verse and prose drama in which about a third of the lines are in verse. There are also lengthy passages of verse in *Lycko-Pers resa*, which is only to be expected in a fairy-tale play. Verse dramas are thus to be found in both Strindberg's early and late production. There is, however, an increasing tendency in the plays after *Inferno* to include song and recitation. Of the twenty-four plays containing songs, only four belong to the earlier period: *Den fredlöse, Lycko-Pers resa, Fröken Julie* and *Himmelrikets nycklar*. But in the post-Inferno dramas there are songs in several of the history plays and the fairy-tale plays as well as in *Till Damaskus* and *Spöksonaten*.

Two of the prose dramas written after *Inferno* contain lyrical passages that tend to create a mixture of two genres. One is *Ett drömspel* in which the preface and epilogue are in verse. Moreover, in the Fingal's Cave scene Indra's Daughter, seeking to establish contact with her father, interprets the sighing of the wind and the song of the waves to the Poet in three stanzas which form a lyrical poem inserted into the drama. Each stanza is introduced with the stage direction 'Reciterar vid Svag musik' (Recited accompanied by faint music — SV 46, p.90), and the stanzas are separated from the surrounding lines by asterisks. The other example of a lyrical register nestling within a drama occurs in the fragment *Holländarn*, the first act of which contains a passage in lyrical prose. A young woman, dressed as a bride, appears in a vision to the protagonist who breaks into a monlogue in which he calls her a 'himlabarn' (child of heaven) and 'af Gudaätt' (of divine ancestry). A reference to Indra's Daughter immediately suggests itself, but in fact the subject is the resemblance between a woman's body and the cosmic lines, the planets and their courses. The monologue begins: 'Hvad är det? Hvem är det? — Ett menskobarn i hvita slöjor; en choeur af linjers harmonier som under slöjan röjes; ett verldssystem, en afbild af den stora Kosmos!' (What is it? Who is it? — A child of man in white veils; a choir of harmonic lines revealed from under the veil, a universe, an image of the great Cosmos!).[16] Strindberg later extracted the passage from the drama, rearranged it in verse, and included it as a poem in *Ordalek och småkonst*.

'Trefaldighetsnatten' in the same collection was originally planned as a verse play. In his excellent edition of *Ordalek och småkonst* in Samlade Verk, Gunnar Ollén includes a dramatic fragment entitled 'Valborgsafton på Fagervik' (The Eve of May Day at Fagervik) which reveals how many traces of the play remain in the final version of the poem. The stage directions and many of the lines spoken by the Customs Inspector, the Postmaster, and the Poet are interrupted by poems. Here, too, Strindberg approaches a mixture of two registers.

The Narrative and the Lyrical Registers

Is it possible to discern a similar mixture of the lyrical and narrative registers? On a few occasions Strindberg in fact chose a genre that is itself based on such a mixture of registers — the Icelandic Saga. There are poems within the prose of the early tale 'Början av Än Bogsveigs saga' from 1872 and the story 'Sagan om Stig Storverks son' (The Saga of Stig, the Son of Storverk) in *Hövdingaminnen*, from 1906. But apart from the field of the saga, there is also a poem inserted into one of Strindberg's very earliest prose works, the sketch 'Huruledes jag fann Sehlstedt' (How I Found Sehlstedt),[17] where the story is presented in a fictitious frame in which the first-person narrator says he has found a large number of scraps of paper that he has pieced together into 'följande dårskap som här nedan meddelas' (the piece of folly to be found below). There then follows the poem which, when Strindberg later incorporated it in his first volume of verse, *Dikter*, he called 'Solnedgång på havet' (Sunset at Sea). In the same volume there is also a prose poem, 'Solrök' (Heat Haze), in which he mixes prose and verse. There are also obvious intrusions from the lyrical register in the novel *Ensam*, which contains two poems, 'Ahasverus' and 'Vargarne tjuta' (The Wolves Are Howling). The first of these is introduced into the narrative when the narrator, a playwright, describes his suffering every spring at the sight of people standing in the street with their vanloads of furniture, about to move house. This arouses memories of a roving life and his impressions coalesce into the poem he calls 'Ahasverus'. Later on in the novel the narrator explains that events sometimes seem to be staged especially for him. One example is the fire he has recently witnessed, when he heard the wolves howling up on Skansen, in the park overlooking Stockholm. He combined his impressions in the poem 'Vargarne tjuta', which then follows. The poems are so loosely attached to the narrative that Strindberg was able to extract them with ease and transfer them to the 1905 edition of *Ordalek och småkonst*. Gunnar Ollén points out that in manuscript both these poems had the subtitle 'Sonata', and were given tempi such as 'Allegro', 'Largo', and 'Presto agitato'.[18]

Experiments using musical terminology are also to be found in the chapter 'Nyårsnatten' (New Year's Eve) from *Götiska rummen*, which contains a conversation between six people on a walk to Skansen. In the text the dialogues, conducted in pairs, are called 'den sexstämmiga fuga' (the six-part fugue). In the original manuscript, this fugue was a good deal longer, but on the advice of his publisher, Strindberg cut parts of it.[19] However, he later succeeded in incorporating it into *Svarta fanor*, where it forms part of the guests' conversation after the so-called ghost dinner at Professor Stenkåhl's.[20] Before Strindberg began *Svarta fanor*, he wrote several fugues which he collected under the title 'Fugor med preludier' (Fugues with Preludes), and sought to publish. They were later slotted into *Svarta fanor* as dialogues in the cloister sections. One of them concerns matter as a living entity which must, in my opinion, be regarded as a piece of lyrical prose. To demonstrate why, I have followed the method which Strindberg employed when he rearranged the monologue in *Holländarn* into a poem in free verse, largely by the typographical redistribution of the clauses and other syntactic groups in the prose original:

Kommer hat och kiv i huset in,
då ryker salslampan,
då brinner brasan ojämn,
så att man icke får skjuta spjället,
då mörknar mässingen,
då blir pianot ostämt
och salsklockan slår på olaga tider.
Uret är känsligt som ett levande väsen;
det mäter ut tiden
och knäpper sina sextio slag i minuten
som människohjärtat;
det ställer in sig efter ditt hjärta och sinne,
och det råder över husets ordning.
Det har satt sig i rapport
med de kosmiska krafterna,
och dess hjul har lika många kuggar
som stjärnorna behöva timmar
att välva sig kring jorden,
som solen behöver minuter
för att rycka fram en grad.
Uret står i förbindelse med världsalltet och evigheten,
med människohjärtat och timligheten.

Kommer hat i huset,
då kan uret slå sju för tu,
då kan det stanna mitt i veckan,
och det bådar ont;
det kan mucka och skråla mitt emellan slagen,
då det eljes blott ger en suck fem minuter före;
och det kan slå tretton slag,
som betyder en varning.

(If hate and strife enter the house, Then the lamp in the drawing-room smokes, Then the fire flares unevenly, And you cannot drop the damper, Then the brasswork is no longer bright. Then the piano goes out of tune And the clock strikes the wrong hours. The clock is as sensitive as a living being; It measures out time And ticks its sixty beats a minute Like the human heart; It adjusts itself to your heart and mind, And governs the order in the house. It is in harmony With cosmic powers, And its wheels have as many teeth As the stars need hours To rotate round the earth, As the sun needs minutes To move forward one degree. The clock is in touch with the universe and eternity, With the human heart and the temporal. If hate enters the house, Then the clock can strike seven 'stead six, It can stop in the middle of the week, And that bodes no good; It can grumble and bellow in the midst of its strike, Where otherwise it merely sighs five minutes before. And it might strike thirteen, Which is a warning.)[21]

By this I naturally do not mean that one can define a text as being in lyrical prose if it can be transformed into verse by a typographical conjuring trick. The object of my version is rather to show how Strindberg used lyrical resources in a piece of prose. This makes it easier to observe what he is doing. The metaphors and the personification of the clock link up with the theme of the text: matter as a living entity. The composition is based on anaphora, as in the opening lines of the two parts 'Kommer hat . . .' and the repetition of 'då'. Other unifying elements are alliterations like 'brinner brasan' and 'mörknar mässingen' as well as assonance and rhyme as in 'kan uret slå sju för tu' and 'evigheten/timligheten'. The first line also contains an inversion. Taken together, tone, rhetorical figures, imagery and the marked rhythm create a tension and a precision of linguistic expression which one associates with lyrical prose.[22] The dialogue on 'matter as a living entity' fills ten pages in Landquist's edition. I have clearly selected a passage that is particularly rich in lyrical elements, but they are prominent in the remaining parts of the dialogue too. I might add that in a letter to his editor, Karl Börjesson, Strindberg suggested that some of the cloister chapters of *Svarta fanor* should be lifted out of the book and published in *En blå bok* under the title 'Hvita Dukar ur Svarta Fanor' (White Flags from Black Banners), among them the dialogue on 'matter as a living entity' (XVI, p.265). However, no 'White Flags' ever appeared in *En blå bok*, but ideas recur there that have already appeared in the dialogue in lyrical prose. Thus, in the essay 'Uret och planetsystemet' (The Clock and the Planetary System), Strindberg develops the notion that the clock has a counterpart in the cosmic system.

The Narrative and the Dramatic Registers

A combination of the narrative and the dramatic registers such as occurs between the narrative and the didactic does not of course exist. I can only repeat what previous scholars have observed: that a great deal of Strindberg's prose is dramatic.[23] The novels and short stories contain plenty of verbal exchanges, though naturally the proportion varies. After *Inferno* Strindberg found other means of dramatizing his prose. The short novel *Ensam* is organized around the occupation of its narrator, a playwright, who spends much time observing scenes that occur in his vicinity. But perhaps Strindberg goes furthest in *Taklagsöl*, which consists almost entirely of a single long monologue interrupted by stage directions and lines from the characters around the speaker. Like 'Trefaldighetsnatten', Strindberg originally planned the work in dramatic form. Here, it is perhaps worth pointing out that Strindberg sometimes utilized the same subject in two different registers. The best known example is probably the dramatization of *Hemsöborna*; otherwise it was mainly in stories and dramas with historical themes that he used the same material more than once. There is a short story with the same title as the play *Herr Bengts hustru* in *Svenska öden och äventyr II* and *Hövdingaminnen* contains two stories based on the same material as *Gustav Adolf* and *Siste riddaren*.[24] The dramas with subjects from world history, *Moses*, *Sokrates* and *Kristus*, are special cases and were transposed into the first stories in *Historiska miniatyrer*. The transformation, which is not particularly impressive from an artistic point of view, was done by inserting isolated narrative passages between the dialogue.

The papers of the Green Sack include numerous plans for dramatizing prose works. Among these were some early short stories, including 'Den romantiske klockaren från Rånö' (The Romantic Organist from Rånö) from *Skärkarlsliv* and an episode in the first volume of *Tjänste-kvinnans son*.[25] There are also more or less detailed drafts of some ten short stories written after 1900 as well as of the novels *Ensam* and *Svarta fanor*.[26] It is also apparent from extant fragments that he had begun the dramatization of three more short stories: 'Sankt Gotthards saga', 'Homunculus', and 'Starkodder skald'.[27]

This survey of the way in which Strindberg's work relates to the four registers permits the conclusion that he shows a greater tendency to mix registers in works that came after *Inferno*, mainly by the insertion of texts belonging to the didactic register into narrative. There are, however, examples of mixed registers even during the earlier period, when it is more usual to find works that are difficult to assign to a specific register.

There are certainly several explanations as to why Strindberg mixed registers more readily after *Inferno*. His return to a Sweden dominated by the writers of the nineties may have had something to do with it. Their view of literature had strong links with the Romantic era, when mixed registers were commonplace, hence novels like Verner von Heidenstam's *Hans Alienus* (1892), which contains long passages in verse, Per Hallström's volume of short stories *Purpur* (Purple, 1895), which also contains both verse and a short play, and Selma

Lagerlöf's *Gösta Berlings saga*, which was originally planned in metrical form and then as a drama, where the principal character recites several stanzas. Given the predeliction of the period for fairy tales, myths, legends, and historical short stories, Strindberg was clearly jumping on a contemporary bandwagon. However, the main reason why he now mixed registers more frequently is to be sought elsewhere, in his increasing interest in experimention, whether in drama, prose or lyric. This led to works like *Ett drömspel* and *Taklagsöl* which, from the point of view of literary history, look forwards rather than backwards.

Notes

1. Morten Nøjgaard, *Litteraturens univers* (Odense, 1975), pp.48-55.
2. *Inferno* is volume 28 of the 55 volumes in Landquist's edition of Samlade Skrifter, almost exactly in the middle of his production. In Samlade Verk it will probably be volume 37 of 75.
3. *Brev* I, p.1.
4. The poem 'Besöket' (The Visit) is from 1868, and if we believe what Strindberg writes in *Tjänstekvinnans son*, it was the following year that he wrote his first play, *Namnsdagsgåvan* (The Namesday Gift), a comedy in two acts now lost. His first short stories were written in 1872. Strindberg's first known published work, however, a translation of Schiller's 'Die Schaubühne als eine moralische Anstalt betrachtet', appeared in *Aftonbladet*, in May 1869. See Gunnar Brandell, *Strindberg — ett författarliv*, I (Stockholm, 1987), p.86.
5. See James Spens, 'De blottlagda känslornas poesi', *Strindberg* (Stockholm, 1981), p.179.
6. Gunnar Brandell, *Strindberg — ett författarliv*, III (Stockholm, 1983), p.179. See also Kerstin Dahlbäck, 'Kristina and Strindberg's Letters and Diary', *Scandinavian Studies*, 62:1 (1990), pp.110-115.
7. The novel was rearranged as the story 'Karantänmästarns andra berättelse' in *Fagervik och Skamsund*.
8. The Svedberg, 'Strindberg som kemist', *Forskning och industri* (Stockholm, 1918), p.100.
9. Svedberg, p.83.
10. Strindberg also saw the connection between his literary and his scientific writing. In a letter to Dr Anders Eliasson he even used the expression 'Kemiska sonnetter' (Chemical Sonnets — XI, p.75).
11. For the structure of the novel, see Margit Pohl, 'Några bärande motiv i *Svarta fanor*', *Meddelanden från Strindbergssällskapet*, 29 (1961), p.13, and Bertil Romberg, 'Strindbergs Svarta fanor. Ett utkast till en romanmonografi', *Svensk Litteraturtidskrift*, 1969:3, p.34.
12. A text of this kind, abounding in chemical symbols, is characterized by denotation, and hence often distinct from the poetic language that is

distinguished by its use of connotation.
13. Raoul Francé and Carl Ludvig Schleich. See *Brev* XV, p.359.
14. See Gunnar Brandell, *Strindberg — ett författarliv*, IV (Stockholm, 1989), p.295.
15. I would also draw attention to the mixing of registers in the hexametric poem 'Skapelsens tal och lagar' in *Ordalek och småkonst*. In this poem Strindberg used a mathematical language characterized by denotation in a lyrical text. His genre model is Lucretius' *De Rerum Natura*. See Gunnar Ollén, *Strindbergs 1900-talslyrik* (Stockholm, 1941), p.230.
16. *Samlade otryckta skrifter I*, (Stockholm, 1918), pp.217-8.
17. First published in *Dagens Nyheter*, 2 August 1874, now in SV 12, p.47.
18. SV 51, pp.286-7.
19. See John Landquist's comments on *Svarta fanor*, SS 41, p.292.
20. Ibid., pp.30-37.
21. *Samlade otryckta skrifter I*, pp. 189-90. Translation by Michael Stevens.
22. See the preface to the anthology *Svenska prosadikter* (Stockholm, 1984), p.25, where the editors point out that Swedish lyrical prose is a product of the 1880s, giving as examples Strindberg's 'Solrök' and Ola Hansson's prose poems in *Notturno* (1885).
23. See for example Martin Lamm, *August Strindberg*, II (Stockholm, 1942), p.391.
24. 'I Bärwalde' and 'Kungshamns-gisslan'.
25. Also 'Mellan drabbningarne' in *Från Fjärdingen till Svartbäcken* (1877) and 'Upp till solen' in *Tryckt och otryckt* (1890).
26. Three from *Historiska miniatyrer*, two from *Hövdingaminnen*, three from *Sagor*, *Taklagsöl* and *Syndabocken* (1907). See Barbro Ståhle Sjönell, 'Strindbergs litterära förarbeten i "Gröna säcken"', *Tidskrift för litteraturvetenskap*, 1984:2-3, pp.25-32.
27. *Starkodder skald* is a dramatization of the short story 'Sagan om Stig Storverks son' in *Hövdingaminnen* and *Homunculus* is a dramatization of the short story 'Anden i flaskan', published in *Strix*, 1905.

'Passions and Interests'

Anthropological Observation in the Short Story

Göran Printz-Påhlson

Cambridge

I

There are few moments in the intellectual history of the human faculties of emotion and volition that can compare in importance with the assertion, in Hume's *Treatise of Human Nature* of 1739, that reason not only is, but ought to be the 'slave of the passions'. This dramatic announcement occurs in the Second Book (named 'Of the Passions'), Section V: 'Of the Influencing Motive of the Will', and has been preceded by a lengthy preamble on the traditional view of this conflict, as it relates to the human will, the first paragraph of which deserves to be quoted:

> Nothing is more usual in philosophy, and even in common life, than to talk of the combat of passion and reason, to give the preference to reason, and assert that men are only so far virtuous as they conform themselves to its dictates. Every rational creature, it is said, is obliged to regulate his actions by reason; . . . In order to show the fallacy of all this philosophy, I shall endeavour to prove, *first*, that reason alone can never be a motive to any action of the will; and, *secondly*, that it can never oppose passion in the direction of the will.[1]

Hume goes on to show that the passions are the prime movers, as aversions and propensities towards certain objects and objectives, and continues his investigation in terms we are perhaps allowed to call

Aristotelian, as they firmly stress the goal-directedness of human actions. It is the 'prospect of pain or pleasure' which provide the driving forces behind human volition, and the calculations of cool reason can only adjudicate between various means available to obtain these goals. Consequently, there is never any conflict between reason and passion: reason cannot on its own produce any action or give rise to volition:

> We speak not strictly and philosophically when we talk of the combat of passion and of reason. Reason is, and ought only to be, the slave of the passions, and can never pretend to any other office than to serve and obey them.[2]

Hume concedes that this view may appear extraordinary and enlarges on the matter with some examples that are no less extraordinary (and must have been even more so to his first readers): 'It is not contrary to reason to prefer the destruction of the whole world to the scratching of my finger. It is not contrary to reason for me to choose my total ruin to prevent the least uneasiness of an Indian, or a person wholly unknown to me.'[3]

In relegating reason to a subservient or instrumental role and in elevating passion to the driving force in human action, Hume turned the tables on the whole tradition of Christian moral philosophy, as it had developed in the Age of Reason. He managed in one fell swoop to side-step some of the thorniest problems in moral psychology, disposing of the problem of cause and effect here as in his better known epistemology of empirics and induction, thus providing the key to a mechanized model of explanation in terms of disposition and aversion, of before and after. There is no longer any point in establishing virtues and vices as dominant psychological forms in the formation of character. And the perpetual crux of *akrasía* or weakness of will, sometimes known as incontinence — when a person is doing what is wrong in full knowledge that it is wrong — is eliminated, as it becomes the norm itself rather than a momentary aberration of the will.

What Hume has to explain is still the question of what remains as anomalies in civilized behaviour, why we occasionally act, not from more or less bestial desire, but from benevolent or unselfish impulses. For this objective, he needs a distinction between the primary passions and those 'calmer' passions that are acceptable in civilized society. These desires he divides in two kinds, simple instincts, 'implanted in our natures', which are exemplified with benevolence or resentment, the love of life and kindness to children, but also a more generalized tendency towards good and aversion to evil, 'considered merely as such'. It is this latter kind which will continue in a radically circumscribed existence as a problematic category in subsequent psychological theory, until it is fully exploded by the advent of Freudian and Darwinist psychology towards the end of the nineteenth century.

Beside the calmer passions, there are, according to Hume's scheme, more violent emotions of a similar kind but with an ever sharper influence on the will. Resentment and anger of an often self-destructive type serve as examples, fear of immediate harm is another. This is the origin and motivation of behaviour which seems to be prompted by *akrasía*, or lack of will. 'Men often act knowingly against their interest; for which reason the view of the greatest possible good does not always influence them. Men often counteract a violent passion in prosecution of their interests and designs.'[4]

It is possible to overcome these violent and immediate passions with the help of interests — and I think it is worth stressing the sudden introduction of this term — which have a long-range effect on the will and, ultimately, on human behaviour.

There is no denying that this sketch of the human passions has had an inestimable influence on the development of ideas and concepts of psychology in the latter half of the eighteenth century. Whereas Humean ideas of empiricism and scientific methodology had a direct impact on philosophy, and were contested and absorbed in the huge construct of Kantian and post-Kantian idealism, Hume's ideas on moral psychology seemed to have a more hidden and subterranean influence which stretched far beyond the small circles of professional philosophers. In freeing the passions from their long subservience to rational will, this new view made possible an unprecedented emphasis on the passionate and emotional life embedded in ordinary human existence. While the moral psychologists of previous centuries — from Montaigne to Descartes — had been most attentive to the classification of the passions and their subsumption under a morally defined scheme of virtues and vices, the morally neutral doctrine presented by Hume makes the subjective quality of relative strength, or violence, the only classificatory basis for an investigation of the passions. In contrast to the Cartesian observer who is — as in Descartes' own *Les passions de l'âme* — following Platonic and Christian prescriptions for the analysis of passion in terms of virtue, the Humean observer is free to *describe* the passions in all their possible variety and with due consideration to their strength. But as civilized society has nurtured the 'calmer' passions and rendered them innocuous, where does this Humean observer of the passions go in order to find his descriptions? He has to go outside civilized society, to make his observations on life among savage tribes and the lower classes, among sailors, servants and criminals and all sorts of 'primitive' people. It is surely more than a mere coincidence that this is exactly the period when anthropology is coming of age.

After virtue come anthropology and observation. This is what we can call the Enlightenment Project, or at least one important component of this project. It permeates the works of Diderot and Rousseau, and its importance has been obscured and confused with a myth of completely different origin and political significance, the myth of the Noble Savage.

The Roman-Catholic moral philosopher Alasdair MacIntyre has in his book *After Virtue* described the Enlightenment Project (the term is his) from a slightly different angle than mine. He links it with what he calls 'emotivism', i.e. the belief that all terms of value can be reduced to terms of approbation or preference. Hume was not an 'emotivist' in this sense: as MacIntyre points out, he refused to draw the full radical consequences of his, potentially emotive, theory, and ended up in his *History* and later works on the passions in a somewhat false position, defending the normal passions of reasonable men, thus 'covertly using [a] normative standard . . . to discriminate among desires and feelings.'[5]

Another name for the enlightenment project is 'realism', then taken in its fuller and more comprehensive meaning, as the restrictive methodological usage of the term cannot be traced back beyond romanticism. This is borne out by the drift of both art and literature in the later eighteenth century, and even if there is no methodological realism, higher standards of probability and verisimilitude are being introduced, giving impetus to the flowering of the novel in England and France. It may be that the probability of some person called Clarissa Harlowe, or something similar, and being in domestic service, writing all these letters printed in the epistolary novel bearing the name of Samuel Richardson on its cover, is extremely low (it has been estimated that she would not have time to do anything else), perhaps as low in real life as hearing persons called Athalie or Phèdre give long passionate speeches in perfect alexandrines, but nonetheless it is difficult to deny that the actions described and — perhaps more importantly — passions displayed in Clarissa's letters are somehow much more accessible, closer to life as we know it, more 'realistic' than those expressed by the characters in Racine's dramas. The Humean observer of passions and interests is himself morally neutral, disinterested as to the question of virtue and vice. However uplifting or sentimental the story is supposed to be, it is presented in Clarissa's own words.

This means that the axiological reductionism, i.e. the reducing of terms of value to emotions, that MacIntyre saw as central to the Enlightenment Project, is in fact secondary to the liberation of passion as a descriptive and psychological category. Even those thinkers who followed closely Hume's analysis of the passions, were reluctant to give up the idea of virtue in their discursive work: it is in literature, and particularly in the novel of the late eighteenth century that we find the open confrontations with rationalist psychology, and there the goodies, the defenders of conventional mores like Richardson or, in his dour and sardonic way, Smollett, are in principle no different from the baddies, in this case the cynical French, Laclos in *Les Liaisons dangereuses*, Diderot in *Le Neveu de Rameau*, or even de Sade. So far from trying to extirpate value from their systems, they are always prone to extol the value of passion, of strong unbridled desire. When, at the tail end of the period in question, William Godwin is closely following Hume in his psychology of the emotions in his *Political Justice*, it is to his novel *Caleb Williams* (1796) we have to go to find one of the first and most radical examples of the novel of crime and crime detection, of persecution and obsession, with an undeniable realist intention, indicated in its alternative title, *Things as They Are*.[6]

II

The Enlightenment Project came to an end before it could generate a fully-fledged realist ideology. Numerous explanations of this failure offer themselves. One such explanation, suggested by MacIntyre, is the appearance of a new relationship between theory and practice, before an emotivist ideology could emerge: this is 'the invention of the *individual*', or the Self of modernity, which is exclusively a child of the ideas of romanticism. There are, however, a number of important points within the Enlightenment context which are residual in relation to the later ideology. I shall enumerate *four* that seem most relevant to our subject matter:

(1) the opening-up of the analyst of passion to anthropological observation, i.e. observations outside his/her accredited cultural sphere;
(2) the revaluation of the passions in terms of other criteria than virtues and vices: strength, pristine naturalness, sincerity;
(3) [following from (2)] the break with the old value system, even, or perhaps typically, in its covert state as a double standard, claiming general applicability from particular cases;
(4) the establishing of forms, better suited for this kind of observation, forms which in their openness and naturalness grant access to the human passions 'as they are' (the 'fleeting moment' in painting,[7] reportorial realism in writing).

Before we can get any further, I must be allowed briefly to review another aspect of the eighteenth-century doctrine of the passions. When Hume opposed the passions to 'interest' in the last quotation given from the *Treatise*, he was invoking and linking up with the discussion which had become a favourite *topos* of political and economic philosophy. Long-term interest can provide a countervailing force to short-term passion. This opposition succeeds and overtakes an earlier one which pitched passion against passion for the benefit of man and society. Both these interwoven concepts might have had their origin in Machiavelli and Spinoza, who both anticipate Hume's ideas in this matter, as does Vico, but are enthusiastically espoused by all apologists for early capitalism and industry, who want to prove that, as Dr Johnson quite blithely announced: 'There are few ways in which a man can be more innocently employed than in getting money'.[8]

There is even a catchphrase, popular far into the nineteenth century, about 'doux commerce': such was in this century the strength of conviction of the ameliorating effects of business and industry.[9]

These and many more fascinating strands in the complicated skein of ideas created by the two terms are skilfully unravelled in a little book by Albert O. Hirschman, *The Passions and the Interests*. He argues, most convincingly, that the opposition between the two terms is quite abruptly ended when Adam Smith, who perhaps had a more matter of fact and less optimistic view of human nature in relation to money-making than his predecessors, decided to treat them as synonyms. The next century will never again see them come together, and utilitarian stratagems of somewhat different origin are to be rallied to the defence of capitalist society. The conjunction had nevertheless had a considerable direct influence on the American Constitution, with consequences that can be experienced to this very day. But on the whole it is safe to say that the two terms retain an unmistakeable eighteenth-century flavour and can, when they appear in later times, be seen as a residue of the Enlightenment Project.

III

Before I am in a position to deal with the short story or Strindberg, I shall have to say something more about the Project of Modernity, if this is to be seen as a continuous process, comprising as integral subparts as disparate and seemingly incompatible idea complexes as romanticism, realism and symbolism. I shall also have to say something about the forms, or genre decisions prompted by realism in particular. It has been suggested — by Stanley Cavell most recently[10] — that romanticism as a project is closely allied to (albeit opposed to) scepticism as a philosophical doctrine, and this is obviously of some importance to Strindberg in his later phase. I have always maintained that we Scandinavians are lucky in possessing in the nineteenth century *two* major writers who in their 'development', be it forced or self-imposed, run through all three main subparts of the Project of Modernity, so that they start in a perhaps reluctantly accepted romanticism, adopt realist strategies for their works of maturity, and end up in something else which we might call, hesitantly perhaps and without much conviction, symbolism. But this 'luck' is as fickle and double-faced as Dame Fortuna herself, and the description seems likewise misleading, insofar as these writers all the time remain themselves. Strindberg's well-known simile when he presents his double affiliation to two traditions, romanticism and realism, in the biological image of the slow-worm, who is a lizard that has taken on the characteristics of a snake, is perhaps more illuminating.

However, I want to consider a text from very late in Strindberg's life which displays a throwback to the very Enlightenment context we have studied so far. It is a passage from the *Blue Books*, and a late one at that (1910), which he rewrote three times. I shall quote from the shorter version in *En ny extra blå bok* which he called *Konversations-logik A*:

> Om man som John Locke ville noga åhöra en konversation, antingen man är deltagare i densamma eller bara åhörare, och sedan reflekterade uprigtigt öfver vad man hört, skulle man förtvifla om möjligheten att komma till klarhet genom diskussion och framför allt inse det lönlöst att bibringa en menniska öfvertygelsen att han misstagit sig om ett faktum.
>
> Åsikter sitta mest i köttet, hafva vuxit ur intressen och passioner, så att det mest förvända uppträder såsom helig öfvertygelse, emedan det står som förpost och bevakar ett intresse.

> (If, like John Locke, one wanted to listen carefully to a conversation, either participating or merely listening, and later, reflecting sincerely on what had been said, one would despair about the possibility to find enlightenment through discussion and, most of all, see the futility in convincing a person that he is wrong about a fact.
>
> Views are located in the flesh, having grown out of interests and passions, so that what is most contrary masquerades as holy   conviction, while it stands guarding an interest. — SOS II, p.199)

I analyzed this passage some years ago in an entirely different context — when discussing Strindberg's philosophy of language[11] — and remarked then that there seems to be some confusion in his mind of two unrelated passages in Locke's Treatise. It would be wrong to make great claims for Strindberg's philosophical sophistication here, trying to make him into a forerunner of the later Wittgenstein or Paul

Grice's 'Conversational logic', but it would be equally unfair to dismiss his observations, given the psychological bias he shared with his contemporaries, as philosophically naive.

Strindberg uses the conjoined terms 'passion' and 'interest' on a number of occasions, always in a derogatory sense.[12] Passions and interests cause a distorted vision of right and wrong, good and evil. One possible and even likely source seems to be Balzac, who is even closer to the Adam Smith position, for instance in *La Fille aux yeux d'or*, a novella dealing with the controversial subject of lesbianism, where he depicts in the introductory chapter the depravity and de-bauches of Parisian life: the inhabitants are driven by a 'tempest of interests' (tempête d'interêts), everybody is wearing masks, not showing their true faces, their physiognomies distorted by their desires. 'What do they want? Money or pleasure?'[13] A few pages later, he makes the conjunction of the two terms explicit, calling Paris 'ce champs de bataille des interêts et passions'.[14]

It takes no great effort to recognize here the favourite psychological observation of Strindberg about the characterless character which he could study in similar passages from Rousseau and Tocqueville. There is, however, another aspect proffered on the psychology of the Parisian: 'A force de s'interêsser à tout, le Parisien finit par ne s'interêsser à rien'.[15] Interest becomes, when leaving the firm economic basis of the Enlightenment Project,[16] dispersed into its opposite: indifference. Again it becomes an adversary rather than an ally of the passions, as it is absorbed into the category of the Interesting, well known to Kierke-gaard and the German Romantics.[17]

IV

Bearing in mind that the Enlightenment Project did not leave much room for *akrasía* or weakness of will, it is easy to see that when this favourite psychological topic is re-introduced by the Romantics, it is bound to have a radically different construction. Hume did stress that we often fail to do what we most ardently desire to do. But with the passions and interests in fine balance, such failures could be blamed on faulty reasoning or outside compulsion. When passions and interest are again conjoined, such cool reasonable explanations seem inadequate, and with the invention of the individual, or rather the identification of the individual with the sum of his passions, the Romantics are forced to seek the explanations within the passions themselves. We can observe this shift happening in *Wilhelm Meister*, in the protracted discussion of the character of Hamlet,[18] as we can see mirrored in the protagonists of that book the semantic shift towards 'realism' as a literary term.[19] The world becomes divided into observers and actors

— subjects and objects if you want to be philosophical about it — and the calmer passions of interest are left to contend with the more violent passions of the observed. This change permeates fiction throughout the nineteenth century.

The distinguished Hebrew scholar Robert Alter has written a book, *Partial Magic*, which highlights this phenomenon and its consequences for the novel, in particular the self-consciousness of the genre that has to be denounced as the claims for reality of the fiction are re-enforced. Thus the author becomes free to impose his views directly on the reader: as he is dealing with 'real' characters, he also feels entitled to manipulate and judge them.[20] This gives a 'Napoleonic' grandeur to the great realist artists, something that also Marthe Robert has pointed out.[21] There is no need to spell out the strong parallel with Strindberg's fictional worlds, either novelistic or dramatic, we here encounter.

It is, however, in yet another genre that the shift in question is even more noticeable: a genre whose origin is clearly connected with the emergence of realism — the short story.

The story, or tale, has always been with us and could sometimes be short, at other times longer. But the short story as a separate and definable genre is probably a creation of incipient realism, in that it was, from the outset, less contaminated by self-consciousness than the novel and offered a more pristine and neutral arena for anthropological observation. Let us consider a story by Prosper Mérimée, who is one of the earliest specialists of the genre, and whose neglect in present-day criticism is quite notorious. He achieved fame with 'Carmen' thanks to Bizet's opera (which Strindberg loathed), but the original short story has a lot more of anthropological interest in its telling in that both Don José, who is Basque and Carmen, who is a Gypsy, belong to minority cultures and are thus alienated from their Andalusian surroundings.[22]

Let us, however, examine a shorter story from Corsica, in fact the first story Mérimée ever wrote or published: 'Mateo Falcone' from 1829.

'Mateo Falcone' tells how the unnamed narrator, whom we have to assume to be Prosper himself, on a tour in Corsica comes across a revered and upright *montagnard*, also a formidable marksman, the eponymous hero of the story. Mateo has settled down, raised a family and has a son Fortunato, now ten years old, who is the apple of his eye. One day when young Fortunato is left alone at the house, a wounded bandit comes out of the bush, asking for shelter as he is pursued by a group of soldiers. After some bartering Fortunato agrees to help him, hiding him in a haystack. When the soldiers arrive, the leader turns out to be a cousin of Fortunato's, and with the help of some bullying and some bribing — a very desirable watch plays a large part in this process — he persuades the boy to reveal the hiding place of the bandit, who is in due course arrested and taken away. When Mateo returns and learns about this incident from the reluctant Fortunato, he immediately takes him out to a nearby ravine and shoots him, after having had him recite all the prayers he can remember.

This grisly story is recorded without any authorial comments whatever in as spare and terse a language as can be imagined. The reader is left to draw the necessary conclusions on his own about a code of behaviour which is alien to him: we have to assume that it is the broken bargain with the bandit that has sullied the good family name of Falcone, and for which such a harsh punishment is meted out. Stories like that, and there are not many as effective and unsentimental, established a pattern that would be at work far into this century: many of Hemingway's earliest (and best) short stories are following it very narrowly, like the early story 'The Killers'.

At the same time this short story offers, in the very reticence of its presentation, a parable about the relations of passions and interest in a society which is guided by codes alien to us today but also presumably to the West European of the post-Napoleonic era.[23] This parable in its insistence on 'realism' formulates a challenge to the 'calmer' passions and 'instincts', like Hume's 'benevolence' and 'kindness to children', thus questioning their very existence in a society which is ruled by an arbitrary but iron code of honour and a bartering attitude to human life. Ethnic information is provided with a minimum of means in this case, although it can be, as in 'Carmen', explicit, with an appended discursive chapter on customs and language. But the medium of language itself is pared down in order to allow bare transparency. This is the meaning of realism within the format of the short story, establishing a model for 'repertorial' writing which goes far beyond what is regarded as fiction and, actually, obliterating the boundary marks between fiction and fact. For all we know, this story, as reported by Prosper Mérimée, could be factual in all its details.

The second story I want to dwell on is very different, although quite as gloomy. James Joyce's 'The Dead' from *Dubliners* (1904) is a very famous story indeed, but it is still not commonly acknowledged how it represents a new turning in the formation of the short story. All of the stories in *Dubliners* display the open-ended, 'impressionistic' narrative structures, which as Harry Levin made clear in an introduction long ago, hardly have been given their due as innovations.[24] The plot, as it is, is now so well known, not least after the faithful rendering on film by John Huston, that the shortest of summaries may suffice. Gabriel Conroy, who is the protagonist and focus of the entire story, is coming with his wife Gretta to a party, around Christmas time, at his elderly aunts', together with a number of acquaintances from Dublin's middle class. He listens to the conversations, takes part in the jollifications, gives an appreciated, albeit sorely cliché-ridden speech. On their way out, his wife stops on the stairs to listen to a tenor singing the old air 'The Lass of Aughrim'. Returned to their home, Gretta tells the story of Michael Furey, the young boy she knew in Galway who used to sing this song,and who died young, probably from his love for her. After Gretta has fallen asleep, Gabriel contemplates his now, as it seems, utterly meaningless life, the lack of passion and emotion in it, the prospects of decline and death which appear to have claimed the entire bourgeois society he is part of. 'Better pass boldly into that other world, in the full glory of some passion,than fade and wither dismally with age.'[25]

The story ends with the famous description of the snow falling outside the room: 'snow was general all over Ireland. It was falling on every part of the dark central plain, on the treeless hills, falling softly on the Bog of Allen and, farther westward, softly falling into the dark mutinous Shannon waves. It was falling, too, upon every part of the lonely churchyard on the hill where Michael Furey lay buried. It lay thickly drifted on the crooked crosses and headstones, on the spears of the little gate, on the barren thorns.'[26]

The Dead are the dead, but also the living, not least Gabriel Conroy himself in his frozen and passionless state. The only reaction of emotion that has been elicited from him during the whole evening is when he is taunted by the young Irish Republican Mollie Ivors with being a 'West Briton' and explains: 'I am sick of my own country, sick of it!' In his inner exile — and he is following his creator's prescriptions of art, exile and cunning only in that respect, as he is pathetically devoid of the other two qualities — in his inner exile, he is as thoroughly alienated from the sentimental gaiety of Dublin society as from his wife's nostalgic epiphany. His is a new kind of *akrasía*, a lack of will, the description of which Joyce may have picked up from his master Ibsen: identical with the death of passion, as delineated in *Rosmersholm*.

Should we call this story realistic or symbolic? Its anthropological credentials are impeccable: it is as if Gabriel (and Joyce) saw the Irish as a strange primitive tribe whose most trivial customs and mores had to be described in detail. The descriptive strategy is, however, not discursive, but strictly in the realist tradition, using dialogue and what the Russian Formalists called *skaz*, i.e. internal oral narration, as its sole instruments. Even the symbolic ending, which has been so often imitated (for instance, to great effect by Scott Fitzgerald in *The Great Gatsby*, a brief novel which has all the characteristics of the short story)[27] is firmly placed within Gabriel's mind and as such serving the realistic purpose of psychological characterization. Already Valéry Larbaud, in his preface to the French translation of *Dubliners*, saw the 'disproportion. . . entre le préparation et le dénouement'[28] and referred it to the incipient modernism of chaotic description and dyslogic conversation (Strindberg's 'Konversationslogik'!). But this seems to be a mistake: the story entirely lacks plot (*muthos*) and its dénouement or *anagnorisis* (recognition) *is* in its preparation. But this is entirely within the tactics and ruse of realism and motivated by the realist impulse: life is not so 'mathematical-idiotic' (Strindberg's word in the Preface to *Fröken Julie*) as to include plot. 'Plot' is the designation for one of the renunciations the realist feels compelled to make, in order to present life 'as it is'.

V

In placing Strindberg firmly within this tradition of the short story, one could be well advised to go to those stories which have an openly avowed anthropological intention, like the sketches of life in the Stockholm archipelago in *Skärkarlsliv*, or else to his major social-psychological case studies in *Giftas*. However, the short story I want to consider is what many may regard as a minor effort, the historical sketch 'Vid likvakan i Tistedalen', written late in 1890 and published in the last volume of *Svenska öden* in 1891. It has the immediacy of his earlier historical short stories, but foreshadows to some extent in style and outlook his later historical work, not least the play *Carl XII* (1904).

> — Smack! sa det, som när man kastar en sten i gyttja; och så var det slut med stora livet som kallats den tolfte Karl! Herren skydde oss alla!

> (— Pluff! it said, as when you throw a pebble in mud; and that was the end of the great life that had been called Charles XII! The Lord protect us all! — SS 12, p.377)

In this brisk and irreverent manner Strindberg begins the tale of the wake at the village of Tistedalen after the death of Charles XII in an atmosphere heavy with the smell of decomposition and ammonia. In its way, it is as death-obsessed as the two other stories we have considered, in its preference for gruesome details perhaps more so. The snow is falling as on the bogs and churchyards of Ireland, but it has no soothing effect: it melts to slush and mud. The Swedish army is in retreat, and various regiments march past the little hut where the once great king is resting on his bier. As the story unfolds, it consists almost exclusively of a long dialogue between Neuman, the king's surgeon, and a young lieutenant Carlberg. It is the older man who, after having attended to the royal corpse, is eager to conduct a post-mortem on the whole life of the ill-fated king, on his character and reign, on his family and the Swedish people.

Strindberg is here, as always, very well served by the breezy matter-of-factness of the medical mind and manages to give, through the mouth of the crabby old surgeon, a virtuoso thumbnail sketch of the history of the royal Swedish Palatine family: the king's grandfather was a drunkard, a brawler and a philanderer, his father was an abstemious skinflint and a misogynist, he himself inherited the worst traits from both of them. He, of German origin, but the most Swedish of all kings of Sweden, was lost in his dreams of grandeur and saw himself as a new Alexander. But as he was fulfilling his destiny, it became gradually clear that Charles XII was just another Viking or Hun, out for what he could get from plunder and pillage, and that the northern tribes were just worthless barbarians set on destruction of all cultural values — here Neuman turns round the climatological speculations later to be launched by Montesquieu and relates the much cruder climatology of the Hippocratic corpus.[29] After having been harangued for a while by the old man, the young lieutenant is at first incredulous and angry and wants a duel or a fistfight but is later convinced against his will, almost hypnotized. The two men decide to get drunk, and in the cold morning light one can see that the mud is mixed with severed limbs and human entrails, as the cannon and waggon-train start rolling again in 'a race towards the inheritance of a people and a country'.

I am not claiming that this raunchy and mostly unpleasant story is of the same order of excellence as the other two which I consider to be masterpieces. Had I wanted excellence, I would have had no difficulty in finding some more appealing Strindberg story. But still, 'Vid likvakan i Tisdedalen' is a minor virtuoso performance which indicates some very intriguing directions for the art of short story writing.

Is it a story in the realist tradition? Again, one could say that it is highly improbable — as in the case of Clarissa Harlowe — that this conversation could take place then and there in this particular fashion, that a simple surgeon would be in possession of all these historical facts and theories (strongly redolent of Strindberg's own historical style and interests), that he would be willing and able to air these and that he also would be able to convince his interlocutor, the callow lieutenant, of their validity. The latter circumstance is of particular interest, as it contradicts the later observation in 'Konversationslogik A' that the conversion rate is extremely low in rhetorical situations, speech acts, as we would perhaps call them today. But this might be just a seeming contradiction, as the passions and interests of the two unlikely interlocutors converge, toward the end of the story, in a desire for strong liquor and raucous song, which might have temporarily reconciled their opposed views and temperaments, and at the same time, given the narrative the desired flavour of Caroline crudeness.

If there is a certain lack of verisimilitude in the setting of the story, there is on the other hand no lack of realism in the more general sense in its contents. The dialogue races along — and this applies to the *non sequiturs* as well as to the *sequiturs* — with only one purpose in mind, the debunking of the received myth of Charles XII. It is realist in its unflinching resolve to tell things *as they are*, however unpleasant. The seeming virtues of the royal leaders of the Swedish people are explained in terms of passions and interests alone, and the rare descriptions of the surroundings — for instance a grotesque account of the Royal corpse itself — are in perfect accord with this analysis.[30] The unpleasantness of the two characters is evident but contingent to the main theme — whether we believe in the crude medical cynicisms of Neuman or not, we are asked to believe in the main drift of the debunking.[31] This in contrast to 'The Dead' where the despairing skepsis of Gabriel Conroy is seen as a direct result of the speciousness of the Dublin society he loathes and frequents, and to 'Mateo Falcone', where the narrator is not asked to comment on the origin of the alien and inhumane code of behaviour he is seen to observe.

Do these three short stories point towards beyond the genres where they originated? Yes, in different ways: 'The Dead', rather obviously, towards the psychological novel of high modernism, perhaps more towards Proust and Thomas Mann than towards the exemplary novels of Joyce himself. 'Mateo Falcone' towards the twilight zone between fact and fiction, the war correspondent's recording of atrocities, for instance. Strindberg's story is at once more old-fashioned and more forward-looking: spurning plot-interest, character portrayal and character development, and epiphanic atmosphere, it is gravitating towards the historical anecdote, what in present-day French historiography is called *La petite histoire*.

One of the adherents of the New Historicism in the U.S.A., Joel Fineman, has recently delivered himself of an analysis of 'The History of the Anecdote', which takes in next to everything, from Thucydides to Derrida on Husserl's *Origin of Geometry* and Jacques Lacan. I quote from one of his least abstruse passages:

> In formal terms, my thesis is the following: that the anecdote is the literary form that uniquely lets history happen by virtue of the way it introduces an opening into the teleological, and therefore timeless, narration of beginning, middle, and end. The anecdote produces the effect of the real, the occurrence of contingency, by establishing an event as an event within and yet without the framing context of historical successivity, i.e., it does so only in so far as its narration both comprises and refracts the narration it reports.[32]

This definition may have got hold of something, although it is not easy to say what. The anecdote may, or may not, have a beginning, a middle and an end: judging from the style of Mr Fineman, it is perhaps more likely to have a beginning, a *muddle* and an end. What is highly debatable, at least regarding this secondary fictional case of what is, after all, a borrowed form, is the question whether it is teleological or not: it seems staunchly reductionist in its reliance on material causes. More importantly, is it really a form or a genre of its own? It seems rather, in Strindberg's nimble hands, the wreckage of a form, the trace of a transgression of the bounds of genre.

VI

The concept of *will* and the entailed conflict between determinism and libertarianism is of paramount and increasing importance to nineteenth-century thinking, in literature as much as in philosophy, as indeed it had been in classical Greek and Roman culture. It is no longer possible to overlook the huge differences in the conceptions of the Self and the human faculties that the classical outlook implied, as to desire and passion on one hand and the regulatory influence of reason on the other.[33] The tripartite division of the human faculties in intellect, emotion and will which had dominated modern psychology at least since Kant, may suggest the platonic tripartite soul as described in *Phaedrus*, but is of an entirely different nature: modular rather than instrumental, topographical rather than allegorical. The will becomes, in particular in the area of interaction between the faculties, in the hands of philosophers like Schopenhauer or Nietzsche, and psychologists like Freud and his many forerunners, no longer a regulatory mechanism, but a mysterious force or substance, which is there to be imposed on a world foreign to the Self.

This leads to a radically changed interpretation of determinism and akrasía. Michel Foucault, whose study of sexuality in antiquity comprises a wonderfully comprehensive psychology, states:

> akrasía is not, like immoderation, a deliberate choosing of bad principles; it invites comparison, rather, with those cities that have good laws but are incapable of enforcing them; the incontinent individual lets himself be overcome in spite of himself, and despite the reasonable principles he embraces, either because he does not have the strength to put them into practice or because he has not given them sufficient thought: this explains why the incontinent person can come to his senses and achieve self-mastery.[34]

Although this self-therapeutic view of willpower as a *cura sui* or *enkrateia* has lasted well into our era, it becomes, with a growing scientific bias of the nineteenth century, somewhat obsolete and cumbersome. The will, being released from its place as charioteer or helmsman, and having let unbridled passions run free, is then in position to project itself on the outer world. But, defined as a substance or fluid, or later on as electric current, it is also obviously and eminently exhaustible. Hence the obsessional preoccupation with mesmerism and hypnosis, and sundry arcane methods of imposing one's will on others, which runs through the nineteenth century from Hoffmann to Freud, from Poe to Strindberg.[35]

Within the field of fiction, Balzac is conspicuously central to this preoccupation, not in spite of but because of his central place in the formation of realist strategies.[36] His novel *Louis Lambert*, ostensibly an 'étude philosophique' with small claims to realism, became a source of inspiration for the heroes of realism, Flaubert (as pointed out by Marthe Robert), also Strindberg, even Henry Miller. Louis Lambert, the mesmerizing genius who wrote a *Traité de la volonté* and ended up as a madman, with all passions and interests spent, formed a model for the realist — the realist, not as craftsman but as searcher, beyond the boundaries of sanity.

Why is determinism such a problem for the intellectual of the latter half of the nineteenth century? It is easy to see that 'neurophysiological determinism'[37] is a philosophical problem of importance in the age of Darwin and Mill, but the iron links of necessity or *Anagke* in tragic fatalism hardly exert the same pressure as in classical tragedy. The ancient forms are being resuscitated in this period, not least by Strindberg, but the psychological contexts of *enkrateia* and *akrasía* are renewed in such forms so as to give free rein to the passions and interests of 'la Bête humaine', even to the point of risking complete exhaustion, or madness, as results.

Why are then *new* genres and forms needed in order to implement these new psychological insights? As Martha Nussbaum has suggested, the novel content demanded a new form — 'anti-tragic theater' — for the creation of a new genre, the platonic philosophical dialogue.[38] The novelty, not of the content but of the 'plots' of moral philosophy, of psychology, and even of politics, demanded new forms that were not easily available: the dialogue, as developed in Athenian tragedy, offered the easiest way out. In a similar situation towards the end of the nineteenth century, the fragmentation in emplotment in modern life demanded new literary forms: the fragmented and plotless genre of the short story offered itself.

How do new genres originate? How do they develop, divide and give rise to further new genres? Rarely by deliberate choice, I would venture. It seems highly unlikely that a writer will sit down and say to himself: — Now I am going to invent a new genre, the way he can say to himself: — Now I'll invent a new metre, a new verse-form, the second-person novel, the science fiction epic, and so on. These are forms and forms can be invented, they are what the ancient Greeks called *tekhnai*. But genres seem to be more fundamental, given, unmovable. The writer can choose between existing genres and he can also mix them, graft new shoots on old branches. But most often, one imagines, he will just start writing in an existing genre, and then find, as he goes on, that there is some new collocation of ideas, or else some intriguing technical innovation that exerts pressure so that the old expectations and the old limitations seem unbearably restrictive. It seems that most generic changes in the arts and literature are of this reductive type. Those huge concatenations of ideas which are partly descriptions of historical periods and partly prescriptions for perceiving the world, like romanticism, realism, modernism, exert this kind of reductive pressure as they drift in and out. But as in global plate tectonics, the continents still bear the imprint of their one-time contiguity in the very shapes and outline of their shores.

Or else, if you prefer metaphors of legal transactions to the insistently common organic ones: — Generic changes are not so much like signing a contract as annulling a contract. You might remember the scene in the Marx Brothers' film — *Animal Crackers*, I believe — where Groucho and Chico are making up a contract. They object to various clauses in it and end up with a very thin strip of paper. — 'The only thing left is the sanity clause,' Groucho says. — 'Didn't you know,' Chico says in his home-made Brooklyn-Italian accent, 'there ain't no Sanady Claus.' — 'Good,' Groucho says blithely, and throws away the last strip.

This is the idealized situation: in reality the writer is not often so lucky as to be left with no contractual obligations; fairly often he is left with a number of strips of contract that make no sense whatsoever.[39]

I don't know if the short story was born out of passions or interests or both, but the comportment of human beings in society is clearly a major theme in its development. The various claims for reduction, the claims of the romantic, the realist and the modernist, are being acknowledged within the genre, but the suspicion remains that it is the same claim. Because the writer is, after all, not setting out to delimit, define or even annihilate a particular genre; he sets out *to say what he has to say*.

Strindberg achieved a remarkable line of reduction in his short stories — as he had earlier and more momentously in his naturalist drama. Where he ended up was in the glorious ragbag called *The Blue Books*, where anecdotes, essays, aphorisms and Jamesian *germs* crowd one another. I still have to find a critic bold enough to tackle this serendipity from a generic point of view, in particular as it is labelled, as a metatext, a commentary on the novel *Svarta fanor*. The passions and interests are not gone, but they are dispersed in some happy *diaspora* outside all genre constraints. Stanley Cavell has produced, taking his cue from Emerson, but perhaps thinking of Poe, a neat definition of genius which seems tailor-made for Strindberg. 'Genius', he writes, 'is the name of the promise that the private and the social will be achieved together, hence of the perception that our lives now take place in the absence of either.'[40]

Whether we agree with this definition or not, and I don't think I do in a more general sense, we cannot but admit that the adhesive needed, but not perhaps always heeded, is provided by Strindberg in his sharply observed *Konversationslogik* which can variously be known as dialogism in a Bakhtinian sense, or diacritics in a Platonic sense. In spite of his late interest in Emerson and Plato,[41] Strindberg was no philosopher — his *skepsis* is a first-order pyrrhonism of instrumental character. But he might have been cheered by Aristotle's generous definition in the *Metaphysics A*:

> It is because of wonder that human beings undertake philosophy, both now and at its origins . . . the person who is at a loss and in a state of wonder thinks he fails to grasp something; this is why the lover of stories is in a sense a philosopher, for stories are composed out of wonders.[42]

The story which we can identify with the anecdote is perhaps the one told by Walter Benjamin from Herodotus, about the Pharaoh Psammenite, who as a prisoner of the Persian king Cambyses was forced to see his children pass by in their humiliating shame and degradation. It was not until he saw his old valet pass by that he broke down and cried. Benjamin (for once rather weakly) can only offer us the variety of choice from Hermeneutics Unlimited.[43] Strindberg no doubt smiles the wicked smile of a true *philomuthes*, saying: 'There ain't no Sanady Claus'. Because the promise of the genius that the public and the private be achieved together can never be fulfilled, unless the Sanity clause is cancelled, and the naive dreams of rationality cannot be honoured as long as belief in the wishfulment of Christmas cheer is the only desire. The pursuit of truth aims beyond the rationality of interest, beyond the abandonment of passion.

Notes

1. Page references are to Henry D. Aiken's annotated edition of David Hume's *Moral and Political Philosophy* (New York, 1949), p.23.
2. Hume, p.25.
3. Hume, p.25.
4. Hume, p.27.
5. Alasdair MacIntyre, *After Virtue* (London, 1981), p.46f.
6. See Raymond Williams, *Writing in Society* (London, n.d.), p.145, originally in a review of Gary Kelly, *The Jacobin Novel* (Oxford, 1976).
7. See Jean Starobinski, *The Invention of Liberty* (New York, 1987), p.119ff.
8. Quoted in Albert O. Hirschman, *The Passions and the Interests* (Princeton, U.P., 1977), p.58.
9. See Peter France, 'The Commerce of the Self', *Comparative Criticism*, 12 (1990), pp.39-56.
10. See *In Quest of the Ordinary - Lines of Skepticism and Romanticism* (Chicago, 1988).
11. See 'Strindberg och "totemismen"', *Konstrevy*, 45:4 (1969), pp.154-60.
12. Relevant shorter pieces and stories of Strindberg's - whether they make the conjunction of the two terms explicit or not - would include 'Över molnen' (SS 15, p.153ff), 'En häxa' (SS 12, p.117ff), several of the Vivisections, both those printed in Swedish in SV 29 and those originally written in French (*Vivisektioner*, translated by Tage Aurell (Stockholm, 1958)), and from Strindberg's later phase 'Jubal utan jag' from SS 38, p.93ff, and various and sundry texts from the Blue Books (SS 46-48).
13. Honoré de Balzac, *Histoire des Treize*, ed. par P.-G. Castex (Paris, 1956), p.371.
14. *Histoire des Treize*, p.388.
15. *Histoire des Treize*, p.372.
16. The term interest had, of course, a much older meaning in a pure economic sense: see Hirschman, pp.32, 36, in particular footnotes j and m.
17. This term was introduced by Friedrich Schlegel in the *Vorrede* to his *Über das Studium der Griechischen Poesi*. For its further history in Schopenhauer and Kierkegaard, see Walter Rehm, *Kierkegaard und der Verführer* (Munich, 1949), and, for a particularly penetrating analysis, Aage Henriksen, *Kierkegaards Romaner* (Copenhagen, 1954).
18. The discussion of *Hamlet* takes place in Book V, chapters 5-7 of Goethe's *Wilhelm Meisters Lehrjahre: Zweiter Teil*, volume 16 of the *Gesamtausgabe* (Munich, 1962).
19. See Göran Printz-Påhlson, 'Realism as Negation', in *Literature and Reality - Creatio Versus Mimesis - Problems of Realism in Modern Nordic Literature*, ed. Alex Bolckmans (Ghent, 1977), pp.133-147.
20. See Robert Alter, *Partial Magic: The Novel as a Self-Conscious Genre* (Berkeley, 1975).
21. See Alter pp.100-101 and Marthe Robert, *Roman des origines et origines du roman* (Paris, 1972), 3me partie, 'Tranches de Vie', although I

agree with Alter that Robert's psychologistic bias makes her miss the point in the long run.

22. The short story 'Carmen' was published in 1845. It is instructive to compare its Gypsy lore with the more compendious presentation by George Borrow in *The Zincali - An Account of the Gypsies in Spain* (1841), and his subsequent very personal account in *The Bible in Spain* (1843).

23. Montaigne had already pointed to the decisive humanist content in parental tenderness in two essays, I:26 and II:8.

24. Harry Levin, ed., *The Portable James Joyce* (New York, 1947), p.18.

25. *The Portable James Joyce*, p.241.

26. *The Portable James Joyce*, p.242.

27. See the interesting, but not quite convincing, Bakhtinian analysis of the novel by Michael Holquist, 'The Inevitability of Stereotype: Colonialism in *The Great Gatsby*', in Paul Hernadi, ed., *The Rhetoric of Interpretation and the Interpretation of Rhetoric* (Durham, N.C., 1989).

28. In James Joyce, *Gens de Dublin*, translated by Fernandez- Pasquier-Reynaud, Preface de Valéry Larbaud, 'L'Œuvre de James Joyce', p.14.

29. See the treatise 'Air, Water, Places', Hippocrates I, edited and translated by W.H.S. Jones (Loeb Classical Library).

30. The story seems to offer a mordant commentary on the great and popular painting by Gustaf Cederström, with almost the same title: 'Likvakan i Tistedalen', where the grief and despair of the attending officers are depicted. But this painting was not in existence at the time Strindberg wrote his story: it is dated 1893 (see Henrik Cornell, *Den svenska konstens historia II: Från nyantiken till Konstnärsförbundet* (Stockholm, 1959), p.182). Cederström's earlier and far more popular painting 'Karl XII:s likfärd' had been displayed at the World Exhibition in 1878, and must have been familiar to Strindberg.

31. For Strindberg's heavy personal involvement in the myth of Charles XII, including this story, see the penetrating comments in Michael Robinson, 'Strindberg: History and His Story', *Scandinavian Studies* 62:1 (1990), p.62.

32. Joel Fineman, 'The History of the Anecdote', in H. Aram Veseer, ed., *The New Historicism* (New York, 1989), p.61.

33. The tentative and weak conceptions of the Self in classical times have been explored in famous studies by Marcel Mauss, *Sociologie et anthropologie* (Paris, 1950), and Bruno Snell, *The Discovery of the Mind* (Harvard U.P., 1953).

34. Michel Foucault, *The Use of Pleasure: The History of Sexuality*, II (London, 1985), p.65.

35. See Maria M. Tatar, *Spellbound: Studies on Mesmerism and Literature* (Princeton U.P., 1978).

36. See the important studies by Tatar, *op. cit.*, Georges Poulet, *La distance intérieure: études sur le temps humain* II (Paris, 1952) and Christopher Prendergast, *The Order of Mimesis* (Cambridge, 1986).

37. John Thorp, *Free Will - A Defense against Neurophysiological Determinism* (London, 1980).

38. See Martha C. Nussbaum, *The Fragility of Goodness* (Cambridge, 1986), pp.122-135 and compare her later plea for ethical genre criticism in 'Perceptive Equilibrium: Literary Theory and Ethical Theory', in Ralph Cohen, ed., *The Future of Literary Theory* (New York, 1989), pp.58-85.

39. Cf. the very important contractual analysis of Balzac's aesthetic economic method in Prendergast's *The Order of Mimesis*.

40. *In Quest of the Ordinary*, p.114.

41. See Lars O. Lundgren, *Den svenske Sokrates* (Lund, n.d.) and cf. his earlier study, *Sokratesbilden - Från Aristoteles till Nietzsche* (Stockholm, 1978).

42. *Metaphysics* 982b12-19. I have quoted from Nussbaum's translation in *The Fragility of Goodness*, p.259. Existing translations of this passage differ to a considerable degree.

43. Walter Benjamin used this anecdote at least twice, both in his essay 'Der Erzähler' and in a fragment in his 'Kleine Kunst-Stücke'. See Walter Benjamin, *Illuminationen - Ausgewählte Schriften* (Frankfurt, n.d.), pp.314 and 391-92.

Strindberg's Autobiographical Space

Kerstin Dahlbäck

Stockholm University

It was no secret to Strindberg's contemporaries that he often ruthlessly exploited intimate biographical material, both about himself and other people. Many of his works were rightly regarded as *romans à clef*, and those portrayed in them often felt the portraits to be unfavourable. Strindberg's lack of reserve with regard to himself and those closest to him was embarrassing, and on more than one occasion publishers hesitated to issue his most indiscreet autobiographical works. In the mid-1880s, for example, Bonniers declined to publish his correspondence from the 1870s with Siri von Essen, although they did eventually issue it after his death in a supplementary volume to his collected works. His German translator, Emil Schering, similarly reported to him that in 1902 the *Norddeutsche Allgemeine Zeitung* regarded *Till Damaskus* as unsuitable for the stage, since it was too close to Strindberg's private life. Strindberg's reaction on this occasion was typical: 'Hvad snackar Norddeutsche Allg. Z. om autobiografi? Säger icke Goethe i Aus meinem Leben att hela hans författeri var en Confession. Är icke Faust en dagbok?' (Why does the Norddeutsch. Allg. Z. go on about 'autobiography'? Doesn't Goethe say in *Aus meinem Leben* that his entire work was a Confession. Isn't *Faust* a diary? — XIV, pp.213-4). But at the same time as he makes such assertions, Strindberg is aware that he exploits those closest to him, and expresses his abhorrence for the 'vampirism' that his writing compels him to undertake.

The autobiographical element in Strindberg's works has been a problem for Strindberg scholars concentrating upon the biographical dimension of his works as well as for those whose prime concern is with the works in themselves. It is possible to speak of two different attitudes or schools: representatives of one school (Oscar Levertin, for example, or Martin Lamm) have regarded even the literary works as obscurely autobiographical while the advocates of the other school have looked upon the autobiographical works as fiction, even though Strindberg himself claimed that they were not. In the first case, there has been a tendency to disregard aesthetic arrangement and fictitious elements, and in the second, a need to question Strindberg's explicit assurances as to their autobiographical nature in the text, in short to break the 'autobiographical contract' that Strindberg draws up with the reader. For the most part, however, the result is the same: we have to work with a canon which continually mingles fact with fiction. And in order to avoid this problem in critical texts, scholars circumvent the most controversial works such as *Tjänstekvinnans son*, *En dåres försvarstal*, *Inferno*, and *Ensam* while their subtle wordings and vague definitions reveal how difficult a problem this is to solve. An increased awareness has contributed to greater restrictions in the use of fictional work as biographical material, leaving only the letters as a relatively reliable source. But even when critics or scholars want to illustrate the texts with the help of biographical material, they are very often so cautious that they prefer entirely to abandon such a connection.

Autobiography has been the centre of attention for the recent lively interest in genre studies. Many serious attempts have been made to define this category of literature, thereby also throwing new light on this specific problem in Strindberg studies. As a way of approaching the letters, I shall here highlight a number of issues raised in two articles where these genre definitions are discussed: 'The Autobiographical Contract' by Philippe Lejeune[1] and Paul de Man's already classic essay, 'Autobiography as De-Facement'.[2]

In 'The Autobiographical Contract', Lejeune makes an empirical definition of autobiography, based on European literature from the 1770s and with the reader's point of view in mind. According to this definition, autobiography is 'a retrospective prose narrative produced by a real person concerning his own existence, focusing on his individual life, in particular on the development of his personality.'[3] Lejeune points out that this definition involves elements from four different categories:

1. Linguistic form: (a) narrative; (b) prose.
2. Subject treated: individual life, personal history.
3. Situation of the author: author (whose name designates a real person) and narrator are identical.
4. Position of narrator: (a) narrator and protagonist are identical; (b) narration is retrospectively orientated.

Two criteria — points 3 and 4a — must be regarded as absolute demands in this genre, i.e. the author, whose real name on the title-page vouches for a connection with 'the reality' outside the text, has the same name as the narrator and the protagonist, although this also applies to other genres within *littérature intime*, like the memoir and the diary.

This identity under a common name can be established in different ways:

> 1. Explicitly: the narrator and the protagonist (the principal character) have the same name as the author (the name on the title-page).
> 2. Implicitly: with the assistance of an 'autobiographical contract' confirming this identity and drawn up either in the title (for example, 'A History of My Life') or in a preface.

Lejeune also allows for other contracts analogous with the auto-biographical, for instance a fictional contract. Such a contract is established when the narrator's/principal character's name is *not* the same as the author's and/or through information in the title or preface telling the reader that the work is a novel, short story, or novella, etc. To clarify his argument, Lejeune produces the following diagram:[4]

Name of protagonist / Contract	≠ name of author	= o	= name of author
fictional	1(a) NOVEL	2(a) NOVEL	/////
= o	1(b) NOVEL	2(b) indeter-minate	3(a) AUTOBIO-GRAPHY
autobiographical	/////	2(c) AUTOBIO-GRAPHY	3(b) AUTOBIO-GRAPHY

into which the previously mentioned works of Strindberg can be inserted by way of experiment.

Tjänstekvinnans son creates immediate problems. That an auto-biography should be in the third person is an unusual device, but not outside the bounds of genre possibility. Indeed, one of Lejeune's essays is entitled 'Autobiography in the Third Person'.[5] However, the main character's name is not precisely that of the author. Johan is certainly August Strindberg's first name, but this is not mentioned on the title-page. Nor is any autobiographical contract established in the title, which is complemented by the explanatory addition 'A History of a Soul's Development'. In May 1886, however, Strindberg wrote a preface in the form of an interview in the then completed first volume of the book. This preface is based on letters to Albert Bonnier from April and May the same year, in which Strindberg discusses *Tjänste-kvinnans son*. The question which Strindberg ascribes to Bonnier in one of these letters is put by the 'interviewer' in the preface: 'Vad är nu detta för en bok herrn kommer med? Är det roman, biografi, memoar eller vad?' (What kind of book have you written, sir? Is it a novel, a biography, a memoir or what? — SV 20, p.370). The author replies by referring to the title, which gives no precise answer, although he confirms that it '[är] inte roman' (isn't a novel — p.370) whereas in the letter he gives a more explicit definition than in the preface: *Tjänste-kvinnans son* is 'en känd och betydelsefull författares fullständiga biografi så litet lögnaktig en biografi kan göras' (a well-known and important author's complete biography as free from lies as a biography can be — V, p.314), and later suggests that this letter might be published in lieu of a preface (V, p.337).

But the preface, once written, did not appear in the first edition; in fact, it remained unpublished until 1912 in Strindberg's Collected Works,[6] and *Tjänstekvinnans son* thus appeared without this contract with the reader. The second edition of 1909, on the other hand, was furnished with a new preface and a postscript.[7] With this preface, *Tjänstekvinnans son* ought to be placed in Lejeune's diagram under 1c (or 3b); without the preface, as in the first edition, it should be placed under 1b (or 3a).

With regard to *En dåres försvarstal*, the situation is both different and more straightforward. This novel about marriage is in the first person, but the name of the main character, Axel, differs from the author's. Moreover, the novel has a preface which draws up a fictional contract with the reader — he is explicitly told that this is a novel (SS 26, p.6). In fact, strictly speaking there are two prefaces, written on different occasions, one dated 1887 and the other 1894, and both signed 'the author', which raises the question whether this is one and the same 'author', and hence whether this 'author' (or 'authors') is/are identical with August Strindberg — in the second preface, for example, the author who signs it describes his meeting with 'the hero of this book'. However, neither this circumstance, nor the fact that *En dåres försvarstal* was published in Germany in 1893 without a preface, affect its positioning in the diagram under 1a. Only one of the two 'absolute genre requirements' has been met. But the situation was different for the book's German public, who read the anonymously published *Die Beichte eines Thoren*. Here, neither the name of the author, nor the preface, proclaimed the book's genre.

In *Inferno* there is also a first person narrator who does not appear at the outset to have a name. But in the second chapter he observes: 'Målade på butiksfönstret finner jag initial bokstäverna till mitt namn: A.S.' (Painted on the shop window I find my own initials: A.S. — SS 28, p.23), and further on he sees 'De sammanflätade bokstäverna F och S' (The intertwined letters F and S — p.45), which remind him of his wife's name (Frida Strindberg). The situation remains unclear until the twelfth chapter, however, when the 'I' of the book is alluded to as 'den olycklige Strindberg' (the unhappy Strindberg — p.168) in a short paragraph from *L'Evénement*, and a named identity is established between the author, the narrator, and the main character. Moreover, *Inferno* has an epilogue in which an autobiographical contract is established: 'Den läsare, som tror sig veta att denna bok är en dikt, inbjudes att se min dagbok, som jag hållit dag efter dag sedan 1895, och varav det föreliggande endast är ett utvidgat och ordnat utdrag' (The reader who believes this book is a piece of fiction is invited to consult the diary that I have been keeping daily since 1895, and of which the above is merely an expanded and reworked version — p.205). But is the contract valid when it isn't drawn up until after the writing of the text, in the epilogue? Lejeune is a little vague here, speaking only of an '*initial section* of the text'.[8] Even if we disregard this epilogue, however, *Inferno* should be placed under 3a and b in Lejeune's diagram.

In the novel, novella or short story *Ensam*, on the other hand, the main character has no name and no contract is established with the reader — this book can thus be classified as indeterminate.

It is of no significance here that from an autobiographical point of view, *Tjänstekvinnans son* must be regarded as in many respects unreliable,[9] or that the novel *En dåres försvarstal* shows what Gunnar Brandell calls 'en nödtorftigt maskerad verklighet' (a barely masked reality),[10] and a first person, Axel, 'som inte kan undgå att identifieras med Strindberg själv' (who can't avoid being identified with Strindberg himself).[11] And nor have the different descriptions that Strindberg gives of his works in the letters any significance here (working on *Tjänstekvinnans son*, for example, he says that this is 'hans lifs saga i besynnerlig romanform' (the saga of his life in a strange novel form — V, p.306)). What matters is the contract with the reader in the book itself, which is more in the nature of directions for use than a declaration of its contents.

These texts by Strindberg, like many of his other works, can be placed in what Lejeune calls 'the autobiographical space', where they not only exist side by side but are also dependent on and presuppose one another. In what follows I hope to show that even the letters are to be included in this autobiographical space.

Lejeune's theory, which I have rendered very briefly, focuses our view of different kinds of autobiographical works, but his diagram hardly permits any infallible genre placings. However, it should be useful, even where Strindberg is concerned, to differentiate between, on the one hand, the contract he establishes with his readers and, on the other, those characteristics which he applies to his works in non-fictional sources. Since we very often meet these commentaries in letters, which are adapted to the addressee, they can be seen as full of contradictions, and Strindberg appears to be more uncertain than he really is. It is only natural that in writing to a fellow author he should stress his audacious creativity in the just finished work, but play down its possibly disturbing originality as a commodity, when describing it to a prospective publisher like Albert Bonnier.

As previously mentioned, Lejeune attaches great important to *le nom propre*. Strindberg's use of naming in respect of autobiography and fiction is both complicated and strange, and must be the subject of a separate essay, but as regards *Tjänstekvinnans son*, the use of his normally unused first name, Johan, can be seen both as a way of dissociating himself from the autobiographical material and as a protective measure, to enable him to part with it. In *En dåres försvarstal*, the main character's name is Axel, a name that underlines the fictional nature of the book but is also borne by many of Strindberg's alter egos.

However, Strindberg's work repeatedly raises the problem of naming, and hence the identity of author and protagonist. The first part of *En blå bok*, for example, is cast in the form of a dialogue between 'The Teacher' and 'The Pupil'. In the supplement to this volume and in the later blue books, 'The Pupil' is replaced by 'I'. Moreover, a great deal of the discussion in *En blå bok* is familiar to the reader of other Strindberg texts. For example, Strindberg discusses the inability of the corncrake to fly, and hence migrate, in a letter to the painter Carl Larsson (XVI, pp.84-5), and 'Kärlekens bok' is largely based on his correspondence with Harriet Bosse.[12] But can 'The Pupil' be regarded as Strindberg? And what about the 'I'? Immediately following the title page the book bears a dedication to his teacher and leader Swedenborg from 'The Pupil'. If the page on which the dedication occurs has the same weight as the title page, an identity is established between the author and the 'The Pupil'. But early on in *En blå bok*, 'The Pupil' is also called 'Johannes', 'Damascenus', and 'Johannes Damascenus', i.e. he bears the same name as the seventh-century Greek Church Father, in a game of hide-and-seek which here primarily prompts associations with one of Kierkegaard's signatures, Johannes Climacus, but also recalls those letters in which Strindberg assumes the role of teacher and appoints an addressee like Lidforss, Heidenstam, or Littmansson as his pupil. And similarly, questions are also raised by the identity that isn't established simply by means of the author's name, or that of a character, but indirectly through the works that the author has previously written: the 'I' in 'Nemesis Divina', in *Vivisektioner*, for example, maintains that he has written *Fadren*, and the 'I' in 'Nya konstformer' professes to be the author of *Samum*, while the 'I' in *Legender* mentions *Inferno* and talks about 'mitt skådespel Herr Bengts hustru' (my drama *Sir Bengt's Wife* — SS 28, p.322).

Lejeune's theories are considered and developed by Paul de Man in his article 'Autobiography as De-Facement'. The genre problem is here pushed aside and instead, de Man focuses on the distinction between autobiography and fiction. To de Man it is 'the effects of language and rhetoric that prevent a direct representation of the real', thus implying 'that "reference" is always contaminated with figurality.'[13] According to de Man, autobiography seems to 'depend on actual and potentially verifiable events in a less ambivalent way than fiction does.'[14] It is true that autobiography can contain fantasies and dreams, but these deviations from reality are rooted in a private subject whose identity is decided by 'the uncontested readability of his proper name.'[15] But an autobiography's dependence on reference to reality can be questioned: doesn't the autobiographical project itself create and determine the life it portrays? And isn't 'whatever the writer does . . . in fact governed by the technical demands of self-portraiture and thus determined, in all its aspects, by the resources of his medium?' And, as mimesis, the depiction of reality, is one way of representation among others, does the referent determine the mode of representation that determines the referent: as de Man asks, 'is the illusion of reference not a correlation of the structure of the figure, that is to say, no longer clearly and simply a referent at all but something more akin to a fiction which then, however, in its turn, acquires a degree of referential productivity?'[16] Reality and fiction merge; the distinction between fiction and autobiography is undefinable and can only be regarded as simultaneously existing 'neither and both'. The term 'neither, and both at once', which is derived from Wordsworth is compared by de Man (in a metaphor he borrows from Genette) to a revolving door: it is impossible to remain in such a door for any length of time, i.e. we are forced to chose one reading or the other. The autobiography becomes 'not a genre or a mode but a figure of reading or of understanding that occurs, to some degree, in all texts.'[17] All texts are, or can be, autobiographical — or none is. The autobiographical element occurs as a treaty between the two subjects involved in the process of reading.

De Man's discussion, which begins with autobiography, will then be valid for all authorial texts. His arguments clear a way for an approach to Strindberg's production, including the letters, as a totality which should involve great advantages, for instance in the study of motifs and metaphors. The biographically interested scholar, however, isn't free from the responsibility to accomplish 'the impossible': to separate fiction from reality. Strindberg's texts differ with regard to the ratio of autobiographical and fictional material. Some of the previously mentioned works but also *Legender*, *Vivisektioner*, the 'Karantänmästarns berättelser' in *Fagervik och Skamsund*, *Taklagsöl* and *En blå bok* refer more clearly and directly to 'reality' than (for instance) *Mäster Olof*, *Röda rummet*, *Fadren*, *Leka med elden*, or *Till Damaskus*, although even these texts are to a great extent autobiographical. I do not intend to classify Strindberg's works according to the relative amount of fiction or fact that each one contains — that is best left as a hypothesis. As early as the mid-1870s, when teaching Siri von Essen the art of writing, Strindberg pointed out that writing permits us to remain silent and talk at the same time. With the help of fiction, it is possible to say everything without indiscretion — we only have to 'uppfinna de ogenomträngliga maskerna' (invent the impenetrable masks — I, p.193). Strindberg knows that he lives within language and that this is both a help and a hindrance to him in reaching the truth: he points out repeatedly in his correspondence that *Tjänstekvinnans son* has been written 'utan stil' (without style — V, pp.339, 350), and that there isn't 'en bild i hela boken' (a metaphor in the whole book — V, p.350). The book is 'ett försök i framtidslitteratur' (an attempt at the literature of the future) and must 'totalt emancipera sig från konsten och bli vetenskap' (totally emancipate itself from art and become science — V, p.339). In spite of this, he is afterwards forced to admit that his descriptions are 'tämligen sannfärdiga . . . [och] kunna icke vara riktigt exakta' (relatively truthful [and] cannot be entirely accurate — SV 20, p.377). On several occasions he expresses the idea, to use de Man's words, that the poet 'whatever he *does* is in fact governed by the technical demands of self-portraiture.' In the later preface to *Tjänstekvinnans son*, Strindberg writes that whether the author has 'experimenterat med ståndpunkter eller inkarnerat i olika personligheter, polymeriserat sig, eller om en nådig Försyn experimenterat med författaren, må framgå ur texterna för den upplyste läsaren' (experimented with points of view or incarnated himself in various personalities, polymorphized himself, or whether a benevolent Providence has experimented with the author, should be clear to the informed reader from the texts — p.377). Strindberg's attitude to his works, and his creativity in general, seems to correspond to de Man's 'neither and both'.

Though he very seldom theorizes about it, Strindberg's output indicates a lack of respect towards, and a ready transgression of, genre boundaries as well as a prolific production of new genres, a production which entailed and presupposed the elimination of concepts such as fictional and autobiographical. This is particularly striking with regard to his letters. Several of the works are close to the letters, and Strindberg frequently regards them as raw material for his literary writing.[18] When, in the mid-1880s, he wished to publish his early correspondence with Siri von Essen, he didn't consider it an autobiographical document but a work of fiction.[19] With minor adjustments, the authentic letters were to function as imaginative literature. It is not the texts that have changed but the contract with the reader. By replacing the names with asterisks, Strindberg arouses certain associations and expectations in his reader, who prepares for an epistolary novel where the connection with reality is of secondary importance.

I am not going to discuss Strindberg's transformation of the letters into *Han och hon* along the lines of my paper at the last Strindberg conference in Seattle, where I compared the letters to Harriet Bosse with the drama *Kristina*,[20] and stressed the verbal and metaphorical correspondences. My intention then was to demonstrate how certain autobiographical material is formulated and transformed in two different kinds of texts, both of which can be read on a biographical as well as on a fictional level. Similar comparisons can be made between the letters and other works from different periods. In his works, Strindberg reshapes his self and allows it to expand in various fictive forms: 'jag kryper ur min egen person, och talar ur barns mun, ur kvinnors, ur gubbars; jag är konung och tiggare, jag är den högt uppsatte, tyrannen och den allra föraktadste, den förtryckte tyrann-hataren' (I creep out of my own personality, and speak through the mouths of children, of women, of old men; I am king and beggar, I am above others, a tyrant, and [also] the most despised, the oppressed hater of tyrants — SS 38, p. 156), as he declares in the autobiographical novel *Ensam*.

In his letters, too, his self proliferates. Strindberg the letter writer appears in many different situations, writes to numerous people, and has a variety of purposes. The signatures, for instance, present him as 'Your humble servant, August Strindberg', 'the head of the household, August Strindberg', 'the Nihilist Strindberg', 'Baron von Strindberg', 'Augustus Rex', 'August Strindberg Deus (optimus et maximus)', etc. But above all, the Strindberg who appears in the letters is something of a Protean figure. The self in the letters incarnates Strindberg's conception of himself and his wishes as to whom he wants to be, but it also comprises the addressee's real or supposed expectations. This can be seen in different stylistic forms — within the epistolary genre — and in varying textual connections. I will briefly exemplify in which way the self in his letters is determined by their context, and how intricate the relations are between fiction and autobiography, also in the textual sphere of the letters.

Röda rummet from 1879 is well-known as one of Strindberg's novels to contain strong autobiographical elements. The main character, Arvid Falk, is the author's alter ego, a fact that is underlined by the similarity in their names: they have both a forename with two syllables beginning with an 'A', and 'Falk' (Swedish for falcon) corresponds to Strindberg's nickname 'Örnen' (the eagle) among his friends. However, there is no absolute identity of name. *Röda rummet* ends with a letter from Borg, the doctor, to the artist Sellén, in which Borg runs through their common acquaintances and relates what has happened to them. In the case of Agnes Rundgren/Beda Pettersson, she has become the subject of an academic dissertation on Caesarean sections, and has ended up as a pelvis in the Academy's pathological collection. Her fate is characterized in this fictitious letter as 'the end of a novel'.

Meanwhile, Arvid Falk's transformation, which takes up the last pages of the letter and consequently of the novel itself, is described by Borg as being 'en så hastigt karaktärsutveckling' (such a hasty character development) that he has only seen its equal 'i dåliga pjäser' (in bad plays — SV 6, p.287). In other words, Borg refers to two fictional genres in order to underline how strange our lives are, and to make his statements credible. Borg's characterization of Arvid Falk, who has 'kastat sig på numismatiken med en iver som icke är fullt naturlig' (thrown himself into numismatics with an eagerness that is far from natural) and 'aldrig läser . . . en tidning' (never reads . . . a newspaper), contains the following well-known passage: 'Falk är en politisk fanatiker, som vet att han skulle brinna opp, om han gav luft åt lågan, och därför släcker han den med stränga torra studier; men jag tror icke det lyckas honom, ty hur han lägger band på sig, så fruktar jag en gång en explosion' (Falk is a political fanatic who knows that he would burn up if he gave vent to the flame, and that's why he extinguishes it by hard, boring studies; but I don't think this will work, for however hard he restrains himself, I fear that one day there will be an explosion — p.289). Borg's views on Falk are voiced by one fictive character about another. At the same time, it is a statement about Strindberg's alter ego and as such it has a certain relevance to Strindberg himself. Naturally, this statement is a part of the fiction, but it has also been seen as an autobiographical declaration; it is neither one thing nor the other, but both at once.

With *Röda rummet*, Strindberg made his name as an author. One of those who became curious about him as a result of reading the book was Edvard Brandes. On 21 July 1880, he wrote to Strindberg as the author of *Röda rummet* and a social critic whose support he wished to enlist for his radical program. Strindberg replied on 29 July in his capacity as the novel's author, but without letting himself be enlisted. Brandes' letter and *Röda rummet* constitute the principal context of this reply in which, at Brandes' request, Strindberg pens a self-portrait:

'Jag har retirerat till mitt hem . . . och håller ifrån mig dagens
frågor, jag gräfver ner mig i det Kongliga Bibliotekets 200,000
volymer . . . öfvar sinologi, geografi, arkeologi — en tid bort
åt, men under detta ligger det och gror och värker tills en sådan
der böld som R. Rummet bryter fram. Då blir jag glad och
befriad!

(I have retired to my home . . . and avoiding current issues, am
burying myself in the 200,000 volumes of the Royal Library
. . . study sinology, geography, archaeology — for a while, but
beneath all this things ache and fester until another boil like The
R. Room bursts forth. Then I'll be happy and free! — II, p.165)

The descriptions of Arvid Falk and the 'I' of the letter are very
much alike: in both cases it is a matter of an outward discipline which
in the end cannot be maintained due to inner pressures. The metaphors
that Strindberg uses are taken from different fields. The 'explosion'
feared by Borg — and here the dry-as-dust studies can be seen as highly
inflammable material — corresponds to the novel's social satire and its
opposition to the spirit of the age. Arvid Falk is a potential revolutionary. The metaphor in the letter to Brandes has two elements: the 'boil',
or abscess, which stands for the malady in society that must be
exposed, and the 'growing' that has to do with artistic creativity; this
creativity is often portrayed in the letters with metaphors originating
in the vegetal world. Thus, two metaphors intersect with another,
which can be said to correspond to Strindberg's dual attitude in the
letter. The addressee, Edvard Brandes, is not only an opposition figure
but also an influential critic, and furthermore he has at his side an even
more famous brother, Georg Brandes. Strindberg has in his letter to
fulfil Brandes' double expectations of him, and also to defend himself
against his demands. The letter's 'I' is hence formed with this in mind.
The two images 'boil' and 'growing' respectively indicate social
concern and creative activity. Since both suggest autonomous pro-
cesses, they underline Strindberg's carefully signalled dislike of taking
sides; he acts out of inner necessity and not due to external pressure.
The metaphor in the letter is explicitly linked with *Röda rummet* but
points beyond the novel and towards new works of a similar kind. And,
since Strindberg, probably consciously, depicts himself in the letter in
words close to those quoted from the novel about Arvid Falk, the
novel's autobiographical character is stressed while the 'I' in the letter
becomes fictional.

When, at the end of 1886, Strindberg writes *Författaren*, the
fourth part of *Tjänstekvinnans son*, and reaches the point of *Röda
rummet*'s conception and reception (incidentally, he characterizes the
novel as both 'dikt' and 'verklighet' (fiction and reality — SS 19,

p.165)), he calls the chapter 'Explosionen' (The Explosion). The metaphorical title combines the statements in the two letters from Borg and Strindberg.

There are many reasons why Strindberg's self in the letters appears in different guises: the varying purposes of the correspondence, the degree to which epistolary conventions are enforced, adjustment to the addressee and the dialogue hitherto established with him, Strindberg's state of mind and sense of style at the time, influences from the surrounding works, etc. may all play a decisive part. The interesting thing in this context is, however, that Strindberg's associative and figurative language gives his 'self' a dimension beyond the ordinary and the 'autobiographical'; the 'self' in the letters often tends to establish kinship or even to identify itself with outstanding religious and literary figures like Jesus, Saul, Jacob and Hamlet, to mention only a few of the heroes with whom Strindberg is fond of associating himself. The metaphorical language of the letters can be seen as casual and passing comment, but also as part of a total literary structure which includes Strindberg's entire textual output. Certain metaphors and groups of images recur constantly both in the letters and in the fictional works. We find ourselves asking whether these complexes of metaphors form some sort of matrix with the help of which Strindberg experiences and transposes himself and 'the world', and whether this means, among other things, that references to reality also become unreliable in the letters.

Notes

1. In *French Literary Theory Today. A Reader* (Cambridge, 1982), pp.192-222, translated from 'Le Pacte autobiographique', *Poétique* 14 (1973), pp.137-162. See, too, *Le Pacte autobiographique* (Paris, 1975). Lejeune's copious writings on autobiography also include *L'Autobiographie en France* (Paris, 1971), *Je est une autre* (Paris, 1980) and *Moi aussi* (Paris, 1986).
2. In *The Rhetoric of Romanticism* (New York, 1984), pp.67-81.
3. 'The Autobiographical Contract', p.193.
4. 'The Autobiographical Contract', p.205.
5. See 'Autobiography in the Third Person', *New Literary History*, 9:1 (1977), pp.27-50.
6. See *Tjänstekvinnans son*, SV 20, pp.354, 370-75.
7. See *Tjänstekvinnans son*, SV 20, pp.376-78.
8. 'The Autobiographical Contract', p.203.

9. See, for example, Gunnar Brandell, *Strindberg — ett författarliv*, II (Stockholm, 1985), p.115.
10. Gunnar Brandell, *Svensk litteratur 1900-1950* (Stockholm, 1960), p.76.
11. *Strindberg — ett författarliv*, pp.76, 194.
12. See Margareta Brundin's essay in this volume *passim*.
13. Raman Selden, *A Reader's Guide to Contemporary Literary Theory* (Brighton, 1985), p.91.
14. *The Rhetoric of Romanticism*, p.68.
15. *The Rhetoric of Romanticism*, p.68.
16. *The Rhetoric of Romanticism*, p.69.
17. *The Rhetoric of Romanticism*, p.70.
18. See Kerstin Dahlbäck, '"Det stängda rummet"' — några reflexioner kring postkontor och brev i *Till Damaskus I'* in *Poesi och vetande*. (Göteborg, 1990), pp.96-110.
19. See Michael Robinson, *Strindberg and Autobiography. Writing and Reading a Life* (Norwich, 1986), pp.94-98.
20. 'Christina: Strindberg's Letters and Diary', *Scandinavian Studies*, 62:1 (1990), pp.108-117.

II

The Drama

Reforming Boundaries

Strindberg and subjective drama

Egil Törnqvist

University of Amsterdam

In his well-known study of the development of modern drama from 1880 to 1950,[1] Peter Szondi makes an important distinction between *Dramatik*, i.e. everything written for the stage, and *Drama*, a particular kind of theatrical work, namely the kind characterized by interhuman conflicts. Shakespeare, Racine, Schiller may be seen as good representatives of *Drama*. This distinction allows Szondi to make another one of utmost importance for his study: that between 'dramatic' and 'epic' elements.

The *terminus a quo* is of course not gratuitous. Around 1880 it stood clear to many that man, far from being created in the image of God, was no more than a super-animal (Darwin), that God was in fact dead (Nietzsche), and that man was not even master in his own house, since his actions are largely motivated by drives unconscious to himself (in due course Freud). The dramatic genre — so palpably human in its staged form — could not be unaffected by such revolutionary revaluations. The classical interhuman conflict now no longer seemed of central interest. Plays became either psychologically *interiorized*, dealing with intrahuman conflicts; allegorically *static*, dealing with the plight of all mankind — often the case in the one-acter; or epically *demonstrative* (Brecht). Whatever solutions were attempted, from around 1880 we rarely find examples of the relatively pure, highly dramatic form, focusing on interhuman conflict, which Szondi calls *Drama*. Instead we get a form blending dramatic and epic elements. It is a well-known fact that just as the novel tends to approach drama in this century (Hemingway, Robbe-Grillet), so drama has tended to approach the novel (Shaw, O'Neill).

Strindberg's essential contributions to this development may be subsumed under the heading 'subjective drama'. Szondi observes:

What was later called *I* dramaturgy, and shaped the image of dramatic literature for decades to come, actually began with Strindberg. . . . His theory of the 'subjective drama' itself seems to coincide with that of the psychological novel . . . in his outline of the literature of the future.[2]

The term 'subjective' is by no means unambiguous. As applied to Strindberg's work, two distinct meanings can be discerned, one biographical, the other textual. To many critics Strindberg is a subjective writer largely because his writings are highly autobiographical. But analysis of subjectivity in this sense obviously presupposes knowledge about Strindberg's biography and therefore excludes the average reader or theatre goer, who is not familiar with the author's life. However, the term 'subjective' can be used in quite another, strictly textual sense: narratological (when applied to epic works) or dramatological (when applied to plays). In this latter sense it would apply to works in which everything or almost everything is seen from the protagonist's point of view. Unfortunately, the two meanings of the term 'subjective' are often used topsyturvy by the critics — including Szondi. In the following, I shall disregard the first, biographical meaning and limit myself to the second, textual one.

Fundamental for Strindberg's subjective drama are two observations made in 1886. In a fictitious interview written in connection with the publication of the first part of his autobiography *Tjänstekvinnans son* Strindberg states: 'Man känner icke mer än ett liv, sitt eget' (You know only one life, your own — SS 18, p. 456). This statement could easily be understood as a rejection of the dramatic genre. But, as Szondi points out, it represents in fact the basic precondition 'for a developmental process which encompasses *The Father* (1887), *To Damascus* (1897-1904), *A Dream Play* (1901-02), and *The Great Highway* (1909).'[3]

The second observation concerns the heterogeneity of the ego. At the end of *Tjänstekvinnans son I* we read: 'Jaget är icke något ett självt; det är en mångfald av reflexer, ett komplex av drifter, begär, somliga undertryckta då, andra lössläppta då!' (One's ego is not a unit in itself; it is a conglomeration of reflexes, a complex of urges, drives, alternately suppressed and unleashed — SS 18, p.218). Applied to drama this idea returns two years later in the Preface to *Fröken Julie*: 'Mina själar (karaktärer) äro konglomerater av förgångna kulturgrader, och pågående, bitar ur böcker och tidningar, stycken av mänskor, avrivna lappar av helgdagskläder som blivit lumpor, alldeles som själen är hopflickad. . . .' (My souls — or characters — are patchworks of various stages of culture, past and present, pasted together from books and newspaper clippings, pieced together from scraps of human lives, patched up from old rags that once were fancy dresses — hodge-podges just like the human soul — SV 27, p. 105). In a more radical form the idea reappears in the Preface to *Ett drömspel*: 'Personerna klyvas, fördubblas, dubbleras, dunsta av, förtätas, flyta ut, samlas' (The characters split, double, multiply, dissolve, condense, float apart, coalesce — SV 46, p. 7).

If we combine these two ideas — the idea that you only know your own life and the idea that the ego is heterogeneous — we naturally arrive at Strindbergian subjective drama, that is, a drama in which one character, the protagonist, tends to embrace all the others, who below a thin realistic veneer function as radiations or emanations of his or her ego, what in German is called *Ausstrahlungen des Ichs*.

A clear case of subjectivism within the epic genre is in the first-person novel. Interestingly enough, the author who stated that 'you know only one life, your own' devoted himself to this egocentric subgenre in *En dåres försvarstal*, written shortly after *Fadren* and dealing with virtually the same subject. A comparison between these two works from, respectively, a narratological and dramatological point of view might yield interesting results as to generic correspondences and differences.

A unique counterpart of the first-person novel in the film medium is to be found in Robert Montgomery's *The Lady in the Lake* (1946), where the camera represents the vision of the protagonist throughout the film. The assumption behind this technique was undoubtedly that it would increase the spectator's sense of identification with the central character. Yet if we may believe the French cineast François Truffaut, we identify with a character not when we look *with* the character; rather, we do so when the character looks *at us*. 'A subjective camera is the negation of subjective cinema.'[4]

If one compares the situation in a first-person novel and a first-person film like Montgomery's with that in a play, one inevitably ends up with monodrama. And so Strindberg's *Den starkare* is a logical result of the idea that 'you know only one life, your own.'[5] But if it is true that this type of novel, film and drama have subjectivism in common, it is equally true that the subjectivism is not of the same kind. While we may speak of a first-person or I-novel and a first-person or I-film, where we are, as it were, inside the protagonist, we cannot in quite the same sense speak of a first-person or I-drama. Given the dramatic genre, Strindberg could go no further than call the protagonist of *Den starkare* Mrs X. It indicates that she is a representative character, an Everywoman. But it does not turn her into a fictive I. This is why I prefer the term 'subjective drama' to the term *Ich-Drama*.

From a completely subjective drama in our technical sense we may demand that the protagonist's point of view rules from beginning to end. This can be done in two ways. The dramatist can isolate the protagonist on the stage, or he can surround him/her with characters, whose primary function is to express his/her thoughts, emotions, etc., that is, characters who incarnate various drives within the protagonist. Also in the second case, it would seem natural to have the protagonist visibly present on the stage from beginning to end; only when the surrounding characters very clearly incarnate qualities within him/her could one momentarily accept an absent protagonist.

Turning to Strindberg's plays, we find that there is not a single one where the protagonist is alone on the stage from beginning to end — as is the case in, for example, Beckett's *Krapp's Last Tape. Den starkare* certainly comes close to this type, since here we deal with only one speaking character. But it should be noticed that the mute character's — Miss Y's — mimicry expresses a point of view which is exceedingly important to the speaking Mrs X. Also in *Paria* the protagonist, Mr X, is on stage almost throughout the play; and here again there is only one other character. But this time the antagonist, Mr Y, has a speaking part. The protagonist in *Fadren,* the Captain, is absent in six of the play's twenty-two scenes. The protagonist in *Till Damaskus I,* the Unknown, rather surprisingly is on stage in only twenty-five of the play's forty-eight sequences, i.e. a little more than half. Indra's Daughter in *Ett drömspel* makes a better case; she is present in all the scenes except the so-called school scene, which dramatizes the Officer's nightmare. In *Spöksonaten,* the protagonist, the Student, is absent in the beginning of Acts I and II. In *Stora landsvägen,* finally, the central character, the Hunter, is present in all the seven scenes.

In other words, if we use stage presence as a criterium for subjective drama, we end up with just a few Strindberg plays: *Den starkare, Paria, Ett drömspel, Stora landsvägen,* and one or two more. The question arises: Do the two pre-Inferno plays, from a subjectivist point of view, have anything in common with the two post-Inferno ones — despite the obvious differences? I believe they do. In the two one-acters, the naturalistic demand for verisimilitude forced Strindberg to create at least a listening partner. But the more intriguing function of these partners is that they at times express views nourished subconsciously by the protagonists themselves. They are there to dramatize what is in fact the protagonist's talking to herself/himself. Especially in *Den starkare,* the second character, being mute, is so suggestive because we cannot tell whether she is a real person or a hallucination on the part of the protagonist, arising from her jealousy and guilt feelings.[6] The major difference between Strindberg's two *quart d'heures* and his two full-length plays — in our context — is that while the latter are openly dealing with extrahuman as well as intrahuman conflicts — the protagonist versus the Powers — the former are disguised as 'objective' plays, acted out in a realistic setting and dealing with interhuman conflicts — although in fact they focus on interior ones. This is true also of *Fadren*. Once naturalism had been replaced by symbolism, Strindberg could make the realistic veneer more transparent — without, however, letting it disappear altogether. It is a common misconception that 'point of view' or 'focalization', so important for the epic genre, does not apply to the dramatic one. Yet also in dramatic works we may distinguish between an authorial point of view (the stage directions) and a figural one (the dialogue). And just as in narrative prose, dramatic dialogue frequently contains one point of view embedded within another — as when one character refers to the opinion of another one, absent or not.

Moreover, since drama-in-performance is an audiovisual phenomenon, the literal meaning of 'point of view' — something *seen* from a particular point or angle — is highly relevant. (This is of course even truer of the film medium with its possibilities of foregrounding, high/low camera angles, etc.) The dramatist can make something visible to a character. He can reveal the character's perceptual point of view in order to inform us of his/her conceptual one.[7] This he can do in two ways. He can limit himself to the character. This is, for example, the case when someone on the stage looks through the window and reports what he sees. He then sees what neither the other characters nor the spectators see. But the dramatist can also have us share the character's perceptual point of view. He can have us look *with* the character through the window. In either case he has found a realistic means of indicating the character's point of view.

Actually, there is a third alternative. The playwright can have us share a perceptual point of view with the character which is strange, dreamlike — because it represents his state of mind. Strindberg incidentally resorts to this latter kind of experience in several of his plays. To make us realize *whose* state of mind is made visible, the 'focalizer' or 'visionary' is isolated on the stage in one way or another, kept separate from his vision.

In the asylum scene of *Till Damaskus I*, a number of inmates are seated at a table next to that of the delirious Unknown. They all look like people he — and the audience — have seen before. 'Ansiktena vaxgula, likvita; och något spöklikt i hela väsendet och i gesterna' (Their faces are waxen and deathly white. Their whole appearance and all their gestures are ghostlike — SS 29, p.89). The inmates clearly incarnate the Unknown's deep sense of guilt; they are all people he has abused. In Act II of *Carl XII*, the King, alone and very sleepy, is visited by an old soldier with the symbolic name of Svält (Hunger). The soldier addresses Charles who does not reply. As soon as he has disappeared, the King, rubbing his eyes, says: 'Jag tror, att jag har sovit! — Var det någon här?' (I believe I've slept! . . . Was anyone here? — SS 35, p.160). In *Dödsdansen I*, similarly, the Captain (Edgar), alone and very tired after his stroke, is visited by 'gamla Maja

101

från fattighuset' (old Mary from the poorhouse). As soon as she has left the Captain says: 'Vem var där i dörrn? Var det någon?' (Who was that at the door? Was there anyone? — SV 44, p.74).

In all these cases Strindberg provides a realistic explanation for the appearance of the dreamlike characters. The Unknown is delirious, Charles XII is dreaming, Edgar has just had a stroke. At the same time he suggests that the incidental characters have a symbolic function; they are either messengers from the Invisible or emanations from the Unconscious. By having us participate in the protagonists' vision — in their point of view — Strindberg tries to heighten our empathy with them. And the point is that *we* no more than *they* can be certain about what we see. *Their* impression of 'half-reality' — Strindberg's own key term in his post-Inferno period — is shared by *us*.

A more radical variation appears at the end of *Spöksonaten,* where we share the vision of *Toteninsel* with the Student, now alone on the stage. In this case there is no realistic explanation for the appearance of the Isle. It is clearly a visualization of the Student's intense hope for a better life hereafter. But the point is that not only he but also we see *The Isle of the Dead.* Not only to him but also to us does this paradisiac life hereafter exist. For how can we deny our own senses? His subjective point of view has become ours.

Nowhere in Strindberg's dramatic *oeuvre* do we sense the emanations of the ego more strongly than in *Till Damaskus,* where at least all the male characters seem to incarnate qualities or drives within the Unknown, whose 'name' indicates that, like all of us, he is alien to himself. But the device resorted to here — the use of what we might term a 'cluster protagonist' — is by no means limited to *Till Damaskus.* It is, rather, standard fare with Strindberg. In play after play he suggests that contrasting characters may well be seen not only as autonomous individuals — this is the realistic surface level — but also as conflicting drives within the same ego. Consider in this respect Olof (the reformist) and Gert (the revolutionary) in *Mäster Olof*; Jean (lusting for life) and Julie (longing for death) in *Fröken Julie;* the socially strong, i.e. pliable, Mrs X and the mentally strong Miss Y in *Den starkare*; the two unsentenced men in *Paria* — in a recent Flemish version dressed up in identical white suits; Gustav (the intellectual) and Adolf (the artist) in *Fordringsägare* — in a Swedish TV version played by the same actor; Erik (the man of imagination) and Göran (the man of action) in *Erik XIV*; the Officer, the Lawyer and the Poet in *Ett drömspel* — three stages on life's way; the Student (youth/innocence) and Hummel (old age/guilt) in *Spöksonaten* — two stages on life's way; the emanations surrounding the Hunter in *Stora landsvägen.* When designing these double or triple protagonists Strindberg has tried to live up to his novelistic credo that we know only one life: our own.

This also goes for *Fadren*, which is a somewhat special case. In *Fadren* the Captain is never isolated on the stage and so his state of mind cannot be made visible to us; at most it is indicated in the storm that arises midway through the play. Nor is the Captain, as we have seen, present on the stage throughout the play. Nevertheless, *Fadren* is a highly subjective play. How can this be? The usual answer is that Strindberg has identified so strongly with the protagonist that he has become partial to the case. Instead of discussing this biographical argument, let us look at the play text and try to establish why we may dramatologically regard *Fadren* as a subjective play, a play in which the Captain's point of view in various ways dominates those of the other characters. The following factors seem to me relevant:

1. The Captain is on stage more than any of the other characters and has more lines to speak. Unlike the others he is drawn in the round. Since his inner struggle concerning Bertha — mama's baby, papa's maybe — is central, we come closer to him than to the others. Moreover, he is intellectually and morally superior to the other characters and fulfils in that respect the Aristotelian demand that the tragic protagonist should be spiritually head and shoulders above average man.
2. His foremost antagonist, Laura, is ignorant, stubborn, manipulative and dishonest.
3. The Captain is struggling against a collective antagonist (besides Laura, the women in his house, later also the Pastor and the Doctor), who by sheer force, manipulation and cowardliness (the men) defeat him. As in any tragedy, we sympathize with the heroic struggle of the victim.

So far the situation compares with that of many other plays. What makes *Fadren* such a special case is that the Captain is not only *a* man and Laura not only *a* woman but that they are, in fact, prototypes of the male and female sex.

To help us realize this, Strindberg resorts to various stratagems:

1. He has the characters use generalizing statements about the sexes, e.g.: 'Nyare forskningar ha givit vid handen att det bara finns ett slag [av kvinnor]!' (Recent research has proved that there is only one kind [of women]! — SV 27, p.61) — 'de [kvinnorna] äro omedvetna om sin instinktiva skurkaktighet' (they [the women] are unaware of their instinctive villainy — p.62.) — 'Tror du att en man skulle gå och basuna ut sin skam?' (Do you think a man goes around trumpeting his shame?) — 'En man har inga barn, det är bara kvinnor som få barn, och därför kan framtiden bli deras, när vi dö barnlösa!' (A man has

no children. Only women have children, and so the future belongs to them, while we die childless — p.96).
2. He provides a mytho-historical background (Hercules-Omphale, Samson-Delilah), demonstrating how man has always fallen victim to the stratagem of woman.
3. He demonstrates how all the men in the play succumb to the women.
4. He shows how the men — the Captain, the Pastor and the Doctor — are initially both balanced and in agreement with one another. And how they later, influenced by the women, notably Laura, become perverted if they are weak (the Pastor, the Doctor) or go mad if they are strong (the Captain).
5. He balances the Captain's seeming misogyny by demonstrating his love for Bertha (the child), the Nurse (the mother figure), and by indicating his past love for Laura.
6. At the end he demonstrates how *l'histoire se repète*. In view of everything we have witnessed before, the ending is inevitable because it is archetypal. It is not only *a* man who is disarmed by *a* woman. It is woman (the lower gender, according to the play) defeating man (the higher one) in the battle of the sexes.

In *Fadren* Strindberg has written a black-and-white fairy tale, where the archetypal male protagonist is very white and the archetypal female antagonist very black. On the basis of the dramatological data just presented one logically arrives at this conclusion without the slightest knowledge of Strindberg's standpoint in the so-called woman question.

But *Fadren* is not only a parable or thesis play describing the prophesied outcome of the battle between the sexes. It is also an interiorized drama, dealing with the Captain's psychic constitution, his unusual — hence not so archetypal — susceptibility to doubts about his paternity.

Ever since Lamm it has been common to see the Captain as a victim not so much of Laura's manipulations as of his own psyche. 'The wife', Lamm writes, 'in fact, merely acts as prompter, whispering in his [the Captain's] ear what he has already been obscurely thinking.'[8] Brandell, similarly, points to the fact that the Captain already years ago has questioned his own mental condition; this makes the ending ambiguous. 'Have we witnessed the destruction of a strong spirit by means of hostile forces or the disintegration of a soul from within, a psychic murder or a psychic suicide?'[9] Lagercrantz goes even further when he equates the Captain's uniform with his straitjacket and concludes: 'It was not Laura who forced him into it [the straitjacket]: it existed within himself.'[10]

What these three interpretations have in common is the suggestion that *Fadren* is essentially an intrahuman drama, dealing with the protagonist's struggle with himself, a fundamentally subjective play forced into the objective straitjacket of operative naturalism. Viewed in this way, the Captain comes exceedingly close to the not so reliable first-person narrator of *En dåres försvarstal*. By its tendency to blot out the borderline between the dramatic and the epic genre, *Fadren* anticipates the subjective dramas of the post-Inferno period.

In this period the epic element in the plays grows in importance. Unity of time and place is replaced by unity of hero, as in *Till Damaskus* (The Unknown), *Ett drömspel* (Indra's Daughter), *Spöksonaten* (The Student) and *Stora landsvägen* (The Hunter). As a result the action in these plays, it could be argued, is a reflection of the protagonist's point of view. It is his or her view of life and death that is dramatized — no more. For — to paraphrase Strindberg — there is only one point of view that is truthful: your own. This appears not least from the key phrase in *Ett drömspel*: 'Det är synd om människorna' (Human beings are to be pitied). The divine Daughter does not say: '*You* are to be pitied' or '*We* are to be pitied'. She uses the third person form, thereby — as Szondi notes — formulating her epic distance to humanity.[11]

To reach out beyond this limiting psychological individualism, Strindberg resorts to the device of reduplication. As we have seen, this happens already in *Fadren*, where the men share the same sad experience with regard to women. On a much larger scale reduplication takes place in *Ett drömspel*, where two connected ideas are constantly illustrated: man lives by illusions and is (therefore) to be pitied.

In *Ett drömspel* Strindberg has used the old device of the outsider visiting an unfamiliar environment in a new and startling way. Here it is a goddess (rather than a human being) visiting our world, that is, an environment unfamiliar to her but familiar not only to the characters on stage but also to the audience. Various representatives of mankind 'report' their experience of life to her. Since the recipient of the play will also be a representative of the human species, it follows that it is with our fellow-men on stage, rather than with the Daughter, that we empathize. And yet, not they but the Daughter, is the protagonist of the play. It is *she* who takes us on a pilgrimage around the world, it is primarily *her* experience of life that we share. *She* is the narrator, the ' "camera" ' between the audience and the fictional world represented on the stage.'[12] In this capacity, she is the 'dreamer' of the play.

Szondi argues that since the protagonist, Indra's Daughter, is merely an observer, to whom 'is shown "what human life is like" ', the play has an epic rather than a dramatic structure.[13] This is certainly overstating the point and disregarding the Daughter's transformation

105

in the course of the drama from an observing attitude to a complete immersion in the human condition, reaching its painful nadir in the infernal matrimonial scene. Just as Indra's Daughter has a double existence (being both divine and human), so her dramaturgic function is a double one: she is both observer and experiencer, both subject and object. In this respect she actually mirrors the situation of the recipient of the play who is a subject insofar as he is an observer of the play (reader or spectator) and an object insofar as he is a human being on a par with those on the stage.

Why did Strindberg gradually turn from objective drama — *Drama* in Szondi's terminology — to subjective drama? Szondi's main explanation is that he happened to be writing in a period marked by a revaluation of traditional values which simply could not but affect dramatic writing at the time. Next to this explanation, one might point to the fact that Strindberg — unlike Ibsen — wrote both novels and plays, and that the question of focalization, so crucial in narrative texts, therefore would present itself more naturally to him. In a letter to his German translator, Strindberg himself pointed to his mingling of the two genres when he wrote: 'Ja, det är hemligheten med alla mina berättelser . . . att de äro dramer' (Yes, the secret is that all my stories . . . are plays — XVI, p.11). More probably, however, Strindberg's preference for a subjective presentation was based on a conviction that an 'egocentric' point of view is a prerequisite for an intense empathy on the part of the recipient. And that empathy with the protagonist's vision is the goal of drama-in-performance. By applying the subjective formula 'You know only one life, your own' — hitherto reserved for the epic (and lyric) genre — to the dramatic one, Strindberg was to pioneer the drama to come.

Notes

1. *Theorie des modernen Dramas: 1880-1950* (Frankfurt am Main, 1956). Published in English under the title *Theory of the Modern Drama*, translated by Michael Hays (Cambridge, 1987).
2. *Theory of the Modern Drama*, p.22.
3. *Ibid*, p.23.
4. Truffaut in Peter Graham, *The New Wave* (New York, 1968), p.93.
5. *Theory of the Modern Drama*, p.25.
6. In a recent play, very similar to *Den starkare* — *A Glass of Water* by Ljoedmila Petroesjevskaja — we do not discover until the end that the

female protagonist has been addressing a woman who probably exists only in her own mind.

7. In his *Story and Discourse: Narrative Structure in Fiction and Film* (Ithaca, N.Y., 1978), p.151f., Seymour Chatman makes a useful distinction between *literal* or *perceptual*, *figurative* or *conceptual*, and *transferred* or *interest* point of view.
8. Martin Lamm, *Strindbergs dramer, I* (Stockholm, 1924), p.295.
9. Gunnar Brandell, *Drama i tre avsnitt* (Stockholm, 1971), p.181.
10. Olof Lagercrantz, *August Strindberg*, translated by Anselm Hollo (New York, 1984), p.164.
11. *Theory of the Modern Drama*, p.29.
12. Freddie Rokem, *Theatrical Space in Ibsen, Chekhov and Strindberg: Public Forms of Privacy* (Ann Arbor, Mich., 1986), p.53.
13. *Theory of the Modern Drama*, p.29.

Strindberg as an Innovator of Dramatic and Theatrical Form

Kela Kvam

University of Copenhagen

After the first performance of *Till Damaskus* at the Royal Dramatic Theatre in Stockholm in 1900, the Swedish author and critic Hjalmar Söderberg observed that he found himself confronted by a play about which it was hardly worthwhile expressing an opinion.[1] Lacking any clue to the latest stage of Strindberg's development, his head was swimming, as were those of his fellow bourgeois theatregoers. From a contemporary standpoint, it is, of course, easy to mock Söderberg and his colleagues and the turn of the century theatre audience, but Strindberg had indeed written a highly original play, which was unlike any other and violated almost every dramaturgical rule.

Strindberg probably knew that it might be difficult to find a theatre for his new play, for shortly after sending the manuscript to Gustaf af Geijerstam in March 1898 — a mere three months after having declared that he had lost all interest in playwriting — he eagerly stressed that the play was intended for the stage: 'Den är ju för scenen' (After all, it is intended for the stage — XII, p.280). For two years he had been trying, both personally and with the aid of go-betweens, to have it performed in Sweden and abroad, but in vain. A planned performance at the Dagmar Theatre in Copenhagen fell through, and so did another at the Venice Opera. His German translator, Emil Schering, did not succeed in selling the play to the theatres in Germany, and even though Strindberg was willing to renounce his author's rights and give him a free hand, Lugné-Poë was not tempted to include it in the repertory of the Théâtre de l'Œuvre in Paris, where *Fadren* had been successfully performed in 1894.

Strindberg was approximately fifty when he wrote the two parts of *Till Damaskus*. He had, in other words, reached the age when few playwrights radically renew themselves. But Strindberg emerged from his Inferno crisis of 1894-96 with a completely personal style. Although he flirted with various fashionable tendencies that he claimed to have anticipated in the past, he was no longer concerned that people consider him the leader of a school, as he had been in the 1880s. Strindberg had that rare ability to carry on growing mentally, and he surely incarnated himself in the two young Hamlets of *Spöksonaten* and *Pelikanen*. He retained to the end the despair of, and an impatience with, the world which is so characteristic of adolescents.

Compared to Ibsen, who in his later years was a highly respected and established dramatist whose plays were performed at all the major European theatres, Strindberg remained avant garde. *Ett drömspel* and the Chamber Plays — his most original plays apart from *Till Damaskus I-III* — were only appreciated by a very limited circle. In fact, the Chamber Plays would probably never have reached the stage during Strindberg's lifetime without the existence of August Falck's Intimate Theatre. When they were first presented to the public, the critics, with few exceptions, agreed that they were the creations of a sick and weakened dramatist's brain.[2] It became customary to emphasize the superior value of Strindberg's great plays from the 1880s so as to diminish the importance of his new works, or to convince him that these might be read with a certain pleasure, but were unsuitable for the stage. Viewed in retrospect, of course, such statements seem grotesque: Strindberg's post-Inferno plays have turned out to be great directors' plays, although he is certainly not the only innovator of dramatic form to have been told that his plays were undramatic because they broke with the conventions of their time.

Strindberg always regarded himself first and foremost as a dramatist. It is characteristic that as soon as he had a theatre at his disposal he produced one drama after another, almost feverishly. But the problem was that for long periods of his life he was a dramatist in search of a theatre. And a dramatist has an urgent need to be performed; a writer of poetry or prose, on the other hand, can afford to be more patient.

It is difficult to find precedents for Strindberg's post-Inferno plays in contemporary drama. There was, of course, a general tendency in the European theatre to free itself from realism, and Strindberg took part in the ongoing discussion about the renewal of drama among the French symbolists at the end of the century. But he still seemed to follow his own path, and it is hard to believe that the models which he himself claimed to follow were much more than superficial. It is difficult, for instance, to see any real correspondence between Strindberg's plays and those of the eccentric French dramatist and occultist, Joséphin Péladan, with whom, as he writes in *Inferno*, after having read his first major Péladan opus (probably *Comment on devient mage*) in May 1897, Catholicism made its solemn and triumphant entry into his life (SS 28, p.201).

For Strindberg, Péladan, the co-founder of the Ordre Cabbalistique de la Rose-Croix and self-appointed Mage, represented a revelation of the superman, of Nietzsche's *Übermensch*; he had wandered from Satanism to Catholicism in much the same way as Strindberg felt he was doing himself. Hence the latter revelled in Péladan's occult writings, with their bizarre mixture of sadism, erotic perversion, occultism and prophetic spiritualism, and maintained a keen interest in his plays, many of which are to be found in Strindberg's library at the Strindberg Museum in Stockholm. He worked on behalf of Péladan's interests in Germany and wrote an introduction to Schering's translation of his play *Panthée*. Before it was decided that the Intimate Theatre should be exclusively a Strindberg theatre, he proposed to Falck that he introduce Péladan into the repertory, along with Wagner (minus the music), Racine, Euripides, Hebbel, Grabbe, and several others.[3]

Of all the available French dramatists, Strindberg had certainly chosen the most bizarre as his model. Nevertheless, it was Péladan, whose plays are set in exotic and remote milieux, and which are written in a mannered and overly elaborate style, who introduced the technique of the Wagnerian leitmotif into drama, a technique which was to become so characteristic of Strindberg's later plays. Moreover, the theme of *Till Damaskus I* may well have been inspired by Péladan's mediocre short story 'Le Chemin de Damas' from 1881, in which the principal character is a disillusioned rogue who is on the point of hanging himself when he meets a priest and is miraculously converted.[4]

A more substantial influence on Strindberg's dramatic work around the turn of the century came from Maeterlinck. In a letter to Richard Bergh from February 1901, Strindberg writes that his house is now filled with the works of Maeterlinck and Péladan, both of whom had their roots in the Paris occultism inspired by Balzac's *Séraphita*, and he adds: 'respekt för Maeterlinck! Plats för Sâr Péladan' (Respect for Maeterlinck! Make room for Sâr Péladan — XIV, p.25). He was greatly fascinated by *Le Trésor des humbles* in which Maeterlinck expounds his theory of the 'static theatre', and (as he likewise told Bergh in a previous letter that January) found it a strange coincidence that it had been published in 1896, 'mitt Inferno- och Damaskus-år!' (my Inferno and Damascus year): 'Jag skulle väl icke få lof att läsa den boken det året; nu fick jag den, sedan min Virgilius — Swedenborg fört mig genom alla Infernos nio ringar' (I was probably not allowed to read the book that year; now I've been given it, after my Virgil — Swedenborg — has led me through all the nine circles of Inferno — XIV, p.16). In a letter to Schering, written the following April, he calls *Le Trésor des humbles* the greatest book he had ever read (XIV, p.82), but adds that he had already anticipated it himself in such plays as *Påsk* and *Midsommar*.

In connection with a German performance of *Brott och brott*, meanwhile, he ironically boasted of belonging to those young artists who are not appreciated until they are old, thus aligning himself with the younger Maeterlinck whose plays had recently been performed in Germany. In 1901-02, when he already entertained plans for a theatre of his own, he tried to obtain the rights to translate, publish and perform Maeterlinck's plays (though ironically Strindberg's dramatic break with August Falck in 1910, which led to the closure of the Intimate Theatre, was provoked by Falck's production of Maeterlinck's *L'Intruse*, which Strindberg regarded as a betrayal in spite of his admiration for the Flemish dramatist). There is without doubt a certain kinship, both in thematic content and dramatic form, between Maeterlinck and Strindberg at this time. It is characteristic that in writing to Bergh Strindberg should quote a passage from *Le Reveil de l'âme* where Maeterlinck heralds a new spiritual age in which souls will see one another without the intervention of the senses (XIV, pp.16-7). Such a spiritual relationship between man and woman is a frequently presented ideal in Strindberg's later plays, in, for example, the brother-sister relationship between Eleonora and Benjamin in *Påsk*. The longing for the elimination of erotic love was, however, part of the general baggage of the spiritual revivalists of the 1890s, as was the interest for the androgyne which is also found in Péladan, and which Strindberg (elaborating the idea for Harriet Bosse when she was preparing the role of Eleonora) had received from Balzac's Séraphita-Séraphitus: 'Engeln, för hvilken jordisk kärlek icke finnes på den grund att hon-han är l'époux et l'épouse de l'humanité. Symbol af den högsta, fullkomligaste menniskotyp, hvilken spökar mycket i den modernaste litteraturen och antages av några befinna sig på vägen hit ner till oss' (the Angel for whom earthly love does not exist because he-she is *l'époux et l'épouse de l'humanité*. A symbol of the highest, most perfect type of man, which often haunts the most modern literature, and which is taken by some to be on its way down here to us — XIV, p.34). Similar ideas could also be found among The Shakers, the American sect which was well-known to Strindberg, as Margareta Wirmark has pointed out in her study of women in Strindberg's theatre, *Den kluvna scenen*.[5]

In such plays as *Kronbruden* and *Svanevit*, Strindberg made a conscious effort 'att intränga i Maeterlincks underbara skönhetsverld' (penetrate Maeterlinck's wonderful world of beauty — the reference, again in a letter to Harriet Bosse which accompanied the manuscript of *Kronbruden*, is to the Flemish poet's use of legend and folklore — XIV, p.22). And in Maeterlinck's 'static theatre' in general, which found its definitive form in the one-acters *L'Intruse*, *L'Intérieur* and

Les Aveugles, he was confronted by an alternative dramaturgy which derived its tension not from external action, nor from the clash of contrasting wills, but from the communication of emotion attained by the duality of spoken words and silence, and from a play of moods and an atmosphere that made room for the irrational and the subconscious. The most obvious example of the inspiration that Strindberg received from Maeterlinck's 'static theatre of the unspoken' is *Oväder*, in which he makes use of the same duality of exteriors and interiors that Maeterlinck employed in *L'Intruse* and *L'Intérieur*.

But although there are many fairly obvious similarities, the difference between Strindberg and his apparent models is greater. Like Péladan's, Maeterlinck's world is a world of unreality and dreams. But Strindberg always retained a firm grip on reality. He dreamt with his eyes open, and created his own personal world of hallucinations. In November 1897, he wrote to Emil Kléen of Péladan among others, that he did not feel called upon to become a prophet or a missionary, and that the fight which is fought in his literary work takes place in his own soul, and no one else's (XII, p.223). He also dissociates himself from Péladan's sentimental Christianity and calls himself a Christian atheist, meaning that for him Christ serves as a source of energy and not as an ideal beyond his reach. The fact that Strindberg dramatized his own inner conflicts and used his private life directly as material for his plays sets him apart from Maeterlinck, even though he may belong to the same spiritual and social world. When using his own life as dramatic material, Strindberg in fact never gets uncomfortably or elliptically private. On the contrary: he writes in a way that enables him to remain accessible to his audience, though reaching deeper levels of subconscious experience than in his pre-Inferno dramas, thus confirming Antonin Artaud's remark about Strindberg's dreams being the dreams which everybody dreams: 'We have lived and dreamed everything this play reveals,' he remarked, of *Spöksonaten*, 'but we have forgotten it.'[6] Typical of Strindberg's relationship to Maeterlinck is the remark he made, again to Harriet Bosse in February 1901, admitting that in *Kronbruden* he has not fully succeeded in attaining to the beauty of Maeterlinck's world: 'Att jag endast stannat vid portarne vet jag; måste bränna soporna i min själ först för att bli värd inträda' (I know I have only stopped at the portal; I must burn the slag in my soul before I am worthy of entering — XIV, p.22). And in letter to Vilhelm Carlheim-Gyllensköld the same month, he says that his Maeterlinck fever, called forth by reading *La Princesse Maleine*, has instilled in him the feeling that something new is entering into him, but that there remains some slag left in his body and soul still to be burnt (XIV, p.30). Fortunately, Strindberg did not succeed in purifying himself of this 'slag', which is precisely what makes him the great and original dramatist he is.

Strindberg's drama has body as well as soul — Maeterlinck's has only soul.

Strindberg's often-stated admiration for Maeterlinck tempted August Falck to transfer the specific Maeterlinck production style, which Lugné-Poë had introduced at the Théâtre de l'Œuvre, to Strindberg's Chamber Plays. But the monotonous sing-song applied to Strindberg's very plastic dialogue proved a catastrophe, as is clear from Anna Branting's review of the première of *Spöksonaten* at the Intimate Theatre, in 1908: 'The words are not enunciated, they are breathed with effort as in panic-stricken visions by actors who have painted their faces as white as chalk to look really starved.'[7] Her judgement is confirmed by other critics. Bo Bergman found the diction unusually languid and felt that the discussion of problems concerning food and domestic servants in stylized, sepulchral voices was not to the play's benefit. In his view, Helge Wahlgren, who played the Student, achieved the most consistent stylization, with the result that Strindberg's Student became a highly affected representative of the lost generation. In so far as he had a directorial role, Strindberg was unable to recognize his own character either; but he was in any case not the right person to guide young and untrained actors through his own text: ''När jag ser min pjäs återgiven utan att jag lägger märke till skådespelarne, så är det bra spelat,' he writes in *Öppna brev till Intima teatern* (When I see my play performed without noticing the actors, it has been acted well — SS 50,p.105). The fact that he could not bear to have actors hammering his own words into his ears every day, but was more fascinated by the text itself, was the reason why he quickly changed from 'ordinary' to 'titular director' at the theatre.

To escape from the prevailing dramaturgy of the well-made play, Strindberg looked backwards, and resumed his reading of Goethe's *Faust* and Shakespeare, especially the philosophical plays *Hamlet*, *King Lear* and *The Tempest*. He loved Shakespeare's pathos, his raging against fate, and the way he incarnated himself in his characters, just as Strindberg himself did: in *Ett drömspel*, for instance, *all* the characters may be viewed as figures appearing in their author's dream. Shakespeare's plays, in which technique is invisible, have been compared to nature, Strindberg states, in his *Öppna brev till Intima teatern*, but Shakespeare is both formless and a strict formalist at the same time. This is also a valid characterization of Strindberg's own plays. Critics frequently reproached him for the lack of pre-meditated form in his post-Inferno plays, since they did not conform to the logical structure of the well-made play or the analytical drama. But if the Aristotelian model is disregarded, a different formal pattern unveils itself, not least if one considers Strindberg's relationship to both painting and music. In many respects he accomplished in drama what his onetime friend Edvard Munch had achieved in painting, though his dramaturgy may well be best expressed in terms of music. The musical structuring of the dialogue is already evident in the so-called naturalistic plays. In the celebrated Preface to *Fröken Julie*, he anticipates the Wagnerian leitmotif technique which entered French drama at the turn of the century and reached its peak with Paul Claudel:

> Jag har undvikit det symmetriska, matematiska i den franska konstruerade dialogen och låtit hjärnorna arbeta oregelbundet, såsom de göra i verkligheten, där i ett samtal ju intet ämne tömmes i botten, utan den ena hjärnan av den andra får en kugg på måfå att gripa in i. Och därför irrar också dialogen, förser sig i de första scenerna med ett material som sedan bearbetas, tages upp, repeteras, utvikes, lägges på, såsom temat i en musikkomposition.

> (I have avoided the symmetrical, mathematical construction of French dialogue and allowed people's minds to work irregularly as they do in real life where in conversation a subject is never fully exhausted, and one mind finds in another a cog which by chance it can engage with. And therefore the dialogue also wanders, providing itself with material in the opening scenes which is later taken up, worked upon, repeated, expanded and developed like the theme in a musical composition — SS 23, p. 109)

At the time, Strindberg felt obliged to follow the conventions of realistic drama — he had to resort to the device of using alcohol, for example, to motivate the long monologues of Jean and Julie. But the difference between dialogue in Ibsen and Strindberg is easily discernible in their naturalistic plays. While Ibsen's dialogue is delivered in small fragments, as bits of a puzzle which must fit together in the course of the play, and none of which can be omitted, Strindberg's dialogue appears spontaneous and almost haphazard. Freed from the conventions of realism, he could sound his full register in *Ett drömspel*, which is a symphonic elegy for solo voices and choir, with variations on the main theme: 'Det är synd om människor'. Strindberg has himself offered the best clue to the composition of this play in the appendix to his original prefatorial note to Victor Castegren, who directed the first performance:

> Vad den lösa osammanhängande formen i dramat beträffar, är även den skenbar endast. Ty vid påseende befinnes kompositionen ganska fast — en symfoni, polyfonisk, fugerad här och där med huvudmotivet alltjämt återkommande, repeterat och varierat av de några och trettio stämmorna i alla tonarter. Inga

solo med ackompagnemang, det är inga roller, inga karakterer eller karikatyrer man borde säga, inga intriger, inga aktslut med applådställen — Stämföringen är strängt genomförd och i finalens offerscen drager allt det förflutna förbi, motiven resumeras ännu en gång, såsom livet med alla dess detaljer lär göra i dödsstunden . . .

(As for the loose, disconnected form of the drama, that is also only illusory. For on closer examination the composition appears rather tight — a symphony, polyphonic, fugal here and there, with the main motif always resumed, repeated and varied by the thirty odd voices in every key. No solos with accompaniments, that is, no roles, no characters or caricatures one should say, no intrigue, no finales inviting applause. The vocal score is strictly carried through, and in the final sacrificial scene the entire past passes in review, the motifs are once again repeated, just as a man's life is supposed to do in all its detail at the moment of death.)[8]

But now these leitmotifs are not only to be found in the dialogue; they are also present in the stage properties, the white Christmas rose and needlework in *Till Damaskus I*, for example, or the green box, the shawl, and the bunch of withering roses in *Ett drömspel*.[9]

With his post-Inferno plays, Strindberg made entirely new demands on the theatre. He did not adapt himself to the theatre, the theatre had to adapt itself to him. And it is worth remarking that we have still not found the proper critical term — a genre definition — to cover Strindberg's later plays, even though the theatre has adapted itself to his associative and often circular dramaturgy, his method of using repetitive structures, and so on. (Or maybe not — for from a recent handbook of drama, *Dramatisk berättande* by the Swedish dramatist Mats Ödeen,[10] it would seem that Strindberg, and a great many other dramatists, has lived in vain. Like many writers of dramaturgical cookbooks, drama for Ödeen is characterized by external action and external conflict. The characters must have specific reasons for their actions, and meet with an appropriate resistance, a view that would easily allow Ödeen to argue that a Hollywood adventure film is of greater value than, say, *Ett drömspel*, in which the characters have no well-defined reasons for doing what they do.)

Certainly when Strindberg delivered *Till Damaskus I* to the Royal Dramatic Theatre, they hardly knew what to do with it. It was impossible to adapt the heavy machinery of the realistic theatre to the rhythm of the play, and to visualize a drama which moved freely in time and space, and where the changing scenes were projections of the main character's unconscious or state of mind. Strindberg had then proposed

115

using pictures projected onto the backdrop to avoid unnecessary breaks in the action, but the technical equipment which was ordered from Dresden (according to a letter to Schering, two sciopticons — XV, p.341) turned out to be ineffective.[11] In spite of this, Strindberg was naturally eager to prove that his new plays were meant to be staged and not read, and experimented with different ways of having them transferred to the stage. Like the English theatre practitioner and theorist, Edward Gordon Craig, he consulted histories of the theatre for ways and means. Herman A. Ring's *Teaterns historia* (1898) provided information about the Oriental theatre and what he came to call the 'Molière Stage', a downstage balustrade which Ring claimed was in use at the Hôtel de Bourgogne, and which Strindberg believed might be employed to indicate a change of scene by the removal or addition of some property or other.[12] From Ring, too, he took the idea of using simultaneous scenography as in the medieval theatre, and hence possibly appropriate to *Till Damaskus* as a modern morality play, in which the Heaven and Hell of the medieval theatre have been translated into the white mill and the black forge of the ravine in Act Two (SS 29, p.63). Strindberg in fact drew several sketches for simultaneous settings with the various localities painted on the side flats, an approach which suited a theatre as poor as the Intimate Theatre, where the play was staged in 1910.

But Strindberg, though a rare visitor to the theatre, was also very well informed of current developments elsewhere in Europe. He had read, for instance, Gordon Craig's brief but important book, *The Art of the Theatre*, shortly after it appeared in 1905, and even though he dissociated himself from Craig's ideas of dethroning the dramatist in favour of the all-powerful 'stage-manager', he was fascinated by his Wagnerian ideas of fusing words, music, movement, lines and colour into an organic whole, and by his new use of theatre lighting, which Max Reinhardt was perfecting in Germany. Strindberg actually met Craig in 1906, but the encounter did not prove very successful. Craig was visiting Stockholm together with the American dancer, Isadora Duncan, who had invited Strindberg to come to the theatre where she was performing and, as she wrote, 'look at her with a *man's* eye'.[13] Strindberg was absolutely terrified. He believed Isadora wished to seduce him and wrote to Harriet Bosse, who was engaged at the Swedish Theatre in Helsinki, asking her to come and save him (see XV, p.238). In fact, Craig's visit to Strindberg's apartment was brief. Strindberg did not like his appearance; with his long hair and camel hair coat he looked too much like a 'teaterbov' (theatre villain). Nevertheless, Strindberg made plans, which were directly inspired by Craig, for a production of *Ett drömspel* at the Intimate Theatre. He envisaged a staging of the play using white drapes which would alter in character with the aid of coloured spotlights, something which at the time in

Sweden was regarded as vulgar and only suitable for variety shows and the like. He also sketched out short dances *à la* Duncan, which were to be inserted into the play along with music by Bach, Mendelssohn and Beethoven.[14] The characters were to wear costumes from different historical epochs in order to stress the dreamlike atmosphere. Dematerialization was a key word for Strindberg at this time. He wanted even a naturalistic play like *Fadren* to be performed on a bare stage hung with drapery. Again he was in accordance with Craig who, many years later in *The Listener* , stressed that *Fadren* could not be staged using a realistic setting.[15] If the father was going to sit in an ordinary chair, it would collapse under him, Craig said, and if the characters were to make their entries and exits through ordinary doors, the whole play would be ridiculous.

Strindberg did not of course realize his radical solutions for staging his plays himself, and he did not live to see Max Reinhardt's productions of the Chamber Plays and *Ett drömspel*, which were performed in the years during and immediately after the First World War, and which led to a complete revaluation of these plays as theatre.[16] Instead, Strindberg achieved what few dramatists have done, namely to be considered posthumously the leader of an avant-garde movement, in this case German Expressionism. *Till Damaskus*, for instance, became nothing less than the model for young German dramatists and provided the name for a specific expressionistic genre, 'Die Stationendrama'. Strindberg was identified with German expressionist theatre to such a degree that when, in 1921, Bernhard Diebold published his polemical attack upon expressionist drama, *Die Anarchie im Drama*, Strindberg was made the scapegoat for all the offences of the expressionists, including their posing as martyrs and their passive expectation of a coming millennium.

The expressionist Strindberg is by no means the whole man, though. What Germans of that generation could identify with was Strindberg's despair, his distortion of reality, and his hope of redemption. The expressionists saw only the suffering Titan. Strindberg's humour, however, was not unveiled until much later, by the absurdists in France and, incidentally, at least once by the English, in Laurence Olivier's marvellously witty representation of the Captain in *Dödsdansen* at the National Theatre, in 1967.

Notes

1. *Ord och Bild*, 10 (1901), pp.51-53.
2. See, for example, the review of *Pelikanen* by Sven Söderman in *Stockholms Dagblad*, 27 November 1907; August Brunius on *Brända tomten* in *Svenska Dagbladet*, 6 November 1907; Bo Bergman on *Oväder, Dagens Nyheter*, 31 December 1907, and *Spöksonaten, Dagens Nyheter*, 22 January 1908.
3. See August Falck, *Fem år med Strindberg* (Stockholm, 1935), p.31.
4. For Strindberg and Péladan, see also Örjan Lindberger, 'Some Notes on Strindberg and Péladan', in Marilyn Johns Blackwell, ed., *Structures of Influence. A Comparative Approach to August Strindberg* (Chapel Hill, 1981), pp.245-255.
5. *Den kluvna scenen* (Stockholm, 1988). See p.189.
6. Antonin Artaud, *Collected Works*, II, translated by Victor Corti (London, 1971), p.97.
7. In *Skådebanan*, 1908.
8. See Helmut Müssener, '*Ett drömspel*. Tillkomst och textproblem', *Meddelanden från Strindbergssällskapet*, 36 (1964), p.26.
9. The Chamber Plays of course invite analysis in musical terms. A valid starting point might be a comparison with sonata form. See e.g. Raymond Järvi, 'Strindberg's *The Ghost Sonata* and Sonata Form', *Mosaic*, 5 (1972), pp.69-84. Shortly after writing the Chamber Plays with chamber music in mind, Strindberg wrote to the composer and violinist Tor Aulin about the possibility of transposing *Ett drömspel* into a chamber opera, much as Peter Brook later did with *Carmen*. See XVI, p.155.
10. Mats Ödeen, *Dramatiskt berättande. Om konsten att strukturera ett drama* (Stockholm, 1988).
11. For a detailed account of the première of *Till Damaskus* at the Royal Dramatic Theatre, see Ingrid Hollinger, 'Urpremiären på *Till Damaskus I*', Gösta M. Bergman, ed., *Dramaten 175 år* (Stockholm, 1963), pp.296-352.
12. Herman A. Ring, *Teaterns historia* (Stockholm, 1898). For the 'Molière scen', which was realized in the 1908 production of *Kristina* at the Intimate Theatre, see p.220.
13. In her autobiography, *My Life*, 2nd ed. (London, 1966), p.203, Duncan recalls: 'When I was in Stockholm I sent an invitation to Strindberg, whom I greatly admired, to come and see me dance. He replied that he never went anywhere, that he hated human beings. I offered him a seat on the stage, but even then he did not come.'
14. See August Falck, *Fem år med Strindberg* (Stockholm, 1935), p.274.
15. *The Listener*, 1956.
16. See Kela Kvam, *Max Reinhardt og Strindbergs Visionære Dramatik* (Copenhagen, 1974).

The Representation of Death in Strindberg's Chamber Plays

Freddie Rokem

Tel Aviv University

To Amitai (1973-1990) in memoriam

> Life's but a walking shadow.
>
> W. Shakespeare

> — Säg far, varför växer blommorna upp ur smuts?
> — Därför att de icke trivas i smutsen, skynda de så
> fort de kunna upp i ljuset, för att blomma och dö!
> (Say father, why do flowers grow out of the dirt? —
> Since they cannot flourish in the dirt they hurry up
> as quickly as possible towards the light, in order to
> blossom and die!)   A. Strindberg

> I was neither
> Living nor dead and I knew nothing.
>
> T.S. Eliot

At the end of the first section of *Repetition* (1843), Kierkegaard's essay on experimental psychology, his fictive persona, Constantin Constantius, eulogizes the sense of loss to which the passage of time inevitably gives rise:

> Travel on you fugitive river! You are the only one who really knows what you want, for you want only to flow along and lose yourself in the sea, which is never filled! Move on, you drama of life — let no one call it a comedy, no one a tragedy, for no one saw the end! Move on you drama of existence, where life is not given again any more than money is! Why has no one

returned from the dead? Because life does not know how to captivate as death does, because life does not have the persuasiveness that death has. Yes, death is very persuasive if only one does not contradict it but lets it do the talking; then it is instantly convincing, so that no one has ever had an objection to make or has longed for the eloquence of life.[1]

In his Chamber Plays, as well as in much of his writing from the post-Inferno period, Strindberg actually, in the words of Kierkegaard, lets death do the talking, directing our attention to death as the great liberator by developing what could be termed a discourse of death. The Chamber Plays have been given a special place among Strindberg's works because of their innovative as well as their enigmatic qualities. Here he created a theatrical discourse of the *peisithanatos*, the persuader to death, who according to Kierkegaard, because of his powerful subject — death — creates a very persuasive and eloquent language.

The voice of the *peisithanatos* can be heard in all of the Chamber Plays: sometimes through an individual character, sometimes through the collective choral voice of several, and sometimes this voice is carried by the whole cast. Finally, however, it is the polyphonic character of the plays as a whole which enables us to listen to the eloquent rhetoric of death. The central argument of this essay is that in the Chamber Plays, Strindberg developed such a rhetoric, which can at least partially be considered as a genre characteristic. I shall first of all present some general characteristics of this exceptional group of plays in the light of Kierkegaard's ideas concerning the literary representation of death, and then go on to analyze some of the more specific rhetorical devices concerned. The feature which makes the Chamber Plays so remarkable, at least in their contemporary context, but even in many respects today, is that they cannot be caught in any prefabricated analytical net in order to be neatly classified and put away in academic formalin.

The Student in *Spöksonaten*, who because of his youth and relative innocence becomes such a powerful character, captures this voice in his confrontation with death, though finally submitting to its inevitability. The Student has been given the final word in the very complex argument presented in the play between an activist position in the reformation of the evils of this world of which the Young Lady is the victim, on the one hand, and the acceptance of death as the final liberator, on the other. When the Young Lady calls for the death screen, the Student calls out, almost triumphantly:

Befriaren kommer! Välkommen, du bleka, milda! — Sov du sköna, osälla, oskyldiga, utan skuld till dina lidanden, sov utan

drömmar, och när du vaknar igen . . . må du hälsas av en sol
som icke bränner, i ett hem utan damm, av fränder utan skam,
av en kärlek utan vank. . . .

(The liberator is coming! Welcome you pale and gentle one! —
Sleep you beautiful, innocent, lost soul, who is not guilty for its
own suffering, sleep without dreams, and when you wake up
again . . . may you be greeted by a sun which does not burn, in
a home without dust, by friends without shame, by a love
without flaws — SS 45, p.210)[2]

During the first months of his fifty-seventh year, in 1907, Strindberg wrote *Oväder, Brända tomten, Spöksonaten,* and *Pelikanen,* as
well as the dramatic fragment *Toten-Insel.* On 15 April, he wrote in
the Occult Diary:

Mina tankar ha den sista . . . tiden sysslat med döden och lifvet
efter detta. Läste i går Platons Timaios och Phaison. Undrar om
jag skall dö nu, eller snart. Skrifver f.n. på ''Toten-Insel'' der
jag skildrar uppvaknandet efter döden och det som verkar [?]
följer, men tvekar och fasar för att blotta livets bottenlösa
elände.

(My thoughts have recently been occupied with death and the
life after this. Read Plato's *Timaeus* and *Phaedo.* I wonder if I
am going to die now or soon. I am presently writing ''Toten-
Insel'', where I describe the waking up after death and what
seems to follow, but hesitate and fear to expose the utter misery
of life.)

Two days later, on 17 April, *Ett drömspel,* written as early as 1901
and perhaps Strindberg's most comprehensive dramatic-poetic
formulation of the relation between this world and the next, was
performed for the first time at Svenska Teatern in Stockholm. And
shortly afterwards, in a letter to Emil Schering, dated 26 April, he
complains that he has lost interest in continuing his work on *Toten-
Insel,* 'liksom jag förlorat intresset vid lifvet, och anar slutet. I tio år
har jag beredt mig på döden och liksom lefvat på ''andra sidan'' ' (as
though I had lost interest in life and sense the end. For ten years I have
been preparing myself for death and have, as it were, lived 'on the
other side' — XV, p.366). The Chamber Plays are definitely a part of
this preparation.

A discourse of death, as well as the paradoxical notion of living 'on
the other side', raises several not easily solved problems for the
dramatic author writing for the stage. How is it possible to find a

theatrical language to express that which is beyond this life? And what is the relationship on stage between this world and the next? Through his reading of Kierkegaard, which began at an early age, Strindberg must have become well acquainted with his enigmatic solutions to the moral as well as the aesthetic problems concerning the literary representation of this world as well as the next. In the passage from *Repetition* dealing with the fascination of death quoted above, Kierkegaard focuses on the question why no one has returned from the dead. The answer he gives is formulated on the level of discourse — the rhetorical power and persuasiveness of death itself. The Chamber Plays are Strindberg's most comprehensive theatrical attempt to cope with this understanding of the relationship between life and death.

In *Ett drömspel*, as well as in *Dödsdansen*, a knowledge of death which is not limited to a metaphorical construction of life as death, is taken for granted. The Daughter's memories of her previous existence in *Ett drömspel* are actually the basis for her intense longings back to where she came from, a motif which Strindberg's reading of Plato must certainly have strengthened. And in *Dödsdansen* the awareness that we shall all, as the Captain says, end up as a heap of dirt — 'Bara så mycket som att köra ut på en skottkärra och lägga på trädgårdslandet' (Just as much as can be taken out in a wheelbarrow and put on the garden — SV 44, p.15) — is the point of departure for this drama.

In this respect, Strindberg's writing is radically different from Ibsen's or Chekhov's. For them, death may serve as an emotional or an intellectual experience, but only as seen from this side of death, from the point of view of the living. For Strindberg, death is primarily a return to a place which has already been inhabited and his protagonists are constantly searching for a language, a discourse, to express this experience. In creating a theatre where the idea of the return to a previous form of existence, which is also the future form of death, the Swedenborgian notion of correspondences, as well as Kierkegaard's concept of repetition (*gentagelse*), have been of great importance for Strindberg. In *Till Damaskus* as well as *Ett drömspel* this kind of Kierkegaardian repetition, in life as well as in the cycle of life and death, serves as the structural, the aesthetic as well as the moral-metaphysical, organizing principle.[3]

In a recent study on Kierkegaard and literature, Louis Mackey has emphasized that the aim of repetition is

> to recuperate every present moment for the ideal and to install the ideal in every present moment, so that the actual becomes the repetition (re-presentation) of the ideal and the ideal becomes the repetition (the meaning and truth) of the actual. In this way repetition would redeem what is lost in hope and recollection alike.[4]

The basic principle of repetition is to undermine or overcome the division between the ideal, i.e. death, and the actual present moment. Death is the experience where the losses and pains of life can be remembered in an extended (post-mortal) sense of the Romantic concept of 'recollection in tranquillity'. From this perspective, even the most trivial details of everyday life can be redeemed. In the Chamber Plays, but in other plays too, like *Ett drömspel*, there is a constant attempt to bridge the conflict between the continual repetition of the menial demands of everyday reality, and the return to the purity and innocence which only death and spiritual redemption are able to grant. In *Ett drömspel* Agnes is confronted with her husband's demand to return to the trivial tasks of the home while she herself chooses to return to the celestial spheres, to her real home. Strindberg is constantly concerned with finding a connection between the two spheres, but it is clear that his emotional preferences for the next world also colour his concept of this one.

The Gentleman in *Oväder* is confronted with a similar dilemma, complaining, just like the Officer in the school scene in *Ett drömspel*, who has to do his homework, that:

— Det är så svårt att ta om igen: det är som bakläxor, som man egentligen kan, fastän lärarn inte tycker så. Jag är så långt ifrån det här — jag var på helt andra trakter — och jag kan inte knyta an vid det förflutna —

(It's so hard to repeat things: it's just like doing homework over again which you already know, even if the teacher doesn't think so. I am so far away from this — I was in completely different regions — and I cannot connect with the past — p. 49)

What the Gentleman really longs for, while being confronted with a schoolteacher asking him to do his homework over and over again, is a static state representing death. The past — the passage of his life — has been lost to sight.

The Stranger in *Brända tomten* meditates on the passage of time in similar terms:

. . . jag har varit rik och fattig, hög och låg, lidit skeppsbrott och haft jordbävning, huru livet än tedde sig, så fann jag alltid ett sammanhang och ett upprepande. — I *den* situationen såg jag resultatet av en föregående; när jag råkade personen *den*, så erinrades jag om personen *den* från det förflutna. Det finns även scener i mitt liv som återkommit flera gånger, så att jag ofta sagt mig: det här har jag varit med om förut.

(I have been rich and poor, high and low, and experienced
shipwrecks and earthquakes, and whatever happened in life, I
always found a connection and a repetition. — In this situation
I saw the result of a previous one; when I met that person I was
reminded of someone else from the past. There are even scenes
in my life that have occurred many times, and I have often told
myself that I have experienced this before. — pp.97-8)

In a passage like this, we simultaneously get the impression that the
Stranger has passed through several consecutive lives and also that the
repetition itself creates a pattern in his life which is at the same time a
prison house of life and a kind of death.

In order to confront these issues, to make them work on the stage,
Strindberg created a theatrical language where the longing to 'the
country which is not', is given both concrete content and form.
Sprinchorn has summarized the thematic core of the Chamber Plays in
pointing out that they

are concerned with death, or, more accurately, they are written
from the point of view of a man who is getting ready to die.
Death is looked upon as an escape from a corrupt and disgusting
world and the portal to the life beyond.[5]

To reach this country of constant negation, of nothingness and
void, the characters in the Chamber Plays have to confront their lives
once again in a gesture of departure and resignation. This gesture,
almost in the Brechtian sense of *Gestus*, is the source of their strength
as well as their weakness, because in their final dissociation from the
triviality of everyday life the characters have to confront this world in
all its different aspects one more time at the same time as they are
already aware of what lies beyond it. The Chamber Plays depict this
threshold between the two worlds.

A much more comprehensive framework than the present one is
needed to discuss the important implications for the theatre of the
meeting between two worlds. I would only point out here that such a
meeting is not simply of central importance for the literary aspects of
drama but is also an essential feature of the theatrical performance —
from the basic facts of 'stage technology' to the metaphysical implications of the theatre. The theatre has constantly competed with official
forms of theology because of its implicit claim to create a contact
between worlds which religious ritual and thinking have tried to
reserve for themselves. The interaction and/or confrontation between
different orders of existence has in the theatre led to the development
of different forms of 'stage language' like, for example, the *Deus ex*

Machina and the stage floor through which different creatures from the underworld appear on the stage. The appearance of Indra's Daughter and Hummel in his wheelchair are two very different variations of the *Deus ex Machina* which enable the meeting between worlds to take place. In the opening scene of *Spöksonaten*, the Milkmaid is an additional creature mediating between the worlds of the living and the dead, setting the key for a whole series of such meetings in this play, which have enriched it with its specific theatrical qualities.[6]

The complex balance between the two worlds was already described quite accurately by Kierkegaard in his reflections on the tragic hero in *Fear and Trembling* (1843). Here, Kierkegaard deals directly with the problem of the literary representation of the end of this life and what comes after it. The question he raised is how explicit and self-conscious the tragic hero can be about the meaning of his own life at the moment of dying. Kierkegaard argues that in a dramatic context where the meaning of the hero's life is an 'external act . . . he has nothing to say', and whatever he says in spite of this 'is essentially chatter'. This chatter only 'diminishes his impact',[7] or as Kierkegaard wrote, in one of his drafts, the hero 'becomes an after-dinner speaker'.[8]

If, on the other hand, 'the meaning of a hero's life is oriented to spirit, then the lack of statement would diminish his impact.[9] Kierkegaard goes on to explain that:

> If an intellectual tragic hero like this culminates in a suffering (in death), he becomes immortal through this last word before he dies, whereas the ordinary tragic hero does not become immortal until after his death.
>
> Socrates can be used as an example. He was an intellectual tragic hero. His death sentence is announced to him. At that moment he dies, for anyone who does not understand that it takes the whole power of the spirit to die and that the hero always dies before he dies will not advance very far in his view of life.[10]

For Socrates to be 'silent in the crisis of death' would even mean that the effect of his life would be diminished, while instead, through the use of language and speech, 'he is required to have enough spiritual strength in the final moment to consummate himself.'[11] The hero is able to clarify not only the significance of his life and his death, but also the relationships between them. In his Chamber Plays, Strindberg has created such a delicate balance between these two heroic types — the one whose life is an external act and the spiritual hero who by preparing for death, like Socrates, already dies. This unconventional combination accounts for the sometimes rather awkward feelings and responses aroused by the Chamber Plays where the trivial and everyday are placed in the immediate context of the spiritual. When this occurs the results can sometimes even be pathetic. In *Oväder* and *Brända tomten* the chattering sometimes takes over as the dominant mode of discourse. In *Spöksonaten* the triviality of the everyday is overcome through mystification and a constant change of focus. We never really know what we are seeing. It is, however, always possible to follow the hero's transformation into what Kierkegaard calls an intellectual hero who dies, not through a death sentence as in Socrates' case, but as a result of his constant awareness of death. The Gentleman in *Oväder* is an example of the mixture between the trivial 'after-dinner speaker' and the intellectual hero reflecting on the meaning of his life: 'Det finns intet närvarande, det som nu går är det tomma intet; framom eller bakom — hälst framom, ty där ligger hoppet!' (There is nothing present, that which is passing now is empty nothingness; backward or forward — forward for preference — because that's where hope is — p.39). Wishing to preserve the purity of the past, the Gentleman is unwilling to meet his own daughter after several years of separation. In a pose of self-imposed isolation very similar to death, he tries to protect himself from the evils of this world. He has created a death *in* life, very different from that of John Gabriel Borkman in Ibsen's play. Borkman has consciously given up his active life as a self-imposed punishment for his financial crimes while the Gentleman never aspired to a successful and active business life. For him, life itself is both the crime and the punishment. His passivity will be transformed into a real death when he has recognized, and accepted, the inherent evils of this world, which cannot, as is often the case in Ibsen's plays, be at least potentially reformed or overcome. The Stranger in *Brända tomten* describes how already as a young boy, at the age of twelve, after having celebrated the memory of the Swedish king Carl XII, whom he calls 'landets förstorare' (the destroyer of the country), he was 'led vid livet' (tired of life). He goes on to say that 'Det var som att gå in i ett stort mörker' (It was like entering a great darkness), not finding an answer to the question 'vad jag skulle här att göra . . . och jag tyckte världen var ett dårhus' (what I was supposed to do here . . . and I thought the world was a madhouse — p.105). He continues:

Jag låg på bårhuset, kära du, som död. Om jag var det, vet jag inte — men när jag vaknade hade jag glömt det mesta av mitt förra liv, och började nu ett nytt, men på det sättet, att ni ansåg mig konstig. — Är ni omgift?

(I lay in the mortuary chapel, my dear friend, as dead. Whether I was, I don't know — but when I woke up I had forgotten most of my previous life and started a new one, but in such a manner that you all thought me strange. — Have you remarried? — p.105)

The Stranger quickly jumps from the comprehensive concerns of his sense of life to the question of marriage. After getting a short answer to his matter of fact question, which is an expression of the sudden moves between the spiritual, other-worldly and the concerns of this world, the Stranger goes on to describe what happened after regaining consciousness. His new perspective on life is a result of what he has experienced on the other side, perceived as a kind of super-sensitivity in this world:

Jag betraktade mig numera som en annan, och jag observerade, studerade denne andre och hans öde, vilket gjorde mig okänslig för egna lidanden. Men jag hade i döden fått nya färdigheter . . . jag såg mittigenom människor, läste deras tankar, hörde deras avsikter. När jag var i sällskap, såg jag dem nakna . . . Var började elden någonstans?

(From that time on, I saw myself as someone else, and I observed, I studied, this other and his fate, which made me insensitive to my own sufferings. But in death I had acquired new faculties . . . I saw through people, read their thoughts, heard their intentions. In company I saw them naked . . . Where did the fire begin? — p.106)

When considered from the point of view of the smallest units of the text, the individual speeches (*repliker*) of the dialogue, there is a move towards different forms of death, and immediately afterwards a sudden and even unexpected return to the everyday perspective. The example quoted above is typical of a dialectics where the post-mortem perspective is interrupted by a question about the immediate surroundings — 'Where did the fire begin?' This sudden move back to the world of the living and the supposedly indisputable facts of the material-social world is an important structural feature of the Chamber Plays. It serves as a tool for applying the knowledge of death in unmasking the hypocrisy of those still living.

The perspective of death imparts to the hero a knowledge which enables him to unmask and discover other characters. And the unmasking is, as several critics have already pointed out, a central theme as well as an important narrative device in the Chamber Plays. The character who is unmasked is actually sent to his death, but even before that, through the hiding of his secrets, he has actually already been dead. All the characters can be unmasked at any moment, because such an act does not have to be previously motivated in the plots of the

127

Chamber Plays. This means that since everyone is a potential victim, they all hide their secrets, and that on some level they are all dead.

In order to achieve the kind of knowledge through which the hero is effectively able to unmask his opponents, death is often accompanied by various expressions of madness. The knowledge imparted only through death is usually expressed in a passive, reflexive, stance to which madness gives an uncontrollable, unforeseeable, quality containing strong theatrical potential. When death and madness are put together they constitute a very powerful symbolic code for the loss of this world. Strindberg has also used other narrative patterns or motifs to enable the unmasking as, for example, the struggle between the sexes or the regression to childhood as a repetition, both of which on different levels also reinforce the meeting between worlds, but they are less prominent in the Chamber Plays than in most of Strindberg's earlier dramatic works. The appearance of death or loss together with madness or near madness has been given a number of different forms in the Chamber Plays: in *Oväder* the resignation of the Gentleman who cannot cope with the loss of his daughter; in *Brända tomten* the Stranger's pain in discovering that the innocence of his childhood was a forgery; in *Spöksonaten* Hummel's fear of the milkmaid, and the Mummy locked up in the closet for twenty years; in *Pelikanen* the letter from the dead father and the effects it has on his son, Fredrik; and in *Svarta handsken* the despair of the mother who thinks she has lost her child.

It is interesting to compare this form of imagined death and the spiritual transformation and knowledge resulting from it with an event in *Fröken Julie* which has a very similar structure. I am referring to Jean's description of his experience when escaping through the dirt from the luxurious Turkish pavilion and hiding beneath a heap of rubbish to get a view of the approaching young lady of the house, Julie herself. Jean compares his entry into the park and the beautiful world of the gentry in terms of a robber entering Heaven. He goes on to tell Julie how a few weeks later he succeeded in getting a glimpse of her in church: 'Jag såg er och jag gick hem besluten att dö; men jag ville dö vackert och behagligt utan smärta' (I saw you and I went home resolved to die; but I wanted to die beautifully and pleasantly, without pain — SV 27, p.142). In order to commit suicide, Jean placed the deadly flowers from an elder bush in an oat chest. He fell asleep and when he woke up, he was very ill. 'Men,' he continues, 'jag dog inte som ni kan se' (But I didn't die, as you can see — SV 27, p.142). This close brush with death, however, was, as Jean tells her after the seduction, an invention. Looking closely at this situation we understand that his desire for Julie, *eros*, is formulated as a desire for death, *thanatos*. In the Chamber Plays, however, *thanatos* has become the point of departure through which the relations between the Student and

Adele in *Spöksonaten*, for example, have to be measured. The young child which the student has lost in the crumbling house before the action of the play itself begins clearly points in this direction. *Thanatos* has taken over in the Chamber Plays and as a result *eros* becomes transformed into a distant memory of things past, of infidelity and pain. The expression of love is here usually a final attempt to overcome the irrevocable forces of death. This is obviously one of the distinctive features of *peisithanatos* — the discourse of death.

The Chamber Plays are, however, not only characterized by a change of perspective from the point of view of *eros* to that of *thanatos*. They strive towards finding a theatrical formulation for the synoptic vision where the accepted borderlines between life and death in the realistic and naturalistic theatre are radically questioned. The dramaturgy of *Ett drömspel* had paved the way for a universal metaphysical theatre and the Chamber Plays are, in spite of their return to the previous, more realistic norms, a continuation of this metaphysical investigation. The Stranger in *Brända tomten*, for example, formulates this quest for a suitable theatrical totality:

> På ålderdomen när ögat blir seende, upptäcker man att alla krumelurerna bilda ett mönster, ett namnchiffer, ett ornament, en hieroglyf, som man nu först kan tyda: det är livet! Världsväverskan har vävt det!

> (In old age, when one's eye starts to see, we discover that all the little curlicues create a pattern, a monogram, an ornament, a hieroglyph, which we only now can interpret: this is life! The world weaver has woven it! — p.97)

Strindberg's plays are in many ways actually such ornaments through which an aesthetic pattern can be made out. On the stage, all the disconnected details can be brought together. In the Chamber Plays themselves, the small details are referred to in theatrical or aesthetic terms, adopting Hamlet's view that 'the play's the thing'. Through the aesthetic patterns of the work of art, the larger pattern can be discovered and interpreted. To the Brother in *Oväder* the red shades on the second floor of the 'Quiet House' look like 'ridåer, bakom vilka man repeterar blodiga dramer' (theatre curtains behind which bloody dramas are rehearsed — p.9). The Stranger in *Brända tomten* has seen life in all its various forms 'men alltid som om det var satt i scen för mig särskilt' (but always as if it was staged especially for me — p.98). The Student in *Spöksonaten*, who in the beginning does not yet understand what is going on, naively exclaims: 'Jag begriper ingenting av det här, men det är som en saga' (I don't understand anything of this, but it is like a fairy tale — p.158), echoing Macbeth's 'tale told by an idiot'.[12] To this, Hummel quickly retorts:

> Hela mitt liv är som en sagobok, herre; men fastän sagorna äro olika, så hänger de ihop med en tråd, och ledmotivet återkommer regelbundet.

> (My whole life, young man, is like a book of fairy tales; but although the tales differ they are held together by a thread and the leitmotif is regularly repeated — p.158)

The world weaver has been here, creating a Kierkegaardian pattern of repetitions. And when the leitmotif has been discovered, when the ornament has been deciphered and the masks have finally been taken off, revealing the individual's true self, the death-screen can be brought in and the mute landscape of the Island of Death, represented by another work of art, Böcklin's well-known painting of *Toten-Insel*, appears.

What then is the structure of these self-referential ornaments? How can the reader/spectator decipher their secrets? These questions will be dealt with only briefly here, and they may, I hope, serve as the basis for a more extensive analysis of the Chamber Plays. I shall concentrate on the meaning of objects and the ostensive function of language where the speaker is pointing at and explaining what we see.

The attempt to make a comprehensive statement about the meaning of life through the use of simple objects is in Strindberg's Chamber Plays not just an expression of what Vershinin in Chekhov's *Three Sisters* calls for when he exclaims, 'let's do a bit of philosophizing'.[13] In Chekhov's play, philosophizing serves many purposes, but it is primarily a more noble way of passing the time than just drinking tea. In passages of reflection, Chekhov usually lets his own special breed of subtle ironies take over, while Strindberg in his Chamber Plays is literally deadly serious. He has attempted to create a perspective of the psychic life of the individual, his social context and sometimes even the whole world by looking at these spheres from the post-mortal point of view of eternity.

For example, in the long speech where the Stranger in *Brända tomten* points at the bed and table, and remarks on the fact that 'allting var färgat i vårt hus' (everything in our house was dyed — p.114), i.e. counterfeit, the objects serve as the point of departure for his philosophizing. This closely resembles another Chekhov figure, Gayev in *The Cherry Orchard*, for whom the old bookcase which he addresses rather serves as a symbol of moral excellence: 'you have devoted yourself to the highest ideals of goodness and justice.'[14] Since the only positive value in the Strindbergian fictional universe is death, the Stranger, from his eternal perspective, reacts more pessimistically when looking at the past as well as the present. Picking up the old living room clock, he considers the vanity of the world, unlike the Chekhov hero, who becomes sentimental and embarrassed because of his own clumsiness. When the clock falls into pieces, the Stranger's attention is drawn to the globe which literally leads him to a vision where the whole world can be viewed from his extra-terrestrial perspective. In a passage which is in many ways similar to the 'birth' of Indra's Daughter into this world in the Prologue to *Ett drömspel*, the Stranger, who is holding the globe in his hand, exclaims:

Du lilla jord: den tätaste av alla planeterna, den tyngsta, och därför så tungt på dig, så tungt att andas . . . villornas och dårarnes värld! — Evige! Har din jord gått vilse i rymden? Och hur kom hon att snurra runt, så dina barn blevo yra i huvet och förlorade förståndet, att de icke förmå se det som är, utan endast det som synes? Amen! Där är studenten!

(You tiny earth: densest of the planets, the heaviest and therefore so heavy on you, so hard to breathe . . . world of illusions and lunatics! — Eternal One! Is your earth lost in space? And how did it start to whirl round so all your children became dizzy and lost their reason and cannot see that which is, but only that which seems? Amen! There's the student! — p.114)

The everyday objects serve as a trigger for the comprehensive philosophical questions, which as usual, without prior warning, lead the Stranger back to the concrete reality at hand — the entrance of the Student.

This mixing of the high and the low, and the bringing closely together of the perspective of this world and the next, have many similarities with the metaphorical conceit of English metaphysical poetry of the seventeenth century. The houses and drawing rooms, as well as the objects they contain, are presented in their realistic concreteness at the same time as they are elevated with an abstract universal and otherworldly significance. The examples given above are only some of the numerous instances where the everyday object becomes a 'symbol', as Gerda, the former wife of the Gentleman in *Oväder*, says about the thermometer. In *Ett drömspel*, which in many ways is close to the Chamber Plays, the conceit can be witty and even humorous like, for example, the Lawyer's explanation after he picks up a hairpin from the floor, parodying at the same time his marriage

131

and the creation of woman from the bone of man, where the two again 'shall be one flesh'[15] in marriage:

> Se på den här! Det är två skalmar, men en nål! Det är två, men
> det är en! Rätar jag ut en, så är det ett enda stycke! Böjer jag
> det, är det två, utan att upphöra vara ett! Det betyder: de tu är
> ett! Men bryter jag av — här! Då äro de tu tu!
>
> (Look at this! It is two bows, but one pin! It is two but it is one!
> If I straighten it, it is one single piece! If I bend it, it is two,
> while it remains one! This means: the two are one! But if I
> break it — here! Then the two are two! — SV 46, p.53)

This relationship to a material object is quite similar to what happens to Peer Gynt peeling the onion, his eyes become filled with tears from the onion itself and from his realization that the core of existence is empty nothingness. But here the theatrical images enable the spectator to view the situation from a distance. In the Chamber Plays this playful dimension has made room for a much more serious approach, and the objects almost inevitably lead the speaker as well as the spectator directly to the profound existential issues. Everything becomes a *momento mori*, in the traditional sense of this rhetorical figure.

In *Svarta handsken*, however, written a few years after the other Chamber Plays, and in many respects different from them, there is a more playful relationship to the everyday objects. Here, the whole house emits small and insignificant sounds which are interpreted by the otherworldly Tomte as a huge, celestial machinery. One of the reasons for this change of mood is that at least partially, the world of death has here been replaced by a spiteful but finally goodwilling and gracious intrusion from the Christmas Angel and its traditional assistant. Also in the argument between the Old Man and the Tomte disputing the unity versus the duality of the universe, which likewise refers directly to the Biblical text on the creation of woman, the movement between trivial detail and a comprehensive synoptic understanding has been expressed in a more light-hearted mood:

> Det våta elementet vattnet
> en enhet är, består dock av de två
> av väte och av syre kan ej disputeras;
> magnetens kraft är delt i nord och syd;
> elektrikans av plus och minus,
> i växtens frö det givs ett hanligt och ett honligt;
> och högst i kedjan aldra överst
> du finner tvåhet, ty allena

var icke gott för mänskan vara;
och så blev man och kvinna till:
Naturens tvåfald alltså konstaterad!

(The humid element water is a unity but consists of two of
hydrogen and oxygen, that cannot be disputed; the power of the
magnet is divided into north and south; electricity in plus and
minus, in the seed of the plant there is male and female; and in
the top of the chain you will find twoness, because it is not good
for man to be alone; and therefore man and woman came into
existence. Thus the duality of nature has been proven! —
pp.318-19)

The whole universe is regarded as a 'toy' which they are picking apart,
letting the pieces fall on the garbage heap.

In the Chamber Plays the objects have become articulate and they
tell their different stories. The most important reason for this, I think,
is that the human characters have become dumb, they can no longer
talk. The houses, the furniture, the trees and the memories of a dead
past all tell their strange tales, they are the yarn of the world weaver,
as the Stranger in *Brända tomten* calls the texture of his counterfeit
life. The human observer merely passes these stories on to the reader
/spectator. Human *speech*, in the true sense, however, has in the
Chamber Plays become almost empty and useless. A few lines from
Spöksonaten reveal this human condition most clearly:

STUDENTEN:. . . Säg! Varför sitta föräldrarne därinne så tysta,
utan att säga ett enda ord?
FRÖKEN: Därför att de icke ha något att säga varann, därför att
den ena icke tror vad den andra säger. Min far har uttryckt det
så: Vad tjänar det till att tala, vi kan ändå inte lura varann?

(THE STUDENT:. . . Tell me! Why do your parents sit in there so
silently, not saying a single word?
THE YOUNG GIRL: Because they have nothing to say to each other,
because one does not believe what the other is saying. This is
how my father puts it: What's the point of talking when we
cannot fool each other? — p.199)

But the objects cannot lie. For this reason, the truth is revealed in
the meeting with death, when the human being becomes monumental-
ized and is transformed into an object; something which he himself can
view from the outside, as a conscious observer, or can be viewed by
others as in the example from *Spöksonaten*. This transformation, as I

have indicated above, is represented fictionally in terms of the unmasking.

According to Peter Szondi, 'these lines [from *Spöksonaten*] mark one source of modern epic dramaturgy.' His reason for drawing such a significant dividing line in the Chamber Plays, and in particular in *Spöksonaten*, is that here the dramatic character has become a raissoneur, a narrator, pointing out, or to use the Brechtian term, demonstrating, what the significance of the surrounding world is. Szondi, however, goes on to claim that the full step towards an epic dramaturgy was never carried out by Strindberg, because Hummel, 'the first example of an epic *I* appearing on the stage,' does not appear in the third act, but leaves the stage completely to Adele and the Student, who are still 'subject to the unfolding of the action'. What Szondi considers to be a 'failed conclusion to a unique work can only be understood in terms of the transitional dramaturgic situation to which it belongs.[16] This transition between two dramaturgies can be most clearly discerned, perhaps, in *Brända tomten*, where the search for a solution to the question of who started the fire, what can be called the detective plot, gradually becomes transformed into a quest for the solution to a much deeper mystery — the enigma of life and death.[17]

This transition is necessary for the simultaneous inclusion of the trivial and the metaphysical spheres, and it is perhaps, as I have argued above, the central rhetorical strategy of the Chamber Plays. At this point, however, I shall not give any more examples of characters involved in mediating or explaining the meaning of the objects which surround them, but rather will try to draw some more general conclusions regarding this quite complex strategy. Such explanations involve what could be called the ostensive function of language, i.e. a situation where someone is pointing at something while at the same time he is explaining what it is — 'This is the house/the person/the object which . . .'

Logicians distinguish between different kinds of definitions and the ostensive definition is the practical response of a parent to a child's question, 'What is an elephant?', which is answered by pointing out a specific animal in an illustrated book or at the zoo. It is important to stress that an ostensive definition is based on making an affirmative connection between a verbal expression and an object or some kind of visual representation of this object — 'This is . . . ' This very simple procedure becomes much more complex when the negative — 'This is not . . . ' — is used, because the negation frustrates the possibility of creating meaning, it postpones the connection between the question and the desired object. It makes anybody in his right mind ask — 'So what is it, then?' Negative ostensivity is also the basic narrative pattern of the detective story where the reader is constantly given information which makes him draw the conclusion 'This is not the murderer'. The surrealist painter Magritte took this procedure one step further in his famous picture of a pipe to which the simple sentence, 'C'est ne pas une pipe' (This is not a pipe), was added. This painting he significantly enough named 'The treason of the objects'.[18]

In the Chamber Plays, Strindberg clearly utilizes the tensions created between the affirmative and the negative ostensive functions of language. On the first level, one character simply tells another as well as the reader/spectator what it is we are seeing in the affirmative mode. On the next level, this object or character is imbued with a symbolic meaning. But then Strindberg makes a further move and goes on to have this character claim that behind appearances a different essence can really be found. What seems is not what really is. Through the negation of appearances the unmasking takes place. The final step in this gradual move towards negation is most clearly worked out theatrically in the scene of the ghost supper, where even language itself is emptied of content and significance. This is the discourse of death. The Chamber Plays abound in situations where the referentiality of the ostensive discourse is denied, where the world is gradually emptied of its known contents, where things just do not exist any more. 'There are no more aspirins,' says Clov to Hamm, the blind, wheelchair-ridden tyrant in *Endgame*, who bears such a remarkable similarity to Hummel. For Beckett, this process of emptying is an axiom: for Strindberg it was a nightmare — and at the same time a possible relief, the relief of death.

Notes

1. Søren Kierkegaard, *Fear and Trembling* — *Repetition* (New Jersey, 1983), p.176.
2. All translations into English of Strindberg's texts are my own.
3. See, for example, my analysis in *Theatrical Space in Ibsen, Chekhov and Strindberg: Public Forms of Privacy* (Michigan, 1986), pp.49-70.
4. Louis Mackey, 'Once More With Feeling: Kierkegaard's *Repetition*', in *Kierkegaard and Literature*, edited by R. Schleifer and R. Markley (Oklahoma, 1984), pp.80-81.
5. Evert Sprinchorn, *Strindberg as Dramatist* (New Haven and London, 1982), p.254. See also Brian Rothwell, 'The Chamber Plays', *Essays on Strindberg* (Stockholm, 1966), pp.29-38.

6. In a not yet published article, 'Gesturality in Acting and the Theatrical Function of the Body', I have developed some notion of meetings between worlds in the theatre in more detail.
7. *Fear and Trembling*, p.116.
8. *Fear and Trembling*, p.255.
9. *Fear and Trembling*, p.116.
10. *Fear and Trembling*, p.116-117.
11. *Fear and Trembling*, p.117.
12. The Shakespearean subtexts in Strindberg's plays and in particular in his Chamber Plays are extremely interesting. See e.g. Egil Törnqvist, '*Hamlet* och *Spöksonaten*', *Meddelanden från Strindbergssällskapet*, 37 (1965), pp.1-17.
13. Anton Chekhov, *Three Sisters*, in *Plays*, translated by Elisaveta Fen (Harmondsworth, 1968), p.280.
14. *Plays*, p.345.
15. Genesis, II, 24. For a detailed analysis of this passage, see Galit Hasan-Rokem, 'And God Created the Proverb', *Semeia*, forthcoming.
16. Peter Szondi, *Theory of the Modern Drama* (Cambridge, 1987), pp.31-32.
17. Egil Törnqvist, *Strindbergian Drama* (Stockholm, 1982), p.163ff.
18. Freddie Rokem, 'The Death of the Apple — Contradictions Between Visual and Verbal Elements in the Same Aesthetic Frame: The Case of Negation', *Semiotics* (1985), pp.139-148.

Frenchifying *Fordringsägare*

Strindberg as his own Translator

Gunnel Engwall

Stockholm University

1. Strindberg and Translation

'Trouver un traducteur Français qui ne dessale le style d'après les règles de l'Ecole Normale rhétorique, ne déflore la virginité de l'expression, est chose impossible' (Finding a French translator who neither desalinates the style according to the rules of rhetoric of the École Normale nor deflowers the virginity of one's expression is impossible — VII, p.203). Thus Strindberg, in a letter to Friedrich Nietzsche in 1888, two months after completing his own French translation of the naturalistic drama *Fordringsägare*. As his own translator, Strindberg effectively killed two birds with one stone: on the one hand, he avoided 'desalinating and deflowering' the text, and on the other, he avoided having to pay for a translator, whom he could ill afford. However (or so he maintained, on finishing his translation in October 1888), the labour of producing a French version of a play which he had originally composed in Swedish in a mere fortnight, immediately after completing *Fröken Julie*, left him exhausted and in still impoverished exile in Denmark, where he and Siri von Essen had entered upon one of the most destructive periods of their complex relationship.

By the time he concerned himself with a French version of *Fordringsägare* Strindberg already had considerable experience of translating and writing in French. He had made his own French version of *Fadren* and spent part of 1887 and 1888 writing the autobiographical novel *Le Plaidoyer d'un fou* directly in French, as he had done with the collection of *Fables* he produced in 1885. Nor would the translation of *Fordringsägare* be his last work in French. Intent on reaching an international audience in what Walter Benjamin was to call 'die Hauptstadt des XIX. Jahrhunderts', and always fascinated by French as a language, he would later use it for his second set of *Vivisektioner* (1894), *Inferno*, and the greater part of *Legender*. He likewise made his own French translation of *Ett drömspel*, and during the 1880s and 1890s he also wrote a great number of letters in French.

Here, however, I shall be focusing only on the French version of *Fordringsägare*, noting especially the differences between the Swedish original and Strindberg's French translation. Strindberg was extremely proud of this play, in which he congratulated himself on having achieved the 'new formula' of psychological naturalism: 'Den är min stora favorit,' he informed the publisher Joseph Seligmann, 'och jag läser den om och om igen, upptäckande nya finesser immer . . . Fröken Julie är ännu kompromiss med romantik och kulisser . . . men Fordringsegare är modernt alltigenom' (It is my great favourite, and I read it over and over again, continually discovering new subtleties . . . *Miss Julie* is still a compromise with romanticism and coulisses . . . but *Creditors* is modern through and through — VII, pp.144-5). As in *Dödsdansen*, the play depicts a monstrous but nonetheless deeply human trio — the heroine Tekla, her first husband, Gustaf, and her present husband, Adolf — who are locked in a seemingly endless battle. Gustaf holds Tekla responsible for their separation and wants to be revenged. He deliberately plunges her towards a trap which she cannot avoid, in spite of her perspicacity. When Adolf collapses at her feet as the curtain falls, she is annihilated.

Strindberg hoped that his translation of the play would be a success in Paris. But how did he proceed? Was he so pleased with his original Swedish version that he translated the play into French complete and with no changes? Or did he try to adapt the play for a French-speaking audience? Or did working in the foreign language hamper him, so that the new version became a simplification of the original? These are the questions addressed in what follows.

2. Modifications in the French *Fordringsägare*

2.1 The Lines

When comparing the layout and the dialogue of *Fordringsägare* in the Swedish and the French versions, one finds that on the whole they differ very little. For the most part Strindberg has translated the original line-by-line, though with a number of important modifications. One of these can be found at the very end of the play, which Strindberg in fact revised several times: firstly, in the Swedish transcript of August 1888, then in the French version of September-October 1888, and finally in the first Swedish edition of March 1890,[1] as is shown in Example 1. (The Swedish transcript, which is a letter-book copy in Strindberg's hand, is used here as the source text, since the original manuscript is lost.)

Example 1

Hon älskar honom! [Swedish copy]	(She loves him)
Elle l'aime! Sans aucun doute, elle l'aime! [French translation]	(She loves him! Without doubt, she loves him!)
Sannerligen, hon älskar honom också! Stackars människa! [Swedish edition]	(In truth, she loves him too! Poor woman!)

In fact Strindberg gradually extends the ending, adding a tone of astonishment to the final line, in order ultimately to emphasize Gustaf's character of *Übermensch*.

An examination of the complete versions, however, reveals that Strindberg removed more than he added. Nevertheless, there are some important additions in the French version which do not figure in either the Swedish copy of 1888 or the first edition. Example 2, in which Adolf refers to Tekla, illustrates this kind of addition, inserted at the end of Adolf's line 'Ja, men den liknar någon! — Det är märkvärdigt att denna kvinna finns i min kropp, liksom jag i hennes' (Yes, but it resembles someone! — It's strange that this woman is in my body, as I am in hers — SV 27, p.204):

Example 2

ADOLF (turning to GUSTAF) Je suis presque certain, que si vous m'abbatiez [sic] sur-le-champ, son image ferait apparition au fond de chaque cellule de mon sang, de mes nerfs!	(I am almost certain that, if you suddenly knocked me down, her image would appear at the base of each cell of my blood, of my nerves!)

2.2 Stage Directions

In contrast to the dialogue, the stage directions are quite often modified in the translation. There is, for example, a remarkable deletion in the very first lines. In the original, Strindberg draws attention to Adolf's poor health in the opening stage directions by placing two crutches by his side. But in the French version, he omits them.

This is significant, since we know that the crutches played an important role in the conflict between the actors and the French adapter of the text, Georges Loiseau, during rehearsals for the first performance of *Créanciers* in Paris in 1894. The controversy arose because Loiseau had used not only Strindberg's French translation as a basis for his revised version, but also Erich Holm's German translation from the Swedish, which appeared in 1893.[2] (Loiseau could not use the original, since he knew no Swedish.) This means that not only did he correct the language in Strindberg's translation but also added lines and stage directions that Strindberg had omitted when turning his text into French. As a rule, Loiseau also retained all the additional phrases in the French translation, which makes his version both longer and heavier than the two Strindbergian texts. In contrast to Strindberg's French translation, Loiseau had in fact added the direction concerning the crutches from the German.[3]

At the rehearsal of *Créanciers*, the Paris actors, who were using Loiseau's version, found the description of Adolf's epilepsy over-emphasized, and wished to tone it down by omitting the crutches. Since they were unable to agree about this, the actors and the director, Aurélien Lugné-Poë, on the one side, and Loiseau, on the other, turned to Strindberg to resolve the dispute, which (having already removed them from his own French translation) he did by postcard on 16 June 1894: 'Rayez les béquilles s.v.p!' (Delete the crutches, please! — X, p.90).

From a study of the text in its entirety it becomes evident that Strindberg has altered many other specific stage directions in translation. The following are characteristic additions, in Strindberg's sometimes idiosyncratic French: 'silence embarrassant', 'des gestes pittoresques', 'foudroyé', 'Espiègle', 'inquiet', 'sur un ton élegiaque', 'tendre'. However, if he has added some stage directions, he has removed others. And while it is not always possible to infer his exact purpose regarding either the additions or deletions, their frequency is worth noting. Stage directions come to play an important role in his later dramatic works, including *Dödsdansen*, *Ett drömspel* and *Spöksonaten*, but it is clear that he was already very concerned about their place while translating *Fordringsägare*.

2.3 Settings, Historical Personages, Language

When writing *Fordringsägare*, Strindberg had the Théâtre Libre, recently founded in Paris by André Antoine, in mind. However, it is in the translation that his wish to adapt the play for a French-speaking audience becomes particularly apparent. This is most noticeable in the changes made with respect to real places and historical personages. In the Swedish version of 1888, Strindberg gives a very general indication about the setting in the opening pages, noting only that the action takes place in a drawing-room at a seaside resort. Later on in the original text, it is made clear that the action is located on the Swedish west coast. The French version is far more specific, and different:

Example 3a

En Salong på en Badort [Swedish copy]	(A Drawing-room at a Seaside Resort)
Aux environs de Stockholm de nos jours . . . dans un hôtel aux Bains de mer de Dalaroe [French translation]	(In the neighbourhood of Stockholm in our time . . . in a hotel at the seaside resort of Dalarö)

Example 3b

Strömstad [Sw. copy]

Stroemstad [crossed out]

Stæket [Fr. translation]

In contrast to the original version, Strindberg gives precise indications about the setting in the opening lines of the translation; he places it in the present, and specifies that the action takes place at a hotel in Dalarö, i.e. in a small seaside resort just south of Stockholm. By changing the setting in this way Strindberg surely hoped that a French audience would recognize and accept the setting more readily than they would have done with the (to them) unknown west coast location of the original version. And having moved the scene to the east coast, he had obviously to modify other indications of its original setting. Strömstad, a town on the north-west coast of Sweden, which is given as the domicile of the doctor mentioned in passing in the dialogue, thus needed changing. As the manuscript reveals, Strindberg at first forgot to make this logical modification, only altering it to Stæket, a village in the neighbourhood of Stockholm. He had started out by following the Swedish original, to which, however, he applied a French touch in spelling Strömstad as 'Stroemstad'.

Strindberg certainly also considers his foreign audience when modifying some proper names. In the Swedish text, for example, Adolf reminds Tekla that she appears in his most beautiful paintings, successively incarnated as Saint Cecilia, Mary Stuart, Karin Månsdotter, and Ebba Brahe. In the French translation, he does not retain the figures from Swedish history but replaces Karin Månsdotter and Ebba Brahe with Charlotte Corday:

> Så målade jag dig i mina vackraste taflor, i rosa och azurblått på guldgrund, och det fans inte en utställning der icke du satt på bästa platsen. Ibland hette du heliga Cecilia, ibland var du Maria Stuart, Karin Månsdotter, Ebba Brahe . . .

> (Then I painted you in my most beautiful paintings, in rose and azure-blue against a gold background, and there wasn't an exhibition where you didn't hold the best place. Sometimes your name was St Cecilia, sometimes you were Mary Stuart, Karin Månsdotter, Ebba Brahe [Swedish copy])

> Et puis je commence à t'introduire dans mes peintures où tu figures en azur et en or, et il n'y a plus un salon où tu n'occupes la cimaise! Parfois tu es baptisée Sainte-Cécile, parfois Mary Stuart, Charlotte Corday [French translation]

Other modifications, meanwhile, may be explained by a difference between the two languages. An obvious case entails the following reference to Swedish orthography in Strindberg's time. Speaking of Tekla in the Swedish original, Gustaf remarks:

> Hon kan ju inte skilja (She can't distinguish between
> på dt och t! dt and t!)
> [Swedish copy]

whereas in the French version he says:

> Elle ne sait pas (She doesn't know how to
> distinguer le régime direct distinguish the direct
> du régime indirect object from the indirect)
> [French translation]

In his translation, Strindberg has thus transformed the spelling difficulty in Swedish into a difficulty of discriminating between different objects in French.

In another line in the second scene, Strindberg plays with pronunciation. Here, Tekla, speaking like a child, mispronounces the name of Jesus: 'Herre Nessus' instead of 'Herre Jessus' or 'Herre Jesus'. In the translation, Tekla's childish way of speaking is shown instead by her not pronouncing the letter 'r' properly in the French adverb 'sérieusement':

Herre Nessus, vill han tala allvarsamt! [Swedish copy]	(Nessus, he wants to talk seriously!)
Bon Dieu, mon petit, il veut parler 'selieusement!' [French translation]	(Good God, my boy, he wants to talk 'seliously'!)

Strindberg's own French translation confirms that the form 'Herre Nessus' in the Swedish manuscript was not a slip of the pen, as has been supposed, but that he really intended this deformation.

2.4. Images

The frequency of Strindberg's use of metaphors and symbols in his writing is well-known. But what use does he make of imagery when writing in or translating into French? This remains one of the most difficult aspects of learning and using a foreign language and translators frequently meet almost unresolvable problems when seeking to transfer images from one language to another.[4]

In fact, several images present in the Swedish text are omitted from the translation. One such instance is Gustaf's vision of Tekla as a snake, another the passage in which she is compared to a malfunctioning watch, and Strindberg has also suppressed the allusions to horse races in reference to marriage, as well as several of the allusions to creditors, appearing to demand what is owed them.

However, this does not mean that there is a general toning down of the language in which Strindberg casts his images in the translation. In fact, the latter contains a number of metaphors and images which have no equivalent in the Swedish original, some of which carry considerable force, as for example when Adolf describes his need for Tekla, 'je la désire comme le cerveau, les poumons, le coeur!' (I need her as my brain, my lungs, my heart!) or Gustaf threatens Adolf with an early death if he doesn't follow his advice: 'Alors, "salut champs que j'aimais!"' (Then, 'farewell fields that I loved!'). Here, the poetic form of the words in quotation marks is puzzling. The Swedish edition is no help, since they have no equivalent there. Is Strindberg translating and quoting Schiller's *Jungfrau von Orleans*, as Heiner Gimmler has proposed,[5] or can it be a quotation from the French *Ode imitée de plusieurs psaumes* by Nicolas Gilbert: 'Salut, champs que j'aimois, et vous, douce verdure'? Whatever the case, it seems a further example of Strindberg's wish to adjust to a new and foreign audience.

Images are sometimes present in corresponding lines in the Swedish and French versions, but are modified for reasons which are not always possible to determine. In each of the following examples, the image is altered in some way:

> (a) Och så skref jag nya texter efter mitt sinne, tills du tyckte att du var fullskrifven (And then I wrote new texts following my own ideas, until you thought you were completely covered with writing) [Swedish copy]

> Et après je la couvre, la chétive ardoise, de nouvelles écritures selon mon sense! (And then I would cover it, the puny slate, with new writing following my own ideas!) [French translation]

> (b) och så hade jag dig i sumpen — och nu är du matt! (and then I had you ditched — now you're checkmate!) [Swedish copy]

> et adieu la boutique! (and good-bye to the lot!) [French translation]

> (c) Du har ett sätt att klippa med högra ögat som om du sköt (You have a way of squinting with your right eye as if you were taking aim) [Swedish copy]

> Vous avez une fa[ç]on de mimer avec l'œil gauche (You have a way of squinting with your left eye) [French translation]

In the first example, Strindberg has modified the metaphor but preserved the image of the slate. The slate is mentioned two lines previously in the Swedish text, where the stress is put on Tekla's conviction that she is perfect. In the translation, Strindberg shifts the emphasis to Gustaf's importance for Tekla's development, and his wish to cover her with new writings.

In the second example, the Swedish 'sumpen' refers to fishing, thus suggesting she is caught, or 'netted'. The meaning of the French version, on the other hand, is not altogether clear, though Strindberg could well be referring to the world of gambling, since Gustaf alludes to a game of chess earlier in the same line. The expression 'adieu la boutique' would then mean that Tekla had lost everything.

In the third example, the substitution of 'left' for 'right' eye in Adolf's observation on Gustaf's expression in the French version is certainly deliberate. It may seem natural for a right-handed person to wink with the left eye when aiming, but there are certainly more important reasons, especially as Strindberg retains the right eye in the first Swedish edition. These have to do with the negative connotations of the French word *gauche*, meaning also 'clumsy' and 'awkward'. It thus points to the expression 'mauvais œil' (evil eye), symbol of the evil which goes with Gustaf's character, and which is certainly fatal for Adolf. According to popular superstition, someone who possesses the evil eye has the disastrous faculty of bringing misfortune to those at whom he looks. The 'evil eye' with this connotation appears several times in Strindberg's later works, including *Inferno, Advent, Fagervik och Skamsund*, and *Taklagsöl*.[6]

3. Vocabulary in *Créanciers*

When reading Strindberg's French texts, one is immediately impressed by the great variety of his vocabulary, by the combination of current words and technical terms. It is evident, too, that he does not avoid theoretical issues. Problems of language have apparently not reduced his vocabulary or simplified his style.

In the first scene of *Fordringsägare*, Adolf and Gustaf compare and contrast the relative value of painting and sculpture. The range of Strindberg's French vocabulary may be illustrated by the following précis in French of this theoretical discussion, where I have employed Strindberg's vocabulary (indicated in italics):

Adolphe avoue que Gustave lui a *ouvert les yeux* sur *les mystères de* son *art*, que *la peinture* ne lui *fournit* plus *le matériel nécessaire* pour *exprimer ce qu'*il veut, et que, à son avis, elle *ne* peut *pas constituer la* forme où se moulera *l'esprit artistique du nouveau temps*. Gustave lui a montré que *les aspirations réalistes*, visent *la pleine réalité, le palpable*, ce qui peut être rendu par *la sculpture seule*, qui *reproduit le corps, l'extension de l'espace* en *trois dimensions*.

(Adolph admits that Gustaf has opened his eyes to the mysteries of his art, that to paint does not provide him with the necessary material for expressing what he wants any more, and that, in his view, this could not constitute the mould in which the artistic mind of the new age will be formed. Gustaf had shown him that realistic aspirations require complete reality, the palpable, and that this can only be realized by sculpture, which reproduces the body, the extension of space in three dimensions.)

Instead of a special terminology or unusual vocabulary, it was rather the links, the interlacing of the sentences, the short, apparently simple, lines of dialogue that created the pitfalls into which Strindberg sometimes fell. In Swedish, he was a master of these aspects of the dramatic text. In French, he had difficulty in finding the appropriate tone and the precise links. The French-speaking reader who is uninterested in linguistic phenomena is therefore often hampered by the morphological and syntactical mistakes in Strindberg's translation.

However, as regards grammar, Strindberg does not always make comparable errors. It is clear that he often knew which form or construction was the correct one; depending on one's point of view, certain errors might therefore be considered mere carelessness or as evidence of real ignorance. In any event, these errors illustrate Strindberg's rather rash approach to grammar, and thus constitute a characteristic feature of his treatment of the French language.

4. Conclusion

In translating, Strindberg does not seem to have tried to avoid abstract reasoning or complicated description because of problems in finding the right word. One is especially astonished to find such a faithful translator in so rapid and vivid a writer, one who generally cared little about proof-reading. He reproduces almost every line of the text word for word, and often retains the same images as in Swedish. To a considerable extent he also resorts to the same stylistic features, e.g. the direct address in the third person that he uses to characterize the relations between Tekla and Adolphe. This is a feature that has frequently been ignored in translations of *Fordringsägare* by other hands. From Strindberg's own translation, however, it is evident that he wished to transfer his Swedish dramatic style, so often admired for its clarity, its conciseness, and its zest, into French.

If there are divergences between the first Swedish text and the translation, it is not by mere chance. It is evident that Strindberg adapted his play to a French audience. In some respects, he also modified the special relationship among the characters: he made

Adolf's submission to Gustaf less pronounced, and somewhat moderated the originally very negative portrait of Tekla. The question concerning man's guilt and his redemption, so often present in his work, is also given less prominence in the translation than in the original. As Strindberg's own translation has never been published without revision, not all his modifications are known. This is regrettable, as the characters and their mutual relations are to some extent modified. These modifications ought at least to be considered, if not followed, in interpreting one of Strindberg's most intriguing plays, either in the theatre or the study.

Notes

1. *Fordringsegare*, in *Tryckt och otryckt I* (Stockholm, 1890), pp.15-102.
2. *Gläubiger*, translated by Erich Holm (pseud. for Mathilde Prager, Berlin, 1893).
3. *Créanciers, Le Lien, On ne joue pas avec le feu*, translated by Georges Loiseau (Paris, 1894).
4. For Strindberg's use of metaphor and symbol, see Karl-Åke Kärnell, *Strindbergs bildspråk. En studie i prosastil* (Stockholm, 1962). For the translation of metaphors, see Peter Newmark, *Approaches to Translation* (New York, 1988), especially Chapter 7, and Sylfest Lomheim, 'Métaphores dans *L'Étranger* par Albert Camus. Analyse et traduction', in Lars Wollin and Hans Lindquist, eds., *Translation Studies in Scandinavia*, (Lund, 1986), pp.118-125.
5. *Fräulein Julie/Gläubiger*, translated by Heiner Gimmler (Nördlingen, 1988).
6. For *Taklagsöl*, where the role of the 'evil eye' is assumed by the 'green eye' of the lamp in the window facing the narrator's bedroom, see Barbro Ståhle Sjönell, *Strindbergs Taklagsöl — Ett prosaexperiment* (Stockholm, 1986), p.73ff.

147

Perspectives on a Genre

Strindberg's *comédies rosses*

Barbara Lide

Michigan Technological University

In an article entitled 'Why We Can't Help Genre-alizing and How Not to Go About It', the American genre specialist Paul Hernadi proposes as one of two main theses that 'all knowledge is genre-bound in both senses of the word: it is tied up with and directed towards conceptual classification.' Hernadi quotes I.A.Richards's statements that 'perception takes whatever it perceives as a thing of a certain sort' and that 'thinking, from the lowest to the highest — whatever else it may be — is sorting.'[1] Or, as Jan Myrdal phrased it, 'it's the human aspect — you sort things out.'[2] As literary scholars, we consistently engage in such conceptual classification of the works we study in order to increase our knowledge of them. To use Hernadi's term, we 'genre-alize.'

Hernadi's second thesis is equally pertinent to our classification of literary texts: 'The superabundance of potential knowledge and the corresponding generic overdetermination of all particulars demand polycentric rather than monolithic classifications.'[3] While this premise is more complex than the first, it certainly is clear enough to those of us who tend to categorize literary works according to our own perception of them, often in the face of opposing classifications. Because of a multiplicity of meanings inherent in all discourse, perhaps especially in literary discourse — meanings dependent upon the perception of readers and spectators representing various cultures and historical periods — literary classification becomes a highly complex and often contradictory endeavour that in many cases not only demands, but also produces, polycentric classifications.

Thus we can read about Molière's contemporaries either applaud-
ing or rejecting Alceste, his misanthrope, as a comic figure; or about
Rousseau's contemporaries perhaps seeing Alceste as 'the unduly
ridiculed hero of a tearful comedy'; whereas Goethe's contemporaries
might regard him as tragic,[4] an opinion echoed later by Brunetière, who
saw both *Le Misanthrope* and *Tartuffe* as 'bourgeois tragedies that
Molière had tried in vain to place in the ranks of comedy.'[5] Today we
might 'align Alceste with such tragicomic misanthropes as Shakespeare's Timon, Lessing's Tellheim, and Ionesco's Béranger in
Rhinoceros.'[6] Or we might see in Alceste nothing more than a ridiculous, pretentious, self-centred ass, without whom the members of his
society — however small-minded they may be — are better off, in
which case *Le Misanthrope* could be described as a comedy with a
happy ending for most of the characters in the play, with Alceste's
withdrawal representing the victory of comedy at the price of his
defeat.[7] Could we not, however, interpret the play as a comedy with a
happy ending for Alceste, since he is perhaps better off to be rid of
Célimène and her circle of friends?

It is in the light of such contradictory 'genre-alizing' that I shall
discuss perspectives on what have been called Strindberg's *comédies
rosses*. In my discussion, which will be limited to the two plays *Första
varningen* (The First Warning) and *Leka med elden* (Playing With
Fire), I shall also engage in some of my own 'genre-alizing', the
purpose of which will be threefold: to perform the kind of sorting out
activity that, it is hoped, will help us to increase our knowledge of the
plays discussed; to argue, even at the risk of appearing to present a
monolithic classification, against opposing views considered by some
to be equally tenable; and, finally, to make a plea for a growing, yet
still minority, view that there are indeed lighter, comic aspects of
Strindberg's *oeuvre* than most people, who know Strindberg primarily
as the creator of unsettling psychological dramas and tragedies of
sexual conflict, are aware of.

Several years ago American theatregoers were treated to a
production of *Playing With Fire*, which enjoyed a six-month run on a
double bill with *Miss Julie* at the Roundabout Theatre in New York.
The play proved to be more than merely a second-rate curtain raiser on
a bill of two one-act plays. Judging by comments of many in the
audience, who 'never knew that Strindberg could be so funny — or so
delightful',[8] people were pleased to be shown a side of Strindberg not
often seen and not sufficiently appreciated, even in Sweden. In 1985,
Eivor and Derek Martinus were involved in a London production of
The First Warning, which prompted a good deal of laughter among the
spectators. Like the audiences in New York who saw *Playing With
Fire*, the London audiences who saw *The First Warning* showed their
appreciation of Strindberg's comic spirit. As we shall see, however,

reception of these two plays by academics has not always been as favourable.

First some background: *Leka med elden* and *Första varningen* belong to a group of six one-act plays — including also *Debet och kredit, Inför döden, Moderskärlek,* and *Bandet* — that Strindberg wrote in quick succession in 1892 and categorized under the heading 'Ur det cyniska livet' (From the Cynical Life — SS 19, p.148). These plays are suitable for an experimental theatre with a small troop of actors and a limited budget, along the lines of André Antoine's famed Théâtre Libre in Paris, where Strindberg had at one time hoped to see productions of *Fadren, Fröken Julie,* and *Fordringsägare.*[9] Their form is that which Strindberg, in his frequently quoted essay 'Om modernt drama och modern teater' (On Modern Drama and Modern Theatre), calls 'den utförde enaktaren', or 'fully executed one-act play' (SS 17, pp.281-303), a form that has its roots in the *proverbes* of Carmontelle, was further developed by Leclerq, Musset, and Feuillet, and continued to evolve in France. It was employed by Strindberg's contemporary Henry Becque, whose play *La Navette* Strindberg not only admired but also regarded as a work approaching the 'fully executed one-act play' that he suggests might become the formula for the drama of the future (SS 17, p.301).[10]

With the exception of the commentary accompanying them in their various editions, relatively little has been written about these plays. Maurice Valency, for example, devotes almost half a book to some of Strindberg's major dramas, but only half a sentence to the six one-acters, writing that the 'short plays . . . [Strindberg] wrote in 1892. . . do nothing to enhance his reputation.'[11] Birgitta Steene includes *Första varningen* among plays which she maintains — and, for the most part, rightly so — appear to be 'mere trifles . . . when compared to most other dramas in the Strindberg canon.'[12] Steene at least classifies *Leka med elden* as 'one of Strindberg's few comedies' (p.64), in contrast to a statement made several years earlier by Atos Wirtanen, that one could question whether Strindberg 'någonsin skrev en enda genuin komedi' (ever wrote a single genuine comedy).[13] Walter Johnson, who customarily wrote lengthy introductory essays to accompany his translations of Strindberg's plays, provides his readers with only a short preface and a brief introduction to the volume *Plays from the Cynical Life,* which contains, with the exception of *Bandet,* the six one-act plays from 1892.[14] Johnson's main judgement of these plays appears to be that they all 'share the same gloomy view of human nature, human behaviour, and human society' (p.v), and that all of them 'are interpretations of human situations from a cynical point of view' (p.3). Nevertheless, he writes that the plays 'should not be disregarded by any student of drama seeking to understand Strindberg's contribution' (p.v). Johnson himself did at least grant *Första varningen* and *Leka med elden* more favourable criticism in another, previously written, context, in which he describes *Första varningen* as 'perhaps the most delightfully amusing of all his [Strindberg's] short plays', a play in which he sees 'such merits as excellent lines, amusing situations, and an interesting set of characters.' Concerning *Leka med elden*, Johnson claims that 'Strindberg never wrote a lighter play', adding that 'the roles are very good indeed, the lines excellent, and the solution amusing.'[15] Egil Törnqvist has made a careful and penetrating analysis of *Första varningen* in terms of its structure, plot, theme, character depiction, setting, and symbolism. Concerning the comic elements and the lighter aspects of the play, however, Törnqvist's remarks are limited. While he does quote Barry Jacobs's comment that the comedy is ' "more witty and playful than anything Strindberg wrote in the preceding period," ' i.e. from 1886 to 1889', Törnqvist himself states merely that 'regarding genre', the play is 'what Strindberg himself. . . called a play "from the cynical life", a comedy of sorts.'[16] It was Børge Gedsø Madsen who linked both *Första varningen* and *Leka med elden* to the French *comédies rosses*, a genre that developed in France in the heyday of the Théâtre Libre (1887-1894). Gedsø Madsen presents brief analyses of the two plays; because he is interested in Strindberg's *comédies rosses* primarily as naturalistic dramas, however, he approaches them more as plays exemplary of the naturalistic tradition than as comedies.[17]

There has also been some decidedly negative criticism. Martin Lamm, for example, regards *Första varningen* as little more than an unsuccessful and 'especially distasteful' comic reworking of the jealousy motif in *En dåres försvarstal*.[18] *Leka med elden* does not fare much better under Lamm's scrutiny. After briefly discussing the play as a comedy in the French manner and comparing it to Sardou's farcical comedy of manners *Divorçons!*, he contrasts it with Sardou's play, a lighter and less cynical comedy, and criticizes Strindberg's play for being 'brutal and depressing.'[19] Lamm's reaction stands in marked contrast to that of audiences who saw the more recent New York and London productions of the plays.

One might suppose that such differing responses to the same works could be attributed to tastes changing throughout the years, allowing for audiences in our post-absurdist and post-theatre of cruelty age to be more receptive to Strindberg's so-called cynical comedies than they were when Lamm wrote his critical comments back around 1924. One must consider, however, that as early as 1910, Felix Salten, reviewing *Mit dem Feuer spielen* in Vienna, called the play 'ein kleines Jewel von einem Lustspiel.'[20] Perhaps Lamm's reaction, in contrast to Salten's, is based not on a response to a theatrical performance of the play that brings out its inherent comic qualities, but on an interpretation of the text determined by and corresponding to the *Erwartungshorizont* prevailing in Sweden in the 1920s, when Max Reinhardt's productions of Strindberg's plays, stressing their demonic, mystic, and chaotic elements, still dominated the stages of Sweden and Germany. In order to help us understand the situation at that time, we might consider a comment by the critic Sven Wetterdal, who observed that, as soon as an actor was given a role in one of Strindberg's plays, he drew down the corners of his mouth as far as he could, spoke with a deep bass voice, wrinkled his forehead, rolled his eyes, hissed, gnashed his teeth, and generally behaved like a lascivious murderer in an older opera. The women transformed themselves into poisonous vampires with long claws and sharp tongues. Such was the so-called 'strindbergstil' (Strindberg style) that had spread throughout Europe.[21] In short, in the 1920s, Strindberg was expected to be 'brutal and depressing.'

This *Erwartungshorizont* still prevails, however, in the minds of many involved in both producing and performing Strindberg's plays and in the study of dramatic literature. If we consider present-day Sweden, where Lars Norén's grim and brutal dramas of family conflict are performed frequently before consistently full houses, and not only receive wide critical acclaim for being some of the best dramas written in Sweden today, but are also praised for their rapier-like wit, we might think that Strindberg's little comedies about jealousy in the marital nest would appear, by comparison, to be mere bits of fluff — or in any case, certainly not as 'brutal and depressing' as Lamm found them to be. Yet it was not too long ago that Hans-Göran Ekman, in an essay on *Leka med elden*, presented an interpretation of the play in which he concentrates on its tragic aspects and seriously calls into question the use of 'comedy' as a proper genre designation.[22] This he does after citing Gunnar Ollén, Sven Rinman, and Gunnar Brandell, who agree that, with *Leka med elden*, Strindberg had indeed written a play that deserves to be called a comedy, and even after quoting Strindberg, who in a letter written in 1908 called the play 'komedi, och icke lustspel: och en mycket allvarlig komedi, der menskorna dölja sin tragedi under en viss cynism' (comedy, and not *lustspel*: and a very serious comedy, in which the characters hide their tragedy under a certain cynicism — XVI, p.167). Strindberg's letter shows that he was well aware of the differences between 'comedy' and 'lustspel', the latter of which is used to designate light comedy, while the former is applied 'to a more serious type of comedy, inclined to the satirical and the expression of human frailty and impotence.'[23] As the German scholar Otto Rommel explains, in a Komödie (as opposed to a Lustspiel), 'through all the merriment, one usually senses the sharpness of satirical anger or the bitterness of impotence.'[24]

Ekman's reading of *Leka med elden* as more tragic than comic recalls the conflicting interpretations of Molière's satirical comedy *Le Misanthrope*, for he regards the character of Axel to be the protagonist of the play, seeing him as an Alceste, an *honnête homme*, a truth-sayer in a corrupt world. Ekman cites a letter written by Strindberg in March 1892 (only about five months before he wrote *Leka med elden*), in which he shows his sympathy for Molière's suffering Alceste by expressing compassion for an acquaintance, Ivar Fock, whom he apparently regarded as an Alceste figure. Strindberg refers to Fock as 'den lidande Fock' (the suffering Fock) and adds, in parentheses, 'Alceste! min Vän!' (Alceste! my friend! — IX, p.16). For further support, Ekman cites Strindberg, writing in 1908, that the play 'är ämnadt tragisk men får halft komisk utgång!' (is intended to be tragic, but has a half-comic ending — XVI, p.172). For Ekman, the play is clearly Axel's tragedy.

Conversely, I regard Axel as a blocking character, whose departure allows re-establishment and reconfirmation of the society, such as it is, depicted in the play. One could also cite at least one letter by Strindberg to support this view. In March 1894, he wrote to his French translator Georges Loiseau, that *Leka med elden* 'n'a pas plû (sic) aux philstres parce que la tradition de la parterre exige à voir le mari ridiculisé et que dans cette comédie l'amant tient le dessous' (did not please the philistines because the tradition of the parterre demands to see the husband ridiculed, and in this comedy it is the lover who is left holding the bag — X, p.29). According to this letter, Strindberg clearly regards Axel as the butt of his comedy, not his suffering protagonist. It appears that by 1908, when he wrote the letter cited by Ekman, Strindberg might have changed his own perspective on the play.

When reading Gunnar Ollén's accounts of critical responses to performances of both *Första varningen* and *Leka med elden*, one becomes acutely aware, especially in the case of the latter play, of the extent to which directors and actors — and critics as well — have, through their interpretations, 'genre-alized' the plays by accentuating, in some productions, the cynical and bitter aspects, and, in others, stressing the comedy.[25] Occasionally Strindberg himself changed his views on plays he had written, and in at least one case — that of *Fordringsägare* — he even altered his original genre designation. His 'genre-alizing' is illustrated by two letters concerning *Fordringsägare* that he wrote to the Danish actress Nathalie Larsen early in 1889, when she was both translating the play into Danish and rehearsing the role of Tekla for the première in Copenhagen. In the first letter, dated 9 January 1889, Strindberg informed Larsen that his tragedy *Fordrings-ägare* 'skall nu kallas: *Tragikomedi*' (will now be called: *Tragicomedy* — VII, p.222 (Strindberg's italics)). This indicates perhaps not only a change in Strindberg's perspective on the play but also an awareness on his part that modern naturalistic drama was showing a tendency to move away from tragedy in the classic sense. In the second letter, dated

26 February 1889, which Strindberg sent to Larsen after having watched a rehearsal of the play, he wrote, 'Om Ni går åt tragedien (den gamla) eller komedien, vet jag ej. Möjligen gå vi alla — tragedien också — åt komedien och då är Ni med!' (Whether you are moving towards tragedy (the old) or comedy, I don't know. Perhaps all of us — including tragedy — are moving towards comedy, and then you're right in step! — VII, p.254).

At this point, I should like to propose a meeting of minds between those who focus on the idea of 'tragedy hidden under a certain cynicism' in *Leka med elden*, and those, including myself, who prefer to regard the play as a comedy even less serious, especially for our time, than its author may have regarded it to be. Perhaps we can resolve our hermeneutic conflict by considering both *Leka med elden*, as well as its companion piece *Första varningen*, as *comédies rosses*, plays belonging to a genre that encompasses both the tragic and the comic and includes many examples which can indeed be called tragicomedies. Considering this possibility might free us from the limited hermeneutic circles we may be caught up in. There is no intent on my part to make any final pronouncement regarding genre on these or any other of Strindberg's plays, for I agree firmly with the American comparatist Herbert Lindenberger, that genre should not be approached 'as a category for which I seek out timeless rules', but 'as a term that opens up opportunities for both formal and historical analysis, that in fact allows the analyst to observe the interactions between the aesthetic order and the social order.'[26]

First, a brief definition of the genre *comédies rosses*: this is not a definition that derives from a theory to be imposed upon a given body of dramatic literature; it derives, rather, from the observations of that literature by André Antoine, director of the Théâtre Libre in Paris; by Jean Jullien, playwright and author of the *comédie rosse, La Sérénade*; and others involved with writing and producing the plays. In a list of plays he considered representative of the *comédies rosses*, Antoine included Henry Becque's *La Navette*, which Strindberg mentions favourably in his essay 'Om modernt drama och modern teater' (SS 17, p.301), as well as another of Becque's plays, *La Parisienne*, with which Strindberg was familiar (X, p.291). Some of the other plays on Antoine's list are Jullien's *Le Maître*, *La Mer*, and the above-mentioned *La Sérénade*, the latter of which Strindberg had in his library;[27] Oscar Méténier's *Monsieur Betsy*, as well as *En Famille*, a play that Strindberg had seen and commended highly (SS 17, p.297); George Ancey's *L'École des veufs*, *L'Avenir*, and *La Dupe*; Edmond de Goncourt's dramatization of *Germinie Lacerteux*, the novel he wrote with his brother Jules in 1864; Jules Lemaître's *L'Age difficile*; and Georges Courteline's *Boubouroche* — all of which were written in the late 1880s and early 1890s.[28]

Because they are works by various authors, these plays differ considerably, yet most of them have in common a number of characteristics. To begin with, the main characters are usually amoral. Many of them are hypocritical, yet they are blithely unaware of their hypocrisy. A straightforward eroticism pervades many of the plays, and love is treated with sophisticated flippancy and regarded from a cynical viewpoint — rarely is it depicted as caritas. The passions that come to the fore in the *comédies rosses* are jealousy, which is often a stimulant to love, and anger, usually that of a deceived husband or lover. These passions are frequently expressed in strong, brutal language, with no attempt on the part of the playwright to shy away from *le mot juste*. Money is very important to the characters in the *comédies rosses*, and many of them devote their entire lives to pursuing it. Their pursuit leads to unhappy marriages and many an unhappy *ménàge à trois*. In addition to the pessimistic view of life reflected in the *comédies rosses*, there is a cynical humour which is usually clothed in witty, flippant dialogue — dialogue which reflects what the French playwright and critic Jules Lemaitre describes as 'le pessimisme essentiellement jovial.'[29] Coupled with the witty dialogue are some comic situations that arise when the wives and mistresses in the plays deceive their husbands and lovers. A fitting, though relatively mild, example of a comic scene in a *comédie rosse* is the opening scene of Becque's *La Parisienne*, which takes place between two of the main characters, Lafont and Clotilde. The spectator does not know what their relationship is, but one might assume that they are married, for Lafont acts like a jealous husband who fears that his wife is about to be untrue to him. He shouts at Clotilde. He demands to see a letter that she is hiding from him. He then pleads with her to remain faithful to him and to maintain her dignity and her honour. Clotilde displays a markedly nonchalant attitude toward Lafont's jealous rantings. Finally, in the midst of his pleading, she calmly cuts him short, goes to the door, listens, and says, 'Prenez garde, voilà mon mari' (Look out, here comes my husband).[30]

Let us turn now to Strindberg's two cynical comedies *Första varningen* and *Leka med elden*. In the first and shorter of the two plays, *Första varningen*, Strindberg presents as his main characters a jealous husband and a wife who displays a flippant attitude toward her husband's jealousy. The primary motif of the play is related not so much to any of the *comédies rosses* as it is to an earlier French comedy, Octave Feuillet's one-act play *Le Cheveu blanc* (1856). In Feuillet's play, a wife has been looking forward to the day when her estranged husband will begin to show signs of ageing, for she hopes that he will no longer attract other women, and that she will then have him for herself. She is delighted when she sees the first white hair on his head, exclaiming, 'That poor white hair! I have waited for it as for a friend;

it seems to me that it marks a happy day in my life.'[31] The single strand of grey hair does in fact bring about a happy reconciliation.

In Strindberg's play, it is the husband who has waited impatiently for his wife to grow older. He tells her:

Hur ofta har jag icke önskat att du redan vore gammal och ful, att du hade fått kopporna, förlorat tänderna, bara för att jag skulle få behålla dig för mig själv och se ett slut på denna oro, som aldrig överger mig!

(How often haven't I wished that you were already old and ugly, that you had become pock-marked and lost your teeth — just so that I could have you for myself and see an end to this anxiety that never leaves me! — SV 33, p.123)

The lines above from *Le Cheveu blanc* and *Första varningen* show that Strindberg's language is decidedly coarse when compared with that of Feuillet's little salon comedy. It is much more in line with the naturalistic, often crude dialogue of the *rosses* playwrights. The ending, too, of *Första varningen* indicates that the play is more closely related to the *comédies rosses* than it is to the more traditional nineteenth-century comedy with which it shares thematic similarities. At the end, the wife breaks a front tooth and, realizing that she is beginning to lose her beauty, fears that she might lose her husband as well. Although the broken tooth, like the white hair in *Le Cheveu blanc*, brings about the reconciliation of husband and wife, Strindberg's conciliatory ending is considerably less optimistic than Feuillet's, as the final exchange of words between the husband and wife suggests. When the wife asks, 'Och är du lugn nu?' (And are you content now?), the husband replies, 'Ja — i åtta dagar!' (Yes — for eight days! — p.146). His answer indicates that after a short time, the bickering, the fighting, and the jealousy can flare up again.

The relationship between the husband and wife in *Första varningen* — characterized by the husband's unrestrained jealousy and the wife's unruffled attitude toward his jealousy — is typical of the relationships between men and their wives and/or mistresses in the *comédies rosses*. The example of Lafont and Clotilde in Becque's *La Parisienne*, cited above, is but one of many that could be mentioned. It should also be pointed out that, as in many *comédies rosses*, jealousy in *Första varningen* — first on the part of the husband, and at the end of the play on the part of the wife — acts as a stimulant to love, or as the glue that holds the love relationship together. As the wife points out to her husband, '. . . det har visat sig att din kärlek blir ganska kylslagen, så snart du icke har anledning att vara svartsjuk' (it is evident that your love becomes rather lukewarm, as soon as you have no reason to be jealous — p.123).

Also in keeping with the nature of the *comédies rosses*, *Första varningen* displays a straightforward eroticism apparently unheard of in the Swedish theatre of Strindberg's day. Strindberg includes among his characters a fifteen year old girl, Rosa, who in her infatuation for the husband rips open the sleeve of her dress and then kisses him passionately. Her rash actions are accompanied by some decidedly spicy dialogue. She invites the husband to come up to the attic to read old love letters written to various women by her father, whom she describes as a man 'som kunde älska, och som vågade älska! Han darrade inte för en kyss och väntade inte tills han blev bjuden!' (who could make love and who dared to make love! He wasn't afraid of a kiss and didn't wait until he was invited! — p.139) That Strindberg, like the *rosses* playwrights, did not shy away from *le mot naturel* is further illustrated by Rosa's lines:

Hahaha! Ni är rädd att jag skall förleda er, och ni ser förvånad ut. Förvånad över att jag, en flicka, som varit kvinna i tre år, har reda på att kärleken icke är oskyldig! Inbillar ni er att jag tror det barn föddas genom örat, — — Nu föraktar ni mig, det ser jag, men det skall ni inte göra, för jag är icke sämre, och icke bättre heller än de andra . . . så är jag!

(Hahaha! You're afraid I'll seduce you, and you look surprised that I, a girl who has been a woman for three years, is aware that love is not innocent! Do you think I believe that children are born through the ears — — You despise me, I see that, but you shouldn't, because I'm no worse, nor am I any better, than the others . . . it's just the way I am! — p.140)

It is generally assumed, as Carl Reinhold Smedmark points out, that it was the frankness in sexual matters expressed in Rosa's lines that prompted the actors of the Royal Dramatic Theatre to refuse to perform the play in 1892 because they regarded it as immoral,[32] even after Strindberg had deleted what he thought were 'uttryck som kunde anses opassande' (expressions that could be regarded as unsuitable — IX, p.29).

Rosa's lines, however, are not typical of the dialogue in *Första varningen*. More characteristic is the polished, quick repartee between the wife and the husband, Olga and Axel, especially in the opening scene, with most of the witty lines spoken by the flippant Olga. Secure in the knowledge that Axel loves her, she can allow herself to treat his jealousy lightly, as she does in the following exchange that takes place when Axel, in the midst of some lightly sarcastic conjugal bickering, begins to finger a bouquet of flowers that an admirer, a captain, has sent to her:

> FRUN: Låt bli och förstör mina blommor!
> HERRN: Har det varit kaptenens förut?
> FRUN: Ja, och sannolikt trädgårdsmästarns, innan det blev blomsterhandlarns. Men nu är det mina!

> OLGA: Stop destroying my flowers!
> AXEL: Weren't they the captain's before?
> OLGA: Yes, and probably the gardener's before they became the florist's. But now they're mine! — pp.121-2)

Axel continues to complain about the attention that the captain was paying to Olga at a party they attended on the previous evening. Finally, venting his anger by flinging the bouquet aside, he exclaims, 'Det är ett vackert bruk här i orten att sända blommor till andras fruar'! (It's a pretty custom they have here — sending flowers to other men's wives! — p.122) His actions, however, scarcely make an impression on Olga, who remains completely unruffled and even assumes a haughty tone, as the following exchange illustrates:

> FRUN: Herrn skulle gått hem och lagt sig litet tidigare, tror jag.
> HERRN: Jag är fullständigt övertygad om att kaptenen önskat etsamma. Men som jag bara hade att välja på att stanna och vara löjlig, eller gå hem ensam och vara löjlig, så stannade jag . . .
> FRUN: Och var komisk!

> OLGA: The gentleman should have gone home and gone to bed a bit earlier, I think.
> AXEL: I am absolutely convinced that the captain wished the same. But since I had only the choice of staying and being ridiculous and going home alone and being ridiculous, I stayed . . .
> OLGA: And were comical! — p.122)

Olga's rejoinders are at times cutting. Consider the following exchange:

> AXEL: Kan du förklara huru du vill vara en komisk herres fru? Jag skulle inte vilja vara man åt en löjlig hustru!
> OLGA: Det är synd om dig!

AXEL: Tycker du inte det! Jag tycker det själv rätt ofta. Men vet du var det tragiska i min löjlighet ligger?
OLGA: Svara själv, så blir det kvickare än om jag gör det!
AXEL: Därute ... att jag är förälskad i min hustru efter femton års äktenskap ...
OLGA: Femton år! Går du med stegräknare på dig?

AXEL: Can you explain why you'd want to be the wife of a comical man? I shouldn't want to be married to a ridiculous wife!
OLGA: You are pitiable!
AXEL: Don't you think so! I think so too — very often. But do you know where the tragical in my ludicrousness lies?
OLGA: Answer that yourself -it will be wittier than if I do!
AXEL: It lies in ... my being in love with my wife after fifteen years of marriage ...
OLGA: Fifteen years! Do you go around with a pedometer? — pp.122-3)

Olga's witty incisiveness loses a good deal of its sting towards the end of the play, however, when she breaks her front tooth. Realizing that she is beginning to lose her youthful beauty, she becomes aware that she is no longer in a position where she can afford to be so flippant, and, consequently, is no longer as witty as she is earlier in the play. Also, since Axel's jealousy has subsided, he ceases to act like the ridiculous figure of a ranting, jealous husband, thereby depriving Olga of an appropriate target for her barbed wit. Still, Axel's final words to Olga, that he will be content for eight days, show promise that he will, after that short period, return to his jealous ways, and that the banter between the two will begin anew.

In *Leka med elden* — a somewhat longer and more complex play than *Första varningen* — both jealousy and a desire for forbidden fruit act as catalysts which set off erotic reactions on the part of several of the characters. These characters, who are listed simply as 'Fadern, Modern, Sonen, Sonhustrun, Vännen, and Kusinen' (The Father, The Mother, The Son, The Daughter-in-Law, The Friend, and The Cousin — p.215), are spending the summer on one of the islands in the Stockholm archipelago. In their summer paradise, they are bored to distraction, and one can perceive an erotic undercurrent ready to surface at any time. In this dull but charged atmosphere the characters begin to play with fire — that is, to play the game of love.

Precisely because it is a game, love is treated lightly, often with a scepticism characteristic of the *comédies rosses*. The friend, Axel, for example, just after declaring to Kerstin, the son's wife, 'Jag älskar dig, med kropp och själ' (I love you with body and soul — p.265), answers her impassioned question, 'Ska vi fly?' (Shall we escape?) with the incisive, yet comic, remark, 'Nej! Men jag skall fly!' (No, but I shall escape! — p.266) Finally, when Axel and Kerstin confess to Knut, the son, that they love each other, Knut appears to gain control of himself rather quickly after being, according to stage directions, 'något förkrossad' (somewhat crushed — p.267) and lamenting, 'vi sökte genom en konstlad öppenhet förebygga faran, skämtade med den, men den har dragit närmare, och slagit ner över oss!' (we tried to prevent the danger by being open about it — artificially. We even joked about it, but it's drawn closer, and now it's come crashing down on us! — p.268). He even appears to display a relatively jovial cynicism in the face of the problem. After asking Axel and Kerstin to help him, and themselves, come to a satisfactory solution, he says to Axel, 'Hör du min vän! Vi måste komma till ett hastigt avgörande, för det ringer till frukost om några minuter' (Listen, my friend! We have to come to a quick decision about this matter because the lunch bell is going to ring in a few minutes — p.269). In a matter of seconds, Knut decides to solve the problem by agreeing to withdraw from the love triangle, but he states as a condition that Axel must marry his wife. It is not long before Axel is seen escaping through the garden 'som om han haft eld i bakfickorna' (as if his pants were on fire — p.272), and the son and his wife are reconciled.

From the beginning of the play up until the *scene à faire* described briefly above, one can observe the motif of jealousy acting as a catalyst to love. Axel and Kerstin have been drawn to each other for some time, but it is not until Kerstin observes Axel talking to Knut's cousin Adèle that her feelings for Axel are aroused. Kerstin acknowledges the connection between her love and her jealousy when she answers Axel's question whether she has never felt as if she could love him by replying, 'Jo, när ni talar med Adèle!' (Yes, I have — when you are talking to Adèle! — p.248). Axel observes that, whenever Knut sees him and Kerstin together, Knut's feelings for Kerstin also seem to flare up. He comments: 'Fröken Adèle och jag tyckas med ett ord ha till uppgift att vara braständare' (In a word, Adèle and I seem to have the same function: we light the fire — p.249).

Another aspect that *Leka med elden* has in common with both the *comédies rosses* and, more generally, with the French comedy of manners, is an interest in money on the part of the main characters. Typical of many French comedies is an intrigue that revolves around marrying for money or inheriting money. Such an intrigue is unusual in Strindberg's plays. Although it is not central to *Leka med elden*, it is, nevertheless, present. Early in the play Knut and Kerstin discuss the possibility of arranging a marriage between Adèle and Axel, because they fear that Knut's father, who apparently is infatuated with Adèle, will leave his money to her and not to them. Their conversation takes on a distinct *comédie rosse* flavour when Kerstin asks, 'Har du tänkt dig den möjligheten att din mor skulle kunna dö?' (Have you thought about the possibility that your mother might die?), and Knut answers flippantly, 'Nå, än sedan?' (Well, so what?). Kerstin explains, 'Sedan kan din far gifta om sig!' (Then your father can remarry! — p.228). Knut catches on and replies, 'Med Adèle? . . . Det måtte man väl kunna hindra för resten. . . Det vill säga att hon skulle bli styvmor och hennes barn dela arvet!' (To Adèle? . . . Well, we'll have to stop that, won't we. . . That means that she would become my stepmother, and her children would share the inheritance — p.229). Characters in several of the *comédies rosses* display an attitude similar to Knut's. One thinks, for example, of Henri, the son in Ancey's *L'École des veufs*, who is cruelly indifferent towards his mother's death but exhibits a strong interest in inheriting his father's money.

Coupled with the cynical and somewhat decadent atmosphere of *Leka med elden* is some of Strindberg's lightest, most playful comic dialogue. In the discussion about where Axel will be staying on his visit to the island, for example, Knut tells Axel rather jovially:

Du stannar bara här, helt enkelt! Låt dem prata! Bor du här, så är du naturligtvis min hustrus älskare; och bor du i byn, så har jag kört ut dig! Då tycker jag det är mer hedrande för dig att anses vara min hustrus älskare, eller hur?

(You'll simply stay here! That's all there is to it! Let them talk! If you live here, of course, you're my wife's lover. And if you live in the village, then I've driven you out! I think it's more honourable for you to be regarded as my wife's lover, don't you? — p.236)

The flippancy of these lines resembles that of *comédies rosses* dialogue. Also similar to such dialogue is the bantering that frequently has erotic or risqué overtones, as in the exchange between Knut and his mother early on in the play, when the mother returns from market with some ducklings in her shopping basket. When Knut, rummaging in the basket, finds the ducklings, and the mother complains, 'De kunde ha varit lite fetare . . . känn här under bröstet,' Knut answers, 'Jag tycker brösten äro vackra jag!' (They could have been a little plumper . . . feel here under the breast. — Oh, I do think breasts are beautiful — p.220). A few lines after he makes the pun on the word 'bröst', Knut answers his mother's question whether he and Kerstin slept well last night with the playful reply, 'Vi ha inte sovit alls!' (We didn't sleep at all! — p.221).

While many similarities can be found between Strindberg's *Första varningen* and *Leka med elden* and the French *comédies rosses*, there are also striking dissimilarities. Unlike the characters portrayed in the *comédies rosses*, for example, the wives and husbands in Strindberg's plays do not deceive each other, nor do they lie to one another. Strindberg includes no secret meetings with lovers, as does Becque in *La Parisienne* and *La Navette*, or Ancey in *L'Avenir*, to name but a few examples, nor are there in Strindberg's plays lovers hidden in closets, as in Courteline's cynical comedy *Boubouroche*. Strindberg presents in neither of his comedies a *ménàge à trois*, as in Jullien's *La Sérénade*, Ancey's *L'École des veufs*, and Becque's *La Parisienne*. In *Första varningen*, although there are two women who attempt to win the affection of the husband, it is clear that he is interested only in his wife. Nor does Strindberg give any hint that the wife's flirtations have extended beyond accepting flowers from admirers, and so an arrangement *à trois* does not enter into the equation. In *Leka med elden*, there is one point at which Knut almost gives the impression that a *ménàge à trois* might be a possible arrangement. Referring to Axel, he tells Kerstin:

> . . . Denna man håller jag så mycket av, att jag icke skulle kunna neka honom någonting! Ingenting!. . . det är galet, brottsligt, lågt, men om han bad att få sova hos dig skulle han få! . . . vet du, jag förföljs ibland av en syn . . . jag tycker mig se er tillsammans; och jag lider inte av det, jag snarare njuter, såsom vid åsynen av något mycket skönt! . . . det är kanske ett ovanligt fall, men erkänn att det är djävligt intressant!

> (I am so fond of that man that I shouldn't be able to deny him anything! Nothing! . . . it's crazy, criminal, base, but if he asked to go to bed with you, I'd let him! . . . you know, sometimes I'm pursued by a vision . . . I imagine that I see the two of you together. And I'm not pained by it. I rather enjoy it, as if I were seeing something very beautiful! . . . it's perhaps an unusual case, but you must admit it's damned interesting! — p.255)

The impression, however, is false, for, as Knut explains later:

> Att för mig fortsätta samliv med en kvinna, som älskar en annan, kan icke bli något helt, då jag alltid skall tycka mig leva i polyandri. Därför — avgår jag, men icke förr än jag har garantier för att du gifter dig med henne.

> (For me to continue to live intimately with a woman who loves another can never amount to anything complete, since I would always regard myself a living in polyandry. And so — I'm

withdrawing, but not until I have your word that you'll marry her — p.269)

Because of such basic differences in the relationships between the husbands and wives of Strindberg's comedies and those of the *comédies rosses*, Strindberg's characters are not hypocritical, as are so many of those portrayed in the French comedies. His plays, therefore, do not depict the kind of society represented in the *comédies rosses*, a society described by the French writer and critic Augustin Filon as one which has the decalogue as its code, but is governed by the seven deadly sins;[33] consequently, Strindberg's plays lack, for the most part, the ironic comedy that arises from the discrepancy between the opinions that the characters have of themselves and the picture that they present to the public. It is precisely in this discrepancy that the French author and literary critic Jules Lemaître believes that the essence of the comic in the *comédies rosses* lies.[34]

The main characteristics, then, that *Första varningen* and *Leka med elden* share with the *comédies rosses* are the theme of jealousy as a stimulant to love, a straightforward eroticism, and an essentially jovial pessimism. Strindberg's plays, like the *comédies rosses*, exhibit a decidedly sceptical attitude toward love and marriage, which — as is well known — many had regarded for some time before he wrote *Första varningen* and *Leka med elden* as a quintessentially Strind-bergian attitude. Although the married couples are reconciled at the end of each play, in *Första varningen* the truce can only last 'i åtta dagar' (a week), and in *Leka med elden* there is no assurance that Knut and Kerstin will be happy; on the contrary, they have already hinted strongly that happiness is impossible for them in a typically Strind-bergian exchange, in which they shout at each other, 'Du har aldrig älskat mig!' (You have never loved me!), and Knut declares, 'Ja, nu ha vi kommit i i det grälet som räcker till döddagar!' (Well, now we've begun the kind of fighting that will last until we die! — p.258).

It should be remembered, however, that no matter how much unhappiness enters into the marriages depicted in Strindberg's two dramas, his plays end with the husbands and wives — who do love each other after a fashion — reunited, their marriages intact. Neither play ends with a *ménàge à trois*, a lover or mistress, or thoughts of infidel-ity. Nor are the characters hypocritical. In a sense, Strindberg's endings are essentially happier — or at least a little more optimistic — than those of the *comédies rosses*. It is noteworthy that even in the comedies that he himself labelled 'ur det cyniska livet', Strindberg, whose reputation for brutality and cynicism is widespread, does not match the cynicism expressed by his Gallic contemporaries in their *comédies rosses*.

This, then, is my perspective on two of Strindberg's comedies, *Första varningen* and *Leka med elden* — the result of my 'genre-alizing.' One of my stated purposes, to bring to light the comic aspects of Strindberg's *comédies rosses*, is partly in response to a largely unheeded plea that Eric Bentley made as long ago as 1946 that Strindberg's comedies 'need to be recovered from the blanket of ignorance and solemnity that hides their author and his work from view.'[35] Not only do Strindberg's comedies need to be recovered, but the comic aspects of his works, so long neglected, need to be brought forth. This is not a task to be appropriated exclusively by academics who gather at symposia to theorize over genre and other aspects of Strindberg's works. We need to cross boundaries, to go beyond the perimeters not only of the academy, but of the written text, to move beyond the word on the page to the word as performed, with all its nuances and accompanying non-verbal, visual aspects of interpretation and performance. The task must be shared by theatre workers, and also by audiences and critics.

In the last decade or so, there have been productions of some of Strindberg's plays that give strong evidence that efforts are being made to recover — perhaps 'uncover', or even 'discover', would be more appropriate — the comic side of Strindberg. Among these are the Fria Proteatern's production in Stockholm in 1984 and 1985 of *Fordringsägare*, directed by Stefan Böhm, with Keve Hjelm, Bibi Andersson, and Tomas Bolme, a production that did not ignore the comic aspects of Strindberg's tragicomedy; the Roundabout Theater's *Playing with Fire*; and Eivor and Derek Martinus's London productions of *Första varningen*, *Moderskärlek*, and other plays. At the Source Foundation in New York, Susan Flakes has directed performances of Strindberg's plays that gave their comic aspects the recognition they deserve. Included in her productions have been *Playing with Fire* and *The Dance of Death*, in translations by Flakes in collaboration with Barry Jacobs. The American actress Geraldine Page, who played in the Source Foundation's *The Dance of Death*, described the play as one with 'many laughs', and suggested that 'it would be good for people to know that and to get the doom and gloom lifted from the play.'[36] (Compare this with John Ward's criticism of the London National Theatre production of *The Dance of Death* in 1969, in which Ward accuses the actors of 'attempting to milk a dour text for laughs, with the result that what should have been demonic inconsistencies appeared as absent-minded absurdities').[37]

If these productions are any indication of what might be brewing in the world of Strindbergian theatre, then I think we can expect that Strindberg's wonderfully incisive, cynical, comic spirit — which has been stifled for so many years — will be free at last to add another dimension, a comic dimension, to what many have come to agree is a disturbingly one-sided critical image of Strindberg. Strindberg was, after all, an observer and recorder of life, and those who approach his works must bear in mind that there is in almost all of them, as in life itself, an intermingling of the tragic and the comic, or, to use Strindberg's own words, 'tragiskt och komiskt, stort och smått omväxla såsom i livet' (the tragic and the comic, the great and the small, alternate, as they do in life — SS 19, p.27).

Notes

1. Paul Hernadi, 'Why We Can't Help Genre-alizing and How Not to Go About It: Two Theses with Commentary', *Centrum*, 6:1 (1978), pp.27-8.
2. Extemporaneous comment made at the Tenth International Strindberg Conference on 2 April 1990.
3. Hernadi, 'Why We Can't Help Genre-alizing', p.27.
4. Paul Hernadi, *Beyond Genre: New Directions in Literary Classification* (Ithaca and London, 1972), p.3.
5. Ferdinand Brunetière, *Études critiques*, Vol. 8, pp. 116-117. Cited in P.J. Yarrow, ed., *A Literary History of France*, Vol. II, The Seventeenth Century 1600-1715 (London, 1967), p.215.
6. Hernadi, *Beyond Genre*, pp.3-4.
7. Cf. Alfred Simon, 'From Alceste to Scapin', *Molière: A Collection of Critical Essays*, ed. Jacques Guicharnaud (Englewood Cliffs, N.J.), p.145.
8. Barbara Lide, heard after performance of the play, 27 December 1981.
9. Letters to Karl Otto Bonnier, 21 August 1888 (VII, p. 105), and Joseph Seligmann, 16 October 1888 (VII, p. 144).
10. I have used Børge Gedsø Madsen's translation, 'the fully executed one-act play.' Børge Gedsø Madsen, *Strindberg's Naturalistic Theatre: Its Relation to French Naturalism* (Seattle, 1962), p.129.
11. Maurice Valency, *The Flower and the Castle* (New York, 1966), p.282.
12. Birgitta Steene, *The Greatest Fire: A Study of August Strindberg* (Carbondale, 1973), p.64.
13. Atos Wirtanen, *August Strindberg: Liv och dikt* (Stockholm, 1962).
14. August Strindberg, *Plays from the Cynical Life*, translated by Walter Johnson (Seattle and London, 1983), pp.3-6.
15. Walter Johnson, *August Strindberg* (Boston, 1976), pp.150-51.
16. Egil Törnqvist, '*Första varningen*/The First Warning — an Effective Drama', *Strindbergian Drama: Themes and Structures* (Stockholm, 1982), pp. 37 and 19.
17. Gedsø Madsen, pp.28-29 and pp.128-137.
18. Martin Lamm, *Strindbergs dramer*, I (Stockholm, 1924), p.393.
19. Lamm, p.402.

20. Review in *Die Zeit*, 2 February 1910, of Josef Jarno's production at the Theater in der Josefstadt.
21. Quoted by Gunnar Ollén in his 1961 edition of *Strindbergs dramatik* (Stockholm, 1961), p.29.
22. Hans-Göran Ekman, 'Sanningssägaren som komediförfattare: En Studie i Strindbergs komedi *Leka med elden'*, *Samlaren* (1979), pp.75-104.
23. Kenneth S. Whitton, *The Theatre of Friedrich Dürrenmatt: A Study in the Possibility of Freedom* (London, 1980), p.20.
24. Otto Rommel, 'Komik- und Lustspieltheorie', *Deutsche Vierteljahresschrift*, XXI: 2 (1943), pp.252-286, here p.273. (Cited in Whitton, p.21.)
25. Gunnar Ollén, *Strindbergs dramatik*, 4th ed. (Stockholm, 1982), pp.204-209 and 218-227. See also Ollén's commentary in SV 33, p.358-368.
26. Herbert Lindenberger, *Opera: The Extravagant Art* (Ithaca and London, 1984), p.20.
27. *Förteckning öfver en Samling Böcker, hvilka försäljes på Stockholms Bokauktionskammare Onsdagen den 30 November 1892* (Stockholm, 1892), p.24.
28. Antoine prepared his list for Heinrich Weber, who quotes it in his study, 'Die "comédie rosse" in Frankreich', *Archiv für das Studium der neueren Sprachen und Literaturen*, Jahrgang 54, 105 (N.S.V.), 1900, p.345.
29. Jules Lemaître, *Impressions de Théâtre*, Troisième Série (Paris, 1889), p.224.
30. Henry Becque, *Oeuvres complètes* (Paris, 1924), Vol. 3, pp.3-9.
31. Octave Feuillet, *Théâtre complet* (Paris, 1897), Vol. 2, p.24.
32. Carl Reinhold Smedmark, ed., *August Strindbergs dramer*, Vol. 4, p.240.
33. Augustin Filon, *De Dumas à Rostand. Esquisse du Mouvement dramatique contemporain* (Paris, 1898), p.70. See also Gedsø Madsen, p.28.
34. Lemaître, p.224.
35. Eric Bentley, *The Playwright as Thinker: A Study of Drama in Modern Times* (New York, 1945), p.163.
36. Cited in *The New York Times*, 28 April 1986.
37. John Ward, 'The Neglected Dramas of August Strindberg', *Drama: The Quarterly Theatre Review*, No. 92 (1969), p.32.

Strindberg's *Advent* and *Brott och brott*

Sagospel and Comedy in a Higher Court

Barry Jacobs

Montclair State College

In *Tjänstekvinnans son*, Strindberg dismisses *Lycko-Pers resa*, the *sagospel* (fairy-tale play) that had been his most popular theatre piece in Sweden, as 'en anakronism och en konjunktur på samma gång' (simultaneously an anachronism and a profitable enterprise — SS 19, p.188). He seems always to have undervalued this work and to have been somewhat embarrassed by its success. In *Tal till svenska nationen*, he claims that because it lacks both artistic form and living characters, it is far inferior to Oehlenschläger's *Aladdin*, the work that inspired it (SV 68, p.100). Therefore when Bernard Shaw tried that same year to persuade him to let Sir Herbert Beerbohm Tree produce *Lycko-Pers resa* at His Majesty's Theatre in London, Strindberg rejected the proposal out of hand. In his initial letter, Shaw explained that ever since 1904, when J. M. Barrie had made a stunning success with *Peter Pan*, every London manager's dream had been to find another play like it — for want of a more precise generic designation in English Shaw describes it as 'a sort of fairy-play for children'. In 1909 Maeterlinck's *The Blue Bird* had been acclaimed by the British public; now, Shaw implied, the pragmatic bourgeoisie of London had not only acquired a taste for make-believe, but also possessed a degree of generic recognition that would enable them to take *Lycko-Per* to their hearts. He apologized for this mild sort of pioneering by intimating that the production of Strindberg's *A Midsummer Night's Dream* would make the London public intensely eager to see his *Hamlet*.[1] Strindberg, who had by no means abandoned this rather frivolous genre, countered

167

with the last of four fairy-tale plays that he had written since his Inferno crisis: a 'lyrical fantasy' entitled *Svarta handsken*, which to this day has never enjoyed much success, except as a radio play.[2] His continued interest in the *sagospel* and his tendency to overvalue plays like *Svarta handsken* raise some interesting questions about his later use of genre.

Genre, as Alastair Fowler observes, is 'a communication system, for the use of writers in writing, and readers in interpreting.'[3] Strindberg's use of generic and modal designations — and even of the more or less interchangeable words *genre* and *form* — often sends confusing messages to his readers. Such is the case with *Gillets hemlighet* and *Brott och brott* which he called comedies, with *Fordringsägare*, which he called a tragicomedy, and with *Advent*, which he called a mystery play (*ett mysterium*). 'Hjärnornas kamp' (The Battle of the Brains), the title of a short story he wrote in 1887, refers to a concept of conflict largely based on Hippolyte Bernheim's findings about psychic suggestion in the waking state that became the dominant theme of the works he wrote during the late 1880s. In January 1887 he proudly proclaimed that he had invented a new *genre*, 'hjärnornas kamp'. 'Denna genre (Edgar Poe),' he wrote to his publisher in 1888, 'blir de närmaste tio årens, och började med Bourget fortsättande i Maupassants Pierre et Jean, implanterades hos oss med Rosmersholm och Fadren' (This genre (Edgar Poe) will dominate the next decade, and began with Bourget, continuing in Maupassant's *Pierre et Jean*, was implanted here [in Scandinavia] by *Rosmersholm* and *The Father*' — VII, p.212). This instructive misuse of the word *genre* shows how Strindberg conceived of the relation between theme and form. Years later (in *Öppna brev till Intima teatern*) he clarified this relationship in the famous dictum: 'Ingen bestämd form skall binda författaren, ty motivet betingar formen' (No predetermined form is to limit the author, because the theme (or motif) determines the form — SS 50, p.12). Using 'form' here in its widely-accepted meaning of genre (or kind), he appears to be saying two things about the relationship between form and content: not only does literature — like genre painting — make its appeal primarily through content, but the content will determine the structure of the plot and the mode of the work.

In 1899 — after his Inferno crisis had culminated in his conversion to a portmanteau belief in 'unseen', corrective powers — Strindberg invented yet another *genre* (in his sense of the word), that is to say, a literary form based on the theme he called 'Nemesis Providentia' in the notes he kept while *Advent* was beginning to take shape in his mind.[4] This genre, which one might call 'the nemesis play', achieves roughly the same prominence in his post-Inferno production as 'The Battle of the Brains' does in the naturalistic works he wrote during the late 1880s. The plot structure determined by the nemesis theme (the content) can be accommodated by various literary kinds: the Strindbergian 'commedia' (*Brott och brott*),[5] the historical play (*Carl XII*), and the *sagospel* (*Advent*). But the true progenitor of the nemesis play would appear to be the *sagospel*.

Shaw's uncertainty about the proper generic designation for *Peter Pan* — 'a sort of fairy-play for children' — points to some of the problems one encounters in trying to define (and confine) the rather nebulous *sagospel* — what is called *Märchendrama* (or *Zauberstück*) in German, *féerie* in French, and *fairy-tale play* (or *extravaganza*) in English. Much as these national variants may differ from each other in emphasis, they are all based on fairy-tale, mythic, or biblical motifs. They usually depict a world in which the laws of time, space, and causality are suspended and where personifications of supernatural beings (gods, spirits, fairies, wizards, and the like) freely interfere in human affairs. Though works by Aristophanes (*The Birds*) and Shakespeare (*A Midsummer Night's Dream* and *The Tempest*) may be regarded as the antecedents of this literary kind, the immediate ancestors of the romantic *sagospel* are Carlo Gozzi (*Fiabe dramatiche*), Schikaneder (*Die Zauberflöte*), Goethe (*Faust*), and Tieck (*Der gestiefelte Kater*).[6] In stories and plays representing the interpenetration of the natural and the supernatural worlds, several Scandinavian writers produced some of their masterpieces: H. C. Andersen's collections of *Eventyr* (*Fairy Tales*), Oehlenschläger's *Aladdin* (1805), Atterbom's *Lycksalighetens ö* (*The Isle of Bliss*, 1824-7), and Ibsen's *Peer Gynt* (1867) — all of which helped inspire *Lycko-Pers resa*.

Somewhat surprisingly, Zola valued the *féerie* very highly, despite its contempt for *le vrai* — or rather because of it. For him, the charm of this fanciful genre is that it lets us escape briefly from earth and takes us into the world of the impossible.[7] The young naturalist Strindberg, on the other hand, clearly felt uncomfortable in the realm of fantasy at this point in his career; yet in 1882, when he got a commission to write a Christmas entertainment, he did not hesitate to employ an elf (*tomte*), a good fairy, a wishing ring, talking rats, a dancing broom, and other *sagospel* conventions to tell the story of Lucky Peter, who has all the characteristics of the typical fairy-tale hero: compassion, humility, and naïveté. The poor lad is cruelly treated by his cynical, misanthropic father, a Swedish Scrooge, whose heart has been hardened not by materialism, but by matrimony. To spare his hapless son from the same fate, he has sequestered him in a church for the first fifteen years of his life. But the spirit of Peter's deceased mother is still very much alive as the protecting, loving fairy godmother who liberates him from his father and sends him out into the world to discover what life is really like and to become 'en människa och en mänsklig människa' (a human and a humane human — SS 9, p.282).

Whereas the path of the fairy-tale hero generally begins in a drab world of everyday reality and moves through a magical realm in order to emerge in a shining new reality, Strindberg reverses this pattern.[8] Departing from a world where rats go into mourning for their lost babies, where a mysterious voice reprimands blasphemy, and where the picture of the madonna nods and speaks, Peter moves out into a more or less recognizable distortion of everyday reality. His mission is not only to search for *lycka* ('happiness', 'good fortune', or 'success'), but to divest that word of its ambiguities and to find its one essential meaning. To help him satisfy his hunger for life and happiness, the elf has provided him with a wishing ring; to help instruct him in the vanity of human wishes, his fairy godmother has given him a female companion, Lisa, a human avatar of herself. For most of the play Lisa remains a supernatural shape-shifter who regularly shows up to rescue him from serious difficulties and to see that he has learned his lesson; but she cannot really become a source of *lycka* herself until Peter overcomes his self-love.

The play ends, as it began, in a church where the fairy-tale realm is reestablished: a broom dances and religious statues speak. Peter sees his own shadow (*skugga*) from whom he learns that it is our failings, not our virtues, that make us human, and that self-knowledge is the only road to real manhood. As a result of his experience of the interpenetration of invisible, supernatural world with the visible world of everyday reality Peter has finally matured to the point at which he can renounce his youthful dreams. When the sexton (Peter's transfigured father) comes to expel Peter and Lisa from the church — from Paradise, Lisa says (SS 9, p.380) — Peter realizes that the enchantment is broken and that they can now take paradise with them. From windows in the church the elf and the fairy godmother watch as the three now fully-human characters reenter the world divested of their dreams and their illusions.

The lasting technical lesson Strindberg learned from this first experiment with the *sagospel* derives from the stage practice of another of his mentors in this genre, the Viennese actor-playwright Ferdinand Raimund, who had made brilliant use of the *changement à vue* (i.e., change of scene without lowering the curtain). This theatrical convention lies well within the reader-spectator's horizon of expectations because the generic paradigm prepares us for the rapid alternation between the two interpenetrating worlds of the *sagospel*. Strindberg experimented with this technique in *Lycko-Pers resa* and later used it with startling effect in the changed context of such post-Inferno works as *Till Damaskus*, *Ett drömspel*, and *Stora landsvägen*. The real trouble with *Lycko-Pers resa* — and surely this is what embarrassed Strindberg about it — is that it deals with the interpenetration of two unreal worlds. In fact, it is easier to accept the talking rats and the wishing ring than it is to believe in Peter and his embittered father as human characters. With *Himmelrikets nycklar* in 1892 Strindberg made an unsuccessful attempt to resurrect this genre, but before he would be ready to reshape the *sagospel*, his world view would have to change. 'Genres survive,' as Harry Levin observes, 'by meeting the conditions that reshape them.'[9] The conditions that reshaped Strindberg's whole outlook on life arose during his Inferno crisis. Strindberg's efforts in youth and early manhood had been to liberate himself first from Pietism (his legacy from his mother), then to reject the ethically-based Unitarianism he had gained from reading Theodore Parker, and finally — in the late 1880s — to espouse a form of nihilistic humanism. This final view, which attempts to reconcile determinism with ethics, is perhaps best expressed by Gustaf in *Fordringsägare*. Arguing that everything happens by necessity, his unfaithful former wife, Tekla, declares herself innocent of any form of wrong-doing in her marriages. 'Oskyldig,' he replies, 'inför honom som icke finns mer; ansvarig inför sig själv och inför sina medmänniskor' (Innocent in the eyes of Him who no longer exists; responsible in one's own eyes and in the eyes of one's fellow man — SV 27, p.270). The moralistic outlook that began to emerge in Strindberg's conscious mind during the last phase of the 'Inferno crisis' forced him to link his inescapable guilt feelings with past misdeeds. When he was at last able to find a connection between suffering and guilt, his anxiety was transformed into remorse.[10] This new sense of guilt and remorse eventually led Strindberg to conclude with Maurice, the hero of *Brott och brott*, that we are guilty of 'thought crimes', even when we are not responsible for committing them.

The Inferno crisis began as a period of intense, apparently innocent suffering for Strindberg. During its early stages he resorted to ideas of metempsychosis, Doppelgänger, or life as a penal colony in order to explain his own meaningless suffering. In 1896 he began to keep an 'occult' diary. This document — part intimate diary, part dreambook, part scrapbook full of Bible quotations, alchemical formulas, and curious facts gleaned from the newspapers — was an attempt to reduce the world to a text that could be read backwards and forwards in order to show purpose, meaning, and causality (or at least probable causality) in the world. On the first page of *Ockulta dagboken* he copied down a dictum from the Talmud: 'Om du vill lära känna det osynliga, då iakttag med öppen blick det synliga' (If you want to learn about the invisible [world], scrutinize the visible [one] with care). This phrase clearly indicates why Strindberg spent so many years (1896-1908) recording and collating his observations of the visible world in this diary: his study of the 'world text' he produced convinced him that the visible world really is interpenetrated by an invisible one peopled with good and evil spirits.[11]

During the Inferno years Strindberg devoted himself to alchemical experiments and became involved with the Paris Occultists (Eliphas Lévi, Stanislas de Guaita, and Dr Papus), who opposed oriental (theosophical) mysticism with a brand of Western occultism based on the hermetic tradition stemming from Paracelsus and Saint-Martin. He also read some of Swedenborg's neo-platonic theological works, as well as Balzac's Swedenborgian novels, *Séraphîta* and *Louis Lambert*. As Swedenborg had done during the crisis that led to his religious conversion, Strindberg began to keep a record of his dreams. Moreover, he developed a strong interest in mystical dramatic works like Maeterlinck's *L'Intruse* and the works of Sâr Péladan. As a reader, he was very like a post-structuralist in that he tended to produce meanings that often had little to do with the intentions of the authors he read. As a diarist, he was a structuralist, hoping to lay bare the systems that underlay his chaotic life. All of his 'occult' interests point in the same direction: he was looking for the hidden narrative, the masterplot for his own life. What he found was a new kind of masterplot for 'nemesis plays', plays about a familiar, visible world in which the manifestations of the invisible world have a terrifying reality.

This masterplot is certainly evident in the first two parts of the *Till Damaskus* trilogy (1898) the so-called '*vandringsdramer*' (sometimes called 'station plays' or 'quest plays' in English) that signalled his return to literature.[12] In the next two plays, *Advent* and *Brott och brott*, one sees a change of direction. That these two plays (in quite different styles) were published together in one volume in 1899 with the overall title *Vid högre rätt* (*In a Higher Court*) points to their thematic similarity. Both plays deal with a man and woman who are unwilling (or unable) to confront their own culpability until they have gone through a hellish series of torments; both works begin in a place of burial and end when the erring characters genuinely repent for their sins and have some grounds for hope of salvation.

When he wrote these two plays, Strindberg was in the process of inventing a new *genre* (in his sense of the word), but he hardly knew what to call it. 'Mitt lif är sig likt,' he wrote to a friend on 10 November 1898, 'kryper, dag efter dag, i arbete och stundom får jag tankar med skön drägt. Skrifver en sagospelstragedi utan fé och tomte; endast de store outgrundlige Osynlige drifva sitt spel' (My life is the same as usual, creeps along, day by day, with work and at times my thoughts come to me beautifully dressed. Am writing a 'fairy-tale tragedy' without either good fairy or elf; only the great, inscrutable Invisible Powers are abroad — XIII, p.35). In the manuscripts of the play he variously designated this work as 'Advent, En Barnpjes', 'Mausolén. Mysterium', and 'Advent. Ett mysterium' ('Advent, a Children's Play', 'The Mausoleum. A Mystery Play', and 'Advent. A Mystery Play'). In one letter (XIII, p.50) he referred to it as his 'nya Swedenborgsdrama (Ett Mysterium) som blir en sagospelstragedi med mystik' (new Swedenborgian drama [a Mystery Play] that will be a fairy-tale tragedy with mysticism). In another (XIII, p.54) he called it 'mitt

Mysterium eller religiösa Sagospel' (my Mystery Play or religious Fairy-Tale Play).[13] On 19 December he noted simply in *Ockulta dagboken*, 'slutade "Advent"', sagospelet' (finished "Advent", the fairy-tale play). These Polonian combinations of generic and modal terms point to a combined genre.

Near the end of the 'Inferno crisis' Strindberg found comfort in some of the visionary works of Swedenborg, who was keenly aware of a dynamic tension between the visible world of human affairs and an invisible world of corrective spirits. Like *Den Andra* (The Other) in *Advent*, these Swedenborgian spirits are charged with the vastation and regeneration of erring man.[14] But if Swedenborg provided a good deal of the content in this new 'genre' of Strindberg's, two other writers gave him the literary matrix that helped him find suitable forms. Before starting *Advent* he had immersed himself in the novels of H. C. Andersen; later, while working on *Brott och brott* he became obsessed with the 'occult' tales of Rudyard Kipling. The conflict between imagination and reality is a major theme in Andersen's novels and the poetic atmosphere in which he develops this theme doubtless explains their immense appeal to Strindberg after the Inferno crisis. In a letter to his children in Finland (XIII, p.59), Strindberg called attention to Andersen's influence on *Advent*. Kipling made an even more profound impression on Strindberg. In early February 1899 he wrote to a friend that [Kipling] 'är ju ett fullt uttryck af nutid. Han är "halfgalen" och alla hans hjeltar äro "galna" ' . . . . Men Kipling är ockult, d. ä. tror på anden hos menniskan och rör lätt vid de Infernoproblem jag lagt ramarne på' (is indeed the complete expression of the moment. He is 'half-crazy' and all of his heroes are 'crazy' . . . But Kipling is occult, that is, he believes that man has a soul and [he] touches lightly upon the problems I got my paws onto in *Inferno* — XIII, p.86). A few days later, he wrote to another friend (XIII, p.92) that Kipling had dredged up all of the mysticism that was lurking in the depths of Strindberg's own being. In other words, reading volume after volume of Kipling's realistically presented stories, in which stolid, pragmatic English colonials are profoundly changed by their brushes with ghosts, gurus, or mysterious Indian divinities, helped corroborate Strindberg's passionate belief that unseen powers are guiding us toward peace in the Hereafter.

Writing about Lucky Peter's quest for self-discovery, as Strindberg said in a letter to Helena Nyblom (II, p.363), was like playing hooky from the grim school of life. While writing *Advent*, on the other hand, he actually lived through some of the same mysterious and disquieting experiences that plague the wicked characters in that play.[15] Like Strindberg, these two characters, the Judge *(Lagmannen)* and his Wife *(Lagmanskan*, the wicked step-mother of the piece), are tormented by a dancing sunbeam *(solkatt)*. In order to perpetuate their relations to the familiar elements of their earthly life, they have built themselves a mausoleum in the midst of their vineyard. Unwittingly, however, they have constructed this monument to their own goodness on what was formerly a place of execution. The newly-completed structure, intended to perpetuate their false, self-serving image of themselves, actually houses the ghosts of all the people who have suffered and died because of their evil. In this modified *sagospel*, familiar fairy-tale motifs are reshaped by being placed in a Swedenborgian context of protective and corrective spirits. Amalia and Adolf, the Judge's daughter and son-in-law, have been deeply wronged: Amalia has been reduced to the status of a servant, while Adolf has been cast out of the family circle altogether. Their innocent children, Erik and Thyra, whom the Judge's Wife has locked in the cellar, are protected by a mysterious, supernatural Playmate, who turns out to be the Christ Child. In this fairy-tale, moreover, it is the ogres, not their victims, who are sent out upon a quest of self-discovery.

The most startling transformation in this play, however, has little to do with the Swedenborgian context. It is the contrast between what the characters see and what is truly to be seen. When the curtain rises *we* see both the visible and the invisible worlds. Though we see the set as they see it (a vineyard, the new mausoleum, a peach tree), the Judge and the Wife look very different to us than they do to each other and to themselves: his costume, dating from the 1820s, links him with his double, the Unjust Judge, who was once executed on the spot where the mausoleum now stands; the Wife (with her kerchief, cane, glasses, and snuffbox) is identical with her double, the Witch, whose ballgown she later borrows. As if we were looking at X-rays of the Judge and the Wife, we see their inner corruption; looking at extremely flattering, retouched photographs of themselves (and each other), they see a Swedish Philemon and Baucis whom we can barely imagine.

The Judge and his wife feel that they have led exemplary lives. He attributes his incredible prosperity to the fact that he was born with a cowl (*segerhuva*). Though both husband and wife greatly fear the heat and light of the sun, the Judge uses sunshine to figure forth their serenity: 'Livets afton,' he observes to his wife, 'har slutligen skänkt oss det solsken som dess morgon lovade' (The evening of life has finally given us the sunshine its morning promised — p. 15). Basking in this metaphorical sunlight, the old couple can almost forgive their envious neighbours and their ungrateful children. The dancing sunbeam (*en solkatt*, literally a 'sun-cat') that suddenly shimmers on the wall of the mausoleum seems to the Wife to be a good omen: 'Det betyder att vi skola se solen lysa ännu en lång tid,' she says (That means we shall see the sun shining for a long time to come — p. 18). Following a familiar Strindbergian pattern, however, events in the rest of the scene soon make it clear that they have misread the omens. The

Judge has illusions of probity, the Wife delusions of pulcritude. The vineyard was not, as the Judge has always believed, once a battlefield, but a place of execution; the new mausoleum stands where the gallows once stood. Though each is still blind to his own faults, by the end of the first scene the dancing sunbeam has become a searing spotlight: the Judge now sees the Wife for the witch she is; his shameful, criminal nature is now fully revealed to her.

The prosperity of the Judge and the Wife is built on a career of misdeeds that has caused untold suffering to others. The Judge has robbed or cheated the living: he has misappropriated a silver coffee service from a poor family and stolen the legacy of an orphan whom he has apprenticed to a chimney sweep. The Wife has plundered the dead: she has stolen the money intended for funeral wreaths for her mother; from her step-daughter, Amalia, she has stolen the memory of her real mother. By substituting a monstrance of silver-gilt for the pure gold one she promised to the church, she has even cheated God. The mausoleum they have built in order to enshrine themselves really houses Death, a Fool mocking the Judge's cowl, the shades of all of the people who have suffered at the hands of the Judge and the Wife, as well as the ghost of the Judge's double, the Unjust Judge. The structure is, in other words, a metaphor for the hidden, inner lives of these two sinners: not a tribute to their goodness, but a barrier to their salvation. Near the end of the play this monument becomes (in the peep show the Judge squints into in Hell) a place of excrement. No hope of forgiveness is possible until it is destroyed.

The Judge and the Wife both have ghostly doubles whose physical defects correspond to the moral defects of their human counterparts: the Hanged Judge has a rope around his neck and is missing an index finger, because he once swore falsely on the Bible; the Wife encounters avatars of herself in her deceased bother, the hunchbacked Prince, whose deformity is obvious to everyone but himself, and in the Witch, who drives her out to wander alone until she freezes to death. The Judge and the Wife are haunted by spectral processions of their victims or of the Seven Deadly Sins. Whereas all of these spectres seem to be projections from within — 'våra egna sjuka drömmar' (our own sick dreams — p.41), the Wife suggests — other corrective spirits seem to have been sent by Providence to drive these sinners back onto the path of righteousness. Chief among these is The Other (*Den Andra*), a seedy, down-at-the-heel devil, who appears from time to time in the guise of a Schoolteacher, a Franciscan Monk, or of the Master of Ceremonies in Hell.[16] In life he was an evil person who fell because he touched the forbidden tree and then went around tempting others to do the same; his punishment in death is to serve the forces of Good: not to tempt with wealth and power, but to punish with whips and scorpions (p.58). Immune to *apotropaia*, this penitent devil cannot be banished by the sign of the cross or by music.

The conflict between good and evil in this play is scenically reinforced by the interplay of darkness and light. Both the Judge and the Wife are extremely fearful of the heat and light of the sun. Not only does the Judge prefer darkness, he blackens everything he touches: the silver service he has stolen is so tarnished that no amount of polishing can brighten it; and the orphan he has plundered and pushed into the life of a chimney sweep seems permanently besmirched. But whereas the imagery of darkness in this play is quite conventional, the light imagery is strikingly original. The Wife first sees the dancing sunbeam ('sun-cat') just after she speaks of dissolving Amalia's marriage; its subsequent appearances always highlight their evil deeds, such as, the expulsion of Adolf and the revelation that the Wife has lied about the monstrance she presented to the church. The 'sun-cat', in short, begins to stalk them like a beast of prey, tormenting and exposing them mercilessly.

One of the theological peculiarities of Strindberg's post-Inferno religion is that though he continued to reject the notion that man could be redeemed by the vicarious suffering of Christ, he eagerly accepted the idea of the Incarnation — even in its highly developed Roman Catholic form. He apparently took quite literally Jesus's words 'Whosoever shall not receive the kingdom of God as a little child, he shall not enter therein' (Mark 10:15). Therefore in *Advent* the Christ Child becomes both the protector and the playmate of the innocent children, Erik and Thyra. The 'sun-cat', one of his attributes, becomes a helpful animal that leads the children directly into the land of enchantment. It literally becomes a cat:

> LEK-KAMRATEN: Kom barn! Ut i solen att fröjdas åt livet.
> THYRA: Få vi ta katten med oss; det ar så synd att han skall stanna har i mörkret?
> LEK-KAMRATEN: Ja, om han vill följa med er! Locka på honom!
> ERIK OCH THYRA: [*gå mot dörren, sol-katten följer dem på golvet.*]
> ERIK: Nej se så snäll han är! [*Jollrar till sol-katten.*] Kisse Misse Plurre Murre!
> LEK-KAMRATEN: Tag honom på armen nu Thrya för annars kommer han inte över tröskeln!

> (PLAYMATE: Come children — out into the sunlight to rejoice in life!
> THYRA: May we take the kitty with us? Such a pity to leave him here in the dark.
> PLAYMATE: Yes, if he'll come along! Coax him.
> ERIK and THYRA: [*approach the door; the sun-cat follows them.*]

ERIK: Oh, look how good he is! [*Talks affectionately to the sun-cat.*] Here Puss Puss! Come, Pusscat!
PLAYMATE: Pick him up now, Thyra. Otherwise he won't cross the threshold! — pp.65-6)

The land of enchantment they enter (Act III, Sc. 2) is a garden full of flowers and topiary hedges in the centre of which is a healing spring (said to have been touched by an angel). Beside the spring stands a giant Fuchsia (called *Kristi Bloddroppar*, 'Christ's Blooddrops', in Swedish), the only forbidden tree in this Eden. Far away we see a field of ripe grain, cliffs, ruined castles, and a gothic archway framing a statue of the Madonna and Child. The only disquieting elements in this earthly paradise are a scarecrow and the sooty chimney-sweep, who enters and timidly watches the children at play. Before revealing himself as the Christ Child accompanied by a lamb, the Playmate allows Erik and Thyra to tear down the scarecrow so that the birds will come to sing to them; then he washes (baptizes) the chimney-sweep in the healing spring and restores him to his lost mother.

Though the Playmate can easily turn punishment to play for the innocent children, their mother, Amalia, finds it impossible to make light of her unjust suffering. What pains her even more than the heavy work she must do is the fact that she cannot love the Wife, the woman she has always taken to be her mother. Though she feels guilty about this unnatural lack of love, she still refuses to accept the idea of suffering as punishment. The wise Neighbour, who becomes the spokesman in this play for some of Strindberg's religious ideas, comforts her by explaining the meaning of suffering: 'Mitt goda barn: att lida rättvist, det göra straffångarne, och det är ingen ära, men att *få* lida orätt, det är en nåd och en prövning som den ståndaktige hämtar gyllene frukter av' (My good child, to suffer justly is what prisoners do — and there's no honour in that; but *to be allowed* to suffer unjustly, that is a gift and a test which bring golden fruits to the steadfast — p.35). As soon as she has undergone the tests set for her, the Neighbour reveals the secret of her life: her real mother is dead and the Wife is her stepmother. After learning this, Amalia can rejoice that God has allowed her to retain an unblemished image of her true mother; now she can understand and accept the cruelty of the Wife.

The tribulations of the Judge and the Wife more than counterbalance the saccharinity of the scenes involving the children in this play. Once the 'sun-cat' has begun the unmasking, the Judge and the Wife are visited by all manner of occult manifestations. In an atmosphere of mounting terror, they begin to suspect each other of poisoning the food they eat and the water they drink. But though they soon think of fleeing from their haunted home, holding a big auction, and starting a new life somewhere else, they continue to find rational explanations for these supernatural warnings. In Act IV the unmasking process begun by the 'sun-cat' is completed. The Wife meets her double, the Witch, at a crossroads and is outfitted for a ball in what turns out to be the Waiting Room in Hell. She meets and dances with the (recently deceased) Prince. When she unmasks him by referring to his hunchback, he pulls off her wig and threatens to remove her false teeth. Thus stripped, they recognize one another as brother and sister. No longer able to conceal her baseness, the Wife finds herself back at the crossroads, where the Witch sends her out to wander until she freezes to death in a marsh. In the mean while the Judge, who still refuses to believe in supernatural powers, is judged by an invisible tribunal (p.102). When he threatens to appeal to a higher court, The Other tells him that his case has been through all the courts except the very highest and that he has been sentenced to be stoned to death. Not until they are reunited in the Waiting Room of Hell on Christmas Eve do the deceased Judge and the Wife, now both fully penitent, become capable of seeing what is truly to be seen. Despite their realization that the wrongs they have done cannot be undone, they still have some grounds for hope: The Other tells them that though the sun never penetrates to this region, on this one night of the year a single star ascends so high in the heaven that it can even be seen in Hell (p.125). The 'sun-cat' has now been transformed into the star of Bethlehem. The mausoleum, the symbol of death and vainglory, is replaced by the nativity scene symbolizing life and hope of salvation. A choir sings the *Gloria*.

Stockenström sees the ending of *Advent* as lapsing into cheap, sentimental theatricality and suggests that if Strindberg had carried out his original plan for the mausoleum motif, *Advent* would have become the first of his Chamber Plays.[17] Disconcerted by what he considers a highly unsuccessful blend of fairy-tale, mystery, nightmare, and stark realism in this play, Ollén too undervalues *Advent*.[18] Both critics appear to ignore the generic paradigm Strindberg was at such pains to provide. Medieval dramatic method presupposed an unsophisticated audience that could easily accept sharp contrasts between comic, often crassly realistic scenes and sacred history. Moreover, it frequently staged simultaneous action: the torments of the damned in Hell juxtaposed to Jerusalem and the Temple. *Advent*, subtitled 'Ett mysterium' ends with a diptych: a nativity scene and an angel chorus — as seen and heard from Hell. The contrast between the two worlds of the play is as naive, as startling, and potentially as effective as the final scene in the 15th century Wakefield Master's *Secunda pastorem*: the thieving Mak has stolen a sheep from his fellow shepherds and his wife Gill concealed it by wrapping it in swaddling clothes and pretending it is her newborn babe; no sooner are these culprits unmasked and punished at the end of this farcical parody of the nativity story, than an angel appears to the shepherds announcing the birth of the Saviour. As at the end of *Advent*, a chorus sings the *Gloria*; then the transposed shepherds go to Bethlehem with touchingly humble gifts for the Holy Infant: a bunch of cherries, a bird, and a ball. They receive the benediction of the Blessed Virgin, who promises to pray her son to keep them from woe. In his modern mystery play, *Advent*, Strindberg is experimenting with a kind of religious theatre that he felt could accommodate both everyday realism and providential contradiction (vastation) and regeneration.

Advent, Strindberg's first attempt to adapt the *sagospel* to religious drama, has proved far less successful in the theatre than *Brott och brott*, his first attempt to use realistic 'comedy' as a medium for dramatizing what he called Nemesis Providentia. In a very famous passage in the *Biographia Literaria*, where Coleridge describes the origin of the plan of the *Lyrical Ballads*, he says that while he directed his endeavours to 'characters supernatural, or at least romantic', Wordsworth sought to 'give the charm of novelty to things of every day, and to excite a feeling analogous to the supernatural' by removing 'the film of familiarity' that makes us blind to the 'wonders of the world before us'.[19] True poetry, he implies, results from the tension between the willing, if momentary 'suspension of disbelief' (poetic faith) and the mind's sudden awakening from 'the lethargy of custom'. Something very like this modal complementarity seems to be at work in Strindberg's 'nemesis plays', where we can see a similar tension between the Andersenian world of make-believe and the nightmarish Kiplingesque realities that make one believe.[20]

The generic subtitle of *Brott och brott* has caused readers problems from the very start. Some early reviewers (Levertin, Warburg, and Wirsén) found 'komedi' utterly inappropriate (SV 40, p.266); when he produced the play in 1902, Max Reinhardt relabelled it 'tragicomedy'.[21] This sort of discomfort with the generic subtitle shows the play to be an early example of a new mixed genre that has been variously described as 'melodrama',[22] 'metacomedy',[23] 'commedia',[24] and as 'dark comedy', the modern umbrella mode defined by J. L. Styan.[25] Hans-Göran Ekman rightly suggests that Strindberg's use of the word 'comedy' is easier to understand if placed in a Dantean context, but one really need look no further than the kind of nineteenth-century well-made play in which conversion, a radical change of mental attitude, 'unties the knot and brings the curtain down'[26] — or to Kipling's short story 'The Conversion of Aurelian McGoggin' — to find the generic paradigms that underlie *Brott och brott*.[27]

Though *Brott och brott* is simply a further development of the material on which *Advent* was based,[28] the realistic demands of the genre Strindberg is using in his second 'nemesis play' occasion a shift in scenic effects: in *Advent* he used lighting to represent the impingement of the transcendent world on everyday reality; here he uses sound to demonstrate the interaction between the two. The play opens in the Montparnasse Cemetery in Paris, where Jeanne and her five-year-old daughter, Marion, have been waiting for two hours for Maurice, Jeanne's lover and Marion's father. In the background is a stone cross bearing the message of the play: *O crux! Ave spes unica!* Though a friendly Abbé translates the Latin words for her, Jeanne is not yet ready to understand the secret of suffering, which is the true meaning of the inscription. A mourning woman kneeling nearby at a flower-bedecked grave seems to be talking with the deceased, but her words are inaudible, and Jeanne, who no longer believes in life after death, rejects the notion that there can be any communication with the supermundane. The interaction between these two worlds gives us the plot of *Brott och brott*. The real hero, the intriguer, as Strindberg said in a letter to his friend Littmansson (XIII, p.120), is 'The Invisible One', who — like Adolphe later in the play — reveals himself in veiled terms through *en halvkväden visa* (literally, 'a half-sung song' — SV 40, p.236).

In the first scene of the play, Jeanne, a good-hearted working-class woman, fears that her long liaison with Maurice may soon end. After years of trying to make his mark as a playwright, Maurice believes that his new play will make him rich and famous, but he is too embarrassed by Jeanne's lack of sophistication to want her by his side on opening night. The only bond that still holds the couple together is their deep love for Marion. Sensing his discomfiture, Jeanne refuses the theatre ticket Maurice half-heartedly offers her, but gives him a package containing a scarf and a pair of gloves that she begs him to wear in her honour on the evening of his triumph. Shortly thereafter at Madame Catherine's Crémerie, the favourite haunt of Maurice and his artist friend, Adolphe, Maurice is transfixed at his first encounter with Adolpe's mistress, Henriette. Fearing that he might lose Henriette to Maurice, Adolphe has tried to prevent their meeting; now his worst fears come true. *Rus* (intoxication) was Strindberg's working title for the play; that word perfectly describes the passion that flares up in Maurice and Henriette, who eagerly accepts the theatre ticket Jeanne refused. Though she and Maurice insist that Adolphe join them at a café after the theatre, they already see him as superfluous.

Though Maurice fancies himself an amoral, bohemian artist, he is really — to an even greater extent than Tonio Kröger — 'a bourgeois *manqué*'. His extremely idealistic play, as described by Adolphe, easily wins popular approval because it rehabilitates mankind and frees the public from lifelong nightmares (p.184). Ironically, though Maurice convinces the public that man is a bit better than his reputation, he himself is attracted to the evil in Henriette. Waiting in vain for Adolphe, who is present only as an empty champagne glass, Maurice and Henriette become intoxicated with passion. Crowning him with laurel, Henriette tempts him to glory in his theatrical triumph, and he worships her as Astarte, the jealous incarnation of sexual pleasure who demands human sacrifice. His best friend, Adolphe, becomes the first sacrificial victim. Jeanne, whose tawdry gift of a scarf and a pair of gloves Henriette-Astarte ridicules and throws into the empty fireplace, is the next. But Maurice cannot betray his bourgeois values with impunity: 'half-sung songs' begin to reach him from the hidden world. In the next room someone begins playing the allegretto movement of Beethoven's Piano Sonata No.17 — now softly, now wildly — ceaselessly repeating the transitional passage (measures 96-107) that Strindberg told his friend Littmansson affected him 'som en centrumborr i samvetet på mig' (like a centre-bit drilling into my conscience — XIII, p.115). The unseen pianist starts playing just at the moment when Maurice begins to regret his failure to join his old friends, as promised, for a celebration at the Crémerie. Next the absent Adolf begins to speak through the mouth of Maurice, who imagines the speech he will make when and if he does show up: 'Ja, jag litar på dig Maurice, dels därför att du är min vän, dels därför att dina känslor äro bundna på annat håll!' (Yes, I trust you, Maurice, partly because you are my friend, partly because your feelings are anchored elsewhere! — p.177). This epideictic exercise proves too much for Maurice, who begins to shudder with cold — or with terror. When Henriette covers him with her pelisse, he feels that he has received her skin, has been invested with a new soul and new thoughts — he even believes he is beginning to assume a female body. At this point Maurice's guilty conscience is fully articulate: the music becomes so obtrusive that it drives the hapless lovers to seek refuge at the pavilion in the Bois de Boulogne.

Henriette is almost entirely motivated by hatred for the bourgeois values that still have such a hold on Maurice. By helping her mother and her siblings wish the life out of her father, she early became guilty of a thought crime, a crime that cannot be punished by any court. Later her bungled attempt to perform an abortion on a friend made her guilty of an actionable crime, manslaughter. Killing both her friend and the unborn child placed Henriette outside society, and cut her off from reality. Since that moment, she tells Maurice, she has only lived a half-life, a dreamlife, in constant dread of discovery and the gallows (p.175). Though Adolphe's goodness attracted her 'som ett vackert försvunnet barndomsminne' (like a beautiful, vanished childhood memory — p.176), she is now too steeped in blood to regain her innocence. Hoping to find a Nietzschean superman in Maurice, she soon discovers that he is neither beyond good, nor truly capable of evil. Embarrassed by the generosity and resignation of Adolphe, whom she had arrogantly hoped to humiliate at the pavilion in the Bois, Henriette-Astarte craves the sacrifice of the child, Marion, and the intoxicated Maurice assents without protest and wishes the child dead. They plan to break old ties unceremoniously and flee south to a new life the very next day. At the moment of her triumph, however, Henriette recoils when she draws the five of diamonds from a pack of cards. This symbolic representation of the supports under the gallows at the Place Rouquette softens her. She sends Maurice to bid farewell to Marion one last time before their departure.

Adolphe does not emerge as a major character in this play until the third act. He too has experienced an artistic triumph: he has been awarded a gold medal for a painting that subsequently fetched a great price in London. But because he shuns success, he has returned the medal. Though he claims not to believe in God, events in his life have made him aware that some eternal power permeates existence and steers our lives; therefore he can easily forgive Maurice and Henriette, because he feels they are not acting of their own free will: they were simply driven into each other's arms by the intrigues of this invisible power. Only those who have needed forgiveness, that is, those who have committed an act for which they are truly penitent, are capable of forgiving others. The thought crime that has altered his life, as he tells Henriette in a 'half-sung song' about a fictional friend of his, was his wish that his father would die (pp.211-12). When his father did suddenly die, Adolphe was so obsessed with the idea that he was a murderer that for a time he was confined in a mental institution. Cured there of all but his sense of guilt, he has continued to punish himself for his evil thoughts. Near the end of the play he advises Henriette to part with Maurice, abandon her artistic career, and return home to her mother. Above all, she must try to turn her hatred against herself, to lance, as it were, her own boils (p.236).

Maurice's thought crime, his wish that little Marion were out of the way, is suddenly fulfilled when the child is found dead shortly after his last visit to her. The testimony of good, (invisible) waiters at the café and the pavilion cast suspicion on him. His play is cancelled, his reputation ruined, his former friends of two minds about his guilt or innocence. Worst of all, he and Henriette begin to suspect everyone else of vengeful acts and each other of murder — like the Judge and the Wife in *Advent*, they poison life for each other. Their lives become hellish: Henriette is mistakenly arrested as a common prostitute; Maurice is accused of being her pimp and is even forced to spend a night in jail, a night that permanently alters his character. Even the discovery that Marion has died of a rare disease — one that she may have contracted from the flowers she was playing with in the cemetery — cannot allay the consciousness of sin that has begun to drive Maurice to accept the Abbé's oft-expressed view that these uncanny events 'är icke människors verk' (pp.198, 202, and 209 — are not the work of man). After two excruciating days, Maurice feels ready to renounce hope of worldly success and to seek refuge in the bosom of the Church.

Not only is Marion dead, but he has also lost both Jeanne and Henriette forever. His final dilemma arises when he must choose between joining penitent prison inmates at a religious service or receiving the homage of his admirers at the theatre, where his play has been reinstated. At the banal conclusion of the play, he solves his problem by deciding to go to church that night and to the theatre the next.

'Mitt pjesslut är nog banalt' (My dénouement is certainly banal — XIII, p.120, n.6), Strindberg admitted to his friend Littmansson, but this kind of ending is, after all, part of the generic paradigm for the comedy of conversion. The shocking peripety, the sudden death of little Marion, removes the 'film of familiarity' from Maurice's bourgeois world and leads him to the awareness that the intrigues of the Invisible One were intended for his moral edification. In other words, *Brott och brott*, no less than *Advent*, is a 'nemesis play', loosely based on Swedenborgian ideas of contradiction leading to regeneration. Sprinchorn makes a very convincing case for a Kierkegaardian-Swedenborgian reading of *Brott och brott*.[29] It is also possible to make a Kierkegaardian reading of the play's generic (or modal) subtitle. Following Aristotle, Kierkegaard saw the unity of the tragic and the comic in the fact that both arise from contradiction (*Modsigelse*). The tragic is a suffering contradiction, the comic a relatively painless one. This is not to say, however, that the comic does not involve suffering; in fact, Kierkegaard felt that suffering is the very source of our sense of the comic. One of his most striking examples of the relation between suffering and the comic occurs in the long fictional diary entitled 'Skyldig?' — 'Ikke-Skyldig?' (Guilty?/Not Guilty?) in *Stadier paa Livets Vej* (Stages on Life's Way):

The more one suffers, the more sense, I believe, one gains for the comic. Only by the most profound suffering does one gain real competence in the comic, which with a word magically transforms the rational creature called man into a *Fratze* [caricature]. This competence is like a policeman's self-assurance when he abruptly grips his club and does not tolerate any talk or blocking of traffic. The victim protests, he objects, he insists on being respected as a citizen, he demands a hearing — immediately there is a second rap from the club, and that means: Please move on! Don't stand there! In other words, to want to stand there to protest, to demand a hearing, is just a poor, pathetic wretch's attempt to really amount to something, but the comic turns the fellow around in a hurry and, by seeing him from behind, with the help of his club makes him comic.[30]

Seen objectively, the suffering of the indignant citizen is laughable; he is the 'fall guy', he who gets slapped, one of the mainstays of the comic tradition. Swedenborgian suffering (vastation), on the other hand, is a painful, totally subjective experience. Strindberg has a remarkable talent for making us experience both sides of the Kierke-gaardian comic at virtually the same time, as when Henriette is picked up by the police as a common prostitute, or when Maurice and Henriette identify themselves with Adam and Eve as they are being driven out of the Jardin de Luxembourg. We experience their suffering as both pathetic and comic, because we are able to see it both subjectively and objectively. In this sense, 'the comic' perfectly characterizes the mode of *Brott och brott*, where the protagonist is turned around in a hurry by his unrelenting, but invisible antagonist. We feel here the same peculiar *vis comica* that Dürrenmatt sensed coursing through *Dödsdansen*, which he reduced to a boxing match in his 'arrangement' of the play, *Play Strindberg*.[31] One critic describes Strindberg's Alice and Edgar as 'tragic characters in a comic situation.'[32] One might say the same about both the Judge and the Wife in *Advent* and Henriette and Maurice in *Brott och brott*.

Though the characteristic mutability of literary genres makes them very difficult to define, generic statements, as Fowler observes, are 'instrumentally critical'.[33] In other words, we cannot fully discover the meaning of a literary work until we have determined the generic matrix from which it issues. The multiplicity of generic and modal terms that have been applied to Strindberg's post-*Inferno* works indicates that his is a particularly difficult case. In creating the religious *sagospel* and the comedy of conversion — or what I have been calling 'the nemesis play' — Strindberg certainly modified two familiar genres. Reading *Advent* and *Brott och brott* together, however, invites us to see these two works not as complementary genres, but as unfused modal variants of the same hybrid genre, the *sagospel*. Both plays involve the interaction between two worlds. In *Advent*, the Coleridgean component, we wander in imaginary gardens with real toads in them, while *Brott och brott*, the Wordsworthian component, excites 'a feeling analogous to the supernatural' in us by placing us in real gardens full of imaginary toads. This kind of modal complementarity would seem to be a key to many of Strindberg's later works. In some of his 'nemesis plays' — like *Dödsdansen* — the Wordsworthian mode prevails; others — like *Spöksonaten* — are cast in a Coleridgean mode. 'A man of genius will create for his theatre a form which has not existed before him,' wrote Théodore de Banville, 'and which after him will suit no one else'.[34] The Strindbergian 'nemesis play' is the perfect example of that form.

Notes

1. Bernard Shaw, *Collected Letters: 1898-1910*, edited by Dan H. Laurence (New York, 1972), pp.907-9. British audiences were, of course, already very familiar with the fairy extravaganzas of writers like J. R. Planché and W. S. Gilbert, whose works inspired the political and philosophical extravaganzas that Shaw wrote in the latter part of his career. See M. Meisel, *Shaw and the Nineteenth-Century Theater* (Princeton, N.J., 1963), pp.380-428.
2. Gunnar Ollén, *Strindbergs dramatik* (Stockholm, 1982), p.574. Strindberg's other four *sagospel* are *Himmelrikets nycklar* (1892), *Advent* (1898; publ. 1899), *Svanevit* (1901), and *Abu Casems tofflor* (1908). See G. Lindström, '*Sagospel*', in *Svenskt litteratur lexikon* (Lund, 1964), pp.440-1.
3. Alastair Fowler, *Kinds of Literature: An Introduction to the Theory of Genres and Modes* (Cambridge, Mass., 1982), p.256.
4. See G. Stockenström, *Ismael i öknen* (Uppsala, 1972), p.426.
5. This generic designation was coined by Cyrus Hoy. See his *The Hyacinth Room* (London, 1964), pp.292ff.
6. See Lindström, pp.440-1.
7. See Émile Zola, *Le Naturalisme au théâtre*, ed. E. Fasquelle (Paris, 1928), pp.285-293.
8. See Maria Tatar, *The Hard Facts of the Grimms' Fairy-Tales* (Princeton, N.J., 1987), p.61.
9. Harry Levin, *Playboys and Killjoys: an Essay on the Theory and Practice of Comedy* (New York, 1987), p.122.
10. See Gunnar Brandell, *Strindberg in Inferno*, translated by B. Jacobs (Cambridge, Mass., 1974), pp.98-159.
11. The manuscript of *Ockulta dagboken* is preserved in the Royal Library in Stockholm. In 1977 Gidlund's Publishing Company brought out a facsimile edition of the handwritten manuscript, hereafter cited in parentheses after a quotation as OD.
12. Besides being the generic ancestor of Strindberg's four post-Inferno *sagospel*, *Lycko-Pers resa* also gave rise to a group of *vandringsdramer* based on the quest theme: *Himmelrikets nycklar*, *Till Damaskus I-III*, *Ett drömspel*, and *Stora landsvägen*. The protagonist in each of these works is involved in a metaphysical quest that brings him into conflict both with other people and with supernatural powers. See G. Ollén, p.59 and Ruprecht Volz, *Strindbergs Wanderungsdramen* (Munich, 1982). Volz defines the Wandrungsdrama as '[ein] Schauspiel . . . in dessen Mittelpunkt ein wandernder Mensch steht, der im Verlauf der dramatischen Begebenheiten die Schauplätze wechselt,' p.29. To confuse matters still further, in the brief preface to *Ett drömspel*, Strindberg refers to *Till Damaskus* as his 'former dreamplay'. This reference has given rise to widespread acceptance of yet another Strindbergian genre, 'the dreamplay'. See Richard Bark, *Strindbergs drömspelsteknik — i drama och teater* (Lund, 1981).
13. Hans-Göran Ekman (SV 40, p.255) quotes Gustaf Uddgren's account of an interview with Strindberg, who said that he chose the generic subtitle of *Advent* to underscore the fact that an age of religious drama

was in the offing — 'liksom dessa mysterier, som inledde Englands dramatiska storhetstid' (like those mystery plays that preceded the great period of English drama). English critics borrowed the distinction between 'mystery play' (a play based on a biblical subject) and 'miracle play' (a play concerned with legends of the saints) from French in the 18th century; see E. K. Chambers, *English Literature at the Close of the Middle Ages* (New York, 1947), p.16. In Swedish, *ett mysterium* means both 'a medieval play based on biblical material' and 'a reality that cannot be understood, but is the object of belief'. Strindberg clearly wishes to activate both meanings in connection with *Advent*.

14. Whether or not one agrees with Karl Jaspers's diagnosis that Swedenborg and Strindberg were both suffering from schizophrenia, it is clear that both shared a poetic or mythic need for the supernatural, for a world where the question of reality does not arise. 'Enfin on peut prouver l'existence de ce monde surnaturel en lui donnant la plénitude sensible d'une chose vécue subjectivement, et c'est cette expérience qui précisément est valable pour Strindberg et Swedenborg,' Jaspers writes in *Strindberg et van Gogh, Hoelderlin et Swedenborg*, translated by H. Naef (Paris, 1953), p.188.

15. On 13 December 1898 he made the following entry in his 'occult' diary: 'På morgonen när jag satt vid skrifbordet . . . syntes en sol-katt pa väggen framför mig så att jag vid en rörelse på hufvudet hade honom i nacken. Jfr. sol-katten bildades af rak-spegeln i sofrummet./ (Jfr. Sol-katten i mitt drama som nu skrifves 'Mausolén' (This morning as I was sitting at my desk . . . a dancing sunbeam appeared on the opposite wall so that when I moved my head it reflected on the back of my neck — OD, p.81). Cf. the reflection came from the shaving mirror in my bedroom./ Cf. the dancing sunbeam in the play I'm writing now, 'The Mausoleum').

16. *Den Andra*'s name is ambiguous. Though the primary meaning in this context would appear to be 'The Other' (i.e. 'The Devil'), this character also uses it to mean 'the second': 'Jag blev den Andre emedan jag ville vara den Förste' (I became the Second because I wanted to be the First — SV 40, p.43).

17. Stockenström, p.403.

18. Ollén, p.268.

19. S. T. Coleridge, *Selected Poetry and Prose of Coleridge*, ed. D. Stauffer (New York, 1951), p.264.

20. Whereas Strindberg apparently saw profound metaphysical implications in the sudden surprising turns of plot in many of Kipling's short stories, Fowler (p.166) sees Kipling as a transitional figure who continued to use *peripeteias* in a way that had been rendered meaningless by the decay of the universe of belief: 'Kipling is a transitional instance: his stories still have plots, and plots still take odd turns (as in *Without Benefit of Clergy*), but the metaphysical implication seems too explicit for the device to hold much potential for future development'. Strindberg obviously felt that sudden turns of plot, such as the unexpected death of little Marion, do disclose the mysteries that are usually concealed from us.

21. See Ollén, p.282.

22. See E. Sprinchorn, *Strindberg as Dramatist* (New Haven, Conn., 1982), p.241, n., where Sprinchorn suggests that Strindberg uses setting to hint that this play is both 'a melodrama with deeper implications and a comedy about crime.' See also M. Valency, *The Flower and the Castle: An Introduction to Modern Drama* (New York, 1963), p.311, where Valency says that 'by exaggerating the conventional effects of melodrama well past the point of credibility, [Strindberg] succeeded not only in giving to a banal action the fabulistic quality of a fairy-tale, but also the glaring realism of a nightmare.'

23. See Levin, pp.123-132.

24. See Hoy, pp.293-4, where he defines Strindberg's comic manner as 'laced with irony, but compassionate'.

25. See J. L. Styan, *The Dark Comedy* (Cambridge, 1962), who regards *Brott och brott* as a prime, early example of the unpopular, implicitly didactic 'drama of the split mind' (p.281) that he designates 'the dark comedy'.

26. See William Archer, *Play-Making: a Manual of Craftsmanship* (New York, 1928), p.339.

27. In a letter to his friend Axel Herrlin (XIII, p.248), Strindberg claimed that the form of the play was inspired by the last movement of Beethoven's Piano Sonata No.17 (Op.31, No. 2). Because Beethoven told his friend Schindler that the explanation to this sonata could be found by reading Shakespeare's *The Tempest*, this work is now usually called 'The Tempest'. In the same letter Strindberg says that his friend Peterson-Berger told him that this piece is called 'die Gespenstersonate' (the 'ghost sonata'), which made the work seem even more relevant to his play that he had at first imagined. For a fascinating discussion of the structural parallels between the allegretto movement of the Beethoven sonata and *Brott och brott*, see Sprinchorn, pp.240-5.

28. See Stockenström, p.428.

29. Sprinchorn, pp.238-9.

30. S. Kierkegaard, *Stages on Life's Way*, translated H. V. & E. H. Hong (Princeton, N.J., 1988), pp.245-6.

31. Dürrenmatt himself claimed that through his efforts a bourgeois marriage tragedy ('eine bürgerliche Ehetragödie') had been transformed into a comedy about bourgeois marriage tragedies ('eine Komödie über die bürgerlichen Ehetragödien'). See F. Dürrenmatt, *Play Strindberg: Totentanz nach August Strindberg* (Zürich, 1969), p.67. For an interesting discussion of the relation between tragedy and comedy in *Brott och brott* see Hans-Göran Ekman, 'Klädernas funktion i Strindbergs *Brott och brott*' in *Läskonst Skrivkonst Diktkonst: till Thure Stenström* (Uppsala, 1987), pp.330-31.

32. K. S. Whitton, *The Theatre of Friedrich Dürrenmatt* (Atlantic Highlands, N.J., 1980), p.205

33. See Fowler, p.38.

34. See 'How to Write a Play', translated D. Miles in *Papers on Playmaking*, ed. B. Matthews (New York, 1957), p.83.

Abu Casems tofflor

Strindberg's Worst Play?

Hans-Göran Ekman

Uppsala University

Strindberg criticism seems to agree on at least one point: that his 1908 *sagospel* (fairy tale) in five acts, *Abu Casems tofflor*, is the weakest of his published dramas.[1] In the final volume of his biography of Strindberg, Gunnar Brandell goes so far as to claim that it is the only one of Strindberg's plays that could have been written by someone else.[2]

My purpose here is not to proclaim *Abu Casems tofflor* a masterpiece out of sheer contrariness. However, I believe that it is unmistakably Strindbergian and as such of great interest to those who are also interested in Strindberg's personality.

Strindberg has for once generously recounted both the origins of this drama and the source of its theme. According to a letter of 8 September 1908 to Knut Michaelson at the Royal Theatre in Stockholm, he received the impulse to write a five-act *sagospel* when he attended a production of his *sagospel* from 1882, *Lycko-Pers resa*, at the Östermalm Theatre in spring 1907 with his daughter, Anne-Marie. As for the theme of the mean Abu Casem, the upright boy Soliman, and Suleika, the girl who hated men, Strindberg refers on the title page to *A Thousand and One Nights* and an unnamed French fairy tale.

This information should afford full knowledge of the genesis of the drama, and permit its interpretation according to the author's wishes, as a simple fairy tale inspired by simple fairy tales, with its prime objective the preaching of love and generosity. This doesn't sound very Strindbergian; nor is it the whole truth about the play.

In other words, there is a case for reacting with suspicion to the author's unusual readiness to account for the play's birth and its literary impulses. One naturally wonders if some personal conflict is once again involved, and if he is leading us astray.

The oriental setting provides a clue, so long as it is not associated exclusively with *A Thousand and One Nights*. It was not the first time that Strindberg had recourse to such a setting. In *Lycko-Pers resa* a wedding is celebrated in an oriental setting; the one-acter *Samum* with its decadent eroticism is set in an Arabian burial chamber; and the novel *Inferno* describes Strindberg's meeting with a woman at a masquerade, whose Eastern attire heightened her beauty and nearly drove him mad (SS 28, p.29). We also know that a large part of Harriet Bosse's attraction for him was her Eastern looks, and when he wrote *Abu Casems tofflor*, his interest in the Orient was reflected in the rugs, fabrics and other materials with Eastern designs, with which he surrounded himself. A journalist from *Dagens Nyheter*, who visited him on 3 October 1908, reported that his room looked like a rajah's secret apartment. For some reason this setting suited his current frame of mind.

Abu Casems tofflor was written during the first days of September 1908,[3] hence shortly after Strindberg moved into Blå Tornet on 11 July 1908, after Harriet Bosse had exited from his private life and the even younger Fanny Falkner had made her entrance. The first time Strindberg saw the latter was at a rehearsal of *Herr Bengts hustru*, in which she was dressed in a page's costume.[4] Female clothes made a strong impression on Strindberg, who had a clear visual memory of how his three wives were dressed when he first saw them. Harriet Bosse was dressed as Puck in *A Midsummer Night's Dream*,[5] Frida Uhl was wearing a fatal green dress,[6] and he would recall Siri von Essen's blue veil[7] just as Dante remembered Beatrice's crimson dress in the *Vita nuova*.

Strindberg's interest in Fanny Falkner increased when they came to live in the same house, and the innocent relationship resulted in September 1909 in a short-lived engagement. Thus Strindberg was preoccupied with his love for this considerably younger woman at the time he was writing *Abu Casems tofflor*, and if the play is seen in this light, it is possible to discover a pattern that transforms the piece into something other than a simple fairy tale, and to see that no one but Strindberg could have written it.

Abu Casems tofflor was thus written by an adorer with a new faith in love but with his old reservations about sexuality intact. Fanny Falkner has affirmed that Strindberg's behaviour towards her was very gentlemanly: 'Han hade ju gått ett helt år och mer och tyckt om mig hela tiden . . . utan att på minsta sätt lägga sina känslor i dagen genom några intimiteter' (He had gone around liking me for a whole year and more without expressing his feelings at all in any kind of intimacy).[8] However, an attentive reading of *Abu Casems tofflor* reveals that

Strindberg was in fact struggling with his sexual impulses in the play. He may have concealed them from Fanny Falkner, but they surface in his drama — in the form of a pair of troublesome slippers. In my paper to the last Strindberg symposium in Seattle, I sought to demonstrate how Strindberg was clearly inclined to shoe and foot fetishism.[9] My point then was not to reveal another side of Strindberg's sexuality but rather to shed light on a characteristic that he made great use of as a dramatist. J.A. Uppvall pursues a similar line in his *August Strindberg. A Psychoanalytic Study* of 1920. Uppval's observations are made with reference to *En dåres försvarstal*,[10] but he fails to develop his theory by relating his observations to other texts, particularly the plays.

If we proceed from the assumption that shoes in Strindberg's work represent sexual impulses, and as such symbolize the 'low' side of life which he increasingly wishes to avoid, then Indra's Daughter's action at the end of *Ett drömspel* acquires great significance. She places her shoes on a fire, and this does not only mean that she is leaving the 'earthly'. Her gesture also symbolically expresses Strindberg's farewell to eroticism, the eroticism that played such a fatal part in his marriage to Harriet Bosse. And giving her this gesture to perform naturally means that Strindberg also wishes to see and hear Bosse take leave of eroticism in the same way, just as in the play *Kristina* from the same period, where the title role was also expressly written for his wife, Strindberg shows that he wishes her to renounce her ambitions. He makes Christina burn her crown, just as Indra's Daughter burns her shoes.

Eroticism does not, however, entirely vanish from Strindberg's life with the shoe-burning in *Ett drömspel*. Nor do shoes disappear from his works. The story *Taklagsöl*, which harks back to memories from a later period of his life with Harriet Bosse, ends with a man fleeing from an island where he is spending his summer holiday, having first thrown his wife's red slippers into a tree. The following summer the man returns, this time alone, only to see the slippers hanging obscenely in the tree-top: 'en flygande häxa med fötterna i vädret, tårna inåt; vinterns snö, regn och sol hade blekt dem, vridit dem vinda, fasliga att se på' ([it looked like] a witch in flight with her feet in the wind, her toes pointing inwards; the winter's snow, rain and sun had bleached them, twisted them, made them frightful to behold — SV 55, p.49). And having been burnt in *Ett drömspel* and thrown into the air in *Taklagsöl*, shoes now resurface in *Abu Casems tofflor* where the principal character attempts to get rid of them in the same way as Strindberg, firstly by throwing them into a lake, then by burying them, and finally by burning them.

The curtain rises on the oriental setting of a Baghdad bazaar. On the left is Casem's perfume boutique, on the right the shoemaker's.

Upstage is the entrance to the baths, in the centre a fountain. This looks like the simple setting for a fairy tale, but slightly more can be perceived if it is regarded in terms of Strindberg's erotic code. The shoemaker's is, of course, linked to sexuality, as is the perfume boutique. Casem sells rose oil, and roses and their scent play an important role in Strindberg's erotic associations. In his diary for 1908 until his first meeting with Fanny Falkner, roses often figure in connection with his telepathic relationship with Harriet Bosse: 'Hon söker mig nu med rosor i munnen, då jag står emot hennes eros' (Harriet seeks me now with roses in her mouth, when I resist her eros), he maintains on 13 June 1908, and there is a wealth of similar examples. Roses were the attribute of the steadfast cavalier in *Ett drömspel*, and it is clear from *Svanevit* that the rose, in contrast to the shoe, stands for an aesthetic and moral element in love which ennobles mankind: 'Rosen på bordet reser sig och öppnas. Styvmodrens och tärnornas ansikten belysas och få alla ett uttryck av skönhet, godhet och lycka' (The rose on the table rises and opens. The faces of the step-mother and the maidens are illuminated with an expression of beauty, goodness and joy — SS 36, p.157).

In scenic terms, therefore, the shoemaker's represents the low side of love and the perfume boutique its nobility. I do not intend to read a sexual meaning into every object on stage, but naturally it is impossible not to interpret the fountain as a phallic symbol and the entrance to the baths as a symbol of the female sexual organ.

On the surface, what happens in the play is that Caliph Harun tests the mean Abu Casem by placing his tattered slippers outside his shop. Casem takes the bait, picks up the slippers, and immediately becomes a laughing stock. Street urchins run after him shouting 'Casems tofflor! Kom och se' (Casem's slippers, come and see! — SS 51, p.112). Then the police chief appears and enters the baths, having taken off his slippers, as does Casem. The street urchins appear and kick away his slippers so that when Casem comes out of the baths, he sees only one pair of slippers, the police chief's, which he believes are a gift from his beautiful daughter, Suleika. Meanwhile Soliman, the shoemaker Hassan's son, returns after winning Casem's old slippers back from the street urchins. Casem is caught wearing the police chief's slippers and is led off stage. At the end of Act One, he realises that the slippers he has acquired only bring bad luck:

Fördömda gåva, olycksgåva, tofflor I, som bringat mig oskyldige betala böter; nu kastar jag er ut i floden.

(You damned slippers are an accursed gift, you caused me to be fined although I'm innocent; I'll throw you in the river — p.126)

He cannot, however, get rid of them that easily. Two fishermen appear, unseen by Casem, with ripped nets and the slippers. They throw the slippers into his shop. The sound of breaking glass is heard as Casem's bottles of rose oil shatter. As the scene demonstrates, shoes and roses do not mix, just as twenty-five years earlier, in *Herr Bengts hustru*, Strindberg had employed another dualism to illustrate the discrepancy between realism and idealism: roast veal and roses.

In Act Two we meet the Prince, who is pining with love for Suleika. Due to a misunderstanding, however, she entertains suspicions about the opposite sex. The character of love in this act is platonic, and its symbolism requires some comment, though not before I have outlined the remainder of the action of a play that is generally ignored by even the most informed of Strindberg's critics. In Act Three we encounter Suleika and her father Abu Casem, who still believes that his slippers are lying at the bottom of the lake. They discuss Suleika's distrust of men. The Caliph enters and in a conversation with young Soliman he speaks highly of the elevated side of love as represented by Suleika. The lovesick Prince also appears. Towards the end of the act an ominous note is introduced when the fountain ceases to flow, for the fountain is associated with the ability to love. Casem says: ' Vad är det här? Fontänen stannat! Har källan sinat, eller drives spel av andra makter som förbannat när du välsignad älskog slog ihjäl!' (What is this? The fountain has stopped! Has the source dried up, or is it driven by other powers that have cursed when you killed blessed love! — p.159). But he is at once presented with a more logical explanation: all the fountains in the town have run dry, and he believes that this is because his slippers have blocked a water pipe. (He is of course unaware that the fishermen have dragged them up.) The audience, on the other hand, is once again reminded of this at the end of the act when 'Apan synes ute på gatan med Casems tofflor' (The Monkey can be seen out in the street with Casem's slippers — p.160).

Act Four begins with Casem burying the slippers, which he seems to have got back from the Monkey. No sooner has he done this, however, than the Monkey appears, digs them up again, and puts a coin in their place, causing Casem to be accused of burying treasure on illegal ground in the final act. The act ends when the Monkey takes the slippers and leaves (p.168).

In the final act, Casem achieves redemption. We discover that his meanness stemmed from a desire to give his daughter a large dowry. He comes downstage and explains that he has now burnt the slippers: 'De äro brända ibland stadens sopor' (They are burnt amongst the refuse of the town — p.175). However, the Monkey reappears, this time on Casem's roof, from where he throws the slippers at the Nurse, though without hitting her. The Caliph gets his slippers back and the

Prince marries Suleika. Abu Casem's soul is set at rest and he arranges a feast for his daughter and her bridegroom. In the eyes of the audience, he has been transformed from a miserly slipper thief into a generous father. Thus the slippers can be seen as a symbol of the sexual urge, and what is characteristic for them in the play is the obstinacy with which they keep reappearing, despite several attempts to get rid of them in water, earth and fire: just as in *Ett drömspel*, Strindberg seems consciously to have worked here with elemental symbolism.[11] To draw a parallel with the present, it could be maintained that Strindberg's use of these recalcitrant objects anticipates something that becomes a convention in the drama of the absurd.

The important thing about the slippers is to a great extent the way in which they are linked to the Monkey. In the list of characters the Monkey is unambiguously described as an 'evil spirit', and Soliman declares in Act Five: 'apan är ej något djur, det är en djävul!' (the monkey's no animal, it's a devil! — p.172). In *En blå bok* it is easy to find evidence for Strindberg's dislike of monkeys. For example, in the article 'Tass eller hand' (Paw or Hand), they are called 'de sämsta av alla djur, bara gjorda av laster och brott' (the worst of all animals, consisting only of vices and crimes — SS 46, p.301). Strindberg's dislike of monkeys stems, of course, from his distrust of Darwinism. Or it may be the other way round: the thought that the monkey could be his ancestor makes him reject Darwinism. In the play, the Monkey is made to symbolize the animal side of man. Its interest in the slippers therefore appears entirely logical.

It has been argued that *Abu Casems tofflor* is about two kinds of love: the sublime, as represented by the Prince and Suleika, and the physical, as represented by the Monkey, and it is into the latter sphere that Abu Casem is drawn when he becomes interested in slippers instead of rose oil. And it is the Monkey who is the real schemer in the play: this is clear from a stage direction where the Vizier gets the fatal idea of placing his slippers outside Casem's shop: 'Apan synes här och spelar som om han ingav de andra tankarna' (The Monkey can be seen here acting as if he inspired the others' thoughts — p.107).

During the Prince's languishing soliloquy on love in Act Two, the Monkey is occasionally visible, but outside the window. In Act Three, set in Suleika's rooms, it is clearly present and turns off the tap to stop the water in the fountain. When the shoemaker Hassan enters, the Monkey hides and listens, grimacing. The shoemaker measures Suleika's feet, and an awareness of Strindberg's particular view of feet, his erotic code, is undoubtedly necessary for this scene to be meaningful:

Se här min fot, tag måttet nätt,
din marockin den ger sig ut i fukten —
Hassan kittlar henne under foten. . . . *Apan härmar Hassan; tar
mått på Ali, Slavinnan och slutligen på Hassan.*

(Here is my foot, measure it neatly,
your moccasin will be going out in the wet —
Hassan tickles the soles of her feet. . . . *The Monkey imitates
Hassan; measures Ali, the Slave Girl, and finally Hassan —*
p.150)

In the same act, Soliman comes upon the Monkey in a scene in which
the two kinds of love confront each other:

Apan härmar en kärlekssjuk.
SOLIMAN (*slår honom en örfil och sätter käringknep för honom*):
Respekt, din hund! Där mänskohjärtat talar,
där tige djuret!

The Monkey imitates a lovesick man.
SOLIMAN (*boxes him on the ear and trips him up*):
Respect, you dog! When the human heart speaks,
the animal remains silent! — p.156)

In Act Four, it is the Monkey that digs up the slippers and then
informs on Casem in sign language. Being a monkey he has to mime,
but we also know that Strindberg's key scenes in his post-Inferno
dramas (for example in *Till Damaskus, Ett drömspel, Dödsdansen,* and
Svarta handsken) are often dumb shows.

Strindberg has thus given the Monkey a substantial if silent role in
the play. It is clear from the original manuscript that this role became
increasingly important : on several occasions Strindberg enlarged the
Monkey's part, inserting additions in the margin.[12] The Monkey directs
people's destinies not as fate but as an evil power. It seems to embody
the lower side of man and largely acts in a world of instinct; it is hardly
evil in a metaphysical sense. It is clearly coupled in the play with
footwear, which in Strindberg's works is generally a symbol of
sexuality. On its final appearance, the Monkey is seated on the roof,
throwing the slippers at the Nurse:

VEZIREN: Se där, se apan, mördarn, och se tofflorna!
CASEM: O ve! Den olycksgåvan lever än?

(THE VIZIER: Look, there's the monkey, the murderer, and the
slippers!

CASEM: Alas! The gift of ill-omen lives on? — p.177)

The gift of ill-omen (the slippers, or sexuality) is regained at the end of the play by the Caliph, which is a prerequisite for its happy ending. One further passage may be quoted in support of the theory that shoes and slippers articulate the secret desires of the subconscious. In Act Two the Nurse comes to the Prince with a letter she claims has been written by Suleika. The Prince is not completely awake and associates freely around the object that he, half-asleep, sees, and which is in fact a large white letter with a red and green seal:

Vad ser jag nu i mörkret, vad?
En ruta vit som golvets marmor,
där liten fot i röda skor, nej gröna,
det är båd rött och grönt,
och det betyder kärlek, hopp!

(What is it I see in the darkness? A white square, like a marble floor, there a little foot in red shoes, no, green, both red and green, and that means love and hope! — p.131)

The Prince's first and slightly far-fetched association (if one is unaware of Strindberg's erotic code) is a pair of shoes. Before he finally recognizes the letter as a letter he has two further associations: 'en duk, en vit, nej, det är ingen duk . . . *Reser sig* . . . att torka tårar med, en svetteduk det är, att hölja likets anlet när som den döde dödens ångest har bestått — den är för mig, ty jag är visserligen död!' (A handkerchief, a white, no, it's not a handkerchief . . . *He gets up* . . . with which to dry tears, it's a shroud to cover a corpse's face when the agony of death remains, like the dead — it's for me, since I am surely dead! — p.132)

These associations are also interesting. Following the shoes, he sees things that recall the symbols of suffering in *Ett drömspel* and *Påsk*. Both Elis' winter coat in *Påsk* and the Concierge's shawl in *Ett drömspel* function as a shroud.[13] In a sketch for the staging of *Till Damaskus* in 1908, Strindberg expressly related the Lady's embroidery to Veronica's shroud.[14] This is one of the motifs that preoccupied him in the early years of the century, and is coupled with the idea of a '*satisfactio vicaria*'. In the dream sequence in *Abu Casems tofflor*, in which Strindberg probably gave his own associations free rein, the shoe is confronted with the shroud, love with sorrow, in images of great relevance, at least for Strindberg himself. The problem with this private symbolism is that it generally fails to find its way over the footlights. In other words, it is inaccessible to semiotic analysis, and requires some sort of psychological analysis.

195

In no other Strindberg play is footwear given such a clearly defined role as in *Abu Casems tofflor*; it is, after all, named in the title. Strindberg could afford to do this since he was able to maintain that the plot was borrowed from a given source, and had not risen spontaneously out of his own, inner self. It is in fact a case of a story which Strindberg had known for a long time. Amongst the books that he left behind in Sweden in 1883 was S.A. Hägg's *Fotbeklädnadens, skomakeriets och namnkunniga skomakares historia från äldsta till närvarande tid* (The History of Footwear, Shoemaking and Celebrated Shoemakers, Past and Present, 1873).[15] This lavishly illustrated history of shoes relates the story of Abu Casem from *A Thousand and One Nights*, as does a German grammar with which Strindberg was also familiar,[16] but in retelling it, he alters and adds to it. In the original version, Abu Casem owns the slippers from the beginning; the action does not have the character of a test, nor does he have to return the slippers to anyone. In the story, Abu Casem also twice throws the slippers into water. The first time, as in Strindberg's play, the fishermen emerge with their damaged nets, but the second time the slippers get stuck in a pipe, causing the town's water supply to be cut off. Strindberg only retains the latter, as something ominous and associated with the ability to love. The Monkey is almost totally Strindberg's invention. A dog makes a brief appearance in the story, dropping the slippers from a roof as does the Monkey in the play, but Strindberg not only changes the dog into a monkey, he also substantially increases its role while the story of Suleika, the Prince and Soliman is taken from other sources. Nevertheless, it is the history of a pair of slippers that inspires him to write this play about the way in which base, animal love is vanquished by sublime love.

The play was sent to the Royal Theatre on 8 September 1908. The theatre took time replying so on the 16th Strindberg promised it to August Falck and the Intimate Theatre if the Royal Theatre would release it, which eventually they did. Towards the end of the month he showered Falck with letters, which indicated his eagerness to get the play staged. He told Falck that he had purchased some expensive oriental fabrics and wished to be present at its casting, and recommended several shops in Stockholm, such as the Oriental Shop and the Indian Bazaar, for the purchase of properties.

It is clear from Falck's account that opinions differed as to the play's quality: 'Jag tyckte aldrig att Abu Casems tofflor var lämplig för Intiman. Trots Strindbergs olika uppsättningsförslag var den svår att sätta i scen; var gång jag kom med en invändning gjorde han ivrigt ett nytt förslag, men när jag till slut i svaga ögonblick var på väg att ge med mig, var det han som ångrade sig' (I never thought that *Abu Casems tofflor* was suitable for the Intimate Theatre. Despite Strindberg's various suggestions about staging, it was difficult to put on;

every time I made an objection, he eagerly made a new proposal, but when I finally weakened and was on the point of giving in, it was he who had misgivings).[18] But Strindberg was also in two minds about the play. 'Lägg undan Casem! Jag är rädd för den!' (Put Casem aside! I'm afraid of it), he wrote, on 4 January 1909 while after rereading it he observed, on the 17th : 'Då jag läste Casem om i kväll, fann jag ingen sak mot den!' (When I reread Casem this evening, I could find nothing against it). The play was never performed at the Intimate Theatre. The fact that Falck regarded it coolly and that Strindberg was in two minds was a poor starting point for a successful production, though towards the end of 1909, Strindberg did renew his efforts, though again to no avail. In any case, by then Karin Swanström had given the play its Swedish première at Gävle, on 28 December 1908.[19] It toured the country under her direction and earned its author 2,000 kronor, which he spent (if Falck may be believed) on a new decor for Blå Tornet.[20] The oriental adventure was over.

But as with all stories, we are bound to ask: 'What happened next?' Are shoes finished with in Strindberg's works? The answer is that they surface one last time, but with a new function, in *Svarta handsken*. Strindberg initially gave this play the appropriate subtitle 'Lyrisk fantasi (för scenen)' (Lyrical Fantasy (for the stage) — SS 45, p.281) but then made it Opus 5 of the Chamber Plays, where it certainly does not belong. *Oväder, Brända tomten, Spöksonaten* and *Pelikanen* form a single unit due to their having been written in rapid succession. They also have a deeply misanthropic tone in common: this begins as melancholy in *Oväder* and ascends to a crescendo of total pessimism in *Pelikanen. Svarta handsken*, however, is more a morality play, ending happily on Christmas Eve itself, with a 'Tomte' blowing kisses to the mother and child. The first four plays were published in one volume in 1907 by Ljus. *Svarta handsken* was written a year and a half later, by which time Strindberg had written several other plays of a different nature, like *Bjälbojarlen* and *Siste riddaren*. He also undertook in his contract with Ljus to let them have the rights to any new chamber plays, and received an advance of 1,000 kronor.[21] It seems, therefore, that Strindberg's rechristening of his lyrical fantasy as Opus 5 was largely a result of his already having spent the advance. Both textual and factual criteria show that the play should not be counted one of the chamber plays. Strindberg's relationship to genres is complex and fascinating.

However designated, *Svarta handsken* is a play about redemption. It demonstrates that, in Strindberg's eyes, redemption can only occur once a woman has ceased to be a wife and lover and become solely a mother and/or daughter. Similarly, the woman must be brought to submission, and this can only happen once she has experienced loss. Perhaps Strindberg's grandest portrayal of this motif is to be found in

197

the poem 'Chrysaëtos' (1902), which describes how a man loses his mind at the sight of his wife's coat in a cloakroom. A pair of galosches also figures in a draft of the poem.[22] This draft could, however, do equally well for *Svarta handsken* in which both items, coat and galosches, are to be found. The great difference is that in the play it is no longer a woman's garment but a little girl's. Strindberg has resolutely placed the woman in the man's role of the bereaved. She expresses her loss in the short second act in a long soliloquy but is otherwise silent in the presence of the lost child's garment; 'faller ner på knä vid stolen, och döljer ansiktet i den lilla barnkappan som hon smeker och kramar' (She falls to her knees by the chair and hides her face in the little child's coat which she caresses and embraces — p.298). She also touches the child's galosches. Here, Strindberg gives the woman a taste of her own medicine. At the same time the old curator is sitting in an attic surrounded by mementos of his wedding. Strindberg himself preserved similar mementos.[23] What is happening here, if we compare it with his previous plays, is that clothes have ceased to be the objects of fetishism and become souvenirs. At this point, in Strindberg's penultimate play, the atmosphere becomes less dramatic and the tone more elegiac.

The theme of redemption can only resound fully once the woman has been given a new role, and it emerges as wholly appropriate that the woman in this play is the Curator's daughter. She is punished like a child. The Curator and the 'Tomte' act firstly as punishers, and then as forgiving fates. The demonic Monkey in *Abu Casems tofflor* has been replaced by kind old men. The function of shoes and other garments has been reworked, and their demonic power is past.

After completing both these plays, Strindberg proposed to Fanny Falkner in September 1909. The engagement was short-lived and the nature of their relationship remains mysterious. Fanny Falkner herself was most mystified by his strange engagement present. Strindberg gave her, to her great surprise, a pair of coarse, brown-striped sports socks, which he wished her to wear so that she would not freeze.

Notes

1. See for instance Martin Lamm, *Strindbergs dramer*, II (Stockholm, 1926), p.422, and Sven Rinman, 'August Strindberg', in *Ny illustrerad svensk litteraturhistoria*, IV (Stockholm, 1967), pp.136-137.
2. Gunnar Brandell, *Strindberg — ett författarliv*, IV (Stockholm, 1989), p.360.
3. He had completed it by 7 September. See Gunnar Ollén, *Strindbergs dramatik* (Stockholm, 1982), p.564.
4. Fanny Falkner, *August Strindberg i Blå Tornet* (Stockholm, 1921), p.9.

5. Brandell, *Strindberg — ett författarliv*, IV, p.144.
6. See August Strindberg, *Klostret*, ed. C.G. Bjurström (Stockholm, 1966), pp.39-42, and Frida Strindberg, *Strindberg och hans andra hustru*, I (Stockholm, 1933), p.117.
7. See the poem 'Segling' in *Dikter*, SS 13, p.107.
8. Fanny Falkner, *Strindberg in Blå Tornet*, p.101.
9. Hans-Göran Ekman, 'Strindberg's Use of Costume in *Carl XII* and *Christina*', manuscript. See also *Klädernas magi. En Strindbergsstudie* (Stockholm, 1991).
10. Axel Johan Uppvall, *August Strindberg. A Psychoanalytic Study with Special Reference to the Oedipus Complex* (Boston, 1920), pp.71-72.
11. See Sven Delblanc, 'Ett drömspel', in *Stormhatten. Tre Strindbergsstudier* (Stockholm, 1979), pp.63-109.
12. Manuscript of *Abu Casems tofflor*, in Kungliga Biblioteket, Stockholm, pp.4, 38, 40, 74.
13. SS 33, p.39. Cf. Göran Stockenström, *Ismael i öknen. Strindberg som mystiker*, Acta Universitatis Upsaliensis: Historia Litterarum 5, (Uppsala, 1972) p.532, n.109.
14. In a letter to August Falck, 26 September 1909. Kungliga Biblioteket, T 36:8.
15. See Hans Lindström, *Strindberg och böckerna*, Skrifter utgivna av Svenska litteratursällskapet 36 (Uppsala, 1977), p.34.
16. See Gunnar Ollén's introduction to his edition of the play in Samlade Verk, forthcoming. Ollén points out that Strindberg's library contained both the German grammar, J.E. Lyth, *Tysk språklära*, 3rd ed, and an edition of *A Thousand and One Nights*.
17. Extracts from the letters are in August Falck, *Fem år med Strindberg* (Stockholm, 1935), pp.187-189.
18. Falck, *Fem år med Strindberg*, p.185.
19. Ollén, *Strindbergs dramatik*, p.565.
20. Falck, *Fem år med Strindberg*, p.187.
21. See Johan Svedjedal, 'Henrik Koppel, Ljus förlag och enkronasböckerna', *Samlaren*, 1988, pp.21-22.
22. Kungliga Biblioteket, SgNM 8:9, 17.
23. See Strindberg's letter to Harriet Bosse, 3 May 1908, XVI, p.289ff.

Strindberg's History Plays

Some Reflections

Margareta Wirmark

Lund University

At the turn of the year 1898-9 Strindberg entered upon an intense period of dramatic writing. 'Jag har nu lagt undan allt annat och ägnar mig uteslutande åt teaterförfatteri' (I have now put everything else aside and am devoting myself entirely to writing for the theatre — XIII, p.59) he wrote, in a letter dated 26 December 1898. In January 1899 he was to celebrate his fiftieth birthday, which may have been one of the reasons for this new start. In the letter Strindberg refers to his youthful masterpiece *Mäster Olof*, which was to be revived for the occasion.[1] The time has come to present Sweden with a dramatic art worthy of the name, Strindberg proclaims, and his intention is to fulfil the promise of his youth, at the same time recreating Swedish dramatic art.

The grandness of Strindberg's plans can be traced from his drafts. One of them, which Claes Rosenqvist dates to summer 1898, lists both written and unwritten dramas: 'Folkunga-Sagan, Mäster Olof, Gustav Vasa, Erik XIV, Karl IX, Gustaf Adolf, Kristina, Karl XI, Karl XII, Friedrich, Gustaf III' (The Saga of the Folkungs, Master Olof, Gustav Vasa, Erik XIV, Charles IX, Gustav Adolf, Queen Christina, Charles XI, Charles XII, Friedrich, Gustav III).[2]

The title of this draft is 'Svenska Historiska Dramer' (Swedish Historical Plays). Strindberg thus identifies the history play as a category of its own, a tradition which has been upheld by scholars from Martin Lamm onwards. We must ask whether this tradition is a useful one. Does it in fact increase our ability to discern and describe what is unique to Strindbergian drama? It is a question to which I shall return in due course.

Walter Johnson's *Strindberg and the Historical Drama* is the most thorough study of this genre. The dramas treated, twenty-one in all, are those that deal with historical figures, usually a king. Johnson tries to distil what is common to this group and finds in all of them a drive towards cosmic order and a struggle for power. He also notes their 'remarkable variety of plots and the variety in the characterizations'.[3]

At first sight Johnson's study seems adequate. But he has neglected one thing: he does not prove that his characteristics are unique to the historical plays. The possibility remains that the same characteristics may, in the same combination, appear in all of Strindberg's dramas.

It is hard to find an acceptable criterion for the history play if the simple fact of its dealing with historical figures proves unsatisfactory. Yet it is even harder to discern the borderline with other types of drama. We may then abstain from a precise definition, and accept this common denominator, that a historical drama deals with a historical person, in order to continue to use the term. This is what I intend to do in what follows.

Most of Strindberg's history plays, including the best ones, were written around the turn of the century. He consciously set out to write history plays, and proclaimed himself the reviver of the genre before he had even started. It was a remarkable venture: he set out to dramatize nothing less than the whole of Swedish history. Today we know that he succeeded. He portrayed the kings in chronological order, covering five hundred years of Swedish history in only three, and devoting one drama apiece to seven kings and one popular hero. As Johnson remarks, only Sweden and Great Britain possess such a treasury of history plays.

When Strindberg embarked upon this scheme, he began with the Middle Ages and the Reformation, epochs he was familiar with from his earlier plays *Mäster Olof, Gillets hemlighet,* and *Herr Bengts hustru.* He followed the order of his draft and completed four plays in one year: *Folkungasagan, Gustav Vasa, Erik XIV,* and *Gustav Adolf.* Three of them were accepted at once by the theatre and *Gustav Vasa* especially was warmly received by the critics as well as the public.[4]

Strindberg then took a pause in writing history plays and switched to dramas with contemporary subjects. But a year later, in summer 1901, he began again. This time he completed a further four plays: *Carl XII, Engelbrekt, Kristina,* and *Gustav III.* But he no longer follows his original plan all that strictly. He jumps over some of the kings and alters the order: after *Carl XII,* for example, he returns to the fifteenth century and writes about Engelbrekt. Nor does he devote himself exclusively to the history play: *Ett drömspel* is written parallel with *Kristina* .

This second quartet of history plays was received quite differently. Some of them were refused, and those which were produced were not very successful. *Kristina* was considered unhistorical, even provocative, and was not performed at all. *Engelbrekt* was withdrawn after only two performances, and *Carl XII* was staged, but met with no success.[5]

In fact these two quartets of history plays, written in 1899 and 1901 respectively, have very little in common. As far as form and dramaturgy is concerned, the first group belongs to the nineteenth century. Strindberg follows the traditional method of constructing a drama. He employs the Freytag model, and it is easy to trace the dramatic curve, from exposition to climax and the denouement. The plot is easy to follow. The drama is based on a selection and concentration of events that cover several years in historical time and the regal protagonist, who is portrayed as powerful and treated as a positive hero even if tyrannical, meets with affliction in the course of the drama and is transformed into a better man. There is no doubt that the king is the centre and the subject of the drama.

The second quartet, written at the dawn of the new century, deviates in almost every aspect from this pattern. It is true that the Freytag model is also used here, but only its last stage. Strindberg focuses on the final period of each reign. *Kristina* deals with her abdication; *Gustav III* centres upon a plot to assassinate the king; and in *Carl XII* the king dies at Fredrikshald. Christina, Gustav III and Charles XII are all engaged in a war, but none of them is seen fighting. Their power is seldom stressed; they do not always know what decision they should reach, and it is hard to tell if the monarch is the subject of the play.

In Strindberg's later historical plays war is already lost and the defeated return to their native country. Both *Carl XII* and *Gustav III* begin with the king re-entering Swedish territory, to be tried by his people and have sentence passed upon him. Several of the plays deal with the king's death, which is never ordinary, though in the case of Gustav III the actual assassination is only anticipated and not portrayed while in *Kristina* another woman becomes a surrogate, stabbed in the street because she resembles the Queen.

Reference to specific historical events is rare in Strindberg's history plays. Sometimes the month or the day of the week may be mentioned, but never the precise year. The spectator has to determine for himself the exact period in which the play is set. In act four of *Gustav III* we learn that the Bastille has just fallen; every spectator familiar with history can deduce from this that the drama takes place in late summer 1789. From the stage directions we see that *Carl XII* begins in December 1715, but the information is never given in the dialogue. The spectator is ignorant of the exact date. There is only one reference to time: we are told that the last scene at Fredrikshald takes place on the first Sunday in Advent.

If one limits oneself to the information afforded by the dialogue, Strindberg's history plays are difficult if not impossible to date. In his *Öppna brev till Intima teatern* he states that this is intentional, and maintains that every dramatist is free to set historical chronology aside. His task is not to teach the audience history, nor is he obliged to give correct information: 'Den som fordrar den kronologiska ordningens iakttagande vid händelsers hopfogande i ett historiskt drama, den har ingen aning om ett drama och borde icke få yttra sig med anspråk på att bli hörd' (Anyone who insists on chronological order in the construction of a historical drama knows nothing whatsoever about drama, and should not be permitted to express himself with any claim to being heard — SS 50, p.248).

In *Gustav Vasa* different events covering between five and ten years are compressed into only five days. Gustav Vasa reigned for almost forty years, from 1523 to 1560. Strindberg selects the years 1542-43 for his drama, the years of Nils Dacke's rebellion in Småland. However, no one in the play mentions the precise year. To locate it, the spectator has to apply his own knowledge of history. Anyone who fails to do so will nevertheless understand the action. In the *Öppna brev till Intima teatern* Strindberg explains why he chose to depict Gustav Vasa at a time when his power was placed in question: 'Denna förtvivlans tid ger bäst tillfälle skildra den stora människan Gustav Vasa med alla hans mänskliga svagheter' (That time of despair affords the best opportunity of depicting the great human being Gustav Vasa in all his human weakness — SS 50, p.247).

But Strindberg is not content to describe only the Dacke rebellion. He also adds some further events which cannot be so easily placed at a particular time. The king is not only shown in conflict with his people, he also quarrels with his son, the future Erik XIV. This conflict between father and son no doubt covered several years but Strindberg abbreviates it to cover the same period as the Dacke rebellion. Furthermore, Vasa is not the only father in the play who is portrayed as fighting against his son; Strindberg augments it with the parallel action of the Hanseatic councillor Herman Israel, who is likewise in conflict with his son, Jacob, thus refining upon the material provided by history in a dramatically effective way.

Despite his afflictions, however, Gustav Vasa is depicted as a strong ruler. His absence from the stage during the first half of the play does not prevent the audience sensing his power, and when he finally appears, carrying Tor's hammer, his resemblance to a god is underlined. *Carl XII*, on the other hand, which may be described as a vacuum, an endless waiting, depicts a monarch who is devoid of Vasa's strength and power. The king's death is anticipated by everyone in the play, but is continually deferred, though he is perceived from the start as a loser.

This is underlined by the setting, which conveys everything to the spectator from the outset. The play opens with 'The Man' (at once a late Adam and a parallel to the king) returned from the war and strolling amidst the debris of his past. What remains of the Eden of his youth is a ghastly place from which all life has departed. His wife and children have succumbed to the plague and the apple tree of life in his ravaged garden bears a single, rotten apple. This use of setting differs from Strindberg's practice in *Gustav Vasa*. Here, everything has to be interpreted as a symbol. Sweden is a tree bereft of all its leaves, the king a rotten apple which refuses to fall.

Throughout the play the king is described with the help of negations. Not only is he a decayed fruit: he is also surrounded by darkness, stillness and silence. He moves little, preferring to remain in bed, and says nothing at all for two acts. Indeed, he is offstage for half a play which contains little specific information about history but much about the terms of human life. It is an existential drama in which man is seen as suffering from guilt but unable to find a solution to his dilemmas.

Carl XII ends with the king's death at Fredrikshald, but Strindberg leaves even this unresolved in the spectator's mind, since no one is able to tell from where the bullet has come, whether from the Norwegians in the fortress that Charles is besieging or 'from above', from God himself. Strindberg leaves the question unanswered, or rather he ends with two evenly weighted and contrasting answers.

However, immediately following the King's death he appends an additional ending: 'Allt upplöses. MANNEN OCH MISSNÖJD kasta sig över Görtz och släpa ut honom. Alla rusa ut i villervalla; lägereldarne slockna; facklor och lyktor bäras ut. Det blir mörkt på scenen' (Everything dissolves. The Man and Malcontent throw themselves upon Görtz and drag him out. Everyone rushes out in chaos, the campfires go out, torches and lanterns are carried out. Darkness falls on the stage — SS 35, p.223).

Thus, *Carl XII* has *two* endings. First, the king is shot down. Then follows an ending in which the dramatic fiction dissolves bit by bit. First of all the actors rush out in chaos, then the lights are extinguished and the stage remains in darkness ('Det blir mörkt på scenen'). At this point, all the instruments of the stage have stopped working.

But Strindberg is not content with this double ending. After a moment of silence a new light is activated. A lantern shines brightly at the same spot where the king was just now shot down. Strindberg's drama is an open one; he leaves the interpretation of this final sign to the spectator.

Gustav Vasa and *Carl XII* were written at almost the same time and they both belong to the same genre. But the two dramas have very little in common: in almost every respect they are the antithesis of each other. In the one people are seated on wooden benches in farms and wine-cellars, in the other The Man stands alone on the seashore, surrounded by darkness and cold. In one the king kills everyone who dares oppose his will, in the other for most of the time the king seems to be asleep. Gustav Vasa changes during his various struggles and learns something about himself whereas Charles XII is never seen fighting against anyone, and he does not change. The one is a hero, the other an antihero.

Is it reasonable to assign two so different dramas to the same genre? We may of course continue to do so if we remember that the term 'history play' is a vague one. One way of being more strict would be to make use of a double classification, to add another term, perhaps just as vague, to the first one. *Gustav Vasa* might be characterized as a historical play (HP) which is also a conflict drama (CD), *Carl XII* is a historical play which is also a modern drama (MD).

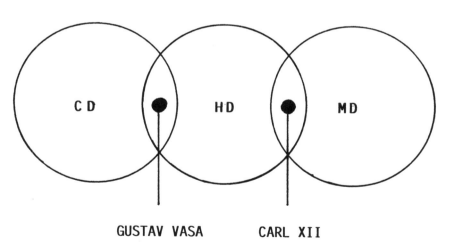

Although not very impressive, this way of classifying these dramas seems to me for the time being the best solution. To describe each drama more adequately, however, we require a new terminology. In order to trace the transformation of the logical drama of the last century into a modern one, we need to invent new tools. No such language is as yet available, and we have to stick to the old-fashioned way of characterizing plays, even though it is now some ninety years since Strindberg's experiments in dramatic form, when he used every possible genre, including the history play, as a melting pot for his explorations.

Not surprisingly, the portrait of the king in *Carl XII* met with little understanding from Strindberg's contemporaries. As a king he appeared odd and bizarre whereas Gustav Vasa was probably easier to comprehend because he accords with conventional notions of a king, being strong and powerful. Today our judgement differs. To us Gustav Vasa stands out as odd and rather bizarre while Charles XII is easier to comprehend. In many respects he can be interpreted as a symbol of Man, an Everyman from our own century. He is our contemporary, the ancestor of Beckett's Vladimir and Estragon in *Waiting for Godot*, for — though written in 1901 — it is evident that Strindberg's history play has much in common with the drama of the absurd.[6]

Notes

1. Svenska teatern performed *Mäster Olof* from 22 to 30 January 1899. See Gunnar Ollén, *Strindbergs dramatik*, 4th ed. (Stockholm, 1982), p.43.
2. Claes Rosenqvist, *Hem till historien. Strindberg, sekelskiftet och 'Gusaf Adolf'* (Umeå, 1984), p.15.
3. Walter Johnson, *Strindberg and the Historical Drama* (Seattle, 1963), p.286.
4. See Ollén, pp.292, 302, 315.
5. Ollén, pp.423, 411.
6. See Margareta Wirmark, '''Skaffa mig en spindel att leka med!'' Strindbergs drama *Carl XII* som förabsurdistisk text', *Strindbergiana* VI (1991), pp.61-94.

III

The Non-Dramatic Works

Genre and Aesthetics in Strindberg's 'Sårfeber' Poems

James Spens

Stockholm University

When Strindberg turned to writing satirical verse in the early 1880s, it was a hazardous enterprise. The literary climate in Sweden was dominated by the academic establishment, particularly that of Uppsala, stronghold of the idealistic and basically conservative philosophy of Christopher Jacob Boström.[1] Meanwhile, through his position as secretary of the Swedish Academy and as critic in the official government controlled newspaper *Post- och inrikes tidningar* ('Posttidningen'), Carl David af Wirsén, himself a devoted follower of the Boströmian tradition, controlled much of the literary scene. This was particularly the case where the 'high genres' of the time, historical drama and lyric poetry, were concerned. Wirsén was of course a lyric poet himself, and a friend of Oscar II, who likewise wrote idealistic poems à la Boström.

Furthermore, the genre of satirical verse had long since sunk into oblivion in Sweden; nothing important had been written in the field since the days of Johan Henrik Kellgren (1751-95) and Anna Maria Lenngren (1754-1817). Imitators of Byron and (particularly) Heine had been numerous, but also generally harmless.[2] The poet of the period was expected to be amiable, writing idyllic poems about flowers, sparrows and brooks rather than social criticism and denunciations of his opponents. The reception of Strindberg's *Dikter på vers och prosa* was scathing, and certainly no better than that of the prose satires *Det nya riket* the previous year.[3] The verse was considered coarse and vulgar, and his allusions to identifiable figures beyond all decency, while there was a general feeling that his obsession with his own person and private sufferings was impudent. The fact that the book was more favourably received in the radical press does not change this general picture. As Per Erik Ekholm has pointed out, *Dikter på vers och prosa* established the negative opinion of Strindberg, which the prosecution of *Giftas* in 1884 only confirmed.[4] As a genre, lyric poetry evidently had no place for a satirist of Strindberg's kind and temperament.[5]

Reviews represent one way of reconstructing the expectation which readers held about genre during the period. Another is to study contemporary aesthetics. Most influential among the aesthetic philosophers in the tradition of Romantic idealism was perhaps the German disciple of Hegel, Friedrich Theodor Vischer. He is accorded a prominent place in Gustaf Ljunggren's survey *Framställning af de förnämsta Esthetiska Systemerna* (Account of the Principal Aesthetic Systems) which Strindberg had to study in Uppsala.[6] As he points out himself in *Jäsningstiden* (Time of Ferment), Georg Brandes' *Kritiker og Portraiter* (Critiques and Portraits, 1870) meant the first serious attack on this kind of aesthetic idealism, which continued to dominate the Swedish literary scene until the early 1880s (SV 20, p.287).

In fact, besides illustrating the kind of aesthetics that Strindberg so bitterly polemicizes against in the 'Sårfeber' (Wound Fever) section of *Dikter på vers och prosa*, Vischer's account of satirical poetry may throw some light on the character of these poems. Vischer treats satirical poetry as an appendage to the theory of poetry proper. Satirical poetry, he writes, shows 'bitter indignation at the perversity of reality'. This perverted reality is then measured by the standard of the ideal 'to make visible its wretchedness'. Vischer also discriminates between two different kinds of satire, one negative or indirect, the other positive or direct. The indirect type makes no statements about how the world should actually be, but allows the objects it describes to articulate its contradictions and deformity. The direct type, on the other hand, attacks reality openly and explicitly by opposing it to the ideal.[7]

Ideal, reality, and indignation are consequently the three basic elements in Vischer's definition of a satirical poem. He would undoubtedly have had some difficulty in fitting Strindberg's 'Sårfeber' poems into his categories. As we have seen, he placed satire outside true poetry, the reason being that it is predominantly mimetic rather than a product of the imagination.[8] Strindberg's tremendous subjectivity and intensity of feeling, however, frequently gives these poems a distinctly lyrical quality, as Gustaf Fröding originally pointed out in his early essay in *En bok om Strindberg*.[9]

The subjective and lyrical elements in the 'Sårfeber' satires can be studied in 'Idealistkritik' (Idealist Criticism, SS 13, pp.69-71). The speaking subject of this poem is a writer who has been accused (we are not informed by whom) of a proclivity for ugliness and dirt, but who has at last written something really beautiful: 'vad vackrast livet har/sitt hjärteblod han giver/det bästa han har kvar' (to the most beautiful there is in life, he gives his heart-blood, the best he has left). However, a man who likes to call himself an idealist writes a cheap parody of this text together with some of his relationships, which leads the speaking subject to conclude that the next time he writes a beautiful idyll, he will protect it from attack by covering it with tulle and sprinkling fly-poison around it.

Here the writer provides no arguments, there are no explicit references to an outer reality, and the theme of the poem seems to be the subject's own hatred, expressed by invectives such as 'tunna hjärna' (diluted brain), 'förfallna suddar' (decayed debauchees), and 'ditt fä' (you beast). But what particularly distinguishes this aggress-iveness is the use of metaphor: the satire's principal author is trans-formed into a human-like fly, equipped with teeth which it is ordered to scrub, not brush, in a bidet (in fact the bidet of the muses). The fly-poison in the concluding lines of the poem suggests an actual killing of the fly, i.e. the author of the displeasing parody, a motif to which I shall return shortly.

Like many of the 'Sårfeber' poems, this satire is directed at the idealists (roughly speaking, the adherents of Boström's philosophy and Vischer's aesthetics). That it was also aimed at Karl Wetterhoff, a dramaturg at Nya teatern who had co-authored a parody of *Herr Bengts hustru* entitled 'Hustru Bengtsson' (Wife Bengtsson),[10] cannot have been apparent to many readers. But its main concern is the unjust treatment meted out to the author, and it is the various expressions of aggression and hate that hold the poem together. In Vischer's terms one could say that the indignation of the speaking subject grows so strong that the bounds of satire are transgressed.

From a metrical point of view, 'Idealistkritik', like most of the 'Sårfeber' poems, consists mainly of iambs. Historically and generi-cally, this links it with the ancient subgenre of the lampoon, especially the epode, with its partly iambic metrical feet and regularly varying long and short lines. A comparison with Archilochus' fragment about a shipwrecked man, the so-called 'Strasbourg Epode',[11] shows that both texts deviate from pure lampoon by giving reasons for their attacks. Just as Strindberg justifies his attack on the grounds of the unfair parody, so Archilochus motivates his cruel vision of an enemy suffering from cold on the seashore after having been shipwrecked with the fact that this man has broken his oath (which is of course also a crime against the gods). There is, however, a difference: Strindberg indirectly attacks a whole group of people, and this attack is part of the continuing aesthetic battle between realists and idealists, which leads to a much wider political and ideological struggle that is explicitly referred to in other poems from the 'Sårfeber' section, e.g. 'Lokes smädelser' (Loke's Blasphemies), 'Folkupplagan' (The Popular Edition) and 'Min jubelfest' (My Anniversary Celebration).[12]

Strindberg repeatedly extends this ancient motif from the lampoon, of a hated person in pain, with their transformation into an animal, which is then put to death. As we have seen, in 'Idealistkritik' the enemy is reduced to an insect, whose end is implicitly accomplished by means of fly poison. In 'Taga rävar' (Catching Foxes) his death is explicit: after having been transformed into a fox, he is caught and poisoned with strychnine in a trap which has been set by the narrator. In 'Den underliga skogen' (The Strange Forest) a fox is killed with a gun. In both cases scholars have suggested that the foxhunt is allegorical, and that Strindberg was actually aiming at Wilhelm Bergstrand, a *littérateur* who had attacked him, under the assumed name of *Michel Perrin*, in a 'svinaktig brochyr' (filthy pamphlet — III, p. 125) upon the publication of *Det nya riket*.[13]

The satirical convention of transforming an enemy into an animal can also be observed in Thomas Thorild's 'Fragment af 1783 års vitterhet' (Fragment of the Literature of the Year 1783), the so-called 'Straffsången' (Song of Punishment),[14] where Thorild directs a furious attack upon Kellgren, who is transformed into a dog and referred to as 'skällare', 'Postens bäste koppel-hund', and 'vitterhetens racka' (barker, the Post's best leash hound, and wit's mongrel) respectively. Thorild's poem was related to a classical satirical tradition, as is shown by the quotation from one of Horace's epodes which he takes for an epigraph: 'Quid immerentes vexas, canis?' (roughly: Why, dog, do you bark at harmless people?). The invectives in Thorild's poem are mostly drawn from the animal world: 'toad', 'chickenbrain', 'ape', 'creepy thing', etc. The general tone of the poem, with its frequent use of imperatives, is also similar to Strindberg's; compare, for example, Thorild's phrase 'Hut! vitterhetens racka; hut!' (None of your sauce! wit's mongrel; none of your sauce!) with Strindberg's 'Gå! skura dina tänder, förrän du bits, ditt fä!' (Disappear! scrub your teeth, before you bite, you beast!). It is reasonable to assume that Strindberg received a direct impulse from Thorild's poem; an extract from the gruesome Song of Punishment is quoted in Arvid Ahnfelt's *Verldslitteraturens historia*, which also seems to have provided him with some other material for the 'Sårfeber' section.[15]

Though personal, there is always a connection in the 'Sårfeber' poems between an attack on a particular individual and the state of affairs that Strindberg wishes to criticize. The attack is aimed simultaneously at the person and the matter in question, the two being in Strindberg's opinion often so hopelessly confused and intertwined that they cannot be separated, as is stressed in the poem 'Person och sak' (Person and Matter):

Jag kunde icke skilja åt
person och sak; det vet nu hela världen,

det är nu så; det var en fåt,
om ock för mycket I begärden,
som gjort personlig varje sak,
som blandat samman Ert och allas
att ej man vet vad fram och bak
egentligen skall kunna kallas.

(I couldn't keep person and matter apart; now everyone knows
that's how it is; it was a mistake even though you were asking
too much, making every matter personal, and then mixing
together your own business with everybody else's, so one can't
tell what's to be called front and what behind — SS 13, p.51)

Strindberg consequently admits having done wrong when attacking
individuals, but reverses the guilt so that it falls upon his enemy, who
has made 'every matter personal'. This apologetical theme is introduced for the first time in the foreword, where Strindberg implies that
he is only counterattacking, and further developed in the 'wound fever'
metaphor, which culminates in the following stanzas from 'Biografiskt'
(Biographically):

När feber honom griper
och yrselns dämon går
med bolmört kring hans kudde
det rister i hans sår!

Då hörs den sjuke sjunga
med hes och bruten röst,
på gamla melodier
som korp i kulen höst.

Om sina sår han yrar,
om sina nederlag,
men ock han höres mana
sin trupp till nya slag.

(When fever catches him and the demon of delirium paces with
henbane around his cushion, his wounds chafe! Then the invalid
is heard singing old melodies in a hoarse and broken voice, like
a raven in bleak autumn. He raves about his wounds, about his
defeats, but is also heard calling upon his troops to new battles
— SS 13, p.18)

This combination of apologetical theme with autobiography, which
characterizes 'Biografiskt', also connects Strindberg's poem with the

classical tradition, where Horace's Satire II.i became so influential that it gave rise to a whole subgenre.[16]

But to return briefly to Vischer's description of satirical poetry. As we have seen, according to Vischer satire criticizes reality from the standpoint of the ideal, either implicitly or explicitly, and in so doing expresses indignation. 'Idealistkritik' was permeated with subjective feeling in such a way that the dividing line between satirical and lyrical poetry was transgressed. However, with the 'Sårfeber' section there are also satires where the balance is very different. Perhaps the best example of a more intellectual, argumentative, ironical kind of satire, a satire of thought rather than feeling, is 'För tankens frihet' (For Freedom of Thought, SS 13, pp.74-87), the major cycle in seven parts that terminates the section. The main theme of this poem may be called 'den offentliga lögnen', or official hypocrisy, and specifically aimed at the recent 250th anniversary of Gustavus Adolphus' death at Lützen. It is interesting to note that Strindberg links 'För tankens frihet' with the genre of occasional poetry by inserting the date of the anniversary immediately below the title. This emphasizes its relationship with the flood of panegyrical poems that appeared in the press and in various anthologies. A particularly interesting contribution to this subgenre of versified homages to the king that appeared during 1882 was Albert Ulrik Bååth's 'STÅT, Epilog till Gustaf Adolfsfesten den 6 November 1882' (POMP, Epilogue to the Gustavus Adophus Festivities, etc). Like Strindberg, Bååth satirizes their pomposity. But the crucial difference is that Bååth regards the king as a great example, whereas Strindberg questions his achievement.[17]

The theme of the anniversary is 'freedom of thought'. But the celebrations have turned into a gala performance characterized by gormandizing, empty rhetoric, and noise. The poem has a logical argument, and makes at least four points: 1. that at this anniversary it is not permitted to question the thesis that the king was an advocate of free thinking, which is in itself a violation of this principle; 2. that the king did not fight for religious freedom, but was on the contrary determined to combat Catholicism; 3. that this enterprise was a complete failure, both morally and ideologically (or as Strindberg puts it: 'Så gick man på med hugg och skott/och klådde katoliker utan ända./Katolska saken stod sig gott/men katolikerna de blevo brända' (And so on they went stabbing and shooting, beating Catholics without end. The Catholic cause survived intact, but the Catholics, they were burnt — SS 13, p.86); 4. the king cannot be regarded as a martyr; he received all the honour he could ask for in life as in death, but the real martyrs must suffer without being honoured.

The discourse of these statements is basically ironic. The repetition of the key phrase 'en fest för den fria tanken' (a festivity for the freedom of thought) may be taken as an example. It is repeated at the end of each of the first four stanzas, each time more imbued with ironical meaning as a result of the satirical text in between. With its many specific references and its logical argument, this would not be a poem by Strindberg if it was not also largely subjective, something that influences its structure and raises generical problems. The events of the first six parts are related by an omniscient and anonymous author, who moves from place to place, reading the minds of his characters, such as the newspaper reporter and the verger in the Catholic chapel. The seventh and last part, however, has the form of a lyrical monologue like most of the 'Sårfeber' satires, and a lyrical 'I' suddenly appears in the text. This fact has led Olof Lagercrantz and others to identify the man spoken of in the final passage, a man 'som för en annan tro/fick ge sin ära men behålla livet' (who had given his honour for another faith but was allowed to keep his life — p.87), with Strindberg. So did a number of critics who were offended by the fact that Strindberg had compared himself to the king.[18] In fact there is no conclusive evidence for such a reading, but the main point to be made here is that this is yet another example of how subjectivity threatens the conventions of the genre.

Related to Vischer's description of satirical poetry, 'För tankens frihet' may be seen as an example of the type of satire which operates through direct confrontation between reality (the anniversary celebrations) and the ideal (freedom of thought). Strindberg's technique of exposing the betrayal of the ideal to the reader, and setting it in sharp contrast to the 'true ideal', is very characteristic for the 'Sårfeber' satires. Strindberg does not intend to tear down the ideal itself, but rather seeks to restore it to its original meaning, and to reconquer it from the hands of the enemy.

Perhaps Strindberg's most original contribution to verse satire is his use of metre and rhyme. In the foreword he defends what may be called a kind of anti-verse, i.e. metrical verse that opposes its own basic rules and gives priority to thought over rhyme or metrical feet (SS 13, p.7), an argument which could of course be — and indeed was — interpreted as simply a bad and somewhat contorted excuse for not being able to write proper verse.[19]

Strindberg chose to attack metrical verse on two different levels simultaneously. He used it in a seemingly casual way while also experimenting with free verse. It is important to note, however, that he used free verse in the 'Stormar' section only, and then on the pattern of Heine. The aesthetically programmatic poem 'Sångare!' (Singers!) in 'Sårfeber' makes no use of rhyme but is metrically quite regular, consisting mainly of iambs and anapests. The first line of every stanza, however, which contains only the word 'Sångare!' with its clearly dactylic character, deviates strongly from this pattern.[20]

From a formal point of view, the predominant characteristic of the 'Sårfeber' poems is their inconsistency. Strindberg generally starts by establishing a basic pattern, metrically and rhythmically as well as regarding rhyme. However, this basic pattern is then violated, particularly by allowing the number of stressed syllables in the different lines of a poem to vary in a seemingly arbitrary way. There are also extreme irregularities in the interweaving of rhyme. The opening poem 'Biografiskt', on the other hand, is completely regular, consisting of cross-rhymed iambic verse with three beats in each line and rhyming the first and third lines, and the second and fourth respectively. The main impression of Strindberg's verse in the 'Sårfeber' section is its unpredictability.

It was this, quite limited, abuse of the formal aspects of poetry that was so immensely provocative to Strindberg's contemporaries; the extreme irregularities within a basic pattern created a quite parodic effect. To some critics, his use of metre and rhyme in the 'Sårfeber' poems seems to have been an insult to an entire genre.[21]

Why, then, did Strindberg choose to violate the rules of metrical verse in this way? To provoke, certainly, and perhaps to parody. But were there other reasons? In 'Sångare!' a much discussed line reads: 'Det sanna är fult sålänge sken är det sköna./Det fula är sanning!' (Truth is ugly as long as appearance is beauty. Ugliness is truth — p.26). As the critic Adolf Lindgren pointed out, this line is a response to a statement by Vischer, which is in itself unclear.[22] What did Strindberg mean? Did he in fact advocate 'ugly' poetry? Is there such a thing as a 'Sårfeber' aesthetics, and in that case, how can it best be described?

I do not as yet have all the answers to these questions, and only intend a brief outline of an intriguing aesthetic problem. Since Strindberg bitterly opposed the aesthetics of idealism, it may be worth considering the views of the Romantic idealists on the question of ugliness in art. Vischer was one of those who tackled the problem of the 'ugly'. According to his definition, ugliness occurs when the image negatively opposes the idea, resists its efforts to penetrate it, and combines this with a claim to form a whole. Vischer maintains that ugliness strives to become extreme so that it can be dissolved, for dissolved it must be unless beauty is to be destroyed.[23] With reference to the 'Sårfeber' poems, we can see that this is exactly what Strindberg does not do, i.e. he abstains from pushing 'the ugly' to its extremes, so that it cannot be dissolved. Christian Herman Weisse, meanwhile, another of the German Romantic idealists to be given a substantial chapter in Ljunggren's *Framställning*, remarks interestingly upon the substance of ugliness as 'the impudently and violently expanding subjectivity'.[24] According to both these philosophers, therefore, most of the 'Sårfeber' poems might lay claim to being 'ugly'.

According to the reviewer of the satirical journal *Figaro*, whose editor, Hugo Nisbeth, Strindberg had attacked in *Det nya riket* (SV 10, pp.93-101, 138-9), it appeared that Strindberg had been struggling in the 'Sårfeber' section with his own method of counting metrical feet on his fingers, but found it increasingly difficult to apply and therefore abandoned it — hence the free verse of 'Stormar' (Tempests).[25] This, it must be admitted, is an amusing twist to the wellknown passage from Strindberg's foreword to *Dikter på vers och prosa*:

Att jag syndat med full avsikt, har man väl ingen glädje av att tro, men då en någorlunda färdighet i fingerräkning kan kontrollera en rads fullmetrighet, må jag väl sålunda hava den billiga fordran att icke anses ha felat av okunnighet om lagar, stiftade av okända, tillämpade mest drakoniskt av obetydlighet-erna, och vilka jag tagit mig friheten bryta, då jag ansett min tanke betyda mer än en versform eller ett rim.

(That I have offended deliberately, one surely does not believe, but as anyone who is fairly competent in counting on his fingers can check that a line of verse is fully metrical, I would surely have the right to claim that I have not failed from ignorance of laws, established by the unknown and rigorously applied by the insignificant, which I have taken the liberty to violate, since I have considered my thought more important than a metrical foot or a rhyme — SS 13, p.7)

If we are to believe Strindberg's own words, therefore, he broke the laws of metrics quite deliberately. And this may well have been in a unique attempt to find an 'ugly' expression for an 'ugly' content, that is, to find an artistically true and adequate form for the 'ugly' reality he had chosen to depict and to satirize.

Notes

1. For a valuable summary of the situation, see Tomas Forser, Thomas Olsson and Per Arne Tjäder, 'Akademikultur och litterär institution på 1880-talet', *Den litterära institutionen*, edited by Arne Melberg (Stockholm, 1975), pp.180-198.
2. For a comprehensive account of the influence of Byron and Heine on nineteenth-century Swedish literature, see Erik Frykman, 'Byron i svensk litteratur', *Samlaren* (1977), pp.58-86, and Walter A. Berend-

sohn, *Der Lebendige Heine im germanischen Norden* (Copenhagen, 1935), pp.79-96 respectively.

3. See *Samlade Verk* 12, pp.136-148.

4. Per Erik Ekholm, *Strindberg och den svenska kritiken 1870-83* (unpublished licentiate's dissertation, Stockholm University, 1961), p.241.

5. See also Gunnar Brandell, *Strindberg — ett författarliv*, I (Stockholm, 1987), pp.335-6.

6. Gustaf Ljunggren, *Framställning af de förnämsta Esthetiska Systemerna*, 2 vols (Lund, 1856-60). Strindberg acquired the book (volume one in its second, 1869, edition) in 1871, and seems to have kept it until his second library was sold in 1892. See Allan Hagsten, *Den unge Strindberg*, II (Lund, 1951), p.41, and Hans Lindström, *Strindberg och böckerna* (Uppsala, 1977), p.53. Cf. also SV 20, pp.286-7.

7. Ljunggren, *Framställning*, II, pp.403-4.

8. Ljunggren, pp.403-4.

9. 'Strindbergs lyrik', *En bok om Strindberg* (Karlstad, 1894), pp.153-169.

10. Erik Hedén, *Strindberg. En ledtråd vid studiet av hans verk* (Stockholm, 1921), p.120.

11. The attribution of the 'Strasbourg Epode' to Archilochus has been questioned by some scholars. See Sture Linnér, *Den gyllene lyran* (Stockholm, 1989), p.101.

12. Cf. Sven Gustaf Edqvist, *Samhällets fiende* (Stockholm, 1961), pp.215-225.

13. *Det nyaste riket. Karaktärisktiska skildringar från tanklöshetens och oförsynthetens tidehvarf. I: Realisten, af Michel Perrin* (Stockholm, 1882).

14. Thomas Thorild, *Samlade skrifter* I, edited by Stellan Arvidson (Stockholm, 1933), pp.105-116. See also Arvidson's commentary in *Samlade skrifter*, VII (Stockholm, 1962), pp.235-249.

15. 'Olika vapen' (Different Weapons) is clearly related to Oscar II's translation (via Herder's German version) of two 'Cid Romances', printed in *Verldslitteraturens historia*, I (Stockholm, 1875), pp.506-7.

16. See Lennart Pagroth, *Den klassiska verssatirens teori. Debatten kring genren från Horatius t.o.m. 1700-talet* (Lund, 1961), pp.335-342.

17. Olof Lagercrantz, 'Strindbergs dikt För tankens frihet', *Meddelanden från Strindbergssällskapet*, 13-14 (1953), p.5.

18. Lagercrantz, p.14; reviews in *Aftonbladet* (24 November 1883), Nya Dagligt Allehanda (22 December 1883), and by Reinhold Geijer in *Ny Svensk Tidskrift*, January 1884, p.80.

19. The best example of this line of interpretation can be found in a review entitled 'Det nya snillet eller Den naturalistiskt-hyperromantiska pannkakan', *Figaro*, 25 November 1883.

20. Cf. John Eric Bellquist, *Strindberg as a Modern Poet* (Berkeley, 1986), pp.31-2. Bellquist rather curiously proposes that the first unstressed syllable in every line of the poem (except the dactylic first line of each stanza) should be regarded as 'extra' so that the poem might then be scanned as generally dactylic and trochaic.

21. For a brief summary of press criticisms of Strindberg's verse, see Ekholm, pp.223-6.

22. See the discussion between Lindgren and Reinhold Geijer in Adolf Lindgren, 'Svenska antologier', *Ny Svensk Tidskrift* (May 1884), pp.359-61.
23. Ljunggren, II, pp.124-5.
24. Ljunggren, II, p.21.
25. 'Det nya snillet', *Figaro*, 25 November 1883.

Inferno: Intended Readers and Genre

Lotta Gavel Adams

University of Washington

When *Inferno* was first published in Sweden in November 1897, it was read and understood as an expansion of Strindberg's diary, a continuation of his 'sjelfbiografiska sammelverk' (autobiographical collection), as is explicitly signalled in the Epilogue :

> Den läsare, som tror sig veta att denna bok är en dikt, inbjudes att se min dagbok, som jag hållit dag efter dag sedan 1895, och varav det föreliggande endast är ett utvidgat och ordnat utdrag.

> (The reader who believes this book is a work of fiction is invited to read my diary which I have been keeping daily since 1895, and of which this book is merely an expansion and arrangement. — SS 28, p.205)

Swedish critics, and even Strindberg's personal friends, took the words in the Epilogue *ad notam* and read the book as an autobiographical document. They reacted to it with consternation, disbelief and even disgust. If this was a true account of how Strindberg experienced the world, he must be insane, they concluded. Strindberg's old friend Pehr Staaff wrote to Gustaf af Geijerstam on 7 November 1897, just after he had finished reading the book:

> Jag kan omöjligen — allra minst när jag resonerat med honom sjelf om boken — fatta den annat än som början till slutet. Och vilket slut! Den äckligaste form af vanvett som jag kan tänka mig, den småskitnaste fånighet grinar ju fram på hvar tionde sida i Inferno. Hvad skall det inte bli när tiden fullbordas?

(I can't possibly — least of all after I have discussed it with him himself — see it as anything but the beginning of the end. And what an end! The most nauseating form of lunacy I can imagine, the most degrading form of stupidity grins at you on every tenth page in *Inferno*. What will come of it in the fullness of time? — XII, p.193)

The Swedish reviewers did not know what to make of the book either. Carl David af Wirsén, for example, saw *Inferno* 'som en bekräftelse på antagandet att strängarne brustit, skriftställarförmågan desorganiserats' (as a confirmation of the suspicion that the strings have finally snapped, that his ability to write has been disorganized).[1] The reasons why Swedish readers rejected *Inferno* as an incoherent autobiography are, in my opinion, twofold. First, they did not recognize the occult world view that Strindberg had encoded into the first part of *Inferno*, and they could therefore not identify with the ideas and values portrayed in the book. Secondly, their assumption that *Inferno* was Strindberg's personal journal, as signalled in the Epilogue, coupled with widespread rumours of his mental illness, prevented them from evaluating *Inferno* from an aesthetic point of view. Instead they proceeded to pass moral judgment on August Strindberg, the author and presumably protagonist of the book, in a way they would never have imagined doing with the other protagonists of Strindberg's novels, such as Carlson in *Hemsöborna* or Axel Borg in *I Havsbandet*.

Though *Inferno* was first published in Swedish, it is clear that Strindberg did not initially sit down to write *Inferno* with a Swedish readership in mind. He composed *Inferno* in French, an obvious clue that he intended it to be read by French readers, readers, moreover, who were well acquainted with the fashionable occultism of the 1890s in Paris. There are several references in his correspondence which indicate that Strindberg first intended the book to be an occult novel, 'un roman occulte d'après nature' (XII, p.165) as he called it in one of his letters to his faithful and supportive French alchemist friend François Jollivet- Castelot.

Since early spring 1896, Strindberg had been convinced that the fashionable occultism which he had come into contact with in Paris was the latest and dominating trend in literature. Passing through Copenhagen later the same year, on his way back to Sweden from Austria, informed Georg Brandes on 30 November 1897: 'De er ikke fulgt med Aandslivets nyeste Udvikling i Frankrig. Vi lever i Occultismens Tidsalder, og det er Occultisterne, der nu beherskar Literaturen' (You haven't followed the latest cultural and spiritual trend in France. We live in the age of occultism, and it is the occultists who now dominate literature).[2] It seems that with *Inferno* Strindberg wanted to position himself in the forefront of this trend.

In May 1896 Strindberg told Torsten Hedlund, who was then publishing his collection of essays in the natural sciences, *Jardin des plantes*, that he was thinking of converting his occult experiences of the past two years in Paris into a book. Three months later, in August 1896, he presented a quite specific plan for his occult book, probably in an attempt to interest Hedlund in publishing it. Strindberg designated the genre of his work a poem in prose:

> En annan sak! Ni sade nyligen att man söker: Ockultismens Zola. Där känner jag kallelsen. Men i stor hög ton. Ett poem på prosa: kalladt *Inferno*. Samma thema som I Hafsbandet. Individens undergång när han isolerar sig. Räddningen genom: arbetet utan ära eller guld, pligten, familjen, följaktligen — qvinnan — modren och barnet! Resignationen genom upptäckten af hvars och ens uppgift gifven av Försynen.

> (Another thing! You said recently that people are looking for: the Zola of Occultism. I feel the call. But in a grand, elevated tone. A poem in prose: called *Inferno*. The same theme as in *By the Open Sea*. The downfall of the individual when he isolates himself. Salvation through: work without honour or gold, duty, the family, consequently — woman — mother and child! Resignation through the discovery of the task assigned to each and every one of us by Providence. — XI, p.307)

It is quite clear that Strindberg in this plan did not intend to focus autobiographically on himself but rather on an *individual* in general, and the downfall of this individual through self-imposed isolation and his eventual salvation through work and family. This plan made no claims to be a true story or an autobiographical account. Instead, the focus is on the theme, which is the same as in his earlier novel *I Havsbandet*. This outline has the finished form of a novel. However, Hedlund was not interested, or was not able financially to publish such a book. Instead he recommended Strindberg to try Bonnier, an idea which Strindberg immediately rejected as he was sure that Bonnier would only return 'en ockultroman med några speglosor som han kallar kritik' (an occult novel with some scornful remarks which he would call critique — XI, p.315). It has generally been considered (by both Lamm and Brandell, for example) that Strindberg gave up this plan because his own personal situation changed. Strindberg wrote the outline after he had received an invitation from his estranged wife, Frida, to go to Austria, where he hoped, forlornly as it happened, that they might be reconciled. However, I would like to suggest that this outline is still quite visible in the first eight chapters of *Inferno*, which I see forming an occult mini-novel in itself, one written with a specific French readership in mind. Strindberg addressed these readers in the text by way of encoded occult messages, the existence of which he explicitly signalled in a letter to Eugène Fahlstedt, who translated the book into Swedish:

Om Du söker nyckeln till den underliga bok Du håller på att öfversätta, så läs G.H.T. för i Torsdag den 5ᵉ Augusti, Bref från Paris om Ockultismen, särskildt om Martinisterna som äro lärjungar af Swedenborg. Forts. utlofvas.

(If you are looking for the key to the peculiar book you are translating, read G.H.T. for Thursday August 5th, Letter from Paris about Occultism, particularly about the Martinists who are disciples of Swedenborg. Cont. promised. — XII, p.139)

Before scrutinizing the text of *Inferno* for evidence of the outline to an occult novel and encoded messages, we might keep in mind that at the end of January 1897 Strindberg — just three months before he sat down to write *Inferno* — had been inducted into the *Association Alchimique de France* as an honorary member and *maître travailleur*. This association had been founded, only five months earlier, by Jollivet-Castelot, and its monthly review, *L'Hyperchimie*, was published by Lucien Chamuel, a lawyer and prominent publisher of occult literature in Paris. It was to him that Strindberg offered his French manuscript to *Inferno* for publication in August 1897. In the first chapter of *Inferno*, the narrator is faced with the choice between Love and Science. By choosing Science over Love, he isolates himself, which causes his downfall, and he ends up in hospital. In the next chapters he encounters his spiritual guides, the French king, Saint Louis, and the Spanish-French chemist and toxicologist Orfila. He is tempted sexually (by Mlle Lecain) and with money (by the representative of all the iodine manufacturers in Europe), and becomes the target of 'envoûtement' (harm caused by sympathetic magic) in nightly attacks. Finally, in chapter eight, 'Béatrice', he is reconciled with society through the love of his little daughter (minus the mother) and a faith in a higher power. The narrator compares meeting his daughter with the reawakening of Faust to an earthly existence. Strindberg probably alludes here to the end of the scene 'Nacht' in Goethe's *Faust*, where Faust in despair over having failed to achieve supreme knowledge through science, decides to commit suicide, but is reawakened to an earthly life by angels singing the praise of God. In the first chapter of *Inferno* we can distinguish what seems to be an encoded message addressed to the members of *L'Ordre Martiniste*. This occult order was headed by a Docteur Papus, an affable medical doctor whose real name was Gérard Encausse. The Martinist order had been inactive for some fifty years when Papus decided to revive it in 1891. A charter member of the *Suprême Conseil de l'Ordre Martiniste* was the publisher Chamuel. On the last Sunday of his stay in the 'purgatory' of the Saint-Louis hospital, the narrator of *Inferno* decides to take a walk. He has received a letter from his wife and feels he is faced with the choice between Love and Science, between returning to his marriage or devoting himself to his research. He leaves the hospital, crosses the Canal Saint-Martin, and continues down the rue Alibert, rue Dieu, rue Beaurepaire, and rue Bondy (today the rue René Boulanger). He has, however, the impression that something inexplicable is going on and wonders whether he is being led by the devil.

The narrator has the habit of interpreting what he sees and what is happening to him as personal messages. Two pages previously, in a reference which might be a clue to the reader to be on the lookout for occult meanings, the narrator remembers walking past a statue of Saint Louis. This, in turn, reminds him of the three great buildings by the thirteenth-century French king Saint Louis, namely Les Quinze-Vingts, the asylum for the blind; Sorbonne university; and the Gothic chapel Sainte-Chapelle. He immediately infers that these buildings are encoded messages to him, telling him that he will pass from a state of suffering, through knowledge to penitence. On his Sunday walk, the narrator reads the street signs and ponders their meaning. In passing the rue Alibert, he remembers that the graphite found in the sulphur sample, which he recently had submitted for analysis, was called Alibert graphite. (In reality, the street was named after Jean Louis Alibert (1768-1837), a dermatologist and head of the Hôpital Saint-Louis. The Alibert graphite comes from the Alibert mines in Siberia, named after another Frenchman of that name, who discovered them.) Next he arrives at the rue Dieu, the name of which he translates as God. This in turn he interprets as a possible sign from above, a manifestation of a divine presence in the secularized Third Republic which had abolished God and converted the Panthéon from a church into a national monument. In reality, the name was more prosaic than the narrator's divination: the street was named after General Dieu, who was mortally wounded in the battle of Solferino in 1859.

As the narrator stops reading the street signs, he gets lost and is accosted by prostitutes and riffraff. Panicking, he starts to run, as rain mixed with snow begins to fall. At the end of a short street, he suddenly sees as in a vision, a triumphal arch outlined against the sky:

> une porte, immense, œuvre de cyclope, porte sans palais qui ouvre sur une mer de lumière . . . Je demande à un sergeant où que je suis. — Porte Saint-Martin, Monsieur.[3]

Without further comment, the narrator continues down the boulevard. No explicit explanation or interpretation is given as to the significance of the 'mer de lumière . . .', which illuminates the interior of the arch of triumph of Saint-Martin. The three dots after 'lumière', however, invite the reader to continue the narrator's train of thought, and challenge him/her to interpret the significance of this vision. Though this cryptic Saint-Martin reference would mean little to his Swedish readers, the Martinists would hopefully understand that Strindberg intended to convey that Saint-Martin, through the reconstituted *l'Ordre Martiniste*, was providing the light in these difficult and confusing times. With this message Strindberg may have hoped to please the Martinists and perhaps smooth the way for the French publication of his book by Chamuel.

The likelihood that the Porte Saint-Martin vision was included in the text as an encoded message is increased by the presence of similar cryptograms in other Strindberg texts from this period. Sverker Hällen has convincingly demonstrated that a passage in Strindberg's essay 'Études funèbres', written autumn 1895, should be read as a cryptogram, an encoded message or warning to Albert Langen and Willy Grétor, and structured to be understood by these two assumed enemies alone.[4]

In the first chapter of *Inferno*, I have also identified a number of expressions with distinct alchemistic meanings, which might be interpreted as encoded messages to Strindberg's alchemist colleagues in France. This chapter has until now been considered very difficult to translate, seemingly full of obscure formulations and expressions that are out of character with Strindberg's usual style. After the narrator has decided to bid his wife farewell and chosen Science over Love, he sets out to reach what he terms 'les connaissances suprêmes'. In existing translations this expression has been rendered as 'kunskapens höjder' by Fahlstedt (SS 27, p.8), literally transferred into English as 'the summits of intellectual achievement' (Sandbach, 1979, pp.101-2) and 'the summit of knowledge' (Sprinchorn, 1968, p.119). 'Les connaissances suprêmes', however, implies something more specific in an alchemistic context: it is 'the supreme knowledge', i.e. the intellectual insight which would enable man to prove the Unity of the Universe, the ultimate goal of the alchemists. It is in pursuit of this ultimate goal that the narrator returns to his miserable hotel room, which doubles as a laboratory. There he experiences 'un sentiment de pureté psychique, de virginité mâle', an expression rendered in English as 'a feeling of spiritual purity, of masculine virginity' (Sandbach, p.102) and 'Conscious of the purity of my soul, of male virginity' (Sprinchorn, p.121)[5] while Fahlstedt translates it into Swedish as 'en känsla av psykisk renhet, av manlig jungfrulighet' (SS

28, p.9). Strindberg's unorthodox juxtaposition of 'virginalité' and 'mâle' has puzzled several commentators, even though startling new imagery is one of his trademarks. But the reference appears to have an occult address, an assumption supported by a passage a few pages later, which has also been considered obscure. In this passage, the narrator talks about being thwarted in his pursuit of 'le grand œuvre' by unknown forces: 'Les inconnus m'empêchèrent de poursuivre le grand œuvre et il fallait briser les obstacles avant de remporter la couronne du vainqueur'.[6] For the general reader, this sentence may sound paranoic. It is difficult to understand why unknown people or powers would have any interest in preventing the narrator's great work. However, to readers versed in alchemy — and there were fifty thousand active alchemists in Paris alone in 1893, if we believe *La Paix* (19 January 1893) — the passage, as well as the earlier expression 'un sentiment de pureté psychique, de virginalité mâle' would not have been difficult to understand. Though the word 'virginalité' may have sounded strange, since it does not exist in French, its connotation 'chastity' and 'purity' (virgin, virginal) would have been quite clear. For an alchemist, psychic purity and chastity were prerequisites for attempting to achieve *transmution*, which they called 'le Grand Œuvre', 'Opus Magnum'. Gold, being the symbol of purity, had to be the result of a completely pure and physically untainted act. Though absolute celibacy was not required, an alchemist should not, according to Jollivet-Castelot's *Comment on devient alchimiste* (1897), become seriously attached to a woman, as his power would then be broken.

Seen in an occult context, therefore, these three textual references can be interpreted as encoded messages which Strindberg was sending to the alchemists. I suggest that they were intended to carry the following deciphered meaning: I have chosen Alchemy over Love. I have set out to reach the supreme knowledge and I have therefore said goodbye forever to my wife. I am pure and chaste and thus worthy to attempt the great work, to achieve Transmutation. I am prepared to break down all obstacles which hinder me from succeeding in making gold, i.e. taking home the victor's crown.

There are other similar encoded messages to the Martinists and the Alchemists in the first half of *Inferno*. They indicate that Strindberg was acutely aware of his potential readers — more so than previous studies of *Inferno* have suggested — and that he was willing to tailor his text to be appreciated (and published?) by them.

However, midway through the book Strindberg seems to turn to a new and Swedish target audience. The occult allusions cease and the structure of the book becomes more disjointed. On 8 June 1897, after completing Chapter VIII, 'Beatrice', he wrote to Gustaf af Geijerstam, the literary editor of Gernandts Förlag, offering him *Inferno* for publication. The two had met earlier, on May 22, and Geijerstam had asked Strindberg about his literary plans. Strindberg, who did not then believe that an 'ockultroman' stood any chance of being published in Swedish, had not even mentioned *Inferno*. However, he now writes:

Till Iª Juli hoppas jag ha min stora bok Inferno färdig (på 350 sidor). Men den är skrifven på dålig Franska och okopierad. Hvar fins Du Iª Juli att jag kan sända dig till läsning eller komma i din närhet?

(By 1 July, I hope to have my big book Inferno ready (350 pages). But it is written in bad French and is not copied. Where are you going to be by 1 July, so that I can mail it to you for reading or go there myself? — XII, p.114)

The following day, 9 June, Strindberg started Chapter IX, 'Swedenborg'. In *Ockulta Dagboken* Strindberg noted on 9 June 1897, 'Skref kapitlet Swedenborg i Inferno' (Wrote the chapter Swedenborg in *Inferno*). In the very first paragraph of this chapter, Strindberg turns to his Swedish readers and explains in an aside that the story they are reading is not a novel: 'ce récit qui n'est pas un roman avec des prétentions de style et de composition littéraire'.[7] Chapters IX to XVI have a more disjointed structure and can be read as an autobiographical demonstration or confession of the futility of pursuing glory and fame, and present the misguided life of August Strindberg as an *exemplum* for the improvement of his fellow Swedes. Strindberg must, of course, also have been aware that an autobiography would have better commercial prospects in Sweden than 'en ockultroman'. By switching his target audience in the middle of the writing of *Inferno*, Strindberg created a work of a double genre, part occult novel, part autobiography.

The double genre of *Inferno* proved problematic for his contemporary Swedish readers, whose genre expectations did not allow them to understand the fictional nature of the work. Nor did Strindberg succeed in reaching or pleasing his intended French readers. *Inferno* was rejected by Chamuel. Not until eight months after the appearance of the Swedish edition, in July 1898, was it published by Mercure de France. His occult book was not widely reviewed in France. I have traced only four French contemporary reviews of *Inferno*. Of these four, only one was positive, that by his faithful alchemist friend Jollivet-Castelot. In *Initiation*, the mouthpiece of *L'Ordre Martiniste*, Strindberg was gently scolded for posing as an 'initié' in *Inferno* when he was not.[8] However, modern readers seem to have a more receptive attitude towards works which violate traditional genres. Thus *Inferno*, Strindberg's once much maligned autobiography, is finding new appreciation today, and proving itself an enduring work of art.

Notes

1. *Vårt Land*, 10 November 1897.
2. Stellan Ahlström, *August Strindberg: Mannaår och ålderdom* (Stockholm, 1961), p.116.
3. Manuscript, p.23.
4. 'Vem förföljde Strindberg? Kryptogram blev utmaning', *Ystad Allehanda*, 19 September 1970.
5. *Inferno and From an Occult Diary*, translated by Mary Sandbach (Harmondsworth, 1979); *Inferno, Alone and Other Writings*, translated by Evert Sprinchorn (New York, 1968).
6. Manuscript, p.9.
7. Manuscript, p.268.
8. *Initiation*, December 1898, pp.202-211.

En blå bok — A Genre of its Own?

Eva Spens

Stockholm University

Strindberg's *En blå bok* presents the reader with an immediate and obvious problem: quite simply, it is difficult, if not impossible, to take the measure of the four published volumes of a work which amounts in all to more than one thousand pages, divided into six hundred and sixty-eight sections, and dealing with a wide range of disparate subjects, which appeared over a period of five years, from 1907 to 1912. Strindberg himself called it 'ett stenbrott' (a quarry — XIV, p.176) in a letter to his editor, Karl Börjesson, in February 1908. Nevertheless, I believe it is possible to find a place for the tetralogy of this Blue Book in terms of literary tradition, and perhaps even to relate it to a genre of some kind.

Strindberg has used colour designations several times in the titles of his works: *Röda rummet, Svarta fanor, En blå bok*. Why blue? There is an obvious link between the colour blue and the idea of heaven, the celestial blue that might consequently be seen as a symbol of Strindberg's spirituality at this time. For example, a similar symbolic use of the colour blue can be found in *Spöksonaten*, also written in 1907 when Strindberg was already preoccupied by *En blå bok*. In the last scene of the play, for instance, there is a blue hyacinth which plays an important part in the setting, and to which Strindberg gives religious significance (SS 45, p.196). Regarded in this light, the colour blue would be one among several other signs (to which I shall come in due course) which Strindberg has given the tetralogy in order to render its elevated purpose evident to everyone.

There is, however, also the old folkloric belief, according to which the colour blue is of benign assistance, a protection against the evil eye, for instance, which in this case comprises the 'böner', 'äfflingar' and 'svarta fanor' (beans, monkeymen, black banners) with which — or whom — its author is in conflict. Nevertheless, though one of the immediate roles of *En blå bok* may have been to act as a kind of pendant to the novel *Svarta fanor*, the colour blue remains an important component in all attempts to analyze the tetralogy as a whole, and not merely any one of its constituent parts.

But *En blå bok* is in addition precisely that, a 'bluebook', a designation which existed long before Strindberg used it for the title of this work. The term 'bluebook' can easily be found in both English and Swedish dictionaries, where it is defined as a government publication, bound in a stiff, blue paper cover, and usually the report of a commission or a committee. Historically, though sometimes with different colours in different countries, the term has generally been used for such a document. Such bluebooks were sometimes controversial, like the Swedish bluebook from the seventeenth century on the financial problems of Karl XI, which aroused a great deal of discussion, and which Strindberg certainly knew from his research for *Svenska folket*, *Svenska öden och äventyr*, the historical dramas, and the later short stories. In one sense such a bluebook had the character of a report or a plea, and accords with what, in modern Swedish, would be called a 'vitbok' (white book; cf. also the English 'white paper').

This aspect, in which the book has the character of a plea, is clearly evident in the Blue Book tetralogy, and particularly in the first volume, or original *En blå bok*, where the title-page bears the clarificatory subtitle 'aflämnad till vederbörande och utgörande kommentar till *Svarta fanor*' (dedicated to those concerned and providing a commentary to *Black Banners*). In delivering the manuscript, Strindberg told Börjesson, on 8 May 1907: 'Hvad skriften beträffar, så innehåller den ju omsägningar från Svarta Fanor till en del, men utgör i sig sjelf mitt manifest, hvarigenom jag afsvär högtidligt all gemenskap med de Svarta Fanorna' (As far as the text is concerned, it partly goes over the same ground as *Svarta fanor*, but is otherwise my manifesto, whereby I solemnly abjure all fellowship with the Black Banners — XVI, p. 14). Here, Strindberg is seeking to justify himself in the eyes of public opinion, the opinion that judged *Svarta fanor* so harshly. This reaction came as no surprise to Strindberg (indeed, he had foreseen it while writing the novel in 1904, three years before it was finally published),[1] and he describes the agonies he experienced when the novel appeared in 'Blå bokens historia' (The History of A Blue Book), which he appended to the first supplement to *En blå bok* in 1908.[2]

En blå bok may be a kind of plea; it is certainly not an apology, however. In those sections where it is possible to observe a clear link with *Svarta fanor*, for example in 'Den klibbige' (The Glutinous One — SS 46, p. 117), 'Vampyren' (The Vampire — SS 46, p. 118), and 'Cinnobers anatomi' (Anatomy of Cinnober — SS 46, p. 119), no attempt is made to soften the attack already made in the novel upon

Zachris, the character based in part upon Strindberg's sometime friend, Gustaf af Geijerstam. The only apparent change seems to be the substitution of 'Cinnober' for 'Zachris' as a name, although as Martin Lamm has pointed out, this is hardly a major change since Strindberg was inspired by E.T.A. Hoffmann's fantasy 'Klein Zaches genannt Zinnober' when he was planning *Svarta fanor*.[3] Cinnober is a vampire and a parasite, who steals people's ideas, friends and peace of mind. Strindberg regretted nothing when he wrote these sections of *En blå bok*, though he may have done so later, in May 1908, when the second part of the tetralogy, *En ny blå bok* (A New Blue Book) was about to appear. He then wrote to Börjesson and suggested that the original subtitle should be eliminated and, if a new edition of the first part could be added to the new one in a single volume consisting of about eight hundred pages, that certain sections should be eliminated: 'skola vi utstryka Cinnobers glasögen och det Moraliskt indifferenta? icke för att det är orättvist, men af menskliga hänsyn? Han har ju barn, fastän icke trefliga, dock barn' (shall we delete Cinnober's spectacles and the 'Morally indifferent'? He has children, after all, although not nice ones, but children all the same — XVI, p.304). This is not a retreat, though it may represent a slight change of purpose in *En blå bok* (certainly, Gustaf af Geijerstam was no longer so immediate a preoccupation). Nevertheless, *En ny blå bok* was edited as a separate volume, with no subtitle, and the sections concerning Cinnober remained in all subsequent editions of the first volume.

There are, moreover, other reasons to believe that the concept of a 'bluebook' was not new to Strindberg. The notion occurs as early as 23 September 1882, in a letter to Hjalmar Branting, where he writes: 'Cronhamn den förrädaren har skallgått i sin korrespondens om den "blå boken" som jag var stupid nog att låna honom öfver en natt, sedan jag beskänkt den uslingen med starka drycker i mitt hem' (Cronhamn, the traitor, has started a hue and cry in his correspondence about the 'bluebook' which I was stupid enough to lend him overnight, after having got the wretch fuddled with strong drinks at my place — III, p.93). According to Torsten Eklund's commentary on this letter, Strindberg was anxious about an anonymous pamphlet entitled 'Victoria-jubel', published in a very small edition by Republikanska klubben (The Republican Club), in which a contemporary royal wedding was satirized in a way that might cause a reader to believe that he (Strindberg) had written it. In fact he had not, although his friends Branting and Pehr Staaff may well have been involved, but whatever the case, it clearly indicates how Strindberg employs the term 'blue-book' for a publication with a powerful message and political or ethical aims.

But a 'bluebook' does not necessarily have to be read on such a pronounced polemical level. There is an early example of a bluebook of a different kind, *Den blå boken* (The Blue Book), published in 1837 by Erik Gustaf Geijer, one of Sweden's foremost authors and historians.[4] It was in opposition to Geijer's historical method that Strindberg wrote *Svenska folket* in 1882. *Den blå boken* is not one of Geijer's most well-known works. It is quite a small volume of eighty-six pages, which are divided into forty-five short sections. The subtitle is 'strödda anteckningar' (miscellanea), and in the foreword Geijer states that *Den blå boken* is 'en minnesbok, hvari författaren plägat uppteckna hvarjehanda' (a memorandum, in which the author has been in the habit of collecting all manner of things). It hardly amounts to a pamphlet, though it is of interest that it was published prior to Geijer's much discussed 'avfall', that is, his desertion of his earlier, conservative ideas, and contains entries which may be connected with that circumstance, for example 'Förändringar inom de arbetande klasserna i England' (Changes within the Working Classes in England).

There are a number of similarities between the bluebooks of Geijer and Strindberg. Like Strindberg, Geijer also includes a section about Goethe. Religion, too, features prominently, with titles like 'Praktisk religion' (Practical Religion) and 'Theologen' (The Theologian). Other titles can be associated with parts of that vague concept which Strindberg called 'Kärlekens bok' (The Book of Love), comprising an unspecified number of sections from *En ny blå bok* about love and marriage.[5] For instance, Geijer's bluebook contains titles like 'Giftemål — Nöd och lust' (Marriage — for Better and for Worse) and 'Första aftonen i det nya hemmet' (The First Evening in the New Home). It is in fact quite easy to list titles from Geijer which could just as well have been found in Strindberg's bluebook, such as 'Det sköna' (The Beautiful), 'Liknelser' (Similarities), and 'Ålderdomens lycka och olycka' (The Fortunes and Misfortunes of Old Age). But there are also major differences: Geijer does not have Strindberg's temperament and force of expression, nor does he include separate sections on science or linguistics, as Strindberg would do. Ultimately, the subtitle of Geijer's *Den blå boken* — miscellanea — is a fair enough description of the book's character, although it could be added, in conclusion, that as with Strindberg, Geijer found it hard to bring his bluebook to a conclusion, a difficulty he finally resolved by founding a literary review, entitled *Litteraturbladet*, shortly after *Den blå boken* was published.[6]

There is yet another bluebook, however: the German periodical *Das Blaubuch*, established in 1906 as a forum for public debate, literature and art. In 1907, Strindberg was sent the journal's twenty-fifth number by a certain Alfons Fedor Cohn, who had written an article 'Strindberg als Lyriker'. But Cohn's letter is dated 4 July 1907,[7] and the first time Strindberg uses the title *En blå bok* for his work is 26 April 1907 (XV, p.366), so it is not possible to claim that Strindberg was given the idea by the German magazine. It merely offered him a further example of what a bluebook might be. Strindberg's *En blå bok* may consequently be seen as an example of a specific 'bluebook' genre. But *En blå bok* is not only a bluebook. As indicated above, the colour blue also refers to the spiritual character of *En blå bok*, and there are still other outer signs which draw the reader's attention to the book's religious tone. The most striking example of this is the dedication to Swedenborg, about which Gunnar Brandell has observed, with great perspicacity: 'To foreign commentators, the combination of these two figures is almost irresistible: two phases in the history of Swedish madness or Swedish profundity![6] The dedication is intended as a tribute to Swedenborg's memory. His remains were to be brought home from England in 1908, for burial in Uppsala Cathedral, which prompted Strindberg to write to Börjesson on 26 July 1907: 'Derför önskade jag se min bok färdig till dess och få helsa min Store Ledare och lärare i en dedikation' (That is why I wished to see my book finished by then, and to be able to greet my Great Leader and Teacher in a dedication — XVI, p.50). And this may well have been his true intention with *En blå bok* where Swedenborg is concerned, that is, simply to extend a greeting to him rather than attempt to follow in his footsteps, for *En blå bok* itself is in no respect a consequential application of Swedenborg's theology, even though Strindberg may frequently refer to him, quote from his works, and (in a letter to Schering, written while working on *En blå bok* in late 1906) call his work a 'Diarium' (XV, p.318). His inspiration here may well have been Swedenborg's *Diarium Spirituale*, and the religious character of *En blå bok* is also sustained by the dialogue form of many of the early entries, with their interplay between a Swedenborgian 'Lärare' (Teacher) and a Strindbergian 'Lärjunge' (pupil or disciple). However, with the supplement to the first volume, these dialogues finally give way to extended monologues.

In 'Blå bokens historia', which is appended to the supplement, Strindberg provides glimpses of the work's creation, its ideas, impulses and models. It is important to keep in mind that this section is also a part of the literary work it describes. The first name mentioned as a source of inspiration here is Goethe. Strindberg informs us that in the summer of 1905 he was inspired by Goethe's plans for writing a non-denominational 'Brevarium universale', containing a word of wisdom for every day of the year (SS 46, p.404). With this in mind, he brought together religious material from all over the world, only to discover that it did not provide him with 'the language' he was seeking. As a result, Strindberg revised his plans and considered a 'Herbarium Humane', a book of worldly wisdom, though again he hesitated. It is possible to discern the outlines of these early plans in the manuscript of *En blå bok*, where entries are dated from 1 January to 28 October (some of the sections having the same date). In the published version, the sections are arranged in a slightly different order. According to 'Blå bokens historia', the 15 June 1906 was something of a turning point: 'På morgon när jag gick ut såg jag först en spårvagn med talet 365. Jag frapperades av numret och tänkte på mina 365 sidor jag skulle skriva' (When I went out that morning the first thing I saw was a tram with the number 365. I was struck by the number and thought of the 365 pages of mine that I was to write — SS 46, p.404). Haunted throughout the remainder of his walk by red flags (one of which was English), Strindberg heeded what seemed to him a warning and on his return had reached a decision as to how he would create his 'krutdurk' (powder keg — p.405), to which he subsequently gave the title *En blå bok*.

This account of the writing of *En blå bok* was written directly after the first two editions of the first volume of the tetralogy, and both the detailed planning and any change of name applies only to this first part. This is also so in the letter which Strindberg addressed to Schering in which he first mentions the title *En blå bok* and the word 'brevarium': 'Mitt brevarium ligger ännu i manuskript och kallas "En blå bok aflemnad till vederbörande"' (My breviary is still only a manuscript and is called 'A Blue Book, dedicated to those concerned' — XV, p.366). This letter is dated 26 April 1907, and *En blå bok* it became, made up of attacks on the targets he had assailed in *Svarta fanor*, scientific analyses, religious reflections, linguistics, and numerous other topics, in an attempt, like Balzac, Poe and Goethe before him, to reach beyond the traditional limits of fiction, to redraw the boundary between what in Swedish are termed 'skön' and 'fack' litteratur.

Writing the tetralogy was by no means a sudden impulse, however. As Strindberg told Börjesson, when trying to place some early manuscripts: 'Har Ni plats för en stor koffert, innehållande flera tusen lappar med 25 års anteckningar till B.B. (kallades först "Gröna Säcken", blef sedan Antibarbarus m.m. och slutligen Blå Boken)?' (Have you room for a large trunk containing several thousand slips of paper with 25 years of notes for B.B. (was originally called "The Green Sack", then became *Antibarbarus*, etc., and finally the *Blue Book*)?).[9] Strindberg's memory is accurate; the genesis of the Blue Book tetralogy goes back as far as the early 1880s since when, in his continual questioning of, and opposition to, the scientific establishment (indeed, of every kind of establishment) he had experimented with different genres — poetry, drama, novels and 'non-fictional' texts like *Antibarbarus* — in order to articulate that opposition. In *Svarta fanor*, for example, which is closely related to the Blue Book tetralogy in so many ways, an alternative science, as presented in the chapters given over to the monastery on Siklaön, is interwoven with the main narrative, which incorporates the figure of Zachris. In one of his many letters to Börjesson, Strindberg calls these chapters 'Hvita Dukar Ur Svarta

Fanor' (White Flags from Black Banners — XVI, p.265), and is clearly aware of the similarities between these monastery chapters and many of the entries in *En blå bok*. In the same letter he even suggests that they could be 'saved' from *Svarta fanor* and reprinted in a further volume of *En blå bok*. In some respects, therefore, these Siklaön chapters of *Svarta fanor*, many of them either in dialogue or as papers delivered in the form of an extended monologue, represent a kind of prelude to *En blå bok*, which is in turn an epilogue to *Svarta fanor*. But while it is consequently difficult to determine the exact point at which the Blue Book tetralogy was conceived, it is certainly true that only there does Strindberg attain the encyclopedic form most appropriate to his purposes.

But it is equally difficult to determine at what point its writing ends. *En blå bok* was printed in three editions, the third including 'The Supplement', in autumn 1907. *En ny Blå bok* and *En ny blå bok, den tredje* (A New Blue Book, the Third), were published in 1908. The last part, *En extra Blå bok* (An Extra Blue Book), was finished in 1912. With the Supplement, Strindberg abandoned the dialogue form of the first volume, and the remaining books are composed as one long monologue, divided into sections, each with a separate title. There is nothing to indicate that the final section of the last part of the tetralogy marks the end of Strindberg's Blue Book project, which is cast in a form that allows its author to continue as long as he wishes, adding section to section as he proceeds. Of course, there is a risk that his readers might get bored. But Strindberg doubtless contrives to avoid that risk through his ability to make poetry out of both 'The Philosophy and Symbolism of Hydrocyanic Acid' and the force of his attacks upon the establishment.

There is also a certain intimacy, or directness, about many of the sections into which the monologue is divided. Strindberg tells us, for example, that he has just bought a new Chinese grammar (SS 47, p.565); several sections later he returns to it and gives us further details about its contents (p.589). It is as though one were reading over his shoulder. Similarly, he invites the reader to take part in his experiments and to view them through his spectacles (SS 48, p.1040). He shares with us his agonies and the hardships of being an author, as well as his ability to make art of life. It is no wonder that scholars have followed the general reader in using the Blue Books as if they embrace the intimate, first-hand material of Strindberg's life and thoughts, in the manner of the letters or the Occult Diary. It is certainly not difficult to trace similarities between the letters and particular sections of the tetralogy, and 'Blå bokens historia', for example, is only one of many sections which can be related to passages in the Occult Diary, though it should be noted that all these texts must be regarded as (at least partly) fictional. The centrality of the Blue Books in Strindberg's life cannot be doubted, however. As he remarked, in a letter of 17 April 1908: 'Jag ville helst sitta till lefnads slut och i B.B. ge menskorna mitt testamente, min donation; bygga och plantera på mina brända tomter! upprätta, komplettera och annulera!' (Most of all I would like to remain here to the end of my days, and in B.B. give people my testament, my donation; build and plant on my burnt sites! restore, complete and annul! — XVI, p.265).

Notes

1. Eva Säfström, 'Publiceringen av Strindbergs *Svarta fanor*' (Stockholms universitet, 1976), pp.4-5.
2. The Supplement was published for the first time in the third edition of *En blå bok* (Stockholm, 1907), pp.318-415.
3. Martin Lamm, *August Strindberg* (Stockholm, 1963), p.366.
4. Erik Gustaf Geijer, *Den blå boken* (Örebro, 1837).
5. See Margareta Brundin, 'Kärlekens bok', below.
6. Published from February 1838 to 1839, continued by a 'Bihang' (Appendix), 1-3, 1840.
7. Letter from Alfons Fedor Cohn, 4 July 1907, in Kungliga Biblioteket, Stockholm.
8. Gunnar Brandell, *Strindberg — ett författarliv*, IV (Stockholm, 1989), p.286.
9. Letter to Karl Börjesson, c. 20 November 1908, in Kungliga Biblioteket, Stockholm. A precursor to 'Gröna Säcken' was 'Den blåa portföljen' (The blue briefcase), containing what in a letter to his brother Axel in 1884 he already called his 'efterlämnade skrifter' (posthumous works) — IV, p.216).

'Kärlekens bok'

Life and Fiction in *En blå bok*

Margareta Brundin

Kungliga Biblioteket, Stockholm

In the spring of 1908 Strindberg performed the striking last act of the drama which was his marriage to Harriet Bosse. It was enacted on three levels and in three genres simultaneously, in the Occult Diary, in his letters to Harriet, and in a collection of essays in *En ny blå bok* (A New Blue Book), which he called 'Kärlekens bok' (The Book of Love). And once again the question arises: What is life and what fiction? And did Strindberg himself know the answer?

'Det var herrliga stunder igår med Edra vackra blad' (What wonderful moments your beautiful pages provided yesterday), Karl Börjesson wrote to Strindberg, on Easter Eve, 18 April 1908, and continued:

> . . . hvar har jag förr läst och varit så gripen? Man skall akta sig för att jemföra, men jag tänker ändock på Balzac, den store och djupa Balzac, som från sitt afskilda vindsrum i nattens ensliga stillhet och fridfulla stämning, diktade så vackert om den rena, varma kärleken.

(what have I previously read and been so moved by? One should beware of comparisons, but I cannot help thinking of Balzac, the great and profound Balzac, who in his remote attic in nocturnal and silent solitude and peace wrote so beautifully about pure, warm love)

What the thirty-one-year-old Börjesson had read were the first manuscript pages of 'Kärlekens bok', which Strindberg had just sent him. It is not clear exactly which essays Strindberg envisaged as belonging under this heading. The genesis of the Blue Books is highly complex, with continuous additions and interpolations, a process which can only be roughly established with the help of the Occult Diary, Strindberg's correspondence, and the various paginations of the manuscripts. After the appearance in mid-December 1907 of the third edition of the first *Blå bok* plus its supplement, Strindberg announced at the beginning of February that he had 'ett nytt supplement på 134 sidor färdigt att aflemna' (a new supplement of 134 pages ready to deliver — XVI, p.175), and the rest of the month saw a flood of new essays for incorporation. On 2 March he notes in the Occult Diary: 'Började 3 Suppl. på en Blå Bok' (Began 3rd Suppl. of a Blue Book). He worked on this while the second supplement was being type-set at the printers and while reading it in proof, and delivered it to Börjesson on 30 March:

> I stället för att plottra med flera supplement sänder jag Er här slutet på Blå Boken. . . Men vi borde nu ordna in, så att det kommer ihop som hör ihop!

> (Instead of messing around with several supplements I am sending you herewith the final part of the Blue Book. . . But we need to see to it that like ends up with like! — XVI, p.233)

Some minor interpolations followed during the next few days and on 7 April he noted in the Occult Diary: 'Lade undan Blå Boken' (Laid aside the Blue Book), whilst writing to Börjesson: 'Hoppas det är slut med B.B. nu!' (Hope that's the end of B.B. now! — XVI, p.243). But a week later Börjesson learnt that:

> Det var icke slut!. . . Om B.B. skulle växa vidare. . . så föreslår jag: titeln *En Ny Blå Bok* . . . Låt dessa sända blad följa i den ordning de ligga.

> (It wasn't the end!. . . If B.B. were to continue to grow. . . I suggest the title *A New Blue Book*. . . Please see to it that the enclosed pages follow in their present order — XVI, p.262)

It was these 'enclosed pages' (which were unnumbered) that Börjesson thanked him for in the letter quoted by way of introduction, that is, pages from 'The Book of Love'.

The Occult Diary allows us to follow what had happened since 30 March, when Strindberg sent Börjesson Supplement 3, 'slutet på Blå

Boken' (the end of the Blue Book). On 4 April he writes: 'På aftonen kom Lillan och hade ett bref från Harriet, att hon förlofvade sig' (Lillan [Harriet and Strindberg's daughter, Anne-Marie] came in the evening and brought a letter from Harriet, that she was getting engaged). The handwriting suggests that the subsequent entries up until 9 April were made at the same time, i.e. written on this date. He relives the period of his engagement seven years earlier and misses and mourns Harriet as dead. 'Gjorde ingenting; gret af smärta öfver kärlekens döda illusioner. . . Söker komma i diktning, men lyckas icke!' (Did nothing; wept with pain over love's dead illusions. . . Am trying to start writing, but without success!). On 10 April he notes: 'Läste hela förmiddagen Harriets och mina bref. Jag gret af rörelse öfver det stora vackra intryck de gjorde. Skref ett exalteradt bref till Harriet' (Read Harriet's and my letters all morning. Wept with emotion at the great impression of beauty they produced. Wrote a highly charged letter to Harriet). At the same time, he reread his diary and assisted posterity by providing his letters from the time of their first acquaintance, their engagement, and 'de 40 dagarna' (the forty days) of a previous crisis in their marriage during August-September 1901, with pencilled dates and explanatory notes. He placed the letters from 'the forty days' in an envelope with the inscription 'Inferno II',[1] and sent several from the period of their engagement to Harriet 'som prof' (as samples), asking: 'Skall jag bränna detta?' (Ought I to burn this? — XVI, p.251). Beset with these impressions, he thus embarks on 'Kärlekens bok' while what he simultaneously dramatizes and details so minutely in the Occult Diary is yet another in a succession of such 40-day crises, with their by now familiar asceticism and suicide mania, including the cyanide, revolver, and 'sista-vilja-brev' (last-will-and-testament-letter) — in short, with all his customary props.

The letters to Harriet Bosse from April-May 1908, his entries in the Occult Diary, and the essays in 'Kärlekens bok', show astonishing, occasionally verbatim, similarities. It is obvious that certain of the essays were written after a reading of the Occult Diary, others in direct connection with the letters, or possibly in response to both stimuli. Strindberg wrote his first letter to Harriet after being informed of her engagement to the actor Gunnar Wingård, on 8 April, but according to the Occult Diary he did not post it until 9 April, when he also (as already mentioned) made the diary entries for 4 April onwards. The entry for 7 April reads:

Erinrade allt vackert från min första tid med Harriet. Hon är nu som död, och jag ser henne derför endast vackert. . . ångrar hvarje hårdt ord, förebrår mig allt. . . gret af smärta öfver kärlekens döda illusioner.

(Called to mind everything of beauty about my early period with Harriet. It's as though she were dead now, and for this reason I see her solely in a beautiful light. . . regret every harsh word, reproach myself for everything. . . wept with pain over love's dead illusions)

In his letter to Harriet, he writes: 'Du var död! Och så började minnets apotheos. . . Förebråelser, samvetsagg, för allt underlåtet, hvarje hårdt ord, allt, allt, alldeles som efter en kär afliden' (You were dead! And then began the apotheosis of my memories. . . Reproaches, pangs of conscience for everything left undone, every harsh word, everything, everything, just as after the death of a loved one — XVI, p.244). In the essay 'Lustgården' (The Pleasure Garden), we read:

Om den oerfarne visste vilket lidande en skilsmässa mellan makar innebär. . . Sorgen i detta fall liknar den efter en död. . . Den bortgångne hägrar. . . och undergår i minnet en apoteos, det fula strykes ut, förebråelserna stiga upp. . . de krossade illusionerna från kärlekens första vårdagar skakar tron på allt; det går ett verop genom världarna. . .

(If the inexperienced man knew how much suffering a separation between a married pair involves. . . The sorrow in this case resembles that which follows upon a death. . . The image of the missing partner haunts one. . . and becomes idealized in memory, ugly traits are obliterated, one begins to reproach oneself. . . the loss of the illusions of the first springtide of love shatters one's faith in everything; a lamentation echoes through the universe — SS 47, pp.725-6)

The short essay 'Apoteos' (Apotheosis) has the same theme and very similar formulations. As I have already mentioned, on 10 April Strindberg notes in the Occult Diary that he had written 'ett exalteradt bref' (a highly charged letter) to Harriet:

I denna morgon har jag återfunnit vår korrespondens. . . Der finns i dessa bref det bästa hos oss, våra själar helgdagsklädda som det kroppsliga lifvet sällan är. Det är icke diktadt, det är sannt; det är icke posering, det är icke illusioner. . . Ser Du, Barn, i dina bref lefver Du och uppenbarar Du Dig som 'Den Stora Qvinnan' jag anade; att hvardagslifvets typ icke motsvarar den, det beror på lifvet sjelft som är så fult, som ger så fula situationer. . . Orden och tungan äro ju så orenade att de icke förmå uttrycka det högsta; det skrifna på det hvita papperet är renare!

(This morning I have rediscovered our correspondence. . . These letters contain the best of us, our souls in their Sunday best, which life in the flesh so seldom manifests. They are not artistically composed, but truthful; there is no posing here, nor any illusions. . . You see, my Child, you live in your letters and reveal yourself as 'The Great Woman' I divined you to be; that your everyday person doesn't match up to this is the fault of life itself, which is so hideous, and affords such foul situations. . . Words on the tongue are so impure that they are unable to express the highest things; what is written on white paper is more pure! — XVI, p.251)

The essay 'Sina bästa känslor' (Our Best Feelings) includes the following passage:

När en människa skriver brev till en riktigt god vän, eller hälst till den älskade kvinnan, så tar han till helgdagsdräkten; det är ju vackert; och i det tysta brevet, på det vita papperet ger han sina bästa känslor. Tungan och det talade ordet äro så orenade av dagligt vardagsbruk att de icke kunna säga högt det vackra som pennan säger tyst. Det är icke pose eller sittning, det är icke falskhet, när man råkar en bättre själ i en korrespondens än i vardagslivet!

(When a man writes a letter to an intimate friend, or better still to the woman he loves, he dons his Sunday best; that's very fitting; and in the silent letter, on its white paper, he expresses his finest emotions. The tongue and the spoken word are so defiled by everyday use that they cannot say aloud the beautiful things which the pen speaks silently. It is not posing or attitudinizing, it is not dissembling, when souls show themselves to be better in correspondence than in everyday life! — SS 47, p.731)

'In the silent letter, on its white paper', not in the spoken word but in what 'the pen speaks silently', Strindberg is himself. And he underlines that it is not a question of 'posing'.
'Kärlekens bok' is also a letter, with an addressee. He writes to Harriet, on 17 April: 'under dessa 14 dagar har jag skrifvit så vackert, talande i mitt hjärta vid Dig! Om du ini den boken, en gång, råkar läsa 36 sidor, skall Du känna igen dem' (during this fortnight I have written so beautifully, speaking in my heart to you! If you should ever chance to read 36 pages in this book, you will recognize them — XVI, p.264). His messages and strategies shift, but the disguise is minimal. He wants

to win sympathy and recalls 'kärlekens första vårdagar' (the first springtide of love), he accuses, warns, and threatens. It is a pattern familiar from previous separations from Harriet Bosse (witness *Kristina*, the poem 'Chrysaëtos', and 'Holländaren'). At the same time he wants to 'skriva ut' (write out) Harriet from his life. He had already tried this once before in *Ovāder*. On 4 May he writes to her: 'Du är ond på mig derför att Du såg en pjäs på Intima Teatern. Jag hade varnat Dig för den! Ty det var en smärtsam dikt, med hvilken jag ville skrifva ut Dig och Lillan ur mitt hjerta! Jag ville ta i förskott de qval jag väntade' (You're angry with me because of a play you saw at the Intimate Theatre. I did warn you about it! For it was a painful work of the imagination, with which I wanted to write you and Lillan out of my heart! I wanted to dispose in advance of the torments I anticipated — XVI, p.293). Strindberg describes the process in the essay 'Mala ont' (Conjuring Evil):

> Det finns människor som ta sina sorger i förskott; och därmed tro de sig neutralisera eller muta ödet, men detta är en dålig uträkning. Jag vet en diktare, som motseende en stor olycka, tog sig för att skriva bort den. Han gjorde ett drama, och därmed trodde han sig vara kvitt olyckan. Men strax derpå kom den, och den verkade lika intensivt som om den varit oskriven
> . . .

> (There are people who anticipate their troubles, hoping thereby to neutralize or bribe destiny. But that is a mistaken calculation. I know of an author who saw a great calamity approaching and tried to write it away. He composed a play, and hoped thereby to have escaped his misfortune. But it occurred soon afterwards, and its effect was as powerful as though it had never been written about — SS 47, p.638)

Literature as conjuration! Or, rather, as drastic cure. On Easter Day, 19 April, Strindberg notes in the Occult Diary:

> Jag har vid hvarje försoning i mitt sinne med Harriet förebrått mig ända till förtviflan det onda jag tänkt, talat och skrifvit om henne. Men vid eftertanke har det kommit för mig att jag liksom 'skifvit ut' hennes ondska, satt dem [sic!] på ett papper och låtit dem gå bort med vinden. . . Då är ju ingen skada skedd!

> (At every reconciliation in my mind with Harriet I've reproached myself to the point of desperation for all the bad things I've thought, said and written about her. But upon

tranquil reflection it has seemed to me that I have as it were 'written out' her wickedness, attached them [sic] to a sheet of paper and let them go with the wind. . . . So no harm has been done!')

As I mentioned at the outset, it is not quite clear which essays Strindberg intended for inclusion in 'Kärlekens bok', and he may possibly not have been sure himself. On 15 April, when Börjesson received the first pages, they were, according to the covering letter, unpaginated. During the remainder of the month, with setting and proof-reading in progress, a steady flow of new pages arrived for 'Kärlekens bok', along with other additions to *En ny blå bok* as a whole. And though he constantly exhorted Börjesson to 'håll ihop Kärlekens Bok' (keep The Book of Love together), his evident failure to do so is hardly to be wondered at. It is likely that the first batch of pages which Strindberg sent him constitutes the sequence of eleven essays starting with 'Lustgården' and ending with 'Viktig skillnad' (Crucial Difference). Internal criteria make it probable that 'Apoteos' and 'Pålen i köttet' (Thorn in the Flesh), which were slotted in some hundred pages earlier, also belonged to this first batch. All these manuscript sheets are unpaginated, and the contents correspond closely to the Occult Diary and letters written between 4 and 14 April, some of which I have already quoted from.

After 'Viktig skillnad' there follow nine essays which Strindberg has numbered 1-9 and 16-34 in blue pencil. Among the various manuscript title pages to *En blå bok* there is one with a note by Strindberg which quite clearly refers to these pages and dates them: 'Kan inskjutas hvar som helst, blott denna (blå) pagineringen behålles, jag menar blott dessa blad sättas i sin följd, emedan ett inre sammanhang finnes här!' (Can be slotted in anywhere, provided this (blue) pagination is observed, what I mean is that provided these pages are kept in sequence, since there's an inner connection here!). Under this note he has written and crossed out '18 sidor' (18 pages) beside the date '19/4'; further down '28 sidor' has been crossed out, along with the date 20/4; and it finally says '34 sidor' (without a date).

Pages 1-18 of the manuscript (dated 19/4), with a lacuna for pages 10-15, correspond to four essays in *En ny blå bok*:

(1) 'Tezla-strömmar' (Tezla Currents), the theme of which is illustrated by the following quotation: 'Hat och kärlek äro polariserade, och genom influens kan den onda kvinnans ondska väcka motsatta strömmar hos den icke onde mannen' (Hatred and love are polarized, and by influence the bad woman's evil can arouse contrary currents in the man who is not evil — SS 47, p.740).

(2) 'Larver eller Tillfälliga materialisationer' (Larvae or Temporary Materialisations), which gives a fairly undisguised account of his onetime flame and old enemy Dagny Juel Przybyszewska and her fate. In the manuscript he first calls her 'Aspasia', but alters this to 'Thais'. Here, Strindberg wishes to underline his previous warning to Harriet in a letter dated 9 April:

> Alla dessa, hvilkas känslor Du väckt, ha återkastat på Dig de strömmar Du framkallat. . . Och Du för in disharmoni i ditt eget lif, ty det är icke bara Du och jag som 'lefva på astralplanet'. Blixten kan slå bakut och åt sidan, och en af oss kan dö, kanske den Du nu skulle mest sakna.

> (All those people whose feelings you've awakened have cast the currents you aroused back at you . . . And you are bringing disharmony into your own life, for it isn't only you and I who 'live on the astral plane'. Lightning can strike backwards or sideways, and one of us could die, maybe the one you would now miss the most — XVI, p.247)

And again, in a letter of 11 April: 'Jag vet att han kan dö, om han träffas af kortslutning i våra förfärliga vexelströmmar' (I know that he [Gunnar Wingård] can die if he is struck by a short circuit in our terrible alternating currents). He writes of Aspasia-Thais: '[Hon] skänkte sig endast för att få avbryta och pina den övergivne med saknadens smärta. Men därmed samlade hon ett sådant block av psykisk ström att hon slutligen slogs ihjäl av urladdningarne' ([She] gave herself only in order to be able to withdraw, and torment the abandoned party with the pangs of longing. But in so doing she accumulated such a build-up of psychic current that she was finally killed by its discharge — SS 47, p.742). The story ends:

> Slutligen blev hon gift; men ledsnade snart, och mot mannens goda mening anträdde hon den nya bröllopsresan långt bort.
> Där hände något som man icke vet, men som jag tilltror mig kunna räkna ut. Mannen sköt henne och sig! Troligen därför att den förre mannen föjlde dem med sitt fjärr-hat och förtog möjligheten till glädje för de två.
> Jag är nästan viss på att jag räknat rätt!

> (Finally she got married; but she soon tired of it, and against her husband's wishes she embarked on her new honeymoon far away. It is not known what happened there, but I believe I can work it out. The man shot her and himself! Most probably

because her former husband pursued them with his hatred from afar and denied the couple the possibility of happiness. I am almost positive that my calculation is correct! — SS 47, p.747)

(3) 'Farliga saker' (Dangerous Things) which deals with psychic adultery and spiritually conceived children, having its point of departure in Goethe's *Die Wahlverwandtschaften*.

(4) 'Deras känslor' (Their Emotions), a sketch in story form about a friend of the family who wishes to be loved, but not to love.

The manuscript lacuna referred to above, comprising pages ten to fifteen, appears between these last two essays, and is explained in a letter to Börjesson, dated 29 April ('Ni bad mig en gång skrifva en 1 Krona berättelse. Hvad bör den helst handla om för att Ni skall gå hem med glans? Och hvad kan Ni ge för en volym som Ensam? 150 oktavsidor?' (You once asked me to write a 1-Krona story. What ought it ideally to be about in order to be profitable for you? And what could you offer for a volume like *Ensam*? 150 octavo pages? — XVI, p.287)), and in another undated letter, written around this time:

Men säg mig, hvilken af bitarne i Kärlekens Bok vi skulle kunna rycka ut och göra berättelse af! Jag ville helst ta ut psykiska Ympar, Afläggare eller hvad den kallas, och förlägga till Riddartid, med Alkemist och Trollkarl etc. Något banalt ämne lockar mig inte, och den tiden är förbi! Jag vill göra upptäckter, och den biten är en upptäckt.

(But tell me which of the pieces in Kärlekens bok we might extract and turn into a story! I favour picking out psychological Grafts, Offshoots, or whatever it's called, and setting it [the story] in the Age of Chivalry, with Alchemist and Magician etc. I'm not interested in a banal subject, and that time is past! I want to make discoveries, and this piece is a discovery! — XVI, p.288)

Nothing came of this plan. Strindberg informed Börjesson briefly, around 8 May: 'Romanberättelsen kom icke!' (The story never came — XVI, p.304). And Börjesson's question of 9 May, 'Då ej berättelsen blef af kunna vi kanske ta med bladen ånyo?' (Since nothing came of the story, might we perhaps reintroduce the pages again?), was left unanswered. The manuscript to this 'piece' from 'Kärlekens bok' with Strindberg's blue pagination is among his papers in the Green Sack, carton seven, under the title 'Personlighetens klyfning. Afläggare och Ympar' (The Splitting of the Personality. Offshoots and Grafts). It was later published by Carlheim-Gyllensköld in the second volume of Strindberg's *Samlade otryckta skrifter*, in 1919.

The central character in the narrative, Léon, is a Parisian 'skulptör med stort namn och ovanlig talang' (sculptor with a big name and exceptional talent — SOS II, p.107). He has a wife, Philomène, and a small son. But she 'tvinar' (wilts) from lack of company, and they part amicably. When she is at liberty and sees her husband from a distance, he begins to 'hägra' (haunt her), and becomes an object of worship for her. She 'söker honom' (seeks him out), and they live together in a sort of spiritual marriage. Attempts to revive the relationship in real terms prove a failure: 'Deras kroppar tålde icke hvarann, men deras själar älskades' (Their bodies could not stand each other, but their souls loved each other). Philomène meanwhile continues to associate with her circle, where she meets a young sculptor, Emile, whom she educates 'i sin mans traditioner' (in her husband's traditions), thanks to which he acquires 'den väldige konstnärens själ i sig' (the great artist's soul within him — SOS II, p.108). One day he meets with a big success and Philomène falls in love with (by implication) Léon's soul in Emile's body. This constitutes the familiar background to the drama which Strindberg is by now adept at presenting, and the sequel can be compared point by point with his letters to Harriet and the entries in the Occult Diary between 8 and 14 April. For example, after Léon has heard about Philomène's and Emile's engagement

> började han bäfva vid tanken på, eller föreställningen om hvad som nu skulle följa. De två, för detta makarne, kunde icke så hastigt afbryta sina förfärligt starka vexelströmmar, och antingen måste Emile träffas af kortslutning, eller Philomène, eller alla tre förgås. Léon, den gamle, hade aldrig sett den unge, hvilket han räknade som en lycka.

> (he began to fear the thought or idea of what will happen next. The two erstwhile marriage partners cannot so swiftly switch off their fearfully strong alternating currents, and either Emile will fall victim to a short circuit, or Philomène, or all three of them will perish. Léon, her former husband, had never set eyes on the young man, which he considered a blessing — SOS II, p.108)

This passage can be compared to the letters of 9 and 11 April to Harriet Bosse, quoted above in connection with the Aspasia-Thais material. Again: on Philomène's engagement night, Léon celebrates a telepathic marriage:

Vid tvåtiden på natten vaknade han, i en månskensstrimma; på sin arm, sofvande, ser han sin lilla hustru; hennes ansigte visade sig som i hvitt vax. . . Han hör hennes andedrägt och mottog en kyss; rummet doftade i det samma af rosor.

(At two in the morning, he awoke in a shaft of moonlight; on his arm, fast asleep, he sees his little wife; her face presented itself as if made of white wax. . . He heard her breathing and received a kiss; the room was instantly filled with the scent of roses — SOS II, p.109)

In a letter of 14 April, Strindberg writes: 'Men när jag så låg i månskenet. . . så var Du på min arm, jag kunde se ditt lilla ansigte, känna din andedrägt' (But then, as I lay in the moonlight . . . you lay on my arm, I could see your little face, feel your breath — XVI, p.260). And in the Occult Diary around this date, there is frequent mention of a scent of roses.

Meanwhile, there is a clear three-way relationship between story, letter, and diary where the appearance of the younger lover in the mind of the older man is concerned. 'Följande morgon kände han det som en helgdag' (The following morning felt like a holiday), observes the narrator of 'Personlighetens klyfning':[2]

Men när han kom ut på avenyen, fick han se Emiles porträtt hänga bredvid Philomènes i ett fönster. Han log först, då han kände igen hennes porträtt taget för sju år sen, då *han* förlofvade sig. Men framför Emiles bild stannade han som förstenad. Det var ju han sjelf, Léon, yngre visserligen, men död! Det liknade ett porträtt af honom sjelf taget för fyra år sedan, då han stigit upp ur en dödlig sjukdom. . . Då började han konstruera fram hvad förlofningen betydde. . . Han erinrade sig först att Emile legat för döden ungefär två år förut. Att Philomène vårdat honom under konvalescensen; och under hans svaghetstillstånd hade hon inympat Léons starka själ i den unga halft liflösa kroppen. Hon had således liksom födt ett barn med Léon, och detta andens barn hette Emile. I denna föryngrade form af sin make hade hon förälskat sig.

(But when he reached the avenue, he caught sight of Emile's portrait hanging next to Philomène's in a window. First he smiled on recognizing her portrait, taken seven years ago, when *he* had got engaged. But in front of Emile's picture he stood frozen in horror. For it was he himself, Léon, young it is true, but dead! It resembled a portrait of himself taken four years ago, when he had arisen from a mortal sickness. . . He then

began to calculate the significance of the engagement. . . He
first of all recollected that Emile had lain at death's door about
two years previously. That Philomène had nursed him during
his convalescence; and during his period of weakness she had
grafted Léon's powerful soul onto the young, half-lifeless
body. She had in this way as it were given birth to a child with
Léon, and this spiritual child was called Emile. It was this
rejuvenated version of her husband with whom she had now
fallen in love — SOS II, pp.109-10)

Similarly, on 11 April Strindberg wrote to Harriet:

Jag har lyckligtvis aldrig sett honom, men såg i går ett porträtt!
Han såg ut som jag; men hans sjelf var dödt och han hade fått
in af min själ en telning, både genom att ha spelat mig och
umgåtts Dig! Han var jag, lik mitt stora Ljusporträtt,[3] jag i en
ung gestalt som jag unnade Dig i byte mott mitt gamla. Men
död var han sjelf!
Hvad är detta? Kan själar föda afkomlingar? . . . Han låg ju
för döden för två år sen. Dog han då, men fick igen en ny själ
af Dig, som han älskat alltsedan Du såg honom i Finland.[4]

(Fortunately, I have never seen him, but yesterday I saw his
photograph! He resembled me; but his self was dead, and he
had become an offshoot of my soul, both from acting in my
plays and associating with you! He was me, as in my large Ljus
photograph, me in youthful guise, which I did not begrudge
you in exchange for my old one. But he himself was dead! What
does this mean? Can souls bear offspring?. . . He almost died
two years ago, as you know. Did he perhaps die, but get a new
soul from you, whom he had loved ever since you met him in
Finland? — XVI, p.254-5)

And on 14 April he noted in the Occult Diary:

Denne W liknar mig, men ser ut som en död; han höll på att dö
för 1½ år sedan (i lues), men kom sig. Är det möjligt att han
genom att spela mig och genom Harriet fått mig i sig? Jag
antager också att de två rotat i mig, i ett års tid, lefvat genom
och på mig och blifvit afläggare [af] mig. Jfr Wahlvervandt-
schaften.

(This W resembles me, but looks as though he were dead; he
very nearly did die 1½ years ago (of V.D.), but recovered. Is
it possible that by performing my plays and via Harriet he has

absorbed me? I also take it for granted that the two of them have
burrowed into me and on me and have become offshoots [of]
me. Cf. *Wahlverwandtschaften*)

Then one day Léon takes out a casket containing Philomène's
letters, and while reading them he reexperiences their first spring days.
He writes her a letter and receives a reply, which is commented on and
quoted:

Hennes fästman var tungsint och hon väntade ingen glädje med
honom. 'Han lider, ty han känner att vi stå i rapport, och han
plågar mig med svartsjuka. Han spionerar, men kan ju ingenting få veta, då Du och jag icke råkas. Detta att han icke kan
förklara hvarför han är svartsjuk, bringar honom till förtvivlan.'

(Her fiancé was gloomy, and she anticipated no happiness with
him. 'He suffers, since he feels that we're in touch, and he
plagues me with jealousy. He spies on me, but naturally without
discovering anything, since you and I never meet. The fact that
he cannot explain why he is jealous, makes him desperate' —
SOS II, p.111)

In view of how closely the story reflects reality, i.e. Strindberg's
reality, it is not entirely inconceivable that this is a summary of a real
letter from Harriet Bosse. It might possibly be the one that Strindberg
answers on 11-12 April: 'Efter ditt kära bref idag, men först efter din
bekännelse' (After your dear letter today, but only after your confession — XVI, p.258), and which he mentions in the Occult Diary on 13
April: 'Hon skref i sitt bref att hon "kämpat, slagits" ' (She wrote in
her letter that she had 'struggled, fought'). Another entry in the Occult
Diary for 9 June seems to confirm this supposition: 'Och nu efter
förlofningen skref hon till mig, att W "lider af att vi stå i rapport; han
känner det på sig" ' (And now, after the engagement, she wrote to me
that W 'suffers because we're in touch; he senses it').
  As previously mentioned, the lacuna in the manuscript with blue
pagination comprises pages 10-15. But the manuscript of 'Personlighetens klyfning' includes a page 16. This is an alteration of '15', and
Strindberg has inserted a new page 15 after having received the
manuscript back from Börjesson. The interpolated material appears to
have been written after the marriage of Harriet Bosse and Wingård on
24 May, and compares with entries in the Occult Diary between 17
and 26 May. Here, too, Strindberg makes a brave (if forlorn) attempt
at disguise: 'Det märkvärdiga är att jag aldrig fått veta slutet på denna
historia, ty jag har bara hört den berättas i Glasgow, på en resa i en

kupé' (The extraordinary thing is that I have never been told the end of this story, for I only heard it related in Glasgow, in a carriage — SOS II, p.112). There is, however, no connection between the five remaining essays with blue pagination 19-34 and the themes developed in 'Kärlekens bok'. Any 'inre sammanhang' (inner connection) of the kind that Strindberg refers to in asking Börjesson to keep the texts together has consequently to be sought on another level, in the fact that three of the texts deal with Shakespeare.

If one counts the unpaginated manuscript sheets of 'Apoteos', 'Pålen i köttet', and the eleven essays in the group beginning with 'Lustgården', which Börjesson is likely to have received around 15 April, and adds to them the eighteen sheets paginated in blue (which Strindberg made a note of on 19 April), the total comes to thirty-six. It seems highly probable that these are the thirty-six sheets which Strindberg refers to in the letter to Harriet of 17 April, from which I have already quoted.

These essays are followed by three others, paginated 1-12 in red pencil in the manuscript, which I also regard as belonging to 'Kärlekens bok': 'Det sköna och det goda' (The Beautiful and the Good), 'Karaktärsförändringar' (Character Changes), and 'Sorgen' (Grief). Another three essays, 'Juvelskrinet eller Hans bättre hälft' (The Jewel Box, or His Better Half), 'Mumiekistan' (The Mummy Coffin — i.e. a coffin containing 'hennes brev, hans bruds, för sju år sedan' (her letters, his bride's, seven years ago — SS 47, p.797)), and 'I vindskontoret' (In the Attic), which are paginated '1-p' in blue in the manuscript and placed roughly twenty pages further on in the book, are similar in kind and tone. One further essay which on internal criteria I have assigned to 'Kärlekens bok' is 'Mala ont', which lacks pagination. I have already compared it with a letter to Harriet Bosse of 4 May. It has been slotted in earlier on in the book, immediately before 'Pålen i sköttet' and after 'Apoteos', but was probably written after both these pieces, which reveal a number of striking similarities with the Occult Diary and the letters of 4 to 14 April.

The total number of essays which I have touched upon here and assigned to 'Kärlekens bok' is twenty-five, including 'Personlighetens klyfning'. It is possible that any such calculation is meaningless: *En ny blå bok* runs on directly into *En blå bok III*, more than half of the book being written in early June.[5] Many of its essays are variations on the theme of 'Kärlekens bok', and could also, depending on the criteria adopted, be placed there.

En ny blå bok appeared on 27 May. On 13 May, Strindberg wrote to Börjesson:

Det var med en viss rörelse jag lemnade ifrån mig sista arket på BB i afton. . . Jag har 70 nya sidor färdiga och kommer icke i

digtning! Det är så mycket oklart och för öfrigt: rena ord äro
bättre! än omsvep! Det är bara omsvep hela digten! och liknar
icke den klara enkla sanningen!

(It was with some emotion that I parted with the last sheet of BB
this evening. . . I have 70 new pages ready and lack the inspiration for imaginative literature! There is so much that is unclear,
and besides: straight words are better! than circumlocution!
Imaginative literature is nothing but circumlocution! and bears
no likeness to the clear and simple truth! — XVI, p.308)

The question of life or fiction appears to be answered here. But in
an entry in the Occult Diary, in March 1901, a few days before his
engagement to Harriet, he was not so sure: 'Tänk om det är och blir en
dikt alltsammans? Hvad så? Så skrifver jag en dikt, då, som skall bli
vacker!' (Supposing it all is and will remain pure fantasy? What then?
I shall compose a work of art, in that case, a thing of beauty!).[6]

Notes

1. He also placed Harriet's letters from the same period in this envelope. The
   originals have not survived, but copies were made by Strindberg's
   executor, Vilhelm Carlheim-Gyllensköld, and are now in the Royal
   Library, Stockholm. For the texts, however, see *Meddelanden från
   Strindbergssällskapet*, 19 (1956), pp.4-8. There are very few extant
   letters from Harriet Bosse to Strindberg; all those returned to her after
   his death, she burnt. See Margareta Brundin, 'Kungliga Bibliotekets
   Strindbergssamlingar', *Strindbergiana*, I (1985), pp.50-70.
2. Strindberg makes the same remark in a letter to Harriet and in the Occult
   Diary on 7 April.
3. Named after the photograph by Herman Anderson, taken 24 February
   1902. It was reproduced in the edition of *Svenska öden och äventyr*
   published by Ljus förlag, in 1904.
4. Harriet Bosse and Wingård had played the leads in the first performance of
   Kronbruden, in Helsinki, in 1906.
5. Letter to Börjesson, c. 1 June: 'Nu ligga 160 sidor ny BB i manuskript!'
   (There are now 160 manuscript pages of new BB — XVI, p.330).
6. I am grateful to Dr Karin Petherick for making the English translation of
   this essay.

IV

Seeing Differently

The Visual Dimension

Strindberg and Visual Imagination

Harry G. Carlson

Queens College, New York

The importance to Strindberg's writing of his responses to forms in life and to the life of forms in art is difficult to overemphasize: they helped to make him the most versatile experimenter in drama in the last century. 'If Ibsen was the Rembrandt of modern drama, its master of psychological portraiture,' I noted elsewhere, 'Strindberg was its master of forms, its Picasso, its restless, inventive spirit, prodigious and prolific.'[1] It was no coincidence that each of the periods when he did a lot of painting — the early 1870s and the early 1890s — were connected, either before or afterward, with periods when his imaginative writing flourished. In fact, in the late 1890s, as we shall see, a new faith in the power of the visual imagination, together with a changed attitude toward nature — thinking it, seeing it, and feeling it as form — were vital mediators in the renewal of his art.

Scholars and critics have generally considered Strindberg's writing and his painting separately, almost like individual, watertight compartments. Comparisons in most cases have been general, rather than specific, such as that he wrote with 'a painter's eye'. Michael Meyer, noting that Strindberg developed into 'an interesting painter,' says that during the first period (1872-74), 'he was . . . painting vigorously, though as a relaxation rather than as a serious means of self-expression.'[2] But it meant much more to him than that. Sometimes painting was a vital way for the writer to get his creative juices flowing, at other times, an alternate form of expression when his writing efforts had been rejected or failed to meet his own expectations. He also found that painting was a more physically satisfying medium, somehow more natural than writing. The art historian W. J. T. Mitchell has observed that 'if writing is the medium of absence and artifice, the image is the medium of presence and nature,' sometimes deceiving us with 'sensory

255

immediacy'.[3] Strindberg must have sensed the power of that 'sensory immediacy', for he believed that the visual artist had greater license than the literary artist, a greater range of expressive opportunities. 'Det fanns nämligen ingen sysselsättning, som så uppsög alla tankar, alla känslor som detta att måla,' he insisted (There was no activity that so absorbed all thoughts, all feelings, as painting). While he felt obliged as a writer to copy directly from nature, as a painter he did not: 'Sittande framför naturen gick det ingen väg' (Sitting in front of nature did not work — SS 19, p.36).

Strindberg comments in his autobiography that as a young neophyte writer he thought of painting as a catalyst. So intimidated did he feel by the challenge of expressing himself on paper, that he felt a physical need to see his 'hazy feelings', as he called them, first take form on a canvas,

> . . . kanske också för att få ett handgripligt sätt att uttrycka dem på, ty de små gnetiga bokstäverna på papperet lågo där döda och kunde ej så öppet och i ett slag visa honom för sig själv. Han hade ingen tanke på att bli målare, utställa i konstföreningen, sälja tavlor eller dylikt. Att gå till staffliet var som att sätta sig och sjunga.

> (. . . perhaps also to find a concrete way of expressing them. His small, crabbed handwriting lay dead on the paper and was incapable of revealing as openly what he felt. He had no thought of becoming a painter, showing in an exhibition, selling paintings or such. Going to the easel was like sitting down to sing. — SS 19, p.8)

The adjective he uses to describe his feelings — 'hazy' (*simmiga*) — is used again by him in an important context two decades later. In 1907 he sent a book of reproductions of paintings by Turner to August Falck, the director of the Intimate Theatre. Included with the book was the instruction: 'Så här simmigt skall målas åt Intima Teatern, särskilt Drömspelet' (This is how hazy (*simmigt*) I want the decor painted at the Intimate Theatre, especially for *Ett drömspel*).[5] Time and again, *simmig* was the kind of word he chose to represent his response to the shadowy zone of expression where the imagination was allowed free flight.

There were times, of course, when expressive needs compelled the use of a different approach. While working as a young telegraphist on an island in the Stockholm archipelago, he enjoyed painting in his spare time, and kept his eye open for likely subjects. One day, a shipwreck

intraffade . . . under särdeles pittoreska omständigheter. . .
Hela sceneriet var så nytt och måleriskt, att han fick lust att
skildra det, men nu räckte icke pensel och färg, utan han måste
taga till pennan. Och så skrev han några korrespondenser till
Stockholms liberala morgontidning.

(occurred under especially picturesque circumstances. . .The
whole setting was so new and pictorial, that he felt the desire to
render it, but now brushes and paints were not adequate. He
had to turn to the pen. And that is how he came to write several
items for Stockholm's liberal morning newspaper. — SS 19,
p.102).

Here is a telling indication of the intimate relationship between the
painter and the writer: while groping for a way to reveal his feelings,
painting offered a more passionate, immediate outlet, but to articulate
these feelings with greater clarity and intensity, he had to turn from
painting to writing.

The art critic Ulf Linde suggests that the relationship between
Strindberg's literary and visual instincts is implied in the following
passage from *Tjänstekvinnanas son*, in which Strindberg defines the
different ways that a botanist, a painter, and a poet interpret a visual
experience:

Vem såg vad skogen egentligen var? Botanisten kanske, som
endast fann en samling fanerogamer och kryptogamer, vilka
omsatte upplösta mineraler och gaser i sina kärlknippen! Den
som såg ytligast och falskast var väl då artisten, som endast såg
på ytan, teckningen och färgen. Men vad hade han sett såsom
poet? Sina känslor återfunna i halvdunkel och heldagrar, i
mossornas färgspel, vilka väckte minnen om hans simmiga
inre, där alla själens funktioner arbetade utan beroende av
viljan.

(Who saw what the forest really was? The botanist, perhaps,
who found only a collection of phanerogams [seed plants] and
cryptogams [spore plants], which convert dissolved minerals
and gases in their inflorescences! The one who saw most
superficially and falsely was surely the artist, who saw only
surfaces, markings, and colours. But what had he seen as poet?
He found his feelings revealed in the half-shadows and half-
lights in the play of colours in the mosses, which aroused
memories of some hazy place deep within him (*hans simmiga
inre*), where the functions of his soul worked independently of
his will. — SS 19, p.93).

The distinction made between artist and poet, says Linde, reveals that as an artist Strindberg wanted to control his subject matter in a subjectively practical way, 'but as a poet he wanted to be controlled by the vision confronting him, to surrender totally.'[6] The idea of 'surrender' suggests someone who wants to lose himself in his work. But I think the importance Strindberg attached to different ways of seeing reveals instead a desire to *find*, not *lose*, himself in that work. The poet — which Strindberg clearly understands to be the true artist, whether he works with words or lines and colours — has an ulterior purpose in his fascination with the 'play of colours' in the world around him: it becomes a means for him to explore his own feelings, to scrutinize the truth of inner essences, rather than outer surfaces. In this way Strindberg echoed the Romantics' emphasis on the wisdom of what Carlyle called the *seeing eye*, which 'is this that discloses the inner harmony of things; what nature meant, what musical idea nature has wrapped up in these often rough embodiments.'[7]

It was Strindberg's discovery of fertile new potential in the visual imagination in the early 1890s — made possible partly through the stimulus provided by a renewed interest in painting — that led him to discern the kind of 'inner harmony of things' that Carlyle talked about. Two documents from the period testify to a growing preoccupation with the role played in the creative process by the visual imagination: a letter of 1892 written to the painter Richard Bergh just before Strindberg set off for Germany in self-imposed exile, and the 1894 essay 'Des arts nouveaux! où Le hasard dans la production artistique'. In the letter Strindberg says: 'I have a number of oil studies to show you, painted from the imagination. A "new direction" that I discovered myself and call "wood-nymphism" '[*skogssnufvismen*] (IX, p.40). This strange new direction is explained two years later in the essay and declared to be the foundation of a new theory of automatic art, first announced publicly, according to the author, to a group of friends in an artist's studio.

Herrarna minns den där berättelsen i folksagorna om gossen som är ute i skogen och upptäcker 'skogsrået'. Hon är vacker som en dag, med smaragdgrönt hår etc. Han närmar sig och rået vänder ryggen till, som liknar en stubbe.

Naturligtvis har gossen bara sett stubben och hans uppspelta fantasi har diktat resten.

(You all remember the story in the folk tale about the boy who is out in the woods and discovers a 'wood nymph.' She was as beautiful as the dawn, with emerald green hair, etc. As he approached her, she turned her back, and now resembled a tree stump. Naturally, the boy only saw the stump — his lively imagination fabricated the rest.)[8]

Two important things are implied in the passage. First, there is a zest for and confidence in the imagination that Strindberg had seldom acknowledged as openly before. In the 1880s he had held a negative view of the imagination and its functions, influenced at least in part by Georg Brandes's espousal of the position of association psychologists, who regarded the imagination as a fundamentally passive, mechanical faculty in the mind, receiving and transmitting sense perceptions. In 1882 Strindberg argued that:

Fantasien som man ansett skapa, det vill säga göra av intet, är endast den arrangerande gåvan, som ordnar minnets större eller mindre rikedomar av intryck och erfarenheter och ställer dem var på sin plats, där de kunna med ljus i händerna lysa tanken dess väg.

(Once considered as creative, that is, capable of making something out of nothing, the imagination [*fantasien*] is only the gift for rearranging the greater or lesser treasures of impressions and experiences stored in the memory, [then] lining them up anew to illuminate the pathway of thought — SS 17, pp.193-4).

By the 1890s, he had developed a totally different perspective on the imagination. No longer either a simple mechanical activity or the infamous source of 'hallucinations' or 'visions' that had once created anxieties for him, it was now a truly creative force. In the essay on chance he proclaims its capacity for not only permitting, but welcoming, the whimsical intrusions of chance in its work, thus asserting its own authority in art, independent of the conscious intent or will of the artist.

Second, the essay passage implies that the character of the relationship between the artist and Nature is collaborative and subjective, rather than, as in Naturalism, only scientific and objective, and this relationship is defined in some detail in 'The New Arts'. The author relates that he himself had experienced 'wood-nymphism' 'many times':

En vacker morgon när jag strövade i skogen kom jag fram till en inhägnad åkerlapp. Mina tankar var fjärran men mina blickar iakttog ett okänt, underligt föremål som låg på marken.
Ett ögonblick var det en ko, därnäst två bönder som omfamnade varann, därnäst en trädstubbe, därnäst . . . Jag

259

tycker om när förnimmelserna växlar på det sättet. . . en
viljeakt och jag vill inte längre veta vad det är . . . jag känner
hur medvetenhetens ridå snart lyfter sig . . . men jag vill inte .
. . nu är det en lantlig frukost, man äter . . . men figurerna är
orörliga som i ett panoptikon . . . åh . . . det är slut . . . det är
en kvarlämnad kärra, där lantmannen slängt sin rock och hängt
upp sin ryggsäck! Allt är sagt! Det finns inget mer att se.
Fröjden är borta!

(One beautiful morning as I strolled in the woods, I came out
onto an enclosed patch of cultivated land. My thoughts were
elsewhere, but I spotted a strange, unfamiliar object lying on
the ground.
The first moment it was a cow, the next a tree stump, the next
— (I like it when sensations alternate in this way). . . . I felt the
curtain of consciousness starting to rise — but I didn't want it
to — What I now saw were some people eating breakfast
alfresco — but the figures were motionless, as if seen through
a panopticon — Oh, oh — it's all over — It was just an
abandoned cart in which a farmer had thrown his coat and hung
up his rucksack! That's all it was! There was nothing more to
see. The joy was over!).[9]

The elements of reality that the artist perceives around him seem to
exist not primarily as objects to be described or imitated with scientific
fidelity, but as grist for the mill of his imagination, which is free to do
almost anything, provided the artist is properly attuned to the messages
emanating either from the sights and sounds of Nature, or the whims of
chance. Whatever imitation that is done is no longer of nature as
object, but Nature as fellow maker and creator.
    The essay also describes a visit to the Scandinavian artists' colony
in France, a setting Strindberg found conducive to transformations that
excited his imagination. He goes immediately to the dining room to
examine the latest batch of impressionistic, improvisational sketches
done by the artists after work on more serious studies. A guessing
game is in order:

Men vad är det? — Det är just denna preliminära fråga som
bereder er den första förnöjelsen. Det gäller söka, erövra; det
finns ingenting angenämare än när fantasin sätts i rörelse. . .
Målarna kaller det 'palettskrap', vilket betyder: när konstnärn
slutet sitt arbete, skrapar han samman resten av färgerna, och
om lusten då faller på, gör han ett eller annat utkast. Jag stod
betagen inför pannån i Marlotte. Där fanns en mycket förklarlig
harmoni i färgerna, eftersom de alla redan utvalts för en tavla.

När målarns själ är fri bekymret att hitta de rätta kulörerna och oppfylld av skarparkraft sätter i gång med att söka fram konturerna, och handen på måfå manövrerar spateln, och han icke desto mindre håller fast naturens förebild utan att han vill kopiera den, då uppenbarar sig resultatet som ett förtjusande virrvarr av omedvetet och medvetet. Här är det fråga om naturlig konst, ty konstnären arbetar som den nyckfulla naturen, utan fastställt mål.

(What is this? — A leading question like this provides the first bit of pleasure. You must search, conquer; and there is nothing more agreeable than when the imagination is set in motion. . . Painters call it 'palette scrapings,' which means: when the artist's work is done, he scrapes together the remnants of colours, and, if he feels inclined, does a study of some kind. I stood enchanted in front of this one panel at Marlotte. There was a harmony in the colours — very understandable, of course, since they all came from the same painting. Once the artist felt free of the trouble of finding the right colours, he was induced to exert all his creative powers in the search for form. His hand guided the palette knife at random, and as he adhered to nature's model without trying to imitate it, the result revealed itself as a wonderful blending of the unconscious and the conscious. This is natural art — the artist working, in other words, like capricious nature, without a prescribed goal.)[10]

The Russian abstractionist Wassily Kandinsky made an almost identical discovery years later. Images created by chance on his palette stirred his imagination in unexpected ways:[11]

In the middle of the palette is a curious world of the remnants of colours already used. . . . Here is a world which, derived from . . . pictures already painted, was . . . determined and created through accidents, through the puzzling play of forces alien to the artist. And I owe much to these accidents: they have taught me more than any teacher or master. Many an hour I have studied them with love and admiration.[12]

In Strindberg's essay the narrator concludes his discussion with advice that he as Zolaesque Naturalist would probably have questioned: 'Konsten som skall komma . . . : Efterbilda naturen på ett ungefär; i synnerhet efterbilda sättet varpå naturen skapar!' (The art of the future . . . : Imitate nature approximately; above all, emulate nature's way of creating!)[13] Strindberg had returned to a fundamental Romantic organic principle. 'Ultimately, in the practice of art,' said Goethe, 'we can only vie with nature when we have at least to some extent learned from her the process that she pursues in the formation of her works.'[14] The focus on *process* brings to mind old terms that were revitalized by the Romantics, terms that distinguish between nature creating — *natura naturans* — and nature created — *natura naturata*, between 'the essential creative power or act', and 'the natural phenomena . . . in which nature is manifested.'[15] Coleridge insisted that 'if the artist copies the mere nature *natura naturata*, what idle rivalry! . . . [He] must master the essence, the *natura naturans*.'[16]

In Paris, in the spring of 1896, Strindberg's interest in experiments that encouraged a free play of the imagination intensified after he moved into the Hôtel Orfila. Some of the experiments, in fact, were regarded as rather bizarre by his friends. He claimed to see unusual images in such commonplace objects as walnuts and pillows. One day, poking a lump of coal out of his hotel room stove, he found:

> den liknade en av dessa demoner, som uppträdde på medel-tidens häxsabbater. Dagen därpå plockar jag fram en ypperlig grupp av två rusiga tomtar, som omfamna varandra med böljande kläder. Det är ett mästerverk av primitiv bildhuggar-konst.

> (it resembled one of the demons who performed in medieval witches' sabbaths. The next day I plucked out a superb pair of drunken goblins dressed in billowing clothes and embracing each other. It was a masterpiece of primitive sculpture. — SS 28, p.46).

When he showed his lumps of coal to Edvard Munch, he says he was pleased when Munch asked him who 'made' them (p.46). Extraordinary resemblances appeared to Strindberg between shelled walnuts and the human brain, and he sketched them to record his impressions. The lumps and folds in pillows presented interesting patterns, and he purposely tossed the pillows about in order to obtain new patterns to interpret, just as, to borrow an image from his own essay on chance in art, weavers might twist and turn kaleidoscopes to obtain new variations.

However bizarre these kinds of experiments might appear, they have long been a common practice among artists. Leonardo da Vinci, for example, advised painters to 'look upon a wall covered with dirt, or the odd appearance of some streaked stones [to discover] things like landscapes, battles, clouds, uncommon attitudes, humorous faces, draperies, etc. Out of this confused mass of objects, the mind will be furnished with an abundance of designs and subjects perfectly new.'[17]

Strindberg was learning to read the Book of Nature in a new way. Instead of just examining natural surroundings as a background for action, he was attempting to understand the essence of Nature's creativity, and the results provide examples of how he anticipated future trends in art. Among the tools he used to record his observations, in addition to sketches, were charcoal rubbings of surfaces of objects, such as the shell of a crab.[18] Thirty years later, Max Ernst, who coined the term 'frottage' to describe such rubbings, was motivated by a similar 'wood-nymphistic' instinct to collaborate with Nature in the creating of art.

Ernst described how a memory served as catalyst. As a boy, while ill in bed with a fever, he had watched a mahogany panel across the room appear to change form, first resembling 'a spinning top, then a nose, then the head of a bird, and so on. And later I consciously tried to recreate similar imaginings by looking at wooden panelling, clouds, wallpaper, unpapered walls, just to get my imagination working.'[19] Years later, in August 1925, cooped up in a little hotel room on a rainy day, he was staring at a wooden floor when suddenly he noticed that the markings in the wood seemed to start to move, and he recalled the childhood incident:

Like my visions then, when I lay half-awake, half-asleep, the lines move and flow into pictures. And then, to keep my concentration going, I try to make a series of drawings from the boards. Quite haphazardly, I drop pieces of paper onto the floor and rub over them with a black pencil. I am astonished at the way suddenly my ability to look, to see, gets stronger.[20]

Ernst later wrote that 'by widening in this way the active part of the mind's hallucinatory faculties I came to assist as *spectator* at the birth of all my works.'[21] Even if Strindberg's intention, unlike Ernst's, had been scientific rather than specifically artistic, he, too, was widening his 'mind's hallucinatory faculties,' and improving his 'ability to look, to see.'

At the time Strindberg arrived in Paris in 1894, the world of art was awash in the latest wave of what Edgar Quinet in 1841 had named the 'Oriental Renaissance': a preoccupation with images culled from Eastern philosophy, mythology, and art. For many Europeans in the late nineteenth century, Orientalism was a synonym for everything in the human spirit regarded as irrational — all extremes of emotional, artistic and imaginative expression. While some artists exploited for sensationalist purposes the lurid appeal these themes suggested, other artists, from Goethe to Delacroix to Matisse, discovered exciting new ways of thinking about art. They sensed that the vital thing about the East was that man's relationships with art and nature were better there than in the West because they were more natural, more organic. A passage in Goethe's *West-östlicher Divan* evokes a mythopoeic view of a world in which man and Nature are one. In the Arabic language, Goethe asserts,

> all the things which man expresses freely and naturally are life relations; . . . the Arab is as intimately connected with camel and horse as is body with soul; nothing can happen to him which does not at the same time affect these creatures and vitally connect their existence and their activity with his own. . . . If we proceed to consider everything else visible: mountain and desert, cliff and plain, trees, herbs, flowers, river and sea and the starry heavens, we find that, to the Oriental, *all things suggest all things.*'[22] [Emphasis added]

Matisse, after spending two winters in Morocco in 1912 and 1913, came to similar conclusions. 'The European Renaissance makes it difficult to bring together the vegetal, the animal and the human,' he wrote, thereby implying, says Pierre Schneider, 'the contrary: that the decorative Orient makes it easy.'[23]

It was precisely this emphasis perceived in the Orient on man's organic relationship to the world around him that attracted Strindberg's interest. His preparation for this stimulation was a long, if selective, history of exposure to Eastern culture and philosophy. Like many Neoromantics in the 1890s, he was ready to be seduced by its imagery. As a young man, he learned a smattering of Chinese and Japanese for his cataloguing duties at the Royal Library. Readings in Schopenhauer then introduced him to aspects of Indic religion and philosophy, and later, in Paris, his readings in theosophy about the same sources encouraged him to undertake further study on his own. By March 1896, his passion for the subject had grown to the point where his reading of a travel book on the East apparently took on the magnitude of a powerful revelation. In what has come to be called his 'Benares Letter' Strindberg confesses to Torsten Hedlund:

> Jag har i dag slutat läsningen af en bok om Indien, och jag vet icke mer hvar jag är hemma. Mig förefaller att författaren till Sylva Sylvarum (och allt det andra!) vore en annan än jag och att denna jag vore en Hindou.

> (Today I finished reading a book about India and I no longer know where I am. I feel as if the author of *Sylva Sylvarum* (and all the rest!) were someone else and that someone was a Hindu. — XI, p.151).

The work in question was by André Chevrillon, who was closely associated with the French symbolists.[24] Cited approvingly in the letter is Chevrillon's description of a building and street scene in the holy city of Benares:

Ini murarne, öfver portarne, skydda nicher vanformade gudar, monster med elefanthufvuden och hvilkas androgynkroppar omslingras af armar. Här och der brunnar hvarifrån uppstiger en stinkande doft af ruttna blommor. . . Man halkar i en gödsel af blommor, man går fram i en smuts af sopor, heliga jasminer som ruttna i detta Gangesvatten, hvarmed man bestänker altarena. . . Midt i menskohopen . . . kor vandra fritt omkring, ätande blommor.

(In the walls, over the doors, niches protect malformed gods — monsters with the heads of elephants, their androgynous bodies entwined with arms. Here and there are wells from which the stinking odour of rotting flowers arise. . . One slips on a dunghill of flowers, one advances over a mire of refuse; sacred jasmines rot in the waters of the Ganges which is then sprinkled on altars. . . In the midst of a throng of people . . . cows wander freely, eating flowers. — p.150).

The description's contradictions may have puzzled many Western readers, but they clearly intrigued Strindberg: a place where flowers are holy and yet trampled under foot, where living growths are revered at the same time that dead and rotting ones are used to anoint altars, where cows are as sacred as flowers. The profusion of images — evoking a picture of life as a turbulent, metamorphic play of forces in which there are no sharp lines of demarcation between the aesthetic and the organic, the spiritual and the sensual — implied a view of man's relationships with art, religion, and nature that was at odds with Western tradition. For Strindberg, it provided a galvanizing imaginative impetus. He would have understood the importance of Matisse's 1947 overview of his own career: 'Persian miniatures . . . showed me all the possibilities of my sensations. I could find again in nature what they should be. . . . Thus my revelation came to me from the Orient.'[25]

In what is probably the most important passage from the travel book cited by Strindberg, in terms of its probable impact on his evolving ideas about art and the visual imagination, Chevrillon describes his reactions to decorations that were 'chased' or hammered onto the surface of a Benares copper vase:

Hvad föreställa dessa ciseleringar? Först vet man ingenting: man ser endast ett snår af hopvirade linier, sammanslingade på en slump. Småningom reder sig härfvan och dunkla gestalter träda fram: gudar, genier, fiskar, hundar, gazeller, blommor, örter, icke grupperade efter ett motiv utan kastade huller om buller som en klump af underhafsgyttjan den man draggat, och ur hvilken oformliga massa man ser framskymta en klo, ett skal, en fena . . .

(What do these chasings represent? At first one knows nothing: one sees only a thicket of entwined lines, twisted together at random. Gradually, the skein untangles and shadowy figures emerge: gods, genies, fish, dogs, gazelles, flowers, herbs, not grouped around a motif, but tossed, pell-mell, and one glimpses in the formless mass, as in a lump of clay dragged from the bottom of the sea, a claw, a shell, a fin — XI, pp.151-2)

To understand how this description could spark Strindberg's imagination, we must imagine that in a flash art and nature became one. Not only do the vase decorations imitate faithfully the interconnectedness in the flow of life, the total effect created can be viewed as a model for the way that art can be read and interpreted. Like life, art too can seem 'only a thicket of entwined lines,' which gradually, with the aid of the imagination, untangles, allowing 'shadowy figures' to emerge. This was precisely one of the points Strindberg had made two years earlier in the 1894 essay on the role of chance in art; now he found apparent support for it in Indic art. In the essay, referring to examples of modern art which a philistine public found inexplicable, the narrator says that at first one notices

bara ett virrvarr av färger, sen börjar det likna något. Det liknar, nej visst inte, det liknar ingenting. Plötsligt fixerar sig en punkt som kärnan i en cell, den vidgar ut sig, färgerna grupperar sig runt om och länkar sig samman. Strålar sprider sig som grenar, i rankor, som iskristallerna på fönsterrutan . . . och bilden framträder för betraktaren, som har biträtt vid tavlans tillblivelse. Och var bättre är: målningen är ständigt ny, den växlar med belysningen, tröttar aldrig, blir ung igen. Därför att den fått livets gåva.

(nothing more than a chaos of colours. Then it begins to look like something, it resembles — no, it doesn't resemble anything. All at once there is a fixed point, like the nucleus in a cell; it grows; colours group themselves around it, accumulate; beams radiate outwards, sprouting branches and twigs, as ice crystals do on windowpanes. . . A pattern appears to the observer, who has himself assisted in the act of creation. More importantly, the painting is continually new; changing with the light, never tiring, ever reviving, endowed with the gift of life.)[26]

The reading of the Chevrillon book must have alerted Strindberg to the cumulative significance of the various experiments with the visual imagination that he had been conducting since 1892: the 'wood-nymph' revelations, the creative patterns discovered in pillows, walnuts, and painters' palettes. What had been evolving in his mind as a result was a new view of the imagination and its role in the creative process; Chevrillon only demonstrated that the same view already existed as part of artistic tradition in Eastern culture. As Matisse said about his own discoveries in Oriental art, 'You surrender yourself that much better when you see your efforts confirmed by such an ancient tradition.'[27]

Strindberg must have also realized that often, throughout his life, his finest work had been done, unknowingly, under the influence of the same broad, liberated view of the imagination as an independent force, collaborating with Nature through improvisations, hallucinations, visions, and dreams. This is why he could admit to Hedlund: 'I feel as if the author . . . [of all my books] were someone else and that someone was a Hindu.' What he probably did not realize at the time was that he was also reactivating a vital Romantic insight. Just as Strindberg talks of a painting being 'continually new', Friedrich Schlegel a century earlier defined Romantic poetry as 'still in the process of becoming; this indeed is its very essence, that it is eternally evolving, never completed. . . It alone is infinite, just as it alone is free.'[28]

Notes

1. 'Introduction', August Strindberg, *Strindberg: Five Plays*, translated by Harry G. Carlson (New York, 1984), p.ix.
2. Michael Meyer, *Strindberg* (New York, 1985), pp.69, 46.
3. W. J. T. Mitchell, 'Visible Language: Blake's Wond'rous Art of Writing', in *Romanticism and Contemporary Criticism*, eds. Morris Eaves and Michael Fischer (Ithaca, New York, 1986), p.48.
4. Except where otherwise noted, all translations are by the author.
5. I am obliged to Björn Meidal for pointing out this reference in August Falck, *Fem år med Strindberg* (Stockholm, 1935; 2nd edition), p.190.
6. Ulf Linde, *Efter hand: texter 1950-1985*, ed. Lars Nygren (Stockholm, 1985), p.469.
7. Thomas Carlyle, *Heroes and Hero Worship* (New York, n.d.), p.124.
8. August Strindberg, *Vivisektioner* (Stockholm, 1958), p.65.

9. Ibid., pp.65, 67.
10. Ibid., pp.57, 59.
11. Roger Lipsey, *An Art of Our Own: The Spiritual in Twentieth-Century Art* (Boston and Shaftesbury, 1989), p.118.
12. Kandinsky, 'Reminiscences' (Rückblicke), *Modern Artists on Art*, ed. Robert L. Herbert (Englewood Cliffs, 1964), p.34.
13. *Vivisektioner*, p.73.
14. Goethe, 'Über Wahrheit und Wahrscheinlichkeit der Kunstwerke', *Sämtliche Werke*, XXXIII, 90. Cited by M.H. Abrams, *The Mirror and the Lamp* (Oxford, 1953), p.207.
15. *The Compact Edition of the Oxford English Dictionary*, vol. 3, s.v. 'natura naturans'.
16. Cited by James Engell, *The Creative Imagination* (Cambridge, Massachusetts, 1981) p.358.
17. Cited by Jean Clay, *Romanticism*, translated by Daniel Wheeler and Craig Owen (New York, 1981), p.174. Da Vinci's advice to artists is cited by Göran Söderström and Max Ernst. Söderström: 'As our friend Botticelli observed, a mushroom, impregnated with different colours and thrown against a wall, leaves stains which can look like a landscape; one can distinguish a mass of images in such stains — a man's head, different animals, pitched battles, cliff scenes, seas, clouds, woods, and so forth — all depending on the disposition of one's soul.' 'Strindbergs måleri', in *Strindbergs måleri*, ed. Torsten Måtte Schmidt (Malmö, 1972), pp.221-22. Max Ernst: 'It is not to be despised, in my opinion, if, after gazing fixedly at the spot on the wall, the coals in the grate, the clouds, the flowing stream, if one remembers some quite admirable inventions. Of these the genius of the painter may take full advantage, to compose battles of animals and of men, of landscapes or monsters, of devils and other fantastic things which bring you honor. In these confused things genius becomes aware of new inventions.' 'On Frottage', in *Theories of Modern Art*, ed. Herschel B. Chipp (Berkeley, 1968), p.429.
18. A reproduction of Strindberg's rubbing of a crab shell appears in Söderström, 'Strindbergs måleri', p.146.
19. From a film documentary series, *The Surreal Eye*, broadcast on American Public Television in 1987.
20. Ibid.
21. Max Ernst, 'On Frottage', p.431.
22. Cited by Ernst Robert Curtius, *European Literature and the Latin Middle Ages*, translated by Willard R. Trask (Princeton, 1973), p.303.
23. Pierre Schneider, 'The Moroccan Hinge', in *Matisse in Morocco: The Paintings and Drawings, 1912-1913* (Washington, D.C., 1990), p.40.
24. Gunnar Brandell, *Strindberg in Inferno*, translated by Barry Jacobs (Cambridge, Massachusetts, 1974), p.243.
25. *Matisse on Art*, translated by Jack D. Flam, (New York, 1973) p.116.
26. *Vivisektioner*, p.67.
27. *Matisse on Art*, ibid.
28. Cited in *European Romanticism*, ed. Lilian R. Furst (London, 1980), p.5.

Strindberg, Chance Images and *En blå bok*

Some Reflections

Magnus Florin

Royal Dramatic Theatre, Stockholm

In *En blå bok* there is a passage on the inner urge which matter displays to develop or become an image. Indeed, throughout *En blå bok* there are essays on optical illusions, projections, clairvoyance, pictorial puzzles, ghostly apparitions, and mirages, but the passage to which I am referring, in the piece 'Nisus Formativus eller omedveten bilddrift' (Nisus Formativus, or Unconscious Image Formation), deals with something quite specific:

> Jag underskrev en gång ett kontrakt med en köpman. När jag sovit om natten, märkte jag att han gjort mig orätt. I vrede tankar gick jag ut att vandra. Hemkommen skulle jag byta kläder; kastade min näsduk på bordet. När jag var omklädd, märkte jag att näsduken av mycket nervöst tummande var tillnycklad och nu bildade, där den låg, en avgjutning av köpmannens huvud, lik en gipsbyst. . . . Jag har läst om indiska vaser som äro så modellerade, att man först ser ett kaos liknande moln, tarmar eller hjärna. Sedan ögat vant sig, börjar utredningen, och alla skapade ting: växter och djur träda fram, tagande form. Om alla åskådare se lika, vet jag icke. Men jag tror att skulptören arbetat utan avsikt, omedvetet, planlöst.

> (I once signed a contract with a merchant. After a night's sleep, I noticed that he had cheated me. With angry thoughts, I went out for a walk. Coming home, I went to change my clothes;

threw my handkerchief on the table. When I had changed, I
noticed that the handkerchief was crumpled up from much
nervous thumbing, and now formed, where it lay, a cast of the
merchant's head. . . . I have read of Indian vases which are
modelled in such a way that at first one only sees a chaos
resembling clouds, intestines, or a brain. After the eye has
grown accustomed to this, the process of unravelling begins,
and all created things, plants and animals, emerge and assume
form. Whether every observer sees the same thing, I don't
know. But I believe that the sculptor has worked without
design, unconsciously and at random. — SS 46, pp.187-88)[1]

Strindberg's abiding interest in images of this kind[2] is linked to one
of his most frequently recurring ideas. The objects through which the
world manifests itself to the eyes of the beholder both conceal and
reveal, and if one is attentive one may discover correspondences and
analogies between objects which point to the truth in a world which is
otherwise governed by falsehood and illusion. But there is a distinction
between the pictures produced by the handkerchief or the vase in this
passage and, say, the celebrated correspondence between a brain and
a walnut, which he describes elsewhere.[3] While this last relationship
emerges as evidence of a mutual biological identity, the images
revealed in the handkerchief or vase have nothing to do with the objects
in which they appear: the latter merely provide a substance in which
the images take shape, like the smoke from a cigar in which figures
may be observed coming into view.

The term for such pictures is 'chance images'. One example that
Strindberg gives of them is taken from Leonardo da Vinci's celebrated
account of how he let his pupils draw the faces that they observed
taking form on a piece of half-transparent linen.[4]

But where do such images come from? They surely have their
origin in the mind of the viewer, just as dreams are understood to
derive from the mind of the dreamer. Strindberg himself suggests that
the picture one sees in an enfolded inkblot is a manifestation of one's
inner, unconscious thoughts. But neither the Swedenborgian notion of
correspondences nor the concepts of psychology offer an adequate
account of Strindberg's interest in chance images. In addition to these
well-rehearsed aspects of Strindberg's thinking, there is, I believe, an
aesthetic motive, which may be traced in a number of his literary
precursors.

The second part of Goethe's *Faust* (1808) ends in the heavenly
spheres, where the harmonious sufficiency of the world (or microcosm)
is reconciled with the unlimited perfection of the macrocosm. Goethe's
way of depicting this is by way of a vision: risen far above everything
petty and mundane, the image of Gretchen is seen in a cloud that has in

turn been created from the dress of the immortal Helen. The meaning of this vision is clear, and it helps Faust finally and definitely to resist Mephistopheles, and thus to take the right direction onward and, ultimately, upward. The vision in the clouds is also the moment of synthesis and exaltation, the fulfilment of everything earthly and unearthly: 'Das Ewig-Weibliche zieht uns hinan' (Eternal Womanhood leads us above).

It may appear a considerable step from the second part of Goethe's *Faust* to Georg Büchner's *Woyzeck* (1837), where the protagonist asks questions of the learned and would-be wise Doctor about the strangeness of nature: 'Die Schwämme, Herr Doktor, da, da steckt's. Haben Sie schon gesehn, in was für Figuren die Schwämme auf dem Boden wachsen? Wer das lesen könnet!' (The toadstools, Doctor, it's all in the toadstools. Have you ever noticed how they grow in strange patterns on the ground. If only one could decipher them!).[5] But both Goethe and Büchner describe pictures that become visible in nature, in the sky and on the ground, as do numerous other writers who similarly describe the images they perceive in mountains and fields, stone or water. They are pictures seemingly without a sender, but with the characteristics of the intentional. Whose, then, is the intention?

Faust's supremacy and Woyzeck's impotence, the triumphant readability afforded the former and the irretrievable illegibility of the latter's world, seem far apart. They both see, but Faust's vision unites him with meaning while Woyzeck's rebounds upon him from the incomprehensible signs he sees about him, signs which leave him bereft of meaning. Yet they both encounter something radically *other*, something, moreover, that recalls the similar striking and absolute kind of image, suddenly apparent through the mediation of something material, which is to be found in a number of H.C. Andersen's tales. When the Emperor in 'Nattergalen' (The Nightingale) is close to death, for instance, he sees strange heads emerging from the folds of the velvet curtain around his bed. The heads are manifestations of his deeds in life, both good and bad. This link between the image and death is, moreover, a frequent one in Andersen: it may be observed, for example, in 'Paa den yderste Dag' (On the Last Day), 'Barnet i Graven' (The Child in the Grave), 'Den lille Pige med Svovlstikkerne' (The Little Match Girl), and 'Iisjomfruen' (The Ice Virgin), and without pursuing these instances in detail, it is worth noting here that the images of death are always seen on or in something material, for example a coat or brick wall. In 'Iisjomfruen', for example, the images of death are formed in clouds, which are compared in turn to different kinds of cloth — veil, curtain, or crepe. The tale as a whole, meanwhile, bears a strong resemblance to E.T.A. Hoffmann's celebrated story 'Der Bergmann von Falun' (The Miner of Falun). Both narratives, for example, indicate a link between this vision and some kind of fall: the character who experiences the vision falls down into the depths, a fall which in both Hoffmann and Andersen invites psycho-analytical interpretation as a fall from identity into chaos.

However, if one compares this vertical movement in Andersen and Hoffmann with Strindberg's approach to the equally forceful images that occur in his work, there is a significant difference. In Strindberg, the movement is horizontal. Image follows upon image, as if they were laid side by side: there is, in short, no fall. In the novel *Svarta fanor* from 1904, for example, there is an interesting passage describing a series of images formed out of smoke:

> Max rökte och blåste ut ringar som vindade upp sig likt garn-härvor eller svängde omkring i älvdansar. Han tyckte sig i dessa bilder kunna se sina tankar, sina icke uttalade ord, vilka behöllo bilddriften och gåvo dunkla former åt röken, blandad med hans lungors inneslutna levande luft .... Ibland såg han bara kaotiska bilder; nebulosen som har äggvitans form eller amnion med allantois, groddblåsan med navelsäcken; men ur dessa sprang sedan fram organiska former: örat, musslan, näsborrarne.

> (Max smoked, blowing rings that wound up like skeins of yarn or swivelled around in fairy dances. In these images he thought he could see his thoughts, his unspoken words, which retained the desire to become an image, and endowed the smoke, which was blended with the living force of his lungs, with obscure forms. . . . Sometimes he saw only chaotic images; a nebula shaped like an egg white or an amnion like an allantois, the vesica of a plant like a navel sack; but from these there arose organic forms: the ear, the cockle, the nostrils. — SS 41, p.22)

What is so attractive about these accidental images and obscure forms that arise fleetingly in the smoke? Certainly, they are not merely passing fancies, peculiar to this novel. For like Max, Strindberg, especially in his later works, was everywhere attentive to such images, which suddenly emerge without reflecting an existing object. Yet it is crucial that these images do not appear immaterial hallucinations but the consequence of material mediation. 'Jag hemsöktes aldrig av visioner, men väl kunde verkliga föremål ikläda sig mänskliga former av ofta storartad effekt' (I was never haunted by visions, but real objects could assume often striking human form — SS 28, p.58), Strindberg writes, in the autobiographical novel *Inferno*. Hence he discovers images in pillow cases, pieces of coal, buildings, and pebbles, on each of which he places an interpretation so that when they are linked together they stand forth as a clear sign that the one who sees them is being led by a stronger power in order that he be made conscious of his hybris. The novel thus becomes a narrative of punishment and possible reconciliation.

But the particular way in which images are seen in *Inferno* can also be considered from a contrary point of view, as precisely exposing such a determining logic in favour of one which is open to the randomness of experience. This receptive attitude may be discerned in the late Strindberg of, for example, *Ockulta dagboken* and *En blå bok*. 'Vem byggde det här?' (Who built this?), is the question posed in *En blå bok*, in the face of a peculiar rock formation. But the answer also takes the form of a question: 'Byggde?'. And again: 'Vem har gjort de här?' (Who made these?), asks the narrator's painter friend in *Inferno*, when confronted by three pieces of coal which resemble statuettes. The answer is again a question: 'Gjort?' (Made? — SS 28, p.46).

There is an eagerness in these books to achieve explanations, interpretations, circumstantial proof. But as soon as light is shed upon something dark, something else obscure is discovered, waiting just around the corner. Thus the source of fascination is not the manic search for truth, but the never ending movement on to the next strange sign, and then the next, and so on.

For me, this movement has more to do with language than with occultism and the like. It touches upon the uncertain relationship between sign and sense, or meaning, and the effect of this uncertainty. Articulating an interpretation holds out the promise of meaning that is always both failed and renewed, as its fulfilment is continually deferred.

What is at issue is the metonymic power of language, the phenomenon of displacement. In H.C. Andersen's 'Iisjomfruen', the clouds were first identified as veils, then as crepe, and then as curtains, a displacement which defers a fixed interpretation as the reader is led on into new fields. Only at the moment of death is this chain broken. The same transposition can be seen in the interpretations which Max places upon the wreaths of smoke, in which he sees skeins of yarn, fairy dances, nebula, an ear, nostrils, and so on.

Images of this kind are almost tangible manifestations but lack a cause: they are signs with an absent referent. Both writer and reader will, however, find a message in such oddities, one that encompasses the rhetorical energy of language. The Invisible One in *Inferno*, who is the power leading the observing writer on from sign to sign, becomes an initiator into the inner realm of language, into its astonishing possibilities and the effects of its displacements and condensations, its fundamental unreliability, its abundant and unending creation of meaning, its continuous deviations.

It can be argued, surely with justification, that the step from the sign as image to the linguistic sign does not take an important difference into account. An ordinary image, like a painting or a photograph, is a sign that resembles its referent, while the linguistic sign is characterized by its arbitrary relationship to what it stands for. But I would suggest that precisely in the case of chance images the visual signs have been infected by the arbitrariness of language. The chance images have no first source, they have been developed by the inherent urge of matter itself to develop pictures.

Moreover, chance images, which are not secondary re-productions of an identifiable first-hand reality, have been a source of difficulty for theories of knowledge and for aesthetics since antiquity. Lucretius, for example, observes in *De Rerum Natura* that objects are visible because they carry their image on their surface like a film or membrane. When we look at ourselves in a mirror our image flows to the surface of the mirror in which we see it. But there are also, Lucretius writes, images without objects:

> There are such images which are spontaneously born and shaped in the sky, that region of the sky which we call the heavens. These assume a diversity of shapes and travel at a great height. So at times we can see clouds come into existence in the heavens, and stain the quietness of the firmament when they caress the air with their movements. Often one can see giant faces sailing by with great shadows behind them. Sometimes one can see immense mountains or crags uprooted from the mountains drifting by across the sun's face, and then a monster hauling a raincloud black with storm behind him. Continuously dissolving they never cease to change their form, assuming the outline now of one shape, now of another.[6]

This is beautifully expressed, and appeals not only to those who, as Strindberg did, enjoy observing cloudscapes. For what Lucretius describes is nothing less than the fantastic theatre of signs.

Notes

1. Cf. Strindberg's letter to Torsten Hedlund, 28 March 1896 (XI, pp.151-3), where the book is identified as *Dans l' Inde* by André Chevrillon (Paris, 1891).
2. See Göran Söderström, *Strindberg och bildkonsten* (Stockholm 1972, new ed. 1990).

3. See, for example, *En blå bok* and the letter to Hedlund of 21 June 1896 with the accompanying sketch of a walnut, which is reproduced in *Strindbergs måleri*, ed. Torsten Måtte Schmidt (Malmö, 1972), p.144.

4. Cf. Harry Carlson, 'Strindberg and the Visual Imagination', footnote 17, above.

5. Büchner, *Werke und Briefe*, herausgegeben von Fritz Bergemann (München, 1965), p.120.

6. *De Rerum Natura*, Book IV, line 131ff.

Strindberg and Scandinavian Painting: 1880-1900

Michelle Facos

Case Western Reserve University

Scholars have always considered Strindberg a maverick painter, whose distinctive style set him apart from his Swedish colleagues. In fact, beginning in the late 1880s, the development of a unique and deeply personal style was a collective goal of all Swedish avant-garde painters. Although these artists shared a set of socio-political and aesthetic convictions, their works rarely bear the family resemblance so typical of earlier Realist or Impressionist painters.

Strindberg became friendly with Swedish avant-garde painters in Paris during the early 1880s, and was drawn to them not only because they were sympathetic compatriots in a foreign land, but also because they shared his profound reverence for nature. Their primary motivation in leaving Stockholm for Paris was the urge to live in an environment where landscape paintings executed out-of-doors were accepted. They began painting open-air landscapes in the mid-1870s under the tutelage of Edvard Perseus, an inspiring and innovative professor at the Royal Academy of Art in Stockholm. This experience so exhilarated these young artists that they could no longer bring themselves to submit to the tedious years of academic study which emphasized drawing after plaster casts of famous ancient sculptures, or people posed like them. Furthermore, there was no place within the academic hierarchy for informal landscapes. The Academy acknowledged only landscapes conforming to the formulas established in the seventeenth century by Nicolas Poussin and Claude Lorrain, preferably ennobled with figures of historical significance. These young landscape painters felt obliged to move to France because they recognized the unfortunate reality that the endorsement of the Royal Academy was essential for a successful artistic career in Sweden.

Several of these artists spent at least part of their summers in the picturesque village of Grèz-sur-Loing, now a virtual suburb of Paris. There they concentrated their attention on the simple, sunlit beauty of the French countryside. Strindberg first visited Grèz in 1883 and developed friendships with Carl Larsson, Georg Pauli and Karl Nordström. During their years in France, the works of the Swedish painters closely resembled those of the French Naturalist artists, such as Camille Corot and the lesser known Jean Charles Cazin, who inspired them.

Toward the end of the 1880s, a strong sense of Swedish national identity emerged in these artists-in-exile.[1] Strindberg, on the other hand, had for more than a decade expressed a similar populist interest in preserving the Swedish cultural heritage which was rapidly falling victim to the forces of industrialization and urbanization.[2] His concern culminated in the publication of his history *Svenska Folket* in 1882. Strindberg's views were shared with escalating fervour by the Swedish avant-garde painters in Paris. A key factor contributing to this change in consciousness was certainly a new appreciation of the unique character of Swedish culture and nature fostered by their immersion in that of a foreign land. Richard Bergh, the primary spokesman and theoretician of the group, exhorted his colleagues to shed their French ways and creep back into their 'peau de suède.'[3]

A dramatic change in the art of the Swedish avant-garde was precipitated by the synthesis of two factors: the discovery of their deep Swedish roots and a belief in the transforming power of the imagination. Richard Bergh's fascination with the workings of the unconscious mind manifested itself in his painting *Hypnotic Seance* (Nationalmuseum, Stockholm), in which a group of interested observers watch while a young woman is hypnotized.[4] Intellectuals of the group were well aware of developments in Parisian Symbolist circles. Pauli attended lectures in Paris given by the Sâr Péladan, guru of the mystical Catholic Rose+Croix artists, and Bergh was familiar with contemporary theosophical writings, especially those of Edward Schuré.

By the early 1890s, the Swedish avant-garde painters had developed a profound belief in an intracultural collective unconscious. Evidence for this was provided by the synthesis of two disparate strains of thought. The mystical theories of the French Symbolists and the Swedish Romantics, combined with scientific (yet at heart, equally mystical) theories of climate and geography. Hippolyte Taine in France and Carl August Ehrensvärd in Sweden popularized in the nineteenth century ideas developed by Charles de Montesquieu in the eighteenth.[5] According to him, the climatic and geographical conditions of a particular region played a decisive role in the moulding of the physique and psyche of its inhabitants. This in turn determined the culture,

277

values, art and traditions distinguishing one society from another. For Sweden, simplicity characterized national tendencies in art.[6] Bergh was particularly fascinated with these ideas and disseminated them to his colleagues in discussions, letters and published essays.

Based on this belief in an intracultural collective unconscious, the Swedish avant-garde painters extrapolated that an art which expressed their deepest, most subjective response to an indigenous subject, particularly nature, would communicate to their countrymen on a preconscious level.[7] This, in large part, accounts for the plurality of styles coexisting among this tightly-knit group of artists. In contrast to avant-garde painters in other countries, they strove neither for a universal art nor for a solipsistic one, but rather for a national art. To the Swedes, imagination was not merely consonant with nature, but it constituted the faculty essential for truly comprehending and interpreting it. In Sweden, in the 1890s, nature and imagination, '*natur och fantasi*', united to produce a body of work marked by an extraordinary diversity of appearance but a passionate unity of purpose.

One painting was pivotal in revealing to Sweden's avant-garde artists the possibility of combining the two seemingly paradoxical urges of truth to nature and truth to one's own imagination: Ernst Josephson's *The Water Sprite*. While hiking in Norway's rugged, mountainous wilderness in the summer of 1872, Josephson encountered the waterfall at Eggedal. There he felt the unmistakeable presence of Nordic folklore's fiddle-playing water sprites *Näcken* and *Strömkarlen*. According to legend, late at night, their plaintive strains entice the curious to the deep waters, where these unwary wanderers drown. The water sprites traditionally symbolize unfulfilled longing, and were understandably of personal significance to Josephson, who repeatedly failed to achieve the critical and financial success he sought. In 1889, he fell victim to the dark forces of nature and succumbed to insanity.

Josephson made his first sketches of this subject in 1878 while in Rome, during a period when he was plagued by loneliness. In 1881, the twin experiences of visiting the imposing Trollhätten waterfall north of Gothenburg and seeing a compatriot's painting of a fiddler beside a waterfall, seem to have prompted Josephson to return to the subject of the water sprite.[9] He completed the first oil version during the summer of 1882. Obsessed by this subject, however, he painted a tempera version during the winter of 1882-83, and a second oil version in 1884 following a visit to Eggedal, the place of his original inspiration. With the exception of Georg Pauli, Josephson's avant-garde compatriots did not immediately understand the painting or its implications, and voted against hanging it in their 1885 Stockholm exhibition. Strindberg apparently *did* like it,[10] no doubt seizing immediately upon the important implications it had for reconciling nature with imagination.

Within several years, the painting began to have a profound effect on Josephson's compatriots. It opened their eyes to the mythic/symbolic potential of Nordic nature and to the emotive dimension of painting. Furthermore, its explicitly non-naturalistic quality helped liberate the imagination of these artists from their preoccupation with the visible world.

By 1887, at the time Strindberg was writing *Hemsöborna*, his ode to the rugged archipelago of his native Stockholm, Sweden's avant-garde painters had begun to return home. In many instances, they not only returned to Sweden, but more specifically to the region of their ancestors. Their attitude about going back to their birthplaces manifested a quasi-biological conviction about the relationship between a creature and the circumstances in which it is nurtured. These artists reexamined what previously had seemed almost contemptibly familiar, and saw it now with new eyes. Interestingly, the new and profound appreciation of the Swedish avant-garde for their ancestral soil, was fuelled not only by their long exposure to French culture and nature, but also by travel to parts of Scandinavia of particular historical importance or natural beauty.

The perfectly preserved, medieval Hanseatic city of Visby, on the island of Gotland assumed a role of central significance in the reorientation of the avant-garde's national consciousness. In the 1880s and early 1890s it was an all but forgotten city, an unspoiled monument of Sweden's historical past. The intact medieval architecture and city plan epitomized for them the living history that they believed was so essential to the development of an authentic indigenous character and the consequent fulfilment of Sweden's destiny as a nation. According to the contemporary poet Verner von Heidenstam

en ålderdomlig byggnad är liksom reliken sammanvuxen med anekdoter, med verkliga eller diktade handlingar, med livet självt, med människor, vilkas blod vi bära och vilkas strävanden vi ärvt.

(an old building is like a relic replete with stories with actual or imaginary events, with life itself, with people, whose blood courses through our veins and whose aspirations we have inherited.)[11]

The moody, silent streets of Visby kindled the visitor's imagination, encouraging him to people the marketplaces and churches with imaginary inhabitants of a time long past. Bruno Liljefors was the first of the avant-garde artists to visit, in 1888, Nordström followed in 1889, and Bergh and Pauli came in the early 1890s. Of these artists, it was only Bergh who painted a work directly inspired by his musings on Visby's glorious and distant past.

In *Vision: Motif from Visby* (Nationalmuseum, Stockholm), completed in 1894, Bergh creatively combined nature and fantasy in a manner clearly indebted to Josephson's *Water Sprite*. In his painting, Bergh envisioned the departure of the Danish fleet under the command of Waldemar Atterdag in 1361. Unable to penetrate the formidable city walls, the Danes plundered the riches of neighbouring towns, slaughtering almost two thousand peasants, while Visby's army watched passively from the safety of the ramparts.

In painting an historical scene, Bergh avoided the 'you are there' realism characteristic of academic history painting. Instead, he made it obvious to the viewer that the scene represented was an imaginative, personal interpretation of an historic event by painting fanciful, toy-like ships in gilt, and by recording the wall in its current state of partial ruin. Thus it is the imagination, not the intellect, by which one gains access to the past, and by which one is able to keep it alive in the present. For Bergh and his comrades, the past did not constitute some remote and inconsequential series of events, but rather comprised a cumulative and integral part of the contemporary 'collective unconscious'. All Swedish myth and all Swedish history were real, if intangible and unrecognized aspects of the modern Swedish psyche.

The sublime and rugged landscape of Norway helped at least two Swedish painters to become more sensitive to the more subtle character of their native land. The younger of the two, Prins Eugen, son of the reigning King Oscar II, was not particularly good friends with Strindberg, but the elder, Richard Bergh, was. In Norway he learned that acute sensory perception alone was not sufficient for the truest transformation of nature into art. In his essay 'Nordic Nature and Nordic Art', Bergh explained:

För att tolka denna motsträviga natur med penseln hjälper det icke att endast öppna ögonen, man måste också förstå att tidtals sluta dem, drömma om vad man skådat, dikta över det, väga ögats mångfaldiga intryck med känslan för att dymedelst utgrunda enheten i denna barbariska mångfald och slutligen finna vägen till den enkelhet i fråga om dekorativ anordning, som ensam gör höghet möjlig inom måleriet.

(In order to interpret this obstinate nature with the brush it does not suffice to open one's eyes, one must also understand that sometimes one must close them, dream about what one has beheld, poeticize it, weigh the eye's varied impressions against one's feelings in order to establish unity among this barbaric multiplicity. Eventually one will find the way to attain that simplicity in decorative composition which alone is the highest achievement in painting.)[12]

At no time did Bergh or any other of his compatriots advocate the liberation of imagination from nature, as did avant-garde Symbolist painters on the continent. For the Swedes, nature remained paramount. Nonetheless, the theories espoused by French Symbolist writers such as Stéphane Mallarmé played a role in the rejection of pure Naturalism that characterized Swedish Symbolist art beginning around 1890. According to Georg Pauli, the Swedes were particularly attracted to continental Symbolism's rejection of sensation and analysis of the visible world and its embrace of subjectivity and emotion.[13]

Strindberg's statement from 1888, that his disembodied self was contained in his paintings and writings,[14] is close in spirit to Karl Nordström's 1891 declaration that he wanted to create pictures with his 'heart's reddest blood'.[15] The urge to create profoundly subjective works that were still in some essential way 'true to nature' was a concern they shared with Sweden's other avant-garde painters. It was during this period 1890-91 that the cantankerous Nordström and Strindberg were closest. One can only speculate as to the impact that each might have had on the other's thinking. In 1891, Nordström saw the paintings of Paul Gauguin for the first time, an experience that seemed to have strengthened his resolve to pursue the daring path on which he had tentatively embarked. Nordström had already begun to simplify his forms, to edit details in the interest of creating a decorative unity. This urge toward distillation characterizes many of Strindberg's paintings as well, but he often chose subjects marked by an inherent simplicity, as in his seascapes. Another lesson Nordström learned from Gauguin was the emotional use of colour. While never going so far as to paint blue tree trunks, as did Gauguin, he did permit his deepest personal feelings for his subject and his individual sense of pictorial harmony to influence his choice of colour. Nordström's statement about wanting to create 'melodies in colour'[16] links him to the synaesthetic trend so prevalent in Symbolism and early modernism, although he never permitted abstract and subjective concerns to dominate his commitment to Nature.

In an 1892 letter to Bergh, Strindberg argued for a pictorial art totally divorced from observation.[17] This statement places him in closer proximity to continental Symbolism than his Swedish compatriots were willing to go. For them, it was Swedish nature that constituted the focal point of their art; all other considerations were subordinate. They sought to create a uniquely Swedish art, and for them that meant an art whose subject and reference point was nature. To further intensify the Swedish, or at least Nordic, dimension of their art, they concentrated their attention on the indigenous and special qualities of Swedish nature.

Transitional times of day and year became a major theme in the work of these artists. Nordström, whose coarse character was viewed as the product of the barren, harsh landscape of his native Tjörn,[18] a peninsula on Sweden's northwest coast, was drawn to the intense afternoon light of late autumn and early spring. At those times, the sun's path stays low in the sky and the long rays of the afternoon sun linger, illuminating the earth with an intense light, in which the colour of objects appears deeply saturated. In works such as *Storm Clouds* (Nationalmuseum, Stockholm) Nordström chose a subject of deep personal significance and portrayed it under the light and atmospheric conditions typical of the northernmost latitudes. In this way he sought to communicate with a public united by its experience of this specific mood of nature, one of compelling beauty and meditative power.

Bruno Liljefors,[19] similarly committed to painting what he knew and loved best, took his subjects from the forests and fields near his native Uppsala and later, the nearby Stockholm archipelago. Since childhood he had been an avid hunter and a passionate and patient observer of animals in the wild. He alone among the avant-garde concentrated on wildlife subjects. In a painting of 1888, *The Mating of the Capercaillies* (Gothenburg Art Gallery), Liljefors shared a rarely witnessed event with the Swedish public.[20] He recorded the moment of the male bird's most characteristic courtship behaviour with uncanny accuracy. Like Nordström, he too chose a transitional time — dawn in early spring. Liljefors also recognized and exploited the suggestive mood: time seems suspended, and the courtship ritual becomes more than a rare and transient episode. The stillness of the painting seems to invite contemplation, and with that Liljefors intended to intensify his public's awareness of the intimate connection between man and nature. The activity of the capercaillies becomes emblematic of inevitable natural forces.

In later works, Liljefors sought to harmonize two seemingly disparate urges: the depiction of animals in their natural environment and the creation of an emotive, decorative ensemble. The latter goal was consistent with that of the avant-garde, which strongly felt that a simple, unified and visually compelling work would communicate most directly and effectively with their Swedish public. In *Settling Wild Geese* (Prins Eugens Waldemarsudde, Stockholm) Liljefors recorded a flock of rare bean geese on their seasonal migration in a dramatic scene just prior to sunset. Liljefors tenaciously studied the aeronautical patterns of these birds as well as their configurations and markings.[21] He combined his acute observations with a profoundly personal sense of colour and composition to produce a work intended to reach the poetic soul of his Swedish audience.

While Nordström and Liljefors, among others, sought to preserve the Swede's intimate relationship with nature, the other pressing concern of avant-garde artists, the preservation of indigenous tradition and culture, was the preoccupation of Carl Larsson. In an effort to reach a broader public, Larsson turned to the mass production of his paintings through books. In them he portrayed the most typical aspects of rural Swedish life in his native Dalarna. He presented them in a manner held up as a cultural ideal. Larsson focused on home life and turned to his own lovingly restored log house as the setting for many of his paintings. He and his wife redesigned the exterior according to the dictates of indigenous traditional architecture, while the interior was largely inspired by native decorative arts traditions. The women of the family designed and wove many of the textiles. The Larssons collected furniture of various styles from earlier periods and often had local craftsmen make pieces based on simple, peasant models. According to Strindberg, this interest in traditional handcrafts constituted an important aspect of the Swedish rediscovery of their unique national character.[22] During the long winter months rural folk had plenty of time to embellish the simple accoutrements of daily life. The Larssons were careful to create objects that were not slavish copies, but ones that reflected the temperament of their makers and their time, while at the same time drawing inspiration from traditional arts and crafts. Underlying this approach is the notion that 'good' or 'true' art results from an organic connection between an environment and its cultural production. This analysis proceeds from a biological model — one where art subtly responds to the changing needs of the culture that produces it. This conviction, underlying the prevailing ideology of the Swedish avant-garde, can ultimately be traced to Darwinian investigations into normative organic growth and the gradual adaptation of organisms to their environment.

The strong ethical impulse to create works that were true to one's time and one's temperament was considered as crucial for painting as it was for crafts. Sweden's avant-garde firmly believed that art must issue from the innermost feelings of the artist, and that the most profound emotions were stirred by that which was most familiar.[23] In expressing his most subjective response to a subject, the artist necessarily articulated the contemporary temperament of his culture as well as the latent, intracultural truths imbedded within it. Thus it was imperative for the artist to engage in an earnest, soul-searching effort to determine his range of appropriate subject matter and to engage his fantasy, his imagination, and not merely his senses, in interpreting it. Despite the plurality of subject matter and style, Sweden's avant-garde painters were united in their goal of heightening public awareness of Sweden's unique national heritage. With this in mind, all of them chose subjects that they considered as particular to and/or typical of the

Swedish experience. With the objective of intracultural communication, these artists selected themes and a visual language intended for an exclusively Swedish audience. These painters expected their public to apprehend the significance of their works with a preconscious intuition, an objective linked to the esoteric aspirations of Symbolism. Their enemies were industrialization and capitalism, forces that destroyed the old commercial relationships and social structures. The Swedish avant-garde fervently believed that these two forces threatened the survival of national culture and values. They wanted to restore to art its curative power, its ability to profoundly affect the spiritual well-being of society, which had been lost since primitive times. All of them felt the urge, in some sense, to reach back in time in order to recover something fundamental which their society had carelessly and dangerously forgotten. That something was the power of the imagination to interpret nature, to make sense of it, and to make people aware of their inevitable if sometimes precarious interrelationship with it.

Notes

1. Richard Bergh, *Vad vår kamp gällt* (Stockholm, 1905), p.10.
2. In his article 'Svenska folkvisor — som icke äro svenska' (Swedish folksongs that are not Swedish), Strindberg wrote: 'De "nationella strävenden" . . . utgingo . . . från det trånga begäret att till varje pris vindicera åt Sverige en självständig plats bland kulturfolken; . . . Följden blev ett vaknade begär hos svenskarne att upptäcka den svenska gent emot både det nordiska och det norska.' (The 'national ambition' . . . proceeds from the narrow desire to claim for Sweden an independent place among cultured peoples. . . .The result was an awakened urge among Swedes to discover the Swedish, at any price, in distinction to the Nordic and the Norwegian), *Dagens Nyheter*, 7 March 1877, reprinted in Torsten Eklund, ed., *Före Röda Rummet. Strindbergs ungdomsjournalistik* (Stockholm, 1946), pp.263-64.
3. Letter dated 22 July 1887 from Bergh to Pauli. Georg Pauli, *Konstnärsbrev*, I (Stockholm, 1928), p.33.
4. Strindberg was also attracted by the workings of the unconscious mind during hypnosis. At the end of *Fröken Julie*, the protagonist asks Jean to hypnotize her. I am indebted to Harry Carlson for bringing this to my attention.

5. Ragnar Josephson, 'Konsten och Nationalkänslan,' *Nationalism och Humanism* (Stockholm, 1935), p.123.
6. Josephson, p.126.
7. See R. Bergh, 'Om öfverdrifternas nödvändighet i konsten,' *Om konst och annat* (Stockholm, 1908), pp.1-10. This essay was first published in *Svea. Folkkalender*, vol. 43 (1887), p.123ff.
8. Sixten Strömbom, *Konstnärsförbundets historia*, I (Stockholm, 1945), p.162.
9. Georg Pauli professed to admire it from the very beginning: 'Redan från första stund blev jag betagen i *Strömkarlen*, då Josephson visade mig arbetet, efter återkomsten från Norge till Paris. Men jag stod ensam i denna beundran . . . ' (Already from the first instant Josephson showed me the work following his return to Paris from Norway, I was taken by *The Water Sprite*. But I was alone in this admiration). Pauli, 'Om Ernst Josephsons teckningar samt utställningen 1893', *Konstnärsliv och om konst* (Stockholm, 1913), p.195.
10. 'Av särskilt intresse är Strindbergs nu helt förändrade och starkt positiva inställning till fantasikonsten, representerad av Josephson vid denna tid av nästan alla oförstådda och begabbade målning *Strömkarlen*. . .' (Of particular interest is Strindberg's now totally changed and strongly positive attitude toward art of the imagination, represented by Josephson's *The Water Sprite*, a painting which at that time was understood by almost nobody). Göran Söderström, 'Strindbergs måleri', in Torsten Måtte Schmidt, ed., *Strindbergs måleri* (Malmö, 1972), p.80.
11. Verner von Heidenstam, 'Modern Barbarism. Några ord mot restaurerandet av historiska byggnader', *Stridskrifter* (Stockholm, 1912), p.54.
12. R. Bergh, 'Nordisk natur och nordisk konst', *Efterlämnade skrifter om konst och annat* (Stockholm, 1921), p.119.
13. See G. Pauli, 'Om Symbolismen', *Konstnärsliv och om konst* (Stockholm, 1913).
14. '[J]ag dör med mig sjelf, endast lefvande i mina verk'. Letter from Strindberg to Brandes, quoted in Göran Söderström, *Strindberg och bildkonsten* (Stockholm, 1972), p.131.
15. Quoted in Bergh, 'Karl Nordström och det stämningslandskapet', *Om konst och annat*, p.121.
16. Letter dated 14 July 1892 from Nordström to Bergh, quoted in Torsten Svedfelt, *Karl Nordströms konst* (Stockholm, 1939), p.15.
17. 'Jag har en del målarstudier, efter fantasien, att visa dig. En ''ny rigtning'' som jag upfunnit sjelf och vill kalla skogssnufvismen. . .' (I have a number of studies to show you, painted from the imagination. A 'new direction' that I have discovered myself and intend to call 'wood-nymphism' — IX, p.40).
18. Bergh, 'Karl Nordström och det moderna stämningslandskapet', p.113.
19. According to one contemporary critic, 'Liljefors . . . som målare har samma betydelse som Strindberg haft som poet' (Liljefors . . . as a painter has the same significance as Strindberg has had as a poet). E.A., 'Konstnärsförbundets utställning. II', *Dagens Nyheter*, 14 May 1898.

20. In an 1894 letter to Bergh, Pauli asserted that 'dekorativ konst och i synnerhet den, som användes i offentlighetens tjänst, anser jag bör vara *enkelt, klar* och uttrycksfull' (Decorative art, and particularly that which is used in the public interest, should, I believe, be *simple, lucid* and full of expression). Quoted in Pauli, 'Om freskomålningarna i Göteborgs museum', *Konstnärslif och om konst*, p.102.
21. Allan Ellenius discusses in detail this aspect of Liljefors's work in *Bruno Liljefors* (Uppsala, 1981).
22. Strindberg, in Eklund, p.264.
23. 'Vår tid har: Ett nytt tro, ett nytt lyckoideal, ett nytt samhällsideal, ett nytt politiskt ideal och kräver en konst inspirerad av nutidsmänniskans idéer och känslor, lidelser och drömmar och formad efter samma nutidsmänniskans belåte' (Our era has: A new creed, a new ideal of happiness, a new ideal for society, a new political ideal and requires an art inspired by modern man's ideas and feelings, passions and dreams and based on the same modern man's contentment). R.Bergh, 'Strödda reflexioner', *Efterlämnade skrifter om konst och annat*, p.150.

Index

The Swedish letters 'å' and ''ä' are alphabeticized in this index as 'a', and 'ö' under 'o'.

287

Strindberg and Genre

Strindberg and Genre